FAR AND WIDE

FAR AND WIDE

by

DOUGLAS REED

FIRST PUBLISHED 1951

CONTENTS

CONTENTS

PART TWO

BEHIND THE SCENE

ALL ABOARD FOR ALABAM'

I TOOK ship one day for Alabama, and this is the tale of that far journey across wide seas and lands. It took me from Africa to, and through, America and back and was much longer than the earth's girth. The calling of political explorer, which chance bestowed on me some twenty years ago, becomes ever fussier, but I seem to be its only practitioner now and enjoy it.

My heart never urgently called me Americaward because it belongs to our cradle-land, Europe, and in serener times I would have stayed there. Today Europe is cut in two and, I believe, will either be wholly crushed into a servile oblivion at one more move in the great game, or rise again. The remaining years of our century should decide that stupendous issue of our age (or, as you like it, that petty incident in time and space).

Much power to sway the decision, either way, has passed from Europe to America, so that I felt an urgent need of the mind to go there. The balance of money-power and manufacture-power has greatly shifted thither; and if 'the world is governed by very different persons from what those believe who are not behind the scenes' (Disraeli's words) then America is today the land which they will chiefly seek to divide, rule and use for the completion of their plan.

The plan, I think, is the old one of world dominion in a new form. It is not merely that of one more Wicked Man, like the Hitler who, in Mr. Chaplin's film *The Great Dictator*, dreamily played with our planet. The political explorer early finds that other men than these spotlighted, evanescent, public figures also play with the globe.

It is, in my belief, the plan of a conspiratorial sect, the members of which wield much power in *all* countries, seldom openly appear, hold sway over the visible public figures, and are able so to direct the acts of governments, friendly or hostile, peaceable or warring, that these in the end all promote their prompters' own destructive ambition.

This ambition (and today I think it is apparent) is to set up a World

7

State to which all nations, having ruined each other, shall be enserfed. The League of Nations was to my mind a first experiment in that direction and the United Nations is a second one, much more advanced.

A wandering journalist, I have gone through the thick of these events for many years and have no doubt left that this is the shape of things intended to come. Two groups, alien in all lands and powerful in all lands, chiefly promote that great design. The political explorer finds Soviet Communism and Zionist Nationalism in all countries to be forces powerful behind the scenes, and in sum their separate efforts serve a converging ambition.

It is, as I judge, to crush the nations into a flat, brazen servitude between the hammer of revolution and the anvil of gold. The founder of Zionist Nationalism, Theodor Herzl, openly described the method: 'The power of our purse . . . the terrible power of the revolutionary proletariat.' It reveals the secret, the great discovery, of politics in our times. Politicians can ever be brought to yield either to the glitter of material reward (perhaps in the shape of votes), or, if that fails, to the threat of agitation and overthrow. Such is the conspirator's road to power, on high and higher to the highest levels.

Today the scene is set for the third act, intended to complete the process. The money-power and the revolutionary-power have been set up and given sham but symbolic shapes ('Capitalism' or 'Communism') and sharply-defined citadels ('America' or 'Russia'). Suitably to alarm the mass-mind, the picture offered is that of bleak and hopeless enmity and confrontation: Black Knight and White Knight. One *must* destroy the other.

Such is the spectacle publicly staged for the masses. But what if similar men, with a common aim, secretly rule in both camps and propose to achieve their ambition through the clash between those masses? I believe any diligent student of our times will discover that this is the case. He will find that in all countries essential to the plan invisible or half-seen men, whose names are publicly little known, are powerful enough to dictate the major acts of governments at vital moments (President Roosevelt's near-deathbed admission that he signed the fatal order to bisect Germany 'at the request of an old and valued friend', who remained nameless, is a recent case in point).

8

In the United States, particularly, these powerful men behind-the-scenes have in the last thirty years been able to give such a slant to governmental actions that these went to promote the ends of Soviet Communism and Zionist Nationalism; at least, it looked like that to me from afar and when I went closer the same picture grew only clearer.

Thus I think that out of the smoke and smother of any new war, begun on the one side to 'destroy Capitalism' and on the other to 'destroy Communism', will at the end be produced (if this situation continues) what those managers really want: the Communist-Capitalist Super-State with all the Capitalist-Communist power over people and gold, and all the nations submerged. For the Second War proved beyond further doubt what the First War began to make probable: that aims and causes tossed to the masses at the start of these great conflicts have no relation to the ultimate plans in truth pursued.

In that matter another incident from the Roosevelt era is convincing. At one point during the Second War the British Government found that Mr. Roosevelt entertained massive ideas about reshaping the globe, and these affected British territories, among many others. The British Foreign Minister, courteously mentioning that they included no American (he might have added, or Russian) sacrifices, gently asked about the President's constitutional powers for redistributing the world while it was still at war.

President Roosevelt then inquired of his legal advisers and was reassuringly told that he could do anything he liked 'without Congressional action in the first instance' and 'the handling of the military forces of the United States could be so managed as to foster any purpose he pursued'.

The last sentence supplies the key to the mysteries of these wars. They are not for the ends publicly announced when The Boys set out. The important thing, apparently, is to get The Boys started; then their military operations may be 'handled' to foster 'any purpose' their rulers may pursue. But *who* are their rulers, today? In the most vital matters, 'old and valued friends', who never emerge from anonymity!

I think the method has become clear, and expect to see it pursued, and any further wars 'handled', until the purpose of setting up the World Servile State is accomplished, or finally fails. Long observation in Europe and Africa brought me to and confirmed these views. America was the essential last stage on my journey of political exploration. I knew all the rest, from Moscow through Berlin to London and Paris, and believed I had a good notion of what went on in America; but the personal experience lacked.

So I went to see for myself, with memories of the two wars and of twenty years of politics in twenty countries in my mind's eye. All those fragments now fitted into the picture of a continuing process, guided by master hands unseen, and I set out to learn how far the American one dovetailed into it. At the end I thought that America, like my own country, was in the business unwittingly but up to the neck. Matters have gone too far for the last great coup, The World State, not now to be tried; only the result, I think, now remains in doubt.

The first part of this book contains the visual picture of America as I saw it at the fateful mid-century during a very long overland journey; my experience is that you need to travel a country far and wide before you try to understand it. The second part contains, for what they are worth, the conclusions which I brought away.

PART ONE

AMERICAN SCENE

CHAPTER I

WAY DOWN IN DIXIE

THE ship crept up the dun-coloured river and Mobile took growing shape, clustered round tall buildings that wore air-conditioning plants like hats atop. Much later, at my journey's end, I was glad to have begun it at Mobile. I doubt if the stranger who descends from the *Queen Mary* straight into the turmoil of New York ever fully recovers from that impact or thereafter gains a fair perspective of America. The better way is to start in Alabama or Maine and see the South and New England first. Having traced the root and stem of America, the traveller will study with more understanding the exotic fruit that has been grafted on at the top, an alien growth on an American stalk. He who arrives first in New York will continue his journey with senses benumbed and confused.

The things which captivate the innocent abroad at the outset are those which are new to him and in America these are, foremost, the gadgets. Already in the taxicab from the docks I wondered what sharp, staccato entertainment the car's radio emitted until I realized that its and other drivers were informing some central command-post of their whereabouts and receiving orders, like tank-commanders in Normandy. My driver took a hand microphone and joined in this brisk exchange. 'Seventy-five heah,' he said, 'coming in from the docks,' and the commander's voice crisply returned, 'Okay, seventy-five, we want yuh for the deepoh.' 'Okay,' he said, and the operation orders continued: sixty-six was heah, forty-nine was at Bienville Square awaiting instructions, thirty-two was sought and twenty-one reported.

Awed at the start, I came to an hotel where the great glass door opened at my approach, without human help. Later I came to know this door well enough to have fun with it. I would stop as I drew near and it opened, and retreat a step; with smooth courtesy it halted and closed. It was the perfect dancing partner, and late one night, when I saw none about, I tried it with a rumba, which it performed perfectly. I was enjoying this dance (it is my favourite) when I felt that I was observed. Looking round I saw a negro porter watching me, not with disdain but with smiling sympathy.

The lifts, too, were playful. Two served my upper floor and faced each other across a wide landing. They were operated by negresses and were noiseless to the point of stealth. When I rang for and awaited the one I would hear a voice behind me say, in accents of suffering, 'Going down', and would spin round to find the other lift-girl looking at me, with some contempt added to the ageless sorrow of her liquid brown eyes. I tried ringing for one and quickly crossing the landing to the other, but then the one originally summoned would silently arrive and behind my back the deep, accusing voice would say, 'Going down'. At the bottom I said, 'Thank you', and she answered, 'You're welcome'; thus, when I finally left the hotel through the unattended door the last words I heard were those which used to greet the coming guest.

From the hotel into the town I followed the trail of such wonders. With a companion I visited the bank, which in America is often placed high among the seeworthy-things (as the Germans say). It seemed full of telephones, iced-water machines, and busy men in large hats from whose mouths cigars pointed like anti-aircraft guns. They incessantly picked up telephones and spoke into them at once, as if the instrument automatically connected them with the folk they wanted, and between calls they visited the iced-water machines. I thought I caught them sometimes telephoning into an iced-water machine or trying to drink from a telephone, but may have been confused. They greeted all, including me, with a cheery wave of the arm, two outstretched fingers at its end, and 'Howdy, pardner. How're yuh t'day? Nice t'see yer.' I at once became the partner of several leading Mobilians and also an officer in some unknown service ('Howdy, cap'n').

These amiable forms are not general in America, I found in time. The slow, unhurried courtesy which was once the accepted manner of an American, of whatever station, widely survives in the South, but gives way to an impersonal brusqueness in other places, particularly those under the spiritual influence of New York, where hurly-burly seems to have been rewritten surly-burly. There a pleasant mien is apparently held a sign of weakness and its wearer 'a smoothy'. 'How strange that it should be a sign of affectation, and even of degeneracy, to be well-mannered and well-dressed, to speak English with correctness and live with a certain elegance;' (wrote Mr. Somerset Maugham in *A Writer's Notebook*), 'a man who has been to a good boarding-school and to Harvard or Yale must walk very warily if he wants to avoid the antagonism of those who have not enjoyed these advantages. It is pitiful often to see a man of culture assume a heartiness of manner and use a style of language that are foreign to him in the vain hope that he will not be thought a stuffed-shirt.' Once, slumped over hot-cakes in a chilly dawn, I saw before me a notice: 'Don't ask us for information; if we knew anything we shouldn't be here.' I wanted to inquire the way somewhither, but forbore, wondering nevertheless why people should deny themselves the ancient pleasure of setting a wayfarer on his road.

The South is still unafraid of civility, or even a little blarney. I felt happier to be told by a waitress here, 'Yes sah, Ah'll gladly bring you that', or by a hotel manager there (when I asked for the bill), 'We hate ter do it, but if you must go . . .'; and by a museum custodian, who had to deny some small request, 'Ah'm jest as sorry as Ah could be, but that's not allowed'. In Mobile the more elegant quality of the earlier time still showed through the shape of the later one. The America of Main Street does not yet compare to advantage with that which first grew out of the wilderness and the fortified settlements.

Mobile was French first, and France bequeathed to these parts an immortal name, that of the dix-dollar notes, or dixies. Its pleasant old houses, now diminishing, with their lacey metalwork balconies, offer a challenge to Main Street which I found repeated all over America, not only in the South and New England. In a thousand small towns of the interior the pleasant white houses of the 'homes section' were projections of those which the early colonists built along the coast, using the timber of the new continent and the best models of the old. In the same thousand small towns the 'business section' was the projection of something different, incongruous and of poorer intrinsic quality. Mobile's Main Street contained a profusion of moneylenders; they were even more plentiful than pawnshops used to be in Camden High Street.

Exploring the town I first came on those suburbs of delightful white houses which continued to charm me all over America. Then I found the districts where the poor whites lived, and those of the negroes. The poor white trash (the name may first have been given them by the sugarfields darkies, for the residue from cane-crushing is 'trash') earned fifty pounds a month but remained an affront to the other white folk. The negroes lived in cheerful slovenry and their girls spent much time with their own beauty specialists, probably having their hair done.

Hair becomes a major problem for the young negress when she lives among white communities. Her own hair is much longer than it looks but clings so tightly to her scalp that white women's hats, which she admires, are too big for her. She cannot stretch it to its full length by plaiting or beading, as the Zulu warrior or baby sometimes does, but achieves this end by heavy grease. This enables her to attain something like the hair-do of her favourite white film-actress. Another method is to wear a wig, and these are manufactured for a lively market.

Down on the levees I found the darkies dreamily angling. They still looked as if they might have known Uncle Tom or Tom Sawyer, and still the ancient conflict racked their souls: whether to do a chore or go fishing. I believe this is for many of them life's major issue. It still is in the Africa from which their forefathers came. Though cast among white men, they do not fully accept the white man's philosophy. The Red Indian (who is neither Indian nor red) seems to reject it completely; prevented from warring and hunting, he huddles together in small reservations and impassively awaits extinction or unforeseeable revival. The negro prefers a compromise; he will work within limits, to gain leisure for fishing or dreaming. He survives and multiplies.

I landed in the Deep South and, therewith, in the middle of 'the colour problem', and was glad Southern Africa had taught me some rudiments of the matter. The question has four distinct aspects. The first, what the black man truly wants, is ignored by all parties to the

great debate. The second and third are the conflicting opinions, between white men who live among black men, about what is good for
him within the limits of what is good for them. The division is in my
experience not very wide, but is broadened by the parties of the fourth
aspect, the political groups far from negro-populated areas who use it
to set white man against white man as a means of achieving votes and
power. This is the chief aspect. The past hundred years have shown
that white folk in New England and Old England may be violently
incited against each other and against white folk in warmer latitudes
by this means, to the point of civil wars. The American Civil War was
the first of these.

The contemplation of sin in others is an ancient human enjoyment,
particularly when the beholder is remote from temptation. It is a
pleasure much enjoyed by unoccupied ladies at lace-curtained windows
in suburban streets. Seated at her New England casement Mrs. Harriet
Beecher Stowe grew wrathful about the goings-on of Simon Legree
and the plight of Topsy, far, far away, to such effect that she similarly
infuriated millions of other window-sitters and became (as President
Lincoln said) 'the little lady who started the big war'. Later, when she
saw the ruined South and Uncle Tom, free but bewildered, she wrote
in alarm: 'Corrupt politicians are already beginning to speculate on the
negroes as possible capital for their schemes and to fill their poor souls
with all sorts of vagaries . . . It is unwise and impolitic to endeavour to
force negro suffrage on the South at the point of the bayonet.'

However, the thing was so enforced, with dire results; Mrs. Beecher
Stowe, had she but known, was herself used by corrupt politicians for
the furtherance of schemes; and *Uncle Tom* could not be unwritten
when she saw the light. At this mid-century the book is used for new
incitement in a land where pale-skinned folk, if not white ones in the
true sense, endure a harsher slavery than her characters knew; time, the
jester, dances on. *Uncle Tom's Cabin*, as a play, is a favourite medium
of the present rulers in Moscow for teaching their herded masses to
hate the Western white man. Moreover, Mrs. Stowe founded a school
of writers, now innumerable. Her success led one Anna E. Dickinson
to delight New York, in 1868, with a novel, *What Answer?* depicting
the marriage of a rich young white man with a negress and since that

17

day the theme has never been let drop. Its true importance seems to be fractional.

Because of this I found life and talk in the South much like those of South Africa; the same note of unease about the future ran through them. The clamour from outside paid little heed to people who were actually worse off than the negroes, namely, the original inhabitants, the Red Indians (so called by Columbus because he thought America was India, reached by a new route; they appear to be of Asiatic origin and to have reached America in remote ages by some icy trek from Siberia, across frozen seas, to Alaska). Mrs. Stowe never wrote the story of Sitting Bull's wigwam, though her own house may have stood on its site. The surviving American Indians are too few for the 'corrupt politicians' elsewhere to bother with.

With a companion I began to discover America, ranging round the Mobile countryside from the luxurious country clubs and fine Gulf-side houses to the poorer farmers' shacks and the coloured quarters. I felt at once the great wealth and energy of the country, also its disquiet and resentments, from which no moving frontier now offers escape. I was fortunate to meet at the outset a companion who gave me a deep insight into many things, at first puzzling.

He was a remarkable man. Born to a hard lot, he had been all over America, afoot or by thumbed-ride. America was his life and being; he felt it as an enormous experience, the shape of which, nevertheless, he could not comprehend. He was full of its lore and in my room sang to me epic poems of the legendary giants of the wood-axe and the trail, Mike Fisk, Paul Bunyan, Johnny Appleseed and the others, the men who boasted they could outfight, outshoot, outjump and outrun all others. In them you could hear the crash of falling timber, the arrow's hiss, the song of the flatboats floating down-stream and of the conquering steamboats churning upriver. He felt himself the child of titans in a stupendous world and knew not which way to turn. He had made himself, from the raw, into an artist and sculptor of talent and found no field or market. He did not feel boundless freedom but an eroding frustration. What could an artist do in America, how could he even live? He sought an answer in a little room among tall build-ings. He saw beauty in the great freight train, with its mile of box-cars, that with clanging bell rumbled straight through the middle of the town. These annihilators of space and distance mean to Americans of his kind something of what ships mean to Englishmen. With him I wandered along the quays, past the darkies daydreamily watching their lines. He knew their soul, too, and put it into his songs. 'Howdy, pardner,' he said to each, 'What you caught?' A sheepish backward grin and 'Nuthin'.' 'What, nuthin'! Gorn, Ah thought you caught a big catfish or somep'n.'

I said goodbye with regret one night and climbed aboard a train. When the midnight choo-choo leaves for Alabam', I hummed as its wheels began to turn. Then I tried to sleep but could not. I had fallen into a trap when a charming Mobilian at the booking-office asked me, 'Upper or lower berth? Upper's cheaper.' Grateful for the hint, I said, 'Upper'.

The sleeping-car was that which England knows as a saloon-car, with a central aisle and sets of seats on either side, facing each other in pairs. By some miracle these were transformed into beds at night, an upper and a lower for each four seats; the aisle remained free, between curtains. The occupant of the lower bed could dress or undress sitting on its edge with his feet on the floor; look out of the windows, sit upright, or even stand by bulging the curtains a little. The upper berth was a windowless cell, only reached or left by a ladder, which was procurable only by ringing for the attendant. The roof of the car was about two feet above the berth itself, so that I found myself undressing and dressing flat on my back in a dark horizontal cubicle, a surprising and difficult predicament. I was glad when, somewhat crumpled, I came to my next abiding-place, a little town in the heart of South Carolina.

CHAPTER 2

WHITE PILLARS, GREEN PASTURES

I T was a quiet, withdrawn place of white houses in a green setting, the relic of a way of life violently interrupted eighty years ago. The houses of the South (and of New England, I later found) share a cool, white dignity and charm. Wood, being abundant, was from the start more used than brick, but design closely followed English models remembered by the early colonists. More shade, however, was needed; and as the classic tradition was then respected and ready-made columns grew in the earth Athenian porticoes were added; the result, in all its variations, is delightful. A few great plantation houses remain in the hands of the original families, who for all their English names still chuckle over the discomfiture of the redcoats as much as they mourn the disastrous sequel of the blue ones. The majority of those that survive have been acquired by rich men of the later time who cherish them, thus using wealth beneficently in a country where great fortunes often go destructive ways in the hands of juniors striving indiscriminately to atone for affluence. While taste and elegance seem to have fled from Broadway and Main Street, the furniture and furnishings of such Southern and New England houses are on the highest level.

These houses were framed in trees that stood like giants; they seemed to grow twice as tall and full as elsewhere. Beneath these overhanging green masses, where blue jays and red admirals sported, and between the pillared, verandaed white houses I wandered, looking at America. Broad roadway, broad sidewalk and broad lawns, all were filled with a tangible hush that seemed not quite peace. The motor car has emptied such residential parts of the walking folk who once enlivened them. To English taste, which might be right or wrong, something else lacked. Americans, from the equalitarian idea or ideal which ever defeats itself, dislike hedges or fences, so that houses rub porches and walls without any line of domain between. That works against the life of gardens, of fathers tending flowers or children playing and the general animation which these pleasant scenes give.

American homes, therefore, somewhat bleakly confront the outer world, usually without any outer, private keep to soften the impact. Later, on Long Island, I saw a private builder's estate of ten thousand small houses where dividing fences were forbidden as a condition of sale. I believe this may cause a spiritual overcrowding, in a huge land, which discomforts many Americans. In a short story about an American girl who sought out her old nurse in England I found the words: 'Frances came upon Ainsty Street and stopped . . . What was life here like? These were pleasant cottages . . . they were not the facile, blank little homes that American developers grind out all over the landscape. The pride and the privacy of each was contained within walls and behind individual wooden gates.' Similarly a wise *Texan in England*, Professor J. Frank Dobie (Hammond, Hammond & Co., London, 1946) wrote, 'As for freedom and pleasance, I'll take a hedged-in cottage and its plot anywhere in England rather than many thousands of acres from which the grass that the buffaloes once grazed has all been destroyed and nothing but dollar wheat planted.'

This may be one cause of the lack of a pleasant domestic vivacity in American residential areas generally, but the South, where other things than buffalo lands were destroyed, is a special case and I ascribed also to its particular memories some of the brooding melancholy which I felt in these green avenues. This sadness, as of a dying strain of music, was caught by the title of Miss Mitchell's book, *Gone with the Wind*. I thought of it as I strolled past quiet white houses and remembered the long queues of people waiting, in London, to see the film that was made from it. They were there before France fell and still there, I believe, when France was freed. It was 'good entertainment' and few of those picturegoers saw anything else in it.

For the South, for the present American Republic, and possibly for the entire white family the Civil War (its true name, I judge) remains of present significance. More Americans were killed in it than in both twentieth-century wars together. Not only for that reason is it a living American reality, whereas the others were more quickly forgotten. Brother fought against brother in it and never knew for what. Few now believe it was fought to free slaves, from whose importation Northern traders once grew rich. The fury of partisanship, on either side, was used to different ends.

It was the first war in which the lot of a third party (and not the aboriginal population) was employed to divide white men against each other in the new worlds they thought to have conquered, and to promote a worldwide revolutionary design. The real aim was to break the political power of the rural South and transfer it to the expanding, industrial North, where the revolutionary forces were strongest. It led to a weakening of the Union, which plainly showed in the Republic of 1950. When that war began America was a country of a homogeneous people, predominantly English, Scottish, Ulster-Irish, German and Scandinavian in origins and recognizably 'American'. In its aftermath, which opened the floodgates of immigration from Eastern Europe, this composition of the population was radically changed. Power passed, not to Northern Americans of the old stock, but more and more into the hands of newcomers. They brought with them schemes for a new Union; that of the world, with America and all other countries servient to it. Like the Republic's tombstone (it has that shape) their headquarters building was rising in New York when I went there; it was called the house of 'The United Nations'.

I think the road to the American Civil War, and beyond, clearly ran from the French Revolution. Today the war against the South continues. It is indispensable to the politics of New York and of the tombstone-building. Crushed in 1865, the South is still too strong. With that obduracy which attends God's processes, it has remained homogeneous, a surviving obstacle to the consolidation of the new power in America and the world.

Travelling in the South Mr. John Gunther (himself of more recent American vintage) remarked in *Inside U.S.A.*: 'The foreign-born and sons of foreign-born, who have been travelling with us for most of the course of this book, now leave our story to all practical purposes. The South is overwhelmingly of native-born Anglo-Saxon origin . . . I might add, "predominantly of Scots-Irish, Ulster or Celtic stock". There are towns in North Carolina almost as Scottish as Aberdeen; there are backwoods in Tennessee and Arkansas as implacably Celtic as anything in Wales . . . In every state except Florida and Louisiana 90 per cent or more of the white citizens come of parents who were both American born. The figure reaches 98.7 per cent in Arkansas . . . That Arkansas should be one of the most unquestionably backward of American states naturally gives the observer slight pause and makes one wonder what peculiar characteristics the Celts and Gaels, when transported, contribute to a civilization.' (However, this writer recorded a notable contribution of the South to what in their day were presented as wars 'for civilization': 'The South from the beginning and most vividly took the Allied side in both World Wars . . . The proportion of volunteer enlistments to conscripts was 85.3 for South Carolina, 92.6 for Georgia, 98.6 for Texas and 123.4 for Kentucky . . . One factor in this is obviously the Anglo-Saxon origin of most Southerners . . . Still another is the peculiar and ineffaceable persistence of the martial tradition, the fighting impulse.')

Mr. Gunther calls the South 'The Problem Child of the Nation'. This characteristically New York conception that the parent is the child and the child now the parent, is unremittingly suggested into the American mind by newspapers, books, plays, films and radio. Any demur is rebuked as racial discrimination. A reviewer in a New York newspaper, discussing a book called *Our English Heritage* said: 'One school of thought insists that the immense influx of people from central Europe makes the future of America belong to them. This reviewer does not agree.' Such words verge on punishable heresy in America today, and are rare to see in print.

The transference of power to a newly-arrived minority is, however, possible if the original stock can be kept fairly equally divided by the wedge of some exterior issue. For this purpose the negroes of the South continue to be used. The matter is explained by Mr. Robert E. Sherwood, one of President Roosevelt's ghost-writers, in *Roosevelt and Hopkins*: 'Roosevelt said to me' (during the fourth-term election campaign) 'that, if there were some fifty million people who would actually vote on election day, you could figure roughly that some twenty million of them were determined to vote Democratic and another twenty million Republican (give or take a few million either way) regardless of the issues or candidates. This left ten million or more uncommitted independents who were subject to persuasion during the course of the campaign, and it was to these that the strongest appeals must be made . . . A substantial number of negroes was included in the independent minority, as Roosevelt reckoned it. It was obvious that anyone with his exceptionally positive social views would be implacably opposed to racial discrimination.'

The Southern negro thus plays in the 1950s, as in the 1860s, the part of stalking horse in the pursuit of political power. The cry of 'racial discrimination' is not genuinely raised on his behalf; the real meaning is that it would be 'racial discrimination' to oppose the new immigration from taking over the American future, as the intrepid reviewer remarked. The ambition, aspirants and method are not peculiar to America; they occur in England, South Africa and all countries known to me.

In England, for instance, the native masses equate two main parties with their beliefs and hopes. They vote Conservative to ensure the liberty of each man and the survival of the nation, and Socialist if they wish individual men to yield their liberty to the State and the State, then, to merge the nation in some international directorate. In fact they get the same thing either way, merely at a different pace, and in America the position is similar, only the labels being different: Republican for Conservative and Democratic for Socialist. Both parties, in both countries, appear to regard the small, indeterminate mass of votes, between the two main parties, as being in the gift of third groups and they court this support by surrender to the aims of those separate forces, which work for the supreme State, first, and the supreme World State, next.

In America, under this masterly manipulation, the two parties have even changed places, or faces. At the Civil War the Republicans, who cried 'Abolish slavery' (or 'down with racial discrimination') as a means to power were the party of the revolutionaries. The Democratic Party was that of the conservative South, and eventually resurrected it. The Republicans then enjoyed seventy years of power, almost unbroken, a period long enough to turn any party conservative. Seeing that, the revolutionary element transferred to the Democratic Party and proved, when President Roosevelt came to power, to be very strong in it; the last seventeen years have been filled again with the specious clamour of 'down with racial discrimination' and the atmosphere of pre-Civil War days has been reproduced. So strong is the memory of what the Republicans did after that war that Southerners still automatically vote Democratic. The most their representatives can do, when they reach Congress, is somewhat to retard the new campaign against the South; on the whole they promote the aim of the new immigration to 'take over the future of America'. The Republican Party, which now professes to stand for the traditional American Republic, in its turn feels ever forced by the thought of coming elections to court the graces of this overriding group. For the present no escape from the blind road offers to the voter, either in England or America.

The clear trail leading from the Civil War to the present was the first of my surprises in America. Like most Europeans, probably, I was ignorant of that war and when I studied it felt like an archaeologist who finds the original of the Communist Manifesto in Greek ruins. What went with that wind was more than the political power of the South; what came with the new one was the enslavement of white men by Soviet methods. Only the peculiar spirit of the South prevented that condition from becoming permanent. I read the records with growing amazement, because I recognized in them a continuing process of today. 'That the Southern people were put to the torture is vaguely understood' (wrote Mr. Claude G. Bowers in 1929 in *The Tragic Era*), 'but even historians have shrunk from the unhappy task of showing us the torture chambers . . . It is impossible to grasp the real significance of the revolutionary proceedings of the rugged conspirators working out the policies of Thaddeus Stevens without making many journeys among the Southern people and seeing with our own eyes the indignities to which they were subjected.'

The key-words are 'revolutionary' and 'conspirators' and they fit today's situation like a glove. That the North, with its newly-discovered gold, growing industry, command of the sea and increasing population would win that war was plain to clear heads in the South from the start, and did not deter them from a war which, they believed, had to be fought. Just as it ended President Lincoln, whose continued presidency would have meant reconciliation, was murdered. The way to the South was opened to persons recognizable today as the revolutionary conspirators we know as Communists.

Of the twelve years that followed, the miracle is that the South survived. Mr. John Gunther, who seems to have been startled by what he learned when he saw the South, says, 'If you read the history of those days you must inevitably be reminded of contemporary analogies. Atlanta in the 1870s must have startlingly resembled Warsaw or Budapest under the Nazis in the 1940s . . . Chopping up the South and ruling it by an absolute dictatorship of the military, while every kind of economic and social depredation was not only allowed but encouraged, is so strikingly like what is going on in Germany at present that the imagination staggers.'

Slightly different comparisons might be more correct. The sufferings of the South compare more closely with those of Budapest, Warsaw and all of Eastern Europe under the Communists after the 1939–45 war ended than even under the Nazis in 1940. It is perfectly true, however, that things happened in the American zone of occupation of Germany after 1945 which strongly recall the years from 1865 to 1877 in the American South. They were chiefly due to the influence, inside the American Army, of the immigration from Eastern Europe and of them Mr. Bowers might today write that 'even historians have shrunk from the unhappy task of showing us the torture chambers'. The American public has not been told much of what went on, nor has the English, though to a lesser extent similar things happened in the British zone. The tale of mock-trials before a black altar, of brutal beatings and confessions extorted in the pretence that sentence of death was already passed, was told by an American Army board of inquiry, headed by a justice, but was not allowed to reach the conscious mind of the American masses. More was revealed in Mr. Montgomery Belgion's *Victors' Justice*, a book to which reviewers in America turned a strangely blind eye.

The close resemblance between the torture of the South in the years after 1865 and that of Europe in those after 1945 proved, to me, the existence of a permanent revolutionary organization, trained to inter-

26

vene at such junctures in human affairs and give them a satanic twist. The day after Lincoln's death Ben Butler was appointed Secretary of State. That was a clear omen; he was the Northern general who ordered his troops at New Orleans in 1862 to treat as common prostitutes any white woman there who 'by word, gesture or movement insulted or showed contempt' for them. Outside the government, real power in the Republican Party passed to Thaddeus Stevens, a dying and malignant man. Club-footed, bald but bewigged, of indeterminate origins, clamant for blood and ruin, he was of the type of Marat, Goebbels, Dzherzhinsky or Szamuely. He lived with a mulatto woman at Lancaster, in Quaker Pennsylvania, and this private factor may have helped inflame his violent public demand for 'absolute equality, socially and politically, between the races'.

Stevens pointed the way: 'Hang the leaders, crush the South, arm the negroes, confiscate the land.' He wanted chaos in the negro-populated area as an essential step towards revolution in the North; the same idea was being taught to American Communists (as an apostate once testified) at the Lenin Institute in Moscow in 1930, and is the ruling aim of American Communists in 1951. The negroes were 'better qualified to establish and maintain a republican government than the whites'. The vote should be taken from the whites and given to the negroes. Attacking 'racial discrimination' he forced through Congress a bill 'establishing for the security of the coloured races safeguards which went infinitely beyond what the government has ever provided for the white race' (President Lincoln's successor, Mr. Johnson, vetoed this bill and narrowly escaped arrest at General Butler's demand).

From the negroless North these white men raved for the extermination of the Southern whites. They tried to suspend trial by jury and, when the Supreme Court resisted, to pack this with compliant judges (President Roosevelt was the next to try that). When the victorious General Grant became president the military commander in Louisiana, General Sheridan, telegraphed asking him to declare the whites there 'banditti', saying 'no further action need be taken except that which would devolve on me'. The real aim of all this was, as Stevens said, 'to secure perpetual ascendancy to the Republican Party'. This continuing attempt to transfer power in the Republic to a more recently arrived section of the community is the reality of all politics there today, though it is now pursued by the other party.

Those fantastic years in the South, I found when I went over the ground, are illuminating for the understanding of the present. The mass of liberated slaves, utterly bewildered, returned to the plantations; chronicles of the day record the gratified surprise of the whites at their general behaviour. Some of them, however, received arms and joined with poor whites of the South and 'carpet-baggers' from the North in a twelve-year orgy of ruin and corruption. The carpet-baggers were men of the kind whom the Western Powers in 1945 forced on the countries of Eastern Europe, thus abandoning them to the Communist Empire. They descended on the South like flies on cadaver, making themselves leaders of the negroes and exerting every means to keep the freed men from returning to their former masters or befriending themselves with the whites.

These carpet-baggers offered the negroes the white man's lands, womenfolk and money, and incited them to take those. The moon looked down on wild festivals of drunken intermingling in the idle cottonfields. Negro superstition was exploited and at black masses (a recognizable feature of any such regime) fearful fates were depicted to any who voted the wrong way. On the ruins of State governments macabre Conventions met and carpet-bagger orators, inciting black audiences, disfranchised masses of the whites. In mock parliaments the people's representatives laughed and yelled, passed bills with their feet on the backs of chairs, sent out for cases of liquor and boxes of cigars, and ran up enormous debts; in Louisiana alone one of these sessions cost nearly $1,000,000 as against $100,000 before, some of the largest items being for champagne and other entertainment. One observer wrote, 'It is a monkeyhouse, with guffaws, disgusting interpolations, amendments offered that are too obscene to print, followed by shouts of glee. Members stagger from the basement bar to their seats; the Speaker in righteous mood sternly forbids the introduction of liquor on the floor. A curious old planter stands in the galleries a moment looking down on the scene and with an exclamation, "My God!" he turns and runs, as from a pestilence, into the street.'

Such corruption at the river's mouth could not come from a source less corrupt. Mr. Bowers wrote in 1929 that 'never have American public men in responsible positions, directing the destiny of the nation, been so brutal, hypocritical and corrupt'. Mr. Truslow Adams, in 1931, spoke of 'the most shameful decade in our entire national history' and of 'a moral collapse without precedent and, let us hope, without successor'. Since President Roosevelt reintroduced the 'racial discrimination' issue into the forefront of American political controversy these comments have become apt to the living present.

The wonder is that the South ever lifted itself from that prostration, and by its own bootstraps. During the worst years the minority of misguided negroes was held in check by the Ku-Klux-Klan, which effectively played on superstitious fears. It was in truth a resistance movement, and only when I saw the South did I understand something that formerly puzzled me; why the Communists in 1950 still rail so much about the Ku-Klux-Klan. They fear future resistance movements, not the one of 1865-77. The negro also played a part in the recovery. He was unable, at little more than one remove from the Congo, to look after himself and turned to the white folks. His natural virtues also contributed. To me he seems, in Africa or America, an innately conservative man in the mass. He is not good revolutionary material, save possibly in the moment of ecstatic excitement to which he is prone, and he is often deeply religious. It was a Negro Senator who wrote in 1876: 'A great portion of our people have learned that they were being used as mere tools and determined, by casting their ballots against these unprincipled adventurers, to overthrow them.' That precisely describes the relationship between the negroes and the white politicians who use the racial-discrimination issue today. Mr. Truslow Adams says of the twelve years, 'There is no parallel for the situation in the history of modern civilized nations, and it is almost incredible that it occurred within our own country.' American politics of today, however, are moving parallel with those of 1860 and again, not for the good of the negro but to divide white people.

I was perhaps better equipped than most, by long experience, to relate the story of those years to our today. I was also in a good town and a good house to study them. The town knew the full brunt of the tragedy and by wonder escaped General Sherman's burning. The house once watched the young men go gaily off to fight, but saw few of them return; it knew also the anguished prayer meetings of 1865, when it was filled with weeping women, the South was in ruins, and no future offered. It had survived to know again the presence of a large and happy family in its fine rooms. Yet the memory of many tears was in it, and all around. I paid a call on neighbours who, I was told, were rich people 'before the war' but now somewhat reduced. I expressed surprise, saying I thought America was richer, not poorer, through the war. 'Ah, I mean the Civil War,' said my companion, and I remembered that in South Africa too 'the war' means the old one, not either of the world wars.

The South has never fully recovered, though it is advancing quickly now. It still has people who have never been able to adjust themselves to the changed order and who live amid furniture and hangings which seem to have 1865 imprinted on them, ancestral portraits then discontinued, and the remnant of family silver, possibly saved by a faithful negro. Like Irish squireens, impoverished but unbowed, they live as in a vacuum suspended in time. Deliberately but without posturing they reject compromise with a time they feel inferior to the one that the wind destroyed. If neighbours arrive from afar these remain 'Northerners, but nice'.

In such a Southern town the America which grew out of 1865 has but one outpost: Main Street, with its drugstore, red-and-gilt five-and-ten-cent stores, movie theatre, hamburgeria, juke-boxes and all. Where hitching-posts may once have stood are now slot-machines which sell the parking motorist time for a dime and with moving finger record the length of his absence. The thought of this mechanical conscience is unnerving; you may see a behelmeted and beshrouded lady rush from a hairdresser's in mid-perm to propitiate the machine. These dime-boxes are often the consolation of American policemen; fearing that their superiors may not wish them to interfere with other forms of evildoing, they apply themselves to watching the red needle and the laggard motorist.

In this Main Street, having let my hair grow for a month at sea rather than submit it to an engine-room hand who claimed he could cut it, I sought a barber's shop. It was like a tonsorial church where barber's masses were celebrated. It had rows of high seats for those who only wanted their shoes polished. If it lacked censers with sweet-smelling herbs, it had brazen pots for another purpose, and music, broken only by announcements that it came by courtesy of Cosmic Cosmetics. While your hair was cut a kneeling black acolyte shone your shoes, and if you spread your hands, as in benediction, another, white and female, at once polished the nails. The barber seemed to be invested with some inner authority; as he pressed a lever and tilted me into a prostrate and helpless position I reflected that he had in fact power of life and death.

I asked for 'a light trim' and received a ruthless shearing; when I returned to the vertical I wondered if the old scalping tradition yet lingered. Not long ago a man could earn good money by bringing in a scalp; in 1800 old Thomas Armit of Pittsburgh lamented that his son legally married a squaw whereas in his own day 'ye could have drawed fifty dollars good money for her skelp'; perhaps my barber had scalping-blood in his veins? He said my hair would look nice next time it was cut, then hurriedly added, 'It looks pretty nice now'. 'I heard you the first time,' I said. 'It sure needed cutting badly,' he said. 'It needed cutting well,' I said, 'I've just made a long sea voyage.' 'You don't say!' he said, 'I was at sea until last fall.' 'An engine-room hand?' I asked. 'Sure,' he said, 'how did you know?' 'I wondered,' I said, 'thank you.' 'You bet,' he said.

I usually try to learn what people read. The Main Street American often says, 'I don't read as much as you could put in your eye'; this self-imposed outlawry from the thought of the ages seemed a lonely thing to me. However, I did not then know this and looked about until I found The Little Bookshop (America has given way to the Quainte and the Olde, a vogue now outlived in England, and I even saw a Gifte Shoppe). The Little Bookshop's large window contained a big stuffed horse; any books must have been in hidden recesses. The main source of literary supply, I later learned, is often the drugstore, which displays racks of paper-covered volumes. These may be classics or shockers, but impartially wear a cover-picture of a girl in a low dress, revealing pumpkin-like contents; I never elsewhere saw books sold exclusively on cleavage-appeal. This seems part of the New America; many planters of the old South had standing orders with booksellers in London and Paris and rare editions are to be found in their houses.

In these early days everything was new, different, delightful, surprising or strange, especially days spent in an American home among young people, all approaching marriage, and their parents. Life moved at speed; the young men came and went by car or aeroplane and the girls rode high-voltage horses, the sight of which made my cracked backbone wince. Had I known, this was to be the last chance of pleasant conversation for some while. In America as a whole time does not suffice for talk.

One girl came, from broadcasting work, late to a meal because she had to deputize for an announcer stricken with hiccups. I thought this was a chance missed, for everybody has heard an announcer *without* hiccups; he should have been introduced to listeners in suitable words, 'We bring you something you have never heard before, the hiccuping announcer.' Then the hiccuper: 'This programme comes to you, hup pardon, by courtesy of Pepper's Anti-Dyspeptic Pepsin, hup sorry.'

(I was glad this amused, for the wayfarer in the Republic, if he is of jesting bent, will leave his ewe-lambs scattered behind him, unrecognized and unwanted. Even my good companion in Mobile was unresponsive to a joke. He first introduced me to the cafeteria, and as he sat down with food and drink asked the negro attendant for a straw. 'No straw, sah,' said the man. 'You don't have a *straw*!' exclaimed my friend in irritable surprise. 'Perhaps they've used it to break the camel's back,' I said. 'I guess so,' he said, looking at me gravely.)

Now the girl who broadcast told the story of the radio-announcement of the executions at Nuremberg. All the 'ace' American broadcasters strained themselves to outdo each other in dramatic effect, and one fell headfirst over the uttermost brink of hyperbole by crying hoarsely into the microphone, 'Goering cheated death tonight by committing suicide!' This reminded me of a wartime headline in London's *Evening Standard* when the boxer Joe Louis was enlisted in the American Army: 'My fighting days are over, says Joe Louis.'

There was a bright moment, too, when a son of the house used the word desultory, pronouncing it desul*tory*. He checked himself and asked me if that were right. I said humbly that, for what it was worth, the word was spoken desult'ry in England; we had been so much intimidated about the word Tory that we instinctively slurred it now. In the South that point immediately took.

One night the negro singers gathered in the music-room, four women and three men. Their faces were still the African ones I knew, though Africa was but a legend to them, like Saxony to an Anglo-Saxon. I often heard negro spirituals before, but found that to be really 'heard' (in the sense the African negro himself uses the word) they need to be sung in an old plantation house of the South which once had its own slaves. In it the most poignant memories of both races mingle; those of the grey-coated young men lightly setting out and the women waiting in fading hope; those of black folk transplanted from their original continent. Perhaps the white man and the black one come nearest together in these songs.

Song was the solitary way in which these people could express their souls when they were slaves and sat in the evenings by their huts, among the cottonfields. A typical figure, at once sorrowful and reassuring, of the American scene today, Mr. Whittaker Chambers, once described the negro spiritual in inspired words: 'It was the religious voice of a whole religious people . . . One simple fact is clear: the spirituals were created in direct answer to the psalmist's question, "How shall we sing the Lord's song in a strange land?" . . . Grief, like a tuning-fork, gave the tone, and the Sorrow Songs were uttered.'

That is the arresting truth; these people sang, on a note of abiding faith, to and of the Christian God. They no longer knew what gods, or idols, their forefathers had. Listening, I wondered whither music has fled from many Christian churches. If passers-by heard singing like this come from a spired building in any mean street of London or New York the churches would be ever full, and that croaking raven of our day, the communist cleric, would flap dismally away from their belfries.

I listened in enchantment to the blending of voices, the harmony and variations, the subtle repetitions and interventions:

33

Nobody knows what trouble I've seen,
Nobody knows but Jesus . . .
Sometimes I'm up, sometimes I'm down,
Sometimes I'm right to the groun'.
Glory Hallelujah!

There was one with a tremendous, infectious beat and rhythm, in which I clearly heard the native dances of Africa. The corpuscle is still in the blood and gives the same itch to feet and shoulders:

I went to the rock to hide my face,
The rock cried out, 'No hiding place,
There's no hiding place down there!'
The sinner man, he gambled and fell,
Wanted to go to heaven but had to go to hell,
There's no hiding place down there!

And then one which rolled and dwindled like a peal of distant thunder echoing down the ages:

Were you there when they crucified my Lord?
Were you there when they nailed Him to the cross?
Sometimes it causes me to tremble . . .
tremble . . .
tremble . . .
Were you there when they crucified my Lord?

The grandchildren of freed slaves sang it to the grandchildren of Southern planters and a harmony filled the pleasant room.

Reluctantly, one day, I left this green and white retreat and set out on my further way, along roads marked to commemorate the battles of the colonists against the King's men and then those of the South against the North. They lead eventually, like signposts, to the different America which emerged from them.

CHAPTER 3

WHERE IT ALL BEGAN

T H E car slid along the road like a ring on silken ribbon as I went through the Carolinas towards Virginia. I wondered if all American roads were as excellent. I found they are; if all human life were suddenly removed from earth, later visitors from other planets might find these roads among the most remarkable works left behind by its dwellers.

On the wayside tablets famous names showed and were gone: Washington and Cornwallis, Grant and Lee. The countryside was much like England in its contours and spring colouring; the white houses, large and small, continued familiar in shape to an English traveller despite the clapboard walls. The names too: I came to Raleigh, so called after that Sir Walter who had named the first colony for his unmarried queen. Not far away was Roanoke Island where at the third attempt in 1587 he landed 150 men, women and children from Devon. The supply ships, four years later, found only empty huts and a mysterious word, 'Croatoan', carved on a tree (today the Roanoke Islanders, in the manner of Passion Play villagers in Germany, re-enact the mystery of those vanished colonists each year). When the next colonists came, in 1607, James was king and they established Jamestown on the James River, a little farther north.

So it all began. Had Drake not sunk the Armada in 1588 the Spaniards might have pushed their civilization northward along this coast from Mexico; had Wolfe not taken Quebec in 1759 the French might have come southward from Canada and clinched their hold on the innerlands. Instead the English spread north, south and west and founded the American Republic.

Raleigh in 1949, was far from all that. Hunger drove me to a drugstore there and I asked for a sandwich. The girl took one readymade out of its wrapping, thrust it into a toaster, and in a recognizable trice a hot sandwich lay before me. I was only starting to learn the stool-and-counter way of eating, the quickfire service, the staccato vocabulary. Soon I knew the 'short stack' and the 'cheeseburger', but never fully accustomed myself to the impersonal haste of it all.

The quieter South fell behind and I met the busy roadside life of the teeming central region. The gaps grew ever smaller between filling-stations, drive-in theatres, diners, cafés, roadhouses, trailer-courts and tourist-camps, stalls and booths. The first entry into a city of size, Richmond, was bewildering. Awed by innumerable signs forbidding the traveller to stop, pause or turn, I was swept along in a traffic-stream from which I could conceive no escape. However, these problems of the newcomer do solve themselves and at nightfall I found myself in an hotel bedroom. Tired out, I put my shoes in the passage and fell asleep. At two in the morning I was wakened by loud knocking and shouts of 'Bellboy, sah, yoh shoes is outside the door'. I opened the door to a smiling negro whose grin plainly said, 'Lawdy, how drunk you musta bin!' Too sleepy to be intelligent, I said the shoes were there to be cleaned. 'Ah never heard of that,' he said in patent disbelief, and waited expectantly. I saw he thought he had saved my shoes from theft and remembered a remote inn in the Carpathians where I suffered such loss.

These are all minor frustrations, for the stranger. Later I realized that shoeshine parlours would complain if shoes were cleaned in hotels, and that hat-blocking parlours might fail if hats were brushed in them. The charm about people is that they are different; Americans seem to feel the day ill begun if they have not had a hat blocked, while I have spent my adult years trying to reduce mine to a devil-may-care shabbiness, always being defied by their obstinate selfwill. Once I rescued one from the debris of a bombed cleaner's in London, thinking its dents would now stay in and its brim remain down, but it was more arrogant than ever. I put three intolerable hats on a rose bush in a Sussex garden during a drenching rainstorm once, hoping to break their spirits. The vicar, calling on a new resident, saw them there and was curious, so that I explained; his visit seemed brief, even for a duty call.

Presumably Richmond-on-James was named from Richmond-on-

Thames, a royal town. Had the South won the Civil War it might be the American capital today. Had the war ended in reconciliation under a living Lincoln, its spirit and influence, with those of an earlier Washington, might have been greater in the shaping of the new America, which is its opposite. The line of the violent break is clear in the picture of America today.

It is particularly plain in Richmond. I looked at Capitol Square with sensations of recognition and pleasure. Thomas Jefferson took the Maison Carrée at Nîmes as model for the Capitol itself, while fine old English-type houses surround it. Here is dignity and, what puzzled me at first, the feeling of age. Later I realized that New England and the South are older than their buildings, because these, through their models, include the best of former centuries. The earlier Americans turned their faces towards, not from, the two thousand years of European civilization; they meant to improve on and not to deny it. This attitude towards life was expressed also in the lives of Americans of that time. The break came with the end of the nineteenth century and the United Nations building in New York is the symbol of the new philosophy.

Washington's statue prompts a question: were men better then, or merely sculptors? What could any sculptor make of Lenin, Stalin, Hitler or Mussolini? Does that which is bred in the bone come out in the bronze? This statue is as near truth as can be, for it is a portrait, to measurement, of a man of fifty-two, over six feet tall, of noble appearance, who saw it when Houdon finished it. The one in Trafalgar Square is a cast from it. Another, in Grosvenor Square, shows an American president erect who in fact could not stand alone. The subject of truth in statuary is of some interest.

From old Richmond I turned to new; Main Street. This was the biggest Main Street yet, though smaller than many yet to come. I found in time that they all reproduce each other; Henry James, who did not like Main Street and its intersections, wrote of 'the dreadful multiplied numberings which seem to reduce the whole place to some vast ledger-page, overgrown, fantastic, of ruled and criss-crossed lines and figures'. Their variety of merchandise is immense, and the personal touch is now that of a vanished hand.

In Capitol Square, Richmond, I felt as I would feel in the Place de la Concorde or Pall Mall. In Main Street, Richmond, though it is but a corner's turn away, I felt as if I were in an Eastern bazaar; and indeed Main Street is an Eastern bazaar that runs from New York to Los Angeles, and puts out branches left and right. There I first felt the speed of life in today's America, that philosophy of pace at any price which the people adopt, either to reach or escape from something. The South has effectively resisted it, and Richmond is very much the South; but its Main Street, like all the others, belongs to New York. In the roadway State Troopers whizzed past on screaming motor-bicycles and as they went talked by microphone with some equally audible Chief, no doubt steely-eyed and iron-jawed, at police head-quarters. On the sidewalks a tomboyish vogue reigned for the moment and the young girls set out to look as if they came straight from a shakedown, not from a make-up; they wore tousled and tumbled hair, a tough air, and crumpled shirts loose outside rolled-up and stained blue jeans, the ensemble being called 'Sloppy Joe'. They looked for the nonce like orphans of the Bolshevist Revolution but soon were to change, at the Garment Centre's next dictate, to the opposite cult of perfect neatness. The men remained recognizably Southerners, the young ones personable and deferential, the older ones quiet and easy-mannered.

By chance I was in Richmond on Army Day and saw a military parade which, to me, vividly symbolized the story of the Republic. It was led by detachments of two famous regiments, the Richmond Grays and Richmond Blues, in their historic shakoes and tailcoats. They fought, in their time, under Washington, with the British against the French and Indians and next, still under him, against the British; then for the South against the North, and later wherever opportunity offered. They were fine lads in the spotlights and marched across Capitol Square towards a question mark: the future. If they and their kind had the making of it the answer would be reassuring, but that was the doubtful point. Next to me a lady watched them with love in her eyes and chatted about them. Though of great age she was in the first fine careless rapture. She put in fourteen hundred hours of war work in the first war, she said, and in the second taught four hundred people how to knit; her simple faith seemed to be impaired by no misgivings about the *results* of those two wars, and in it she was plainly ready to spring to her knitting needle again at any alarm.

I remember Richmond for a quite different spectacle, too, that offered by a Human Cannonball. I was interested in Human Cannonballs because, many years ago, I met a pretty one in Berlin who said her painful profession frustrated all maternal hopes, so that I asked why she didn't get herself fired. That left me with an idea, never pursued but never quite abandoned, for a novel about a Human Cannonball. I saw it as a story of frustrated love and motherhood, of a feminine Pagliacci flying ever above the gaping crowd with aching heart behind the goggles and crash helmet, as it were; how could a girl aspire to settle down to conjugal joys, with all those bruises! Now I went to watch Richmond's Human Cannonball. A lover of fireworks, I was enthralled by the great howitzer, the fine explosion, the smoke and the white figure flying over the wheel to the net. Best of all, I found that my unwritten comedy had a happy ending. Despite the bruises (which are the least injuries to be feared in the calling) this Human Cannonball was the mother of two fine children; I hoped my earlier acquaintance, who by now must have put her projectile days behind her, similarly found her fears empty and her arms full.

Within a few jumps of Richmond are the still older places from which it, Virginia, the group of English colonies, the American Republic and today's heterogeneous Union all sprang. This region, even more than New England to the north, is the cradle of the giant who has now reached adolescence and, on that brink, looks uncertainly into what lies beyond. First comes Williamsburg, the colonial centre before Richmond rose. Its historic Colonial Capitol and Sir Christopher Wren's College of William and Mary have been restored to complete beauty by Rockefeller money, and stand monuments to the quality of the early pioneers and a challenge to the present. Next door to it is Jamestown, where all began, with the ivy-covered ruin of an English church. A little farther on is Yorktown, where Cornwallis surrendered to Washington and the second stage in the American odyssey began; the fortifications of that siege remain.

This is the perfect route for the understanding of America. Richmond, Washington and New York are the successive tiers of the edifice. Richmond was the capital-city of the thirteen Colonies; Washington was that of the Republic of thirty States which grew out of them and pushed inland from the eastern seaboard; New York is the real capital of today's transcontinental empire of forty-nine States. Whose is the inheritance? Were the War of Independence and the Civil War but two wars of the succession, which new pretenders are following with a third, possibly unarmed one, in the twentieth century?

The process looked to have that shape. A new struggle for power in the Republic was in progress. I set out for Washington, through a hundred miles of history as momentous as Napoleon's hundred days.

CHAPTER 4

CAPITAL OF THE CONTINUATION

A GREAT city gleamed softly ahead in the haze and roads curved towards it between green expanses. In that dulcet early morning light it might have been Camelot but for the clamant throng of four-wheeled traffic, which gave it the look of an anthill and made me halt while afar off, like a foraying commander in a strange land, to consider how I might best enter. Once in the main torrent, I knew, I would be swept on, the helpless captive of stop-signs, traffic-lights and policemen's whistles. Carefully I studied the lie of the land, saw a roadside advertisement offering cheap rooms, went into a filling-station and telephoned. Yes, I might have a room; when would I arrive? 'That,' I said, like King Harry's soldier before Agincourt, 'is more than I know.'

Bracing myself against the shock, I plunged into the maelstrom. To travel in America with sleeping berths, rooms and air-liner seats forebooked is one thing; to explore it alone and humbly is another. I was carried through and out of Washington, then back and out again, and at the third attempt, like an unwelcome guest repeatedly re-entering swing-doors from which he has been thrown, contrived to turn quickly into a parking-lot with one vacant place. Then, blessing the three Rs, I set out afoot to unravel the lettered or numbered streets and find a particular conjunction. Arrived, breathless, I fell into a seat and ordered a coffee. A pleasant young man at once appeared and asked if I would try a camel. While I still wondered how one could help me, in Washington, he handed me a packet, said 'It's a mild smoke, sir', and vanished.

These initial encounters with American cities are major experiences. The traveller's feeling of hopeless homelessness changes to triumph when he succeeds in dodging the hooting pursuers, doubling up and down side streets, sighting a lodging, and being accepted. It deepens into a fugitive's misery when he enters a crowded convention city at dusk, is whirled along by a Mississippi of motor cars, and finds any door he can reach closed against him.

From this furious chase I took brief, happy refuge in Washington. Standing, like Belgrade, where two rivers meet, it is of the world's fine cities, and plainly a cousin of the European ones. Here the era of the Colonies merged, without violent change, into that of the Republic just as the Corinthian columns grew on to the Southern mansions. These splendid white buildings and memorials descend from Greece and Rome, like those of Munich. The formal gardens and vistas speak of Fontainebleau and Versailles. Likewise, the surrounding country-side, and Washington's house there, reflect the firm dignity of domestic architecture in seventeenth-century England. In Washington the sym-bols of the Republic's unexampled rise run to and from each other across shining river and green parkland in a straight line, itself symbolic: the Capitol, Washington's obelisk, Lincoln's temple, Lee's house. With them the straight line fades into an enigmatic future. If it is to be pro-longed to the tombstone building in New York, that is a sharp turn to the left and a leap into obscurity.

Of Athens, Cicero said that its glories in stone delighted him less than the thought of the great men who lived, worked, debated, dis-puted, died and were buried there. In Washington the feeling of a group of great men, Washington, Jefferson, Lee and Lincoln, is tangible and the buildings express their quality. The question mark at the end of them is equally palpable. Great presidents may make a great republic, but what happens if the noble breed gives out? The four-yearly election is not merely that of a prime minister, but of a head of State. Henry Adams thought 'the succession of Presidents from Washington to Grant is almost enough in itself to upset the whole Darwinian theory', and Mr. Albert Jay Nock in 1943 added: 'Had Adams lived to see the succession extended to the present time he would perhaps say it was quite enough.' Mr. Nock did not see the events of 1944-50; he died calling himself *A Superfluous Man* in an American era which alarmed him.

Despite the still living echo of Northern armies tramping along Pennsylvania Avenue to crush the South, Washington remains a Southern city; the memory of great Southerners and their works fills it.

It owes much of its beauty to the original plan, which was the child of L'Enfant, a French military engineer. Urbane charm often grows better in towns laid out for defence than in those conceived on draught-boards by civic planners. L'Enfant designed long, broad boulevards, similar to those of Haussmann, which intersected each other at circular junctions; from these round-points the military could mow down invaders or rioters from all directions.

Time plays its pranks. The result is a delightful place to live but one indefensible against today's infiltrators, who may arrive at Capitols and government departments, in Washington or Westminster, by limousine, and be saluted by janitors as they enter. L'Enfant's roundabouts today impede only the American motorist, and tunnels are being made beneath them so that he may gain the world a few seconds quicker. The beauty of Washington cannot be impaired in its basic quality, but is much blurred or masked by the enormous mass of traffic, moving and standing. I could see no final answer to the parking problem, unless by some new device of claws or grappling hooks, cars become enabled to scale tall houses and hang themselves from the window-sills.

The human scene of the city, at this mid-century, was not congruous to the classic dignity of its inanimate shape. The effort to dethrone Washington, with all other national capitals, in favour of the super-national committee in New York gave the tone to life in it and all the political intrigues of the world seemed to have moved into it. Congress, when I looked down on it, was a pleasant place, but in its lobbies prowled the 'fixers' and priority-pedlars, who courted politically influential men with flattery and gifts, usually small. In Washington, as in London, committees inquired into such practices and, again in both capitals, missed the important point, which was not that of petty venality or of 'priority' gained for 'a project' of the fixer's friends. Politicians, once caught in such toils, may later find themselves under pressures, then less easily resisted, in major affairs of State, especially foreign ones. The political affiliations of well-known 'fixers', in Washington and London, might be instructive if they were more publicly known, but this aspect of the matter is never examined by the commissions which, in both capitals, are periodically charged to investigate the evil.

Congressmen and Senators seemed unaware of the fish that might be fried at barbecues and cocktail parties given for them by newcomers to the capital. Political Zionists, Communists, Irish Republicans and others wooed the powerful by flattery or covert intimidation. At the top level Political Zionism looked like a ruling power; to express doubt about its undertakings was like confessing heresy before an inquisition. Beneath the surface, the Communists rose by permeation to ever higher levels. Always denying their real allegiance, they had in twelve years come to infest the capital. Partial disclosures were recurrently made of this fermenting mass at the Republic's centre and each time some master hand pulled down a blind between the matter and the public gaze. Washington was become rather like the medieval courts of Naples, on a greater scale. I later learned, from one of these fragmentary exposures, that a drugstore where I sometimes drank coffee was a clearing-centre between Washington's Communists and Moscow, where papers purloined from official files were handled.

This corrosive influence displayed itself in curious ways, alien to the Christian principles on which the Republic was founded. In a busy street I saw a large covered vehicle from which a loud, mechanical voice invited all to 'come in and see Goering's treasures', and as admission-fee to make a donation to the United States Marine Corps League. The United States Marines (like the Royal Marines) are an elite corps of the highest tradition, whose recruiting posters say:

> First to fight for right and glory
> And to keep our honour clean,
> We are proud to bear the title
> Of United States Marines.

They may have had little to do with this exhibition, which redounded to nobody's honour. The truck contained wedding-gifts (presumably looted) made to Goering when he married his second wife, the actress Emmy Sonnemann, in Berlin about 1934: a silver dinner-set from Hitler, a silver inkstand from the City of Berlin, a vanity-set from the German Air Force and so on. The mechanical voice roared into the streets of Washington that this or that gift was made to Goering on his wedding-night 'by his mistress, Karin'. Karin Goering married him just after the first war, when he was a penniless and out-of-work young ex-officer, and died long before Hitler even came to power. This was the first word I ever heard uttered against a woman twenty years dead; the owner of the mechanical voice apparently knew and cared nothing about the facts of Goering's life.

Washington was filled with a kind of whispered, muttered tumult, that of the world's conflicting political ambitions, nearly all pursued behind the cloak of other purposes. In this conspiratorial hubbub a quiet spot held me most absorbed. I liked to eat in a restaurant facing Ford's Theatre, where Lincoln was murdered. From my table I looked across at the door through which he was carried, to a house adjoining the restaurant, where he died. I went into the theatre and saw the door of the box in which he was shot. I began to study the event itself and soon felt again like a man who finds unexpectedly familiar things in an old tomb. This was not something that merely happened seventy-five years ago, but part of something that continued today. I drove to the Anacostia Bridge, over which the murderer fled, and followed the line of his flight to the Potomac River. Then I read the accounts of the crime and the evidence.

Here was something I recognized. . . .

CHAPTER 5

OF MURDER AND MOTIVE

... This mystery has four chief parts: the man, the moment, the murderers and the motive.

The man, like the victims of other comparable crimes, was a unifier and reconciler. He fought the South to preserve the Union, *not* to abolish slavery: 'My paramount object is not to save or destroy slavery ... If all earthly powers were given me I should not know what to do with the existing institution' (of slavery). Though he unwillingly issued the slave-freeing Proclamation he never departed in conviction from the original, declared aim of the war: 'It is not for any purpose ... of interfering with the rights or established institutions of the Secession States but to preserve the Union with all the dignity, equality and rights of the several States unimpaired.' He intended to defeat only the claimed right to secede;* then to restore the Union and leave the legal institution of slavery to be gradually modified into abolition by judicial courts.

In that policy the Leftist Republicans around him saw the danger of the conservative Democrats returning to power. They introduced the false issue of slavery into the war to perpetuate the Republican Party in power by taking the vote from the Southern States and the Southern whites and giving it to the negroes, of whom not one in a hundred could then read. (Similarly the aims of the Second World War, when it was half run, were changed from the liberation of countries overrun and the restoration of parliamentary governments to 'the defeat of Fascism', which meant their re-surrender to Soviet Communism.)

Lincoln's Republican Party contained the mass of Leftists, who were near to dominating it. Lincoln knew that they raised the bogus issue to inflame passions and prolong the war; his own Secretary of War,

---

* ¡The secession dispute itself is one of history's recurrent jests, summed up by an American humorist in these words: 'If you admit the right of secession, sir, my sympathies are with the South; if you deny it, God bless his Majesty!'

46

Edwin Stanton (who with Thaddeus Stevens headed this group), said so: 'The great aim of the war is to abolish slavery. To end the war before the nation is ready for that would be a failure. The war must be prolonged and conducted so as to achieve that.' (The Second World War was similarly prolonged, through wasteful detours, to achieve 'the defeat of Fascism', but *not* the original aim.) Lincoln was an obstacle to the forces of destruction in his own party.

Such was the *man*. The *moment* of his murder was that at which he was about to fulfil his policy of reconciliation and accomplish the declared aim of the war. Two days before Lee at last surrendered and Washington was lit up. At the very moment Lincoln's emissary, General Sherman, was negotiating with the Southern leaders a truce following Lincoln's constant line: no confiscation or political disablement, recognition of the Southern States governments if they took the oath to the Constitution, reunion, conciliation. (That was as if President Roosevelt, at Yalta, had upheld the war aims originally understood by the Western peoples, instead of surrendering half of Europe to a regime resembling that endured by the South after Lincoln's death.) At Lincoln's last cabinet meeting, on the day he was killed, he said he was glad Congress was adjourned; the extremists in it would not be able to hinder the work of reviving State governments in orderly fashion. 'There must be no bloody work', he would have no part in hangings or killings; the task was 'to extinguish resentments'.

At that moment the man was killed. In the choice of time and victim the crime startlingly resembles four others, which also struck down unifiers and conciliators just when they seemed likely to impede the process of universal revolutionary destruction. Alexander II of Russia emancipated twenty million serfs in 1861 and pursued his work of reconciliation until he was murdered in 1881; of that crime Soviet Communism and Political Zionism were born. In 1913 the Archduke was killed at Serajevo; he had the reputation of a unifier and conciliator who might have saved the Austro-Hungarian Empire from war and disintegration, *had he lived*. In 1934 Alexander of Yugoslavia was killed at Marseilles; he was a unifier who could not have been turned from his throne by an ally, as his little-known eighteen-year-old son Peter was in effect in 1945 by Mr. Churchill, and a Communist dictator set in his place. In 1948 Count Bernadotte was murdered as he completed a plan of truce and pacification in Palestine.

Each of these events changed the course of history for the worse. Together with the wars and annexations to which they led and the revolutionary movements which profited by them, they produced the state of affairs with which the Western world finds itself faced at this mid-century. In each case the men marked for death were ones who stood for reconciliation, unity, orderly judicial reforms and 'the extinguishing of resentments', as Lincoln said. In each instance (save that of Count Bernadotte, where no pretence of justice was done), nondescript individuals were publicly presented as the culprits. On each occasion a powerful organization obviously stood behind those puppets and each time all was done to prevent its exposure.

None can doubt today that Lincoln was removed to prevent the reconciliation of North and South and the consolidation of the Union. Though the wound did seem later to heal, the events of today show it still to be raw, so that the conspirators' aim of 1865 cannot yet be said, in 1950, to have failed. Time has yet to show this result, with all others.

The culprits displayed to the populace were the usual group of obscure individuals, who clearly could not have carried out the deed unaided. Lincoln's killer, the actor John Wilkes Booth, escaped for a while. A benchful of generals promptly executed one Lewis Paine,* a youth called David Herold who accompanied Booth in his flight, a mysterious German, George Atzerodt, and a woman boarding-house-keeper, Mrs. Suratt. Pending trial, the prisoners were kept in solitary cells, with empty cells on either side, and made to wear thick padded hoods, with small holes for nose and mouth, over head and shoulders. The only plausible explanation is that communication with any other person whatsoever was to be prevented. These four, and four men sent to a remote island, all *knew* Booth and his associates. Men who helped him escape, but did not know him before, were not even charged.

---

* Who simultaneously attacked, but did not kill, the Secretary of State, Frederick Seward, the only other man in Lincoln's Cabinet who unfalteringly pursued reunion and reconciliation.

That looks as if the capital offence was to be in possession of information about Booth's movements and acquaintances in Washington. For that the State prosecutor seems to have demanded death and the four men sent to an island only escaped it because the generals shied at wholesale hangings without evidence of complicity. Studying this aspect of the matter, I recalled van der Lubbe, the vagrant found in the burning Reichstag. I believe he was kept drugged during his trial and until his beheading; he alone could have said who put him in the Reichstag. The demeanour of Rudolf Hess, at the Nuremberg Trial, was similar to that of van der Lubbe; none but he could publicly explain the wartime mission on which he was sent to England.

The circumstances of Lincoln's murder speak for themselves. Booth fired the shot into his neck as he watched the play. The door of the box was unlocked, but on the inner side of it someone had placed a wooden bar and a mortice, so that Booth could ensure that none entered it *after* himself! At the door should have been Lincoln's armed bodyguard, a Washington policeman, recently enlisted, called John F. Parker. Only his empty chair was there and no word survives in the records to say why he was not in it! This collapse of protective vigilance was a feature of the Serajevo, Marseilles and Jerusalem murders. President Lincoln's danger was well known. That very afternoon he asked his Secretary of War if Stanton's stalwart aide, a Major Eckert, could accompany him to the theatre for his protection. Stanton refused and Eckert, asked by the President himself, also declined (on the next day Stanton telegraphed to General Sherman that he too was in danger 'and I beseech you to be more heedful than Mr. Lincoln was of such knowledge').

The missing bodyguard, Parker, was appointed less than a fortnight before the murder, during Lincoln's absence from Washington, so that the usual presidential confirmation of his appointment was never obtained. In three years service serious complaints of 'neglect of duty' were several times made against him and in April 1864 he was dismissed. In December 1864 he was reinstated and in April 1865, immediately before the deed, allotted to the President's personal protection! After the murder he was again charged with 'neglect of duty'; the trial was secret, the complaint was dismissed, and the records of the hearing have vanished from the files. Three years later he was once again charged with dereliction, dismissed, and at that point vanishes from history!

Thus Booth walked into an unguarded box, shot the President, jumped on to the stage, ran through unguarded wings to the back door, jumped on a waiting horse and rode away. He caught his spurred boot on some bunting as he jumped, fell awkwardly and broke a small bone in his leg.

This alone seems to have prevented him from getting clean away. He rode across the Anacostia bridge and along the well-known route to Virginia which the Southerners, throughout the war, used for spies and communications with the North. Behind him galloping cavalrymen were sent to scour the country, north and west, which he obviously would avoid. This one southward route, which a flying Southerner would clearly take, was left open long enough for him to escape. His unforeseeable injury prevented that; unable to go on the actor went into hiding.

If his escape was desired, this naturally threw up a new problem. After a few days his whereabouts became known and the chase was converging on him when the military Provost Marshal, who led it, was suddenly recalled to Washington and the pursuit entrusted to the head of the secret service, one Colonel Lafayette C. Baker. He was given 'twenty-six cavalrymen' commanded by 'a reliable and discreet commissioned officer', Lieutenant Doherty. This officer, however, was placed under the orders of two of Colonel Baker's detectives, his cousin, ex-Lieutenant Luther B. Baker, and an ex-Colonel Conger, who 'by courtesy was conceded the command'. Whose courtesy is not recorded, though Lieutenant Doherty's chagrin is. This force eventually surrounded the barn where Booth lay hidden, with strict orders to take him alive. Of the twenty-nine men none could clearly say later who fired the shot which killed him. Baker thought Conger did; Conger denied it.

Clearly Booth would have escaped but for his damaged foot. With his death none remained who could tell the whole truth; those who knew most were quickly hanged or exiled.

Thus the *man*, the *moment*, and the *apparent murderers*. The *motive* today seems as clear as the organization behind it remained, and remains, obscure. It was to remove Lincoln because he was an obstacle to the destruction of the South. The student from afar, who finds Lincoln honoured equally with Washington, on deeper study learns how lonely he was when he died. To the collapsing South he was the destroyer; to the North he was the enemy of further destruction. To-day's traveller may perceive a great flaw in the array of memorials erected to Lincoln in his country. Suggestively, they commemorate him as the slayer of slavery, first and foremost. It is the continuation of a falsehood; that was not his primary aim, he was against violent demagogic actions, preferred judicial gradualness, and had at heart only the unity of the Union. Thus his memory is misused today in the further pursuit of ulterior schemes; the false issue, the falsity of which he saw, is raised in his name and his words and monuments are pre-sented as its also.

In the South the news was received as a last unaccountable blow of destiny. In the North different feelings were expressed. Clerics, frequently thirsty for a vengeance claimed by God, avowed that the deed must be a divine act, albeit mysteriously performed. A Republi-can Congressman, Mr. George Julian, later recalled that his party met the day after the murder 'to consider a line of policy less conciliatory than that of Mr. Lincoln'; while everybody was shocked the feeling of the meeting was overwhelmingly that the accession of a new President 'would prove a Godsend to the country'.

Mr. Truslow Adams's *Epic* dismisses 'the conspiracy of a handful, led by a half-madman, which destroyed the one man who stood between his country and the powers of evil and plunged us all into a sea of infamy and misery'. The description of the deed and its effects is accurate, but the theory of the recurrent madman grows thin. Coincid-ence did not drop Gavrile Princep at the spot where he could kill the Archduke, Vlada the Chauffeur into a Marseilles street as King Alexander went by, and the deadbeat van der Lubbe into the Reichstag (I saw him and his trial and can vouch for that). Even if coincidence's arm were so long, it could not always reach to the suppression of inquiry in these cases.

This is a chapter by itself in our times, and in my opinion the most important. I remember how governments combined, at the League of Nations in 1935, to shelve the inquiry into the complicity of other governments in the murder of King Alexander. The same thing happened in the case of Count Bernadotte; the United Nations dropped the matter of its own emissary's murder as if it were a hot coal. The truth is not, as American writers put it, that 'history shrinks' from exposing these things. Politicians recurrently cover them up and conceal the continuing process. The study of Lincoln's murder did more than anything hitherto to convince me that it *is* a continuing process, with an enduring organization behind it. It shares identical and recognizable features with the later series of murders, which all led to the spread of the area of destruction. These conspiracies cannot be improvised; obviously the experience of generations, or centuries, lies in the choice of moment, method, line of retreat and concealment. The little folk who are trotted out after each such deed may be 'the handful', but the hand is never seen. Particularly in this matter of covering-up is Lincoln's murder of present-day significance in America. The same resolute and efficient methods are used to defeat public curiosity about Communist infiltration into government departments, the public services and high places. In America (and for that matter in England and Canada), a cat sometimes slips out of the bag, a Dr. May, a Dr. Fuchs, a Mr. Alger Hiss. But then the bag is tied more tightly than before, and the public mind forgets.

Booth was not a madman. He kept a diary and the entries he made while he lay hidden show a sane man, even though pages were apparently removed before its existence became known, two years after it was taken from his body! He wrote among other things, 'I have almost a mind to return to Washington and in a measure clear my name, which I feel I can do' (the anonymous bullet effectively prevented his return to Washington). A Congressman asked, 'How clear himself? By disclosing his accomplices?' A parliamentary commission also set about to find who were the persons 'many of them holding high positions of power and authority . . . who acted through inferior persons who were their tools and accomplices'. Nothing much came of that in 1865, or of similar efforts in 1950.

Among high persons of that time the eye of today's curiosity falls chiefly on Edwin Stanton. As Secretary of War in a country at war he was almost supremely powerful. All communications were under his personal censorship. All acts tending to deflect Booth's pursuit, or after Booth's death to obscure the trail, seem traceable to him and the Leftists around him. Within a few hours of the murder he wrote to the American Minister in London of 'evidence obtained' to show that the murder was 'deliberately planned and set on foot by rebels, under pretence of avenging the South'. Just so did Goering claim to have proof that Communists fired the Reichstag, while it still burned. Stanton may have pictured himself as dictator; he nearly achieved such status in the sequel of events. He forced through Congress a Reconstruction Bill to dissolve the Southern States and degrade them to military districts, and a Tenure of Office Bill framed to deprive the new President of the constitutional power to dismiss himself, Stanton. When President Johnson did dismiss him he refused to resign and only failed by one Senator's vote to secure the President's impeachment. Andrew Johnson proved a stauncher man than the Leftists expected when he succeeded Lincoln. Among the most arresting questions of American history is, what would have ensued had Johnson's impeachment succeeded by one vote, not failed. Since President Roosevelt revived the political issues of Reconstruction days the conundrum has gained new and current interest.

Sitting at my restaurant window I pictured Booth riding away from Ford's Theatre. 'There you go,' I thought, 'Wilkes Booth, Gavrile Princep, Marinus van der Lubbe, Vlada the Chauffeur: whatever your name, your unimportant shape is clear, but the darkness around you hides your masters. . . .'

CHAPTER 6

STRICKEN FIELD

Early rising is proverbially profitable and to this habit I owe the sight of a man who came out of Blair House one morning and strode briskly towards Fourteenth Street. While I would not turn a corner merely to 'see' either Naples or Napoleon, I have always welcomed accidental encounters with notable men in the flesh. It adds another dimension to the subjects about which I write. Having seen most of the leading figures of our time, I have a kind of collector's interest for such glimpses; I do not go out of my way to increase the collection but contentedly add to it when chance insists. This was such an occasion; not every day, even in these times, can you see a man who took on himself the burden of ordering the death by atom bomb of some scores of thousands of civilians.

Therefore I looked with much interest at this other early riser. The White House was falling down and being shored up for repair, so that he used Blair House for a time. He was of medium build, energetic, and when saluted by those he met responded with the beaming smile which party-managers like prominent party-men to wear; they believe it to reassure the populace about the state of the world. The weight of his formidable decision seemed to lie lightly on him. American newspapers said that the four years following it had left him 'four pounds heavier and a good deal more confident'. They added, however, that the decision 'was still on his mind', and he himself, about that time, said at a social gathering, 'I had to make that decision on the basis of the welfare of not only this country but of our enemy country. And I made that decision because I thought 200 thousand of our young men and some 300 or 400 thousands of the enemy would be saved . . . Now I believe that we are in a position where we will never have to make that decision again, but if it has to be made for the welfare of the United States, and the democracies of the world are at stake, I wouldn't hesitate to make it again.'

I thought, four years later, that the area of what might by any stretch be called democracy was much diminished in the sequel to that event. The argument seemed dubious, but the tone of the words was arresting. American presidents seemed truly much more confident than in a day when one, Thomas Jefferson, said, 'I tremble for my country when I reflect that God is just'. So much faith appeared nowadays to be invested in the personal pronoun, the leanest letter of the alphabet, where it stands like a weak sapling among robuster growths.

The day after I saw the confident man I drove out of Washington, with regret, on my further way. I crossed a river and saw people waiting for a great river-steamer, with tall chimney and many, windowed decks, that moved towards them. It was called the *Robert E. Lee*, and I found myself humming, 'Waiting on the levee, waiting for the *Robert E. Lee*'. A little later I ran into Maryland. 'Maryland, my Maryland,' I thought, and suddenly realized how much Englishmen of my age have grown up with songs of the American South. They accompanied me all the way from Mobile, and made me think of leave from the trenches and shows in London, for I was of the generation that first began to sing of coal-black mammy down in Alabamy, of peaches down in Georgia, of Carolina where nuthn' could be finer, of Virginia and the loveliness that's in yer. This was a musical ride back through my own lifetime, and I wondered how these Southern songs, with their negro rhythm and their attendant, jungle-born dances, gained such appeal for the youthful British mind. Mainly it was the result of the mass-production of songs in New York during this century and their dissemination through paid 'song-plugging'. However, the original appeal of primitive folk to ones less primitive was genuine.

I made a detour in order to visit Gettysburg, a hallowed place where a gentle peace intervenes in the hurried American scene. It must be unique, this battlefield stricken, as it were, at the combat's height. Breast-works and gunpits remain; every gun is in place; homestead walls show bullet holes; the famous peach orchard has been replanted as it was in 1863 and bloomed before me in Arcadian tranquillity. Nothing but the soldiers and the din are absent, and eight hundred memorials mark the position of every company, troop, battalion, brigade, division and corps.

I looked down on the scene of Pickett's charge from Cemetery Ridge, where the Southern tide reached its high-water mark and then fell back. The unanswerable questions of history! What if Blucher had not come in time; if the sea had not been calm at Dunkirk; if the South had won at Gettysburg? The South would not then have won the war, for the Southern leaders never expected to and only fought because they felt they must; but there might have been an earlier and better peace, with all that would have meant for today. Instead the war was prolonged, the false issue inserted, and the Leftists at Washington were enabled to pursue their aim of exterminating and depopulating the South, almost to success. The Civil War was America's real revolutionary war, not the one Washington fought. When brother fought brother at Gettysburg, and father even son, they comprehended nothing of the destructive conspiracy in Washington.

I went on through Lancaster and York, ever nearer to the central throng and tumult of America, and felt more and more the awesome, almost distressful energy of the land. The mind can hardly picture an immense further multiplication of the road-traffic and when it asks whither that road finally leads, echo only answers 'Where?' The American devotion to machine-driven progress baulks at no such imaginings, but drives on. Mountains, ravines and torrents are there to be tunnelled, surpassed, by-passed or bridged, no matter what their size. This process, without an apparent spiritual goal, alarms some, like the American-born poet, Mr. T. S. Eliot. Living in Chelsea rooms over those once inhabited by an earlier fugitive who was filled with similar misgivings, Mr. Henry James, he wrote:

> . . . The rabbit shall burrow and the thorn revisit,
> The nettle shall flourish on the gravel court,
> And the wind shall say: 'Here were decent godless people:
> Their only monument the asphalt road
> And a thousand lost golf balls. . . .'

For Americans, however, the process is its own spiritual goal; God is in the machine. A different view of it was offered by an Englishman of much American experience, Mr. Bertrand Russell: 'In America the hopefulness and enterprise that circumstances permit increase the success that is achieved beyond what would be possible for men of a different temperament. Obstacles, it is felt, exist to be overcome, and therefore they are overcome. All this is admirable. It existed in Elizabethan England, and to a lesser degree in Victorian England. A little more of the American spirit would do us far more good than any amount of austerity unrelieved by hope.' That seems reasonable, for austerity unrelieved by hope is also a road without a spiritual destination; between the two might lie one with a goal.

These reflections are for poets and philosophers. The Americans in bulk do not delay with them but drive with quickening materialistic gusto along the asphalt road. I thought, as I whirled over huge bridges that bestrode wide rivers, 'They do these things like shelling peanuts'. The Americans have much enriched the English language. They picture a thing in two or three vivid words by reflecting it in some dazzling glimpse of the American yesterday or today. 'Shelling peanuts' is perfect. 'The horse-and-buggy age' and 'climbing aboard the band wagon' depict a whole era. 'We must hang together or we shall hang separately' and 'a necktie party' put a matter in terms plain to any child who ever read Zane Grey or saw a Western. 'The calm confidence of a Christian with four aces' sharply conveys truth through a sudden peep into a gambling-saloon. When the long-levered gaming-machine is called 'a one-armed bandit' the last word has been said (not that it has been heard, for Americans adore to hand cash to these. If they once feared the hold-up man, they love this mechanical one, and in many parts well-advised sheriffs leave him alone).

Thinking on these things I found myself off to Philadelphia one morning, or at all events through it, on my way to New York.

CHAPTER 7

SPEED THE COMING GUEST

I FELT myself within the aura of New York long before I saw it. Its effluence filled the air, which contained a sense of quickening, nervous haste. The traffic thickened, and the specklessness of town and countryside deteriorated a little; I saw more litter and lumber and even a few inferior houses. Through it all ran the superb road, so marked that the traveller was drawn along as by invisible strings. A child could find its way all over America; I only once went astray, through a missing detour-sign.

It was like sleep-walking, and then sleep-sprinting. Ten miles away, at length, I saw the city's mountainous shape and the race began. I was drawn by the hypnotic force of the signs on to a motor-road where all life ceased but that of the wheeled traveller. It led straight towards Manhattan, the core of New York. Manhattan is an island, long and narrow from north to south, in a loop of two rivers. It can only be reached by bridge or tunnel, or from the east by ocean liner.

I became a fly on a wheel. Signs commanded a low speed but the traffic moved at some forty miles an hour and, tightly contained in it, I was carried along. Wayside notices forbade all further stopping to think or looking before leaping. For the initiated exits offered, but not for me. The road became a bridge, miles long. It did not merely span a river, though I fleetingly saw one or more beneath; on huge stilts it strode over water, fields, houses, factories and sped the newcomer towards Manhattan, while the concrete mountains loomed nearer. My ears were filled with an unaccustomed noise, the unbroken whoosh-whoosh of wheels. I sought the Lincoln Tunnel, having been told to use it, not the Holland Tunnel. Signs flashed by announcing the Holland Tunnel. Suddenly, when I was nearly past it, one said 'Lincoln Tunnel, turn left.' A quick turn at forty miles an hour, a dizzy roundabout, a run downhill, a brief pause to make payment at a turnstile, and I was in the Lincoln Tunnel beneath the Hudson River.

It was about two miles long, but felt much longer. It seemed dark, though it was bathed in a ghostly fluorescent lighting. The whooshing noise was amplified in this cylinder and speed seemed greater; it was not low, at that, but I felt as if I hurtled to some whirling destiny, pursued by furies. Placarded orders flashed by, and from a narrow platform policemen watched on their observance; they looked like the saints of some strange religion as they stood in niches in the curved walls. 'Unlawful to cross the line,' said a sudden proclamation, immediately gone; I strained to keep my side of the line of glittering, mesmeric metal knobs. 'Stop at the red lights,' said another; seeing none, I assumed these appeared when some mishap piled up all the traffic in this vault. 'Keep intervals of 75 feet,' abruptly ordered a third; in the mirror I guiltily saw a car treading on my heels and accelerated to sixty to overtake the one in front, which was a quarter-mile ahead, fearing that some unwitting transgression would bring out all the red lights and down on me, like dark avenging angels, all those sentinels. Whoosh-whoosh went the scourging refrain of the tunnel; it stretched ahead like the corridor of doom; dazed but dogged I gripped the wheel. Then the dark pin-point at its end brightened and, like a mariner on a spar, I was thrown ashore, bruised and breathless, into daylight and Manhattan.

A rare but fortunate impulse of caution led me to attempt this first invasion of Manhattan on Sunday; had I emerged into an exitless stream of work-a-day traffic I should have had to circulate until night fell or fuel failed. Now the streets were empty and I was able to seek a lodging. I found, on a sixteenth floor, a small but astonishingly complete room, with cupboards that concealed a cooker, pantry, refrigerator, bath and lavatory. Hunger then led me to an automatic restaurant. I knew the *Automat* from Berlin, but this was a later model, where a hot-dish slot impersonally presented me with macaroni-cheese and a hot-coffee slot aloofly poured me a cup, adding milk from another tap just as I feared this was forgotten. I took these to a table where a man talked to himself in Viennese German; he seemed filled with *Weltschmerz* and twice told himself not to talk nonsense: 'Red'n S' do' ka' Unsinn.'

Feeling smaller and lonelier than ever before, I went out, always the busy worker, to look at New York. Making the most of Sunday, I contemplated it afoot and awheel, from subway and elevated, from the Brooklyn Bridge and from a Hudson River ferryboat. It is easy to unravel, for the short and narrow east-west thoroughfares are called streets and are numbered and the long and broad north-south ones are called avenues (save for one, called Broadway, which is narrower). Thus the newest newcomer can at once find 'Fifth Avenue and Fifty-Fifth East', or any other conjunction.

I wandered with apprehensive curiosity through the empty canyons on this springtide Sunday, and compared this marvel of the twentieth century with older ones of Europe and of America. Most of all my mind's eye compared it with Richmond and Washington, the capitals of the first and second phases. This was the third tier in the edifice. The violent break in the tradition was plain even at first sight. It looked rather like a pagan banner planted on a Christian rampart.

CHAPTER 8

VIA COLOROSA

A DISTANT glow at the end of a rather sombre street between dark, high walls led me that Sunday evening, when I wanted a late breath of air, to Broadway. It was more than I expected. Checked by the first impact, I blinked and then saw that the Great White Way was not white but multi-coloured, and the dominant hue was red. Around me were more lights than I ever saw in one place, red, green, yellow, orange, mauve and blue, all twinkling, coruscating, scintillating, revolving, jumping and jerking. Had all human sound and movement suddenly ceased, the effect would still have been that of pandemonium; there was even less room for one more bulb than in the tulip-fields of Holland.

Among the lesser lights rose great setpieces of salesmanship-by-night. From a huge face, with O-shaped mouth, came puffs of smoke (to advertise a cigarette), that mingled with clouds of steam from manholes in the roadway, below which I supposed the subway trains ran. A neon waterfall played, fifty feet above the pavement. Above a beer-restaurant a train ran through Bavarian mountains, eternally vanishing into and reappearing from Alpine tunnels. Two enormous nude figures, a man and a woman, dazzlingly surmounted a clothing store; their meaning alone was veiled. Between crammed and glittering shops, packed with buyers at this eleven o'clock of the Christian Sabbath, surged thick, human masses. Loud-speakers blared, pin-tables rattled, barkers hoarsely praised the girls within their dance-halls and night-clubs, a man without legs propelled himself on a truck, playing a kind of hurdy-gurdy in this street of dollars and of dolours. Sirens wailed as riot-car or ambulance screamed past, with warning red lights tumbling like a juggler's clubs. Confusedly I scribbled in my mind the song of the Innocent on Broadway:

A roseate, roaring, coruscating roadway
(and rather narrow, too; it isn't broad).

I wonder, did they only call it Broadway
To obfuscate the innocent abroad?

From manhole covers, steamy clouds ascending
(Are dragons down below, or demon's fires?)
'Walk in, walk in, and see The Happy Ending!'
(The screech of brakes on rims, and tortured tires).

Polychromatic taxicabs a-honking,
('Here's Swingland, come on in, we've Lovely Girls!')
Bright honky-tonks all brazenly a-tonking,
Kaleidoscopic lights, all whirls and twirls.

Strident strains cacophonously clashing,
A legless beggar grinding out a tune,
The great white moon beholds a great red Fasching.
('O mon amour, comme elle est blanche — la lune!')

The change of pace, like one of altitude, is merely a matter of adjustment. The body and soul quickly key themselves to the speed of life in New York. When I went to bed that first night the attunement was not complete; my senses hurt, like the ears of an air traveller who quickly descends from 10,000 feet to land. I could not sleep and lay listening to the sirens. I found in time that all urgent public services in American cities carry these frenzied warnings; whether the call be one of fire or sickness, burglary or riot, the missioners' clamour is the same. It was like London during the air-bombardment and, as I lay awake and read, I received a jolt of surprise from some words of Mrs. Angela Thirkell's latest novel:

'Suddenly the air' (of tranquil Barsetshire) 'was rent by the hideous wail of a siren, rising and falling, rising and falling. The war was long over . . . "The only Aubrey," said Jessica, "he had that siren fitted to his car to show Americans the horrors of war, but I think it's stopped being funny." '

Aubrey was deluded. Far from showing Americans the horrors of war, his siren probably made them homesick (for I do not imagine American sirens were copied from war-time London; assuredly they were first in the field. They belong essentially to the pursuit strenuous and are the tantivy of the machine age).

CHAPTER 9

NEW BABYLON

I SPENT some time in New York at various visits and set down here my final feeling about it, not the surface impression of a first encounter. Whatever it may be, it is unlike anything in America or the world as far as I know them, save that a group of American cities, Chicago and Los Angeles chief among them, and Johannesburg in South Africa are in their nature its satellites, while Tel Aviv, I am told, visibly relates to it. If a new force is rising in the world, which aspires to transcend and rule all nations, these cities may be its citadels.

Its chief characteristic is a nervous unease, palpably felt in an island where millions of people pursue each other between tall buildings, each of which at morn and eve absorbs and releases the population of a small European town. In midsummer the high walls make the streets steambaths from which the citizen may only find refuge in an air-conditioned store; midwinter gales, hurtling through them, may drive him to that same shelter, then warmed. New York is without repose. The traffic moves at speed, for all the congestion, and furious clamour assails any driver who dares pause. The bus-drivers must collect fares and count takings while braking and accelerating between the frequent stops and such tension arises between them and their passengers that one of them once set his whole cargo on the street, then driving off empty to the garage with the remark that he had wanted to do this for years. There are boulevards and bouleversements, but no boulevardiers; here is no time for strollers. The New Yorkers themselves fear the strange thrall and their journals mourn 'the lost art of doing nothing' and 'the sad cult of going nowhere quickly'.

The outer world formerly thought of the average American as an unhurried, deliberate and imperturbable being. Is today's strained impatience a new thing, and is it now an American trait in general, or a symptom of New York? Mr. Truslow Adam's *Epic* attributes it to Americans in mass, and even to pre-American Americans (the Red

Indians), for he says, 'For the most part the climate throughout the continent seems to have been one which tended to produce a high nervous tension in the living beings subjected to it, even the savages, not only from its sudden changes, but from some quality which we do not know ... The Red Indians' nervous systems were unstable and they were of a markedly hysterical make-up, peculiarly susceptible to suggestion.'

Mr. Jay Nock, who thought the haste aimless, wrote of his own New York boyhood in the 'nineties, 'Our people had resources in themselves which enabled them to get on with few mechanical aids to amusement'. He quoted Edison's words, 'I am not acquainted with anyone who is happy', and Stendhal's, 'The springs of happiness seem to have dried up'. Once I stood in Fifth Avenue with a well-known American writer much hounded for his opinions. He watched the throng with apprehensive interest and said, 'No people in history were ever clothed or fed like these. But where are they going, and why are they so unhappy?'

The tortured unease of New York seemed to me a separate thing, distinct from any native 'nervous tension', born of climate and geography, which may inhabit the mass of Americans. So many folk are squeezed into the central island, all hastening, in the steambath or the wind-tunnel, as if from some pursuant fate. The galley-slaves used to call for the lash, when the uttermost was demanded of them; so do New Yorkers seem to scourge themselves. The reasons why 'Manhattan had to be that way' are oft proclaimed; because the island was small the buildings had to be tall, and so on. Anyway, it *is* that way, and is as different from Richmond and Washington as cloudy from clear; here the shape of things American was abruptly changed.

It is in effect the city of the later immigration, which followed the Civil War. While the landings, the settlements, the War of Independence and the conquest of the wilderness went on the population remained homogeneous; it was predominantly of British, German and Scandinavian stock, continually renewed, which merged smoothly into the 'American' whom the world then knew. When all those clearances were finished the new and different immigration began, from Eastern and Southern Europe, which today (as the reviewer remarked) claims to take over the future. 'Between 1860 and 1880,' (says the *Epic*) 'less than 250,000 Eastern and Southern Europeans came to us; between 1890 and 1910 they numbered over 8,000,000 . . . These people were much more 'foreign' in their background and outlook than those who had come previously, and less easily assimilable to our social life and institutions . . . They kept themselves from the desire to assimilate themselves to American social life, to learn English and to adapt themselves to American ways. They thought adaptation should come from the reverse direction and with much success pursued that belief.' 'Before 1882' (says *The American People*), 'most of the immigrants were from Germany, the British Isles and the Scandinavian peninsula; after 1882 they came from Southern and Eastern Europe . . . By 1900 one-third of all white people in the country were either themselves foreign-born or had parents one or both of whom were foreigners.'

New York today is the monument to that sudden change in the American course. It is the city of the later comers, whose resolve to remain apart may have been obscured by a misleading phrase, 'The Melting Pot'. The new immigration did not melt into the mass and this mid-century has shown that it aspires to rule America and the world, through American strength. It set out to make New York a state within the State, and then a super-State; the United Nations building is the signpost of that ambition. The charter of this new, transcendent body omitted the name of God, as its flag, if all nations submitted to fly it, would banish the cross from any national banners that still display it. That was logical, for in such a universal directorate the Christian peoples would be far outnumbered and reduced to correspondingly inferior status. In this body the long American trail might find a strange end.

From these things springs the peculiar feeling of New York. Soil and climate may generate a 'nervous tension' in Texas and Oregon as well as Brooklyn and the Bronx, yet the 'nervous tension' of New York is different. It is in its temper and passion recognizably Asiatic or Eurasian to any man who knows those parts. New York was once New Amsterdam, the foreordained capital of the New Netherlands. It became New York, pendant to New England. Today it may be

New Minsk, New Pinsk or even New Naples; it is distinctly not New *York* or New *Amsterdam*. Mr. John Gunther quoted a friend 'who always says that Manhattan is like Constantinople . . . He means not merely the trite fact that New York is polyglot, but that it is full of people, like the Levantines, who are interested basically in only two things, living well and making money.'

The words where opinions differ are 'living well'. The new masses changed New York from a place where 'there were values other than the beastly rent values' to one where 'there are no reasons but of dollars', as Henry James, returned to New York in middle age, wrote when he looked back on his New York youth. The New Yorkers I knew did not feel they lived well, save in material things not conclusively material. They lived to get out of New York, and that was a criticism. Its thrall was all-possessing while they were in it; it is without quiet backwaters, secluded places and the rustic corners which seem essential to urbanity. Its people eat well but often in discomfort; the stool, food-machine and self-service counter make for speed but not for content. They may drink what they please, without the bans and adulterations of other lands, and in doing so sit in rows in a dim light, all gazing one way; they seem to await some coming but in fact watch the television screen.

Eating and drinking can hardly count among the day's amenities in New York now. Once, with an American friend, I went to the Pierpoint Morgan Library, a quiet corner in the tumult where early printed books were on display. From the open page of a very early one, John Lydgate's *The Horse, the Sheep and the Goose*, printed by William Caxton in 1477, words sprang out at us: 'Atte thy mele be glad in contenance. In mete and drynke be thou mesurable. Beware of surfite and misgovernance. They cause men oft to be Unresonable. Suffre nothing be said at thy table that ony may hurte or displese.'

'Sound rules for living well,' I said. 'Not in New York,' he said, 'we must have slipped back a long way if those standards were generally accepted in 1477.' 'They weren't,' I said, 'but the idea of a standard was accepted, if not the standard itself.' 'The only standard here is that of the quick-lunch counter,' he said, 'sit, eat, pay, git. I guess the guy was right who said American society is the only one which has passed directly from barbarism into decadence without once knowing civilization.' 'Who said it?' I asked. 'Some Frenchman,' he said. 'It sounded smoothly Gallic,' I said, 'sparkling but paste. It might fit New York. It isn't true of America. A clear line of civilization shows in the South' (and later, after travelling farther, I would have added 'and New England'), 'New York seems to be a bogus façade, subsequently imposed.'

Here and there, in this city of mountains and canyons, were remains of that earlier period so plainly to be seen north and south of it. They needed search, the pleasant streets in the East Fifties, the Little Church Round The Corner, Gramercy Square, Wanamaker's Store left downtown by the uptown tide, the Battery, a few nooks and corners by the East River. Each time I found such relics I had a mental picture of the city that might have been. It is a vision that haunted Henry James. His last story, *The Jolly Corner*, shows an American expatriate (obviously himself) returning to the old New York house of his boyhood and finding it haunted by the ghost of the self he would have become, had he remained in America. The spectre reveals a face 'evil, odious, blatant, vulgar', from which he recoils.

Henry James's whole life was shaped by a prescient fear of what was coming over America, and it drove him to take his body abroad, though not his heart. But for an injury he would have fought for the North against the South, like his brothers; nevertheless some revelation disclosed to him the changed shape which that war was to give his country and some of his novels seem to me allegorical treatments of this theme. The corrupted characters (usually Americans, as are the innocent ones) impart a sinister feeling of possession by an evil spirit; the later New York made that same effect on him, whereas his boyhood memories of it were filled with grace, charm and happiness. He wrote with more foreknowledge than knowledge and New York today is the full reality of his presentiment.

It is polyglot, but one of its breeds is paramount. 'New York is a Jewish city' (wrote the *Zionist Record* of Johannesburg), 'when you have got over the first terrific impact which New York makes on you, you wake up to discover that New York is a Jewish city.' That is true and to my mind is the secret of New York's especial tension; it is that of Jewry in ferment. Any man who knew the Jewish quarters of Warsaw, Berlin, Vienna, Prague and Budapest in this age of Political Zionism recognizes the condition, and it is tauter and more vibrant in New York than it ever was anywhere. It has more Jews than any city in the world and is the stronghold of Political Zionism, which now grasps all of Jewry, Zionist and anti-Zionist, as firmly as the Nazis held all Germans and the Communists hold all Russians.

The unease which this causes among Jews would alone be enough to fill it with unrest. It stirs them, for or against, to the depths of their natures, for they (if not the Gentiles) know what it portends: that though the world has made peace with the Jews the Jews refuse to make their peace with the world (as Mr. Shaw, by report, once said). They are anew to be torn between the teaching of Jeremiah, 'Seek the peace of the city whither I have caused you to be carried away captive', and that of the nameless psalmist, 'How shall we sing the Lord's song in a foreign land?'

If Mr. Shaw did use those words, however, they were wrong; not 'the Jews' but Political Zionism refuses peace and scourges Jewry towards new wanderings. From New York the Political Zionists persist, so far with success, that the American Republic must hitch its wagon to the star of David. The same claim has been made with success in England, but the strength of America is apparently considered decisive for the final ambitions; the expansion of the Zionist State and the setting-up of a world one. This seems to me the chief cause for the uncanny sense of a sinister destiny which overhangs the nervous tumult of New York. I met many Americans, including native New Yorkers, and foreigners who felt it. Mr. Priestley (who would presumably not agree about its cause) described the condition in words which fit my own sensations:

'. . . I would be visited, after the first enchantment of landing in New York had vanished, by a growing feeling of spiritual desolation. . . . In this mood, which has never missed me yet in New York, I feel a strange apprehension, unknown to me in any other place. The city assumes a queer, menacing aspect, not only to me, I feel, but to all the people I know there . . . When Americans say that New York does

not represent America, they are leaving much unsaid . . . My deep
uneasiness remains, grows, even accompanying me into the houses of
friends there, calm, smiling, hospitable friends. Outside those houses,
it begins to take on a nightmare quality. I feel like a midget character
moving in an early scene of some immense tragedy, as if I had had a
glimpse in some dream, years ago, of the final desolation of this city,
of seabirds mewing and nesting in these ruined avenues. Familiar
figures of the streets begin to move in some dance of death. That
barker outside the Broadway burlesque show, whose voice has almost
rusted away from inviting you day and night to step inside and see the
girls, now seems a sad demon croaking in hell. The traffic's din sounds
like the drums in the March to the Gallows of a Symphonie Fantastique
infinitely greater, wilder, more despairing than Berlioz's. Yes, this
is all very fanciful, of course, the literary mind playing with images;
yet the mood behind it, that feeling of spiritual desolation, that
deepening despair, are real enough. And nowhere else in America do
I catch a glimpse of this Doomsday Eve. Only New York does that
to me . . . Has something been seen, some faint glimmer of writing
on one of these walls, some echo of the voice that was suddenly heard,
pronouncing judgment, at Babel?' (*Midnight on the Desert*.)

So it is, precisely. It is what I and many whom I know feel. It is
the same spectre that Henry James saw. I often went by day and night
to look at this astonishing city from the Staten Island ferryboat. The
ferryboats offer the one easy way of brief withdrawal from a town
where the only other form of relaxation is the seventh-inning-stretch
(also, I heard cricket was played somewhere in Staten Island and wanted
to see so strange an affair, but I never found it). My chief reason was
that New York can only be seen as a whole from the ferryboats.
When you are deep in the canyons it is incomprehensible; when you
look at its shape from afar you may hope to find a meaning. Also,
the excursion is pleasant. It still costs but five cents, and hardly anything at that price is now offered in the five-cent store. You may see
the *Queen Mary*, coming in or going out, and refresh your spirit in the
ocean breeze. You pass the Statue of Liberty, with the curious lines
on its base:

Give me your tired, your poor,
Your huddled masses yearning to breathe free,
The wretched refuse of your teeming shore. . . .

The goddess wears a strange, spiked coronet, rather like a crown of thorns. At night the ferryboats afford New York's one romantic retreat to lovers, who fill them. These busy craft have their own histories, sometimes eventful. Even in their brief voyages mates have delivered babies and men have jumped overboard. I often used a ferryboat with a macabre story to tell. A passenger came aboard with a bundle containing the head of a man killed by him and in midstream elbowed it off the broad rail; another passenger caught it as it fell and restored it to him with a friendly smile.

From these decks I looked in spellbound conjecture at New York's silhouette. If it is beautiful, it may be New York's one beauty. It is arresting, bizarre, exotic, wonderful as Babylon was wonderful. It rises like a mountain range without foothills. Its huge but impotent fingers point at or appeal to heaven.

The name Babylon is no cliché; it jumps unbeckoned to the beholder's mind. The drawbacks of the hundred-story buildings having been learned, new 'baby-scrapers' are going up. The regulations demand that the upper stories of these shall be set back, so that they taper towards the top and are crowned with blockhouses containing the elevator-and-air-conditioning equipment. In this form they are replicas of the step-storied *ziggurats* of Babylon, surmounted by blockhouses. Remarking that, an American pastor wrote, 'The ziggurat was none other than the Tower of Babel, a culture centre for men intent on creating a world unified without God; alas, alas, that great city!' (To point his comment, the United Nations building was at that moment rising alongside the East River.)

A Soviet newspaper recently compared New York to disadvantage with Moscow (that is, the Moscow yet to be, not the present one, where anything of beauty is the work of pre-Communist Czars). 'The new skyline,' it said, 'will bear no resemblance to the chaotic and unharmonious New York skyline, in which ugly stalagmites rear between streets that are dark gloomy cracks into which the rays of the sun cannot penetrate.' The Soviet architects would avoid the mistakes made in such buildings as the Empire State one in New York. The new Moscow buildings would be limited to thirty-two stories. From this vision, and the details of New York's 'baby-scrapers', it seems that New Moscow (which will also be as un-Russian as New York is un-American), will in fact closely resemble New York; another Babylon arises.

One day, with an American friend, I looked from a high window of the huge Empire State Building (presumably by some perverse mischance, its hundred stories are crowned by what looks like the phallic symbol, limned in red at night). On a misty day some years ago he looked from this window and saw a bomber flying towards him. It hit two stories higher, destroying itself but not deeply denting the edifice. With native celerity he telephoned the radio authorities and immediately broadcast an eye-witness account of the affair.

· Another American, gazing down at the scene far below, said 'I sometimes think I am looking at something that will be vanished to-morrow, never to return.' He added, 'Is this not great Babylon, that I have built for the house of the kingdom by the might of my power and for the honour of my majesty?'

'How does that go on?' I asked. He continued. 'While the word was in the king's mouth, there fell a voice from Heaven, saying "O king Nebuchadnezzar, to thee it is spoken; the Kingdom is departed from thee. And they shall drive thee from men, and thy dwelling shall be with the beasts of the field; they shall make thee to eat grass as oxen, and seven times shall pass over thee, until thou know that the most High ruleth in the kingdom of men, and giveth it to whomsoever he will. The same hour was the thing fulfilled upon Nebuchadnezzar; and he was driven from men, and did eat grass as oxen, and his body was wet with the dew of Heaven, till his hairs were grown like eagles' feathers, and his nails like birds' claws." '

'Is that what you feel about New York?' I said. 'Well, it fits,' he said, 'there's some menace in this fevered air.'

CHAPTER 10

STREET SCENE

M Y mind's eye retains a thousand pictures of the street scene of New York as it stood, in 1949, on the verge of something, yet to be revealed; some decision possibly fateful for the entire white family. I see, near my hotel, the early morning breadline outside the Franciscan monastery. An industrious man cannot easily stay workless in America today, yet a residue of human beings remains, unable or unwilling to earn a livelihood: the bums and deadbeats. After the monk came with the sandwiches they would disperse to pick up cigarette ends, beg a nickel for a cup of coffee, mooch around, lie down somewhere at night and join the breadline again next morning. Farther on I see two prosperous and well-fed men, one gesticulating and the other listening. 'How'd I do it? Why, I gotta hardship-priority, see!' says the voluble one as I pass.

Still farther away was the Garment Centre, the preserve of the suit-and-cloak trade. I will risk a massive generalization and say the world has nothing like it. Here, block on block, clothing factories and warehouses stand, inhabited by Eastern European and Italian tailors and seamstresses. The narrow streets are choked with great trucks, the narrow pavements with heavy, wheeled racks of clothing, pushed about by negro, Puerto Rican and other labourers. During working hours the Garment Centre is congested enough; at mealtimes, when the cutters and sewers surge into the streets and remain there, shouting, jostling and gesticulating, it is almost impassable. The Garment Centre belongs to them and this ownership is demonstrated in a 'Keep out if you don't like it' spirit. This is the new immigration showing that 'the future of America belongs to it'.

The Garment Centre decides what America shall wear tomorrow and spreads its influence through all the Main Streets. Soon after Christmastide those myriad shop-windows fill with the attire of spring; long before spring ends the gossamer clothing of summer invades them;

while New York wilts in the heat the autumn fashions supplant that; and before the leaves are red furs and topcoats are there. Each clearance is early and ruthless, and the window-shopper who liked a beach-frock in May will vainly ask for it when the sun fries the skyscrapers; by then the Garment Centre is reaping the fall harvest. The pace is terrific.

All this energy does not end with apparel. The garment industry is politically organized, for political ends. The vote of New York is held to be of decisive importance in elections and the Garment Centre controls a large section of this, so that party-managers urge aspiring mayors, governors and even presidents to court it, and Garment Centre leaders have the entry to the highest places. The two garment industry unions (in New York and Chicago) have as yet always been led by men from the revolutionary areas of Russia or Russian-Poland where Soviet Communism and Political Zionism were born. Together their membership forms an inconsiderable fraction of the American population but their political claims are imperious. In 1950 the Chicago union 'demanded' that the State Department should 'consult American labour on foreign policy' and 'draw on the labour movement for its personnel'. Zionist newspapers state that the influence of these bodies 'has long since gone beyond mere matters of wages and hours and entered wider political, national and even international spheres of influence', which is clearly true. In 1949 and 1950 the two unions supplied two million dollars to the Zionist State. These contributions were 'suggested' to the branches, but 'imposed an obligation on members'; if members objected their union benefits, such as holiday pay, were stopped. The two unions claim at present to be 'anti-Communist', but the description might resemble one of their own reversible garments, which may be turned according to vogue.

In any case, the Garment Centre is powerful in American politics, openly supports one of the two foreign adventures into which the Republic has been drawn, and may not wear its heart on its sleeve in the other case. It is the most striking example of the progress of that new immigration which began when all conquests were completed. 'The old immigration' (says the *Short History*), 'spread out pretty evenly throughout the North and West, and went in about equal numbers into farming and industry . . . The new immigrants congregated in the industrial centres of the East and Middle West.' The political results are now being seen.

The Garment Centre, the symbol of this new power in America, stands at the leftmost extreme of the New York street scene. At the other end (though not far away) stands the Rockefeller Centre, the symbol of the earlier civilization and its puzzled striving to maintain and build up the old tradition and virtues. The amassing of money produces a problem: what to do with it when acquired. In America (said John Adams) wealth became an end in itself; 'the conception of work as a moral virtue' (says the *Epic*), changed into 'the further conception of moneymaking as both a personal virtue and a patriotic duty'. The giants of gain came by this road to a signpostless land; they may not have had more money than they knew what to do with, but often did not know what to do with the money they had.

Some of it began to devour its begetters. In early days the tradition was followed which bore good fruits in Europe, where rich men endowed almshouses or schools for poor scholars, founded universities, became the patrons of poets and painters; money fructified life. In the Republic, when music, reading and all culture came to be scorned as things effeminate, best left to women's clubs, rich men often lost the instinct of direction. Their huge but unmeditated generosities sometimes had unforeseen effects, for money, unskilfully employed, may take on the nature of a cur, biting the giving hand. Great libraries, passing into the care of committees, often became propaganda centres for subversion, or, in farming and cattle states, the resting-places of deadbeats. The juniors, too, often played havoc. The inheritors of great fortunes, cast into the stormy twentieth century without spiritual goal or the need to toil, sometimes sought a facile popularity by showering money into Communist coffers, especially if they bore the label, Liberal. Much money found this level and famous grandsires in the shades may have wept like anything to see it. The instinct of nursery rebellion against parental restraints often produced this effect in affluent adolescents. The titans of money in the last century, who publicly declared that gain was its own self-blessed goal, bear much responsibility for the spiritual anchorlessness and adriftness of American youth today, for by elevating this puny creed to the standard of a national ideal they deprived the next generation of all others, such as God and country. Their descendants found that this patrimony was not enough. In their spasmodic striving to rediscover faith they are the prey of worse misleaders than the dollar Colossi, and this is one explanation of the doubts and confusions which beset America today.

The Rockefeller Centre is a case of money wisely spent and improving itself. It is a lonely example, in Fifth Avenue, of what New York might be, were not Henry James's 'beastly rent-values' the general rule. It is the proof that light, air, trees, flowers and fountains may survive between high buildings; for a few blocks New York becomes an urbane metropolis. Even here the good purpose was turned aspishly against itself. A painter living in Mexico was invited to do the murals for its great entrance hall. The contractual theme was 'Man at the Crossroads looking with uncertainty but with Hope and High Vision to the choosing of a course leading to a New and Better Future'. His murals showed this choice in the form of a group of Rockefeller Americans drinking, gambling and wantoning, on the one hand; and a benevolent Lenin presiding over happily united workers on the other. The painting was rejected and now, aptly, adorns the lounge of the garment-workers' holiday home in the Pennsylvania mountains.

In the street scene of New York the Communist (or Political Zionist) picket-line, too, was a constant feature. I met it first when, looking in a restaurant window, a voice behind me cried, 'Passa-them by, passa-them by, they are no good, passa-them by.' I turned, saw a lonely striker, and resumed my reading of notices in the window, which proved to be the proprietor's answer to him. 'Do notta-reada them,' cried the voice to my back, 'it issa alla-lies, passa-them by.' From then on voices soft or hoarse, wheedling or intimidating, repeatedly told me not to enter this shop or store, and the thing went on all over New York. People on twentieth floors were suddenly left without elevators, and the liftmen traipsed up and down the sidewalk crying 'Unfair!' while milkless breakfasts were eaten far above and unemptied ashcans overflowed. When peace was made in one sector the war at once broke out in another, ten blocks away.

A major picket-line, of Communists, Zionists and a negro or two, revolved slowly and endlessly before a small German exhibition, crying 'How much for human lampshades?' 'What price Belsen!' and 'Who said Ilse Koch?' To me a repugnant sequel to the Second War was the persecution of the womenfolk of defeated enemies, apparently for their wifehood alone. Neither the British nor the American people ever associated themselves with such barbaric things before. I recalled the horror with which, in 1933, I saw a Socialist woman in Berlin who was thrashed by Nazis. My report of that, to *The Times*, went over the world; I would not then have believed that the American or British name could ever be linked with anything similar.

This Ilse Koch was the wife of the commandant of Buchenwald concentration camp, and her name was strung to a story about the making of lampshades from human flesh. In every war this story recurs, in such similar form as to suggest a continuing source of fabrication. In the American Civil War Northern tales were spread of Union soldiers' bones being crushed to make fertilizer for the South and of their skulls being fashioned into drinking-cups. In the First World War Allied propaganda unhappily produced the story of soldiers' bodies being made into German soap. The truth of it later came out, yet in 1945 at Danzig, after the Second War, an American ambassador was again persuaded that he saw 'the remains of human bodies, still lying in vats of alcohol, the fats from which were to be converted into soap', while 'dried human skin was still stretched out in the laboratory for the manufacture of lampshades'.

Some unknown hand appears to direct an especial malignity at this particular woman, Ilse Koch. An American occupation-zone court sent her to life imprisonment for 'participating in the management of a concentration camp', which is a bad but much lesser thing. Mr. Montgomery Belgion later disclosed something of the methods of these courts (in the British zone as well) and in 1949 the sentence was reduced to four years 'for lack of evidence' (which was once ground for acquittal or possibly redress). At that clamour broke out in New York and her release (sentence, on lacking evidence, served) was prevented; she was handed over to some 'German court' which arranged to try her for 'twenty-nine murders', and presumably the world will learn as little of what transpires as it did before. These things make talk of an Iron

Curtain illusory; one can only be said to exist if different principles prevail on either side.

The purpose of the picket-lines seemed to be that of fanning hatreds of race, class and creed in the pretence of combating them. They piled unrest on unrest in the restless street scene of New York:

> Round about the cauldron go,
> In the poison'd entrails throw . . .
> For a charm of powerful trouble,
> Like a hell-broth boil and bubble.
> Double, double toil and trouble,
> Fire, burn; and cauldron, bubble.

Soviet Communism and Political Zionism stirred the brew and sometimes the Irish Republicans helped. Their pickets, around a building which contained the British Consulate, thrust at me leaflets bearing the names of Zionist rabbis, whose words were used to portray Southern Ireland as a happy sanctuary for Jews, harassed by 'religious discrimination' in the British Island and Ulster! However, Irish Republicans are not without native humour. 'You have new allies against Partition!' I said, 'are you for or against Partition in Palestine?' The picketer grinned and said, 'That's a long way away'.

New York seldom knows a respite from such incitements. I came to a small riot around the New York High School. Students milled to and fro, yelling and waving placards; a few policemen uneasily tried to keep order. These demonstrations went on for some days and I learned they were directed against two professors; one was supposed to be anteye-semidick and the other to have put white and negro students in separate dormitories. The besieged Rector issued deprecatory bulletins, intimating that he could hardly dismiss his two colleagues, though they were rather naughty and the salary of one had been reduced. Beyond that (he implied) he could not go unless pushed very hard.

Then in Madison Square Park I found the President of Israel, Chief Rabbi of Jerusalem, other speakers and a fair crowd gathered to celebrate the anniversary of Israel. Angry applause followed attacks on Britain and 'Bevinism' and glad tumult greeted references to 'our be-

77

loved America'. Having heard similar voices speak earlier of 'our beloved Germany', 'our beloved Austria' and 'our beloved England', I felt that Americans were like folk in the Political Zionist barber's shop, waiting for the words, 'Next, please!'

As the permanent United Nations building in New York was not ready, I took train to a place outside, that looked like wasteland, where a lonely sign said 'United Nations'. The temporary headquarters was a repellent place, like some remote base in wartime, where only the bar seemed busy, butterfly-ladies sat about in club-chairs, and the members of the new bureaucracy, immunized from taxation and other discomforts of life, lounged aimlessly around. It had also the distinctive atmosphere, recognizable to any experienced visitor, of a Communist cell. Its first Secretary-General, who also helped draft its Charter, was a Communist who betrayed his country's secrets to the Soviet Empire, and when it was founded, in the confusion of 1945, its organization was wide open to the Communist technique of infiltration. Today it runs a kind of shop in Fifth Avenue which distributes to all-comers literature full of the teachings of subversion. If this body should become supreme above nations the future would be bleak indeed.

As to that, the temporary home sufficed for the first ill-omened deed, in Palestine. Count Bernadotte was dead and in New York the Mayor turned out a police band to welcome a leader of the organization which claimed his death. Americans, and most others, do not know what that first act may imply for them; if the partition of Palestine can be ordered, so can that of the United States or any other country. While I was in America an appeal judge in California set aside a judgment, involving property ownership, on the ground that it 'conflicted with United Nations law'. The Charter of the United Nations, he declared, was not only 'the supreme law of the land' but also 'paramount to every law of every State in conflict with it'. If that should become true, every law born in the history of America or any other land will have been swept aside without a question put to the peoples concerned. Fitting is the tombstone shape of the new United Nations building in New York.

In a city where such huge ambitions gather and hatreds are unremittingly incensed, the nervous tension must needs be great. It was never small; before all this began New York and its 'cold, dreary streets' moved the negro singer Daniel Emmett yearningly to compose that rollicking national anthem of the South, 'Way down south in Dixie'. Today it has an added excitement, a kind of suppressed frenzy. Once a suicide stood for many hours on a sixteenth-story window-ledge, contemplating the jump. The policeman who vainly tried, while time ticked by, to lure him back said afterwards that his nerves suffered most from the screaming of women in the street far below; it never ceased.

From the ordeal of uncomprehended suspense few escapes offer, save by wheel to the distant country. To my own surprise I often sought respite and repose in various hospitable and friendly New York clubs. In my London youth I thought clubs the resorts of a selfish affluence, fortified against the unemployed young man. Experience has taught me to prefer Colonel Blimp to Commissar Blimp, on the Kremlin walls or in the United Nations Assembly. The New York clubman was being lampooned as Colonel Blimp was in England twenty years ago, or ten. He was 'Mr. Groton', the butt of the party-line comedians (Groton is a leading New England school). 'Have you selected your chair for the winter, Mr. Groton?' asks the club servant, or, 'I think you should wake up now, Mr. Groton; spring is here and the Socialists have taken over.' Alternatively he appears as 'Senator Claghorn of the Deep South' ('I'm so anti-North, sir, I won't wear a union suit').

The New York clubs, anyway, were places of peace among an instigated turbulence. One of them awoke in me memories of an affair which gratified the sensation lovers many years ago, for I learned it was designed by Stanford White, who was shot by Harry Thaw at Madison Square Garden. That had a sequel, to me amusing. Years later Marie Lloyd was denied entry to America for 'moral turpitude'. Many years after that again, Harry Thaw, now free, was refused admission to England. An American newspaper said this was a neat tit-for-tat; I doubt if it was ever so meant, but the point was well taken.

The little matters that mutually irritate related peoples are often diverting. Unthinking travellers in either direction tread in the foot-steps of old clichés; Americans complain of warm beer and cold coffee in England and Englishmen feel superior about flatulent beverages drunk from the bottle. Americans are often made uneasy by small things about Englishmen, and sometimes are affronted when, his attention being drawn to them, he admits their unreason and smilingly continues in error. I have known Americans almost indignant because Englishmen draw shirts over their heads instead of buttoning them like jackets. They dislike English affectations of speech, for instance, the pronunciation of clerk as clark or Berkley as Barkley. They think words should be pronounced as spelt, like P'ke'psy. The long 'a' frets their ears and 'tomarto' seems to them an intolerable quirk implicitly admitted by 'potehto'; 'a' should be spoken short as in Kansas (not long, as in Arkansas).

They will forgive an Englishman much if he can strike the right note. Once I found myself the only guest at a dinner in New York of former students of the University of California, and knew no soul save my host, who was seated far from me. Everybody else was on Al-and-Ed terms and between the excellent courses, and after, speeches continued until I realized, with alarm, that everyone present would be called on to say something. All spoke lovingly of distant California, to me unknown. I did not want to appear stupid or give offence, but I thought several highballs had gone to my eyeballs and my mind would not work. When the inexorable moment came I said, on the moment's spur, that in a company of Californians I could only offer the slightest of pretexts for being present; I believed, on my mother's authority, that as a child I had on several occasions made passing acquaintance with California Syrup of Figs. A dead pause of about five seconds followed, in which I heard the dwindling tinkle of lost ewe-lambs' bells. Then a crash of laughter filled the room and honour was saved.

One morning I left New York; it was Friday and the 13th. I did not look forward to a second acquaintance with the tunnel, but did not then know New York well enough to try and find one of the bridges. I thought of taking the second tunnel, the Holland one; from my map it looked better for my purpose. However, better the tunnel I know, I thought, and went out through the Lincoln Tunnel. At that moment a 16-ton trailer truck carrying four thousand gallons of inflammable carbon disulphide blew up in the Holland Tunnel. It held, the river did not come through, and none was killed, by wonder, but sixty-six people were injured or half-asphyxiated, while a long line of trucks, jammed hard against each other at the moment of halting, was destroyed; their drivers escaped miraculously by running from the blaze through falling tiles and chunks of concrete. At the entrance to the tunnel thousands of cars piled up and all their drivers honked in a fury of frustrated haste.

However, I only learned about that later. I ran blithely through the Lincoln Tunnel on Friday the 13th and found it much less alarming at the second experience.

CHAPTER II

IN YANKEELAND

FROM the old South, through New Babylon, to the old North, then on to the newer West: that is the best way to understand America, if it can be understood. It baffled an eminent American, Walt Whitman:

How can I pierce the impenetrable blank of the future?
I feel thy ominous greatness, evil as well as good;
I watch thee, advancing, absorbing the present, transcending the past
I see thy light lighting and thy shadow shadowing, as if the entire globe.
But I do not undertake to define thee — hardly to comprehend thee.

After the political witches' cauldron of New York the cool beauty of Connecticut and all New England was like a benison. The differences from the South were mainly those of latitude. The South has low-lying, sandy pine barrens, swamps, mud-brown rivers, even snakes and alligators (I once saw a snake bigger than any personally met in Africa); the Gulf and the tropics are not far away. The North has green downlands, rolling hills, low mountains covered with forest, sparkling streams and innumerable lakes; here you think of trout, salmon and hushed winter snows. The longitudinal line of the same civilization, however, runs clear from South to North along this seaboard, and is broken only by New York. It springs from a common Christian and European root.

I began this journey in a quiet, white village of fine houses set around a green. Only in New England and a few places in the South do you find villages and village greens, and they reveal the continuing Saxon tradition, carried into these American lands. The colonists, remembering disputed commonages, laid out a common ground where all men's rights were equal. Thus many New England villages remain homogeneous communities clustered round the green, and Main Street has to step aside.

This village was almost deserted. It waited for Decoration Day at the end of May (when flags are placed on American war graves) to bring the brief summer season and the holidaymakers. Mist, rain and snow fill the other nine months and often, on western highways, you may meet New Englanders migrating towards Arizona's or California's sun (or encounter them returning to the damp green lands, which they find they prefer when they go away).

From this first Connecticut village I explored New England, travelling always along green aisles beneath green arches and being ever astonished by what the earlier colonists built. The feeling of a mellow culture accompanied me through Litchfield, Sharon and Salisbury, on to Stockbridge and Williamstown in Massachusetts; again, these places seemed older than they were because they contained so much of a parent civilization. The early colonists, when they took home names and clapped 'New' on to them, must have meant 'another', not 'different'. It was a confession, not an apostasy. They meant to build another place on foundations they knew, not a 'new' one, the newness of which would be a denial of the old. They used the old models for their houses, for the excellent inns, for their schools and above all for their exquisite churches. Architects or master-builders from England built many Southern mansions. New England was harder and poorer soil and men fended for themselves, but with equally fine results. Taste was good and many valuable builders' manuals were available, especially one, the *Country Builder's Assistant*, published by an enterprising Jew, Asher Benjamin. All contained drawings after Wren and to them and the skill of local craftsmen New England owes these delightful white churches.

I found one of the loveliest in Vermont, the Old First Church at Bennington, a little town still lively with the memory of battles against the redcoats (near it was the old First Meeting House where the Vermonters 'met in prayer for assistance against the oppressive measures of New York and the overwhelming power of King George', a prayer, the first part of which might not be inapt today). The model is Wren's, but the tall columns from foundations to roof are single white pine trees. The inner dome is held in the arms of a cross, 'the cross triumphant over the world'; the UNO building in New York is today's answer to that.

Bennington interested me also because of its part in a very strange affair; here, in the early 1800s, two men were sentenced to death because their uncle dreamed they had murdered someone. Two toenails were all that could be produced of the *corpus delicti*, and fortunately for them the victim appeared while they were awaiting execution.

The mass and speed of motor traffic blur this countryside of endless delight to today's traveller. I wished I could explore it by bicycle, or in a surrey. Either method is theoretically possible, but in practice a wanderer afoot, a-cycle or driving something horsedrawn is almost as inconceivable as a woad-painted caveman in Piccadilly Circus. New England calls for time and leisure, to enjoy it, but that style of travel is dead in America. A trace of it remains only in the New England inns, which are survivals of the colonial past.

The rich men or companies that now operate them maintain them with care, furnish them with taste and serve excellent food, so that they combine the best of old and new. I stayed at one, at Wallingford in Vermont, which was a model in both respects. It was a fine house, aged in the wood and full of good furniture, which took thought of everything a modern guest could possibly need. Hotels in America are not all of this standard, and as the wayfarer delves into the West, seeking humble lodgings, he may fare pretty roughly. A novelty to me, in those parts, was the cutaway lavatory door, which saved the proprietor the cost of a lock and some wood, for the newcomer needed merely to look for a pair of feet. At one, quite large though modest hotel in Colorado, economy was carried farther still; no doors were provided.

I went on through New Hampshire to Maine, pondering on the immense quiet of New England, beneath the surface noises of the road. Norwich and Hanover, Orford and Haverhill, Bethlehem and Bethel: English, Royal Georgian and Biblical names marked the way. Save for Bethlehem, which was much overrun by New Babylonians, as if to spite its name, they breathed the spirit of the early colonists and a deep respect for these grew in me. This was all bitter wilderness when they came. Their remoteness from civilization was daunting to think of even now, yet they seemed to have remained nearer to its heart, as they built these white towns in green groves, than the masses of people are today.

CHAPTER 12

LIFE OF A SALESMAN

THROUGH the woods of Maine I came, in quest of a night's lodging, to a little place called Skowhegan, and stopped at a modest-looking inn where a very fat, wheezy and jovial landlord rocked himself on the stoop. To my surprise he took my heavy bags one in either hand and sped lightly upstairs with them; I never knew a man's appearance so deceptive. He surprised me again by showing me a cheap room and saying he had one cheaper and just as good, if I cared to use a public bathroom. Such probity may once have been general among innkeepers but is rare now. I was tired and hungry and asked where I could eat. This is often a major problem for the stranger in America; the stool and hamburger pall in time and his being calls for a solid meal, a chair beneath him and a table before him.

'Down by the river,' he said, 'half a mile away.' I went and found a log-cabin restaurant and a table by a window. Outside, logs were floating gently downstream and the senses were restored after the rush of the road by their reassuring movement. In a smooth partnership of man and nature, they were cut in the mountains, slid down the slopes, and then the river did the rest; it brought them to some distant boom which fed them to the mill where they were pulped for paper. It was an enchantingly primitive arrangement, slow, but surer than speed. Of course, there were libertarians among them and these sought to gather in any corner where they might escape the stream; then they set up log-jams, another American expression which has enriched the English language. It is the perfect image for any obstructive congestion in industry, traffic or aught else. English politicians, liking the mixed metaphor, usually prefer 'bottle-neck', which is the opposite of what they mean; the neck of a bottle ensures smooth, uncongested efflux, neither rudely swift nor obdurately slow.

While I mused on these things a good-looking and engaging young man asked to share my table. 'Gladly,' I said, and either this one word or my look told him I was English, so that he invited me pleasantly to be his guest, adding a word about friendliness received in England. He suggested, from the menu, 'Chicken in the rough'. 'I'd like that,' I said, 'what *is* chicken in the rough?' It proved to be all the most toothsome parts of the fowl, served to be eaten with the fingers, and restored me after hard travel.

Forthwith he told me all about himself. He was training to be a salesman of refrigerator parts and expected to spend five years learning the craft. That showed me graphically the place which salesmanship holds in the respect of Americans. Five years seemed to me a long probation. From casual reading and hearsay I thought until then that salesmanship was a natural gift, quickly tested by practical success or failure. I saw it was a high science demanding long novitiate; a talent acquired, not inborn.

To him I owe much lore of the road. When he began his five-year travels, he said, he stayed at hotels and ate regular meals, but soon found this used up both his expenses allowance and his salary. He systematically applied himself to economy. He stayed only at the cheapest tourist-camps, lived during the day on a carton of milk and a packet of crackers, and allowed himself one good meal, at night (thereafter a lone rider, one D. Reed, travelled America with carton and packet beside him). He never drove faster than forty miles, because his fuel bill was lowest at that speed. He put his laundry in a machine which washed, rinsed and dried it all for twenty-five cents; to press these things he ran a little travelling-iron from the electric light in his quarters. Thus his salary remained intact and he saved something from his expenses allowance too.

His life, perfectly organized, lay before him like a smooth, straight road, with a desirable haven five years away. It seemed an excellent plan, the exact opposite of that of the young American in the days when he set out for the uncharted West. 'You are not married?' I said.

'No,' he said, and spoke of a turning missed on life's road, to which, I thought, he would have liked to return. Like many other youngsters whom I met, his thoughts were much in Europe, whither his military service led him; it holds an appeal for which they cannot account. He lived in memory in days spent with an Italian girl, and talked with a romantic nostalgia of 'three beautiful months' spent in her company. For two years after leaving her, he said, he was utterly miserable.

'Two years!' I said, 'then it was no fleeting fancy. Why didn't you marry her?'

'I couldn't ever make up my mind whether she loved me or my food,' he said.

I knew what he meant. The American soldier was thrown among hungry people in strange lands in wartime, with a cornucopia in his hands. Nevertheless, if he was so happy with her, I thought he might have dismissed his doubt about what attracted her in the first place and have set himself to ensure what should hold her in the last. I felt that a shadow of regret darkened his straight, secure road. 'Yeah, she married another guy in my regiment,' he continued, 'he stayed on in Italy and married her. I guess my ideas were in a jam.'

He fell silent and we both watched the floating logs. The movement of those endless, unformed battalions, drifting, drifting downstream was impressive; it looked like destiny at work.

CHAPTER 13

MAINE TO MASSACHUSETTS

AFTER the verdancy of New Hampshire and Vermont, Maine was higher and wilder; towns grew fewer and farmland rarer. I went through this country of mountain and forest, lake and river, which the French and English disputed until Wolfe prevailed at Quebec, on my way to Bar Harbour and the sea. New England now is a holidaymaker's land and it was sleepy and empty between the two high seasons of winter and summer sports. Nevertheless, the sun was already hot and rain was needed, so that lonely dwellers in the immense woodlands, though barely freed from snow and ice, were beginning to worry about forest fires.

Bar Harbour, which is almost on the edge of Canada, was the northernmost point on my route, and is one of the world's lovely places. All down this coast the mountain's footlands fall away into islands and islets as if the earth shed hard tears at the ocean's victory. It is a scalloped battleline, where green promontories and peninsulas resist the amethystine siege of coves and bays and the endless combat joins in a smoke of white spume and spray; where the scents of firs and newly-sawn wood meet salt breezes. No road could follow these convolutions, which are like those of an uncompleted jigsaw puzzle, so that, although you continually see landlocked water, the ocean remains distant. This is the coast which gave the Republic most of its ships, fisherfolk and seamen.

Having seen the inner countryside of New England I set off southward along its coast for New York again. The day was astonishingly hot and I pulled up at a place which seemed to offer food and shade. There was a mile of beach, the smell of mussels and cockles which pleases English nostrils, a few tables beneath striped umbrellas, and two sheds, which promised 'Lovely Food' and 'Lobster Picnic Plate'. I saw visions of a succulent trifle nestling in crisp green leaves, and of a cooling plunge. On closer view I forewent the bathe; the beach was rockier than Brighton's. I entered one shed and ordered Lobster Picnic Plate.

The counter-hand looked hot and troubled and was too busy, over some sizzling dish, to serve me at once. He turned from his cooker to a box, touched a switch, and spoke to 'Joe' (in the other shed, I supposed). 'Joe,' he said, 'Al here, how's about you coming over and giving a hand with this hamburger?' (a child waited, presumably for the hamburger). Joe's answer was inaudible, but he did not come, and Al turned wearily to me, leaving hamburger and child to fate. He looked happier when I asked for Lobster Picnic Plate and said, 'Sure'.

He took a deep papier mâché dish and filled it with clam-shells, damp from the sea. Then he lifted the lid from an urn, releasing hot clouds of vapour, and with tongs extracted a huge scarlet lobster, intact and steaming like a locomotive, which he laid on the clam-shell bed and proffered to me. I pictured myself rending a boiling lobster with my hands and recoiled. 'You don't wannit?' he said; he was of few words. 'No,' I said. 'Okay,' he said, and put it in the urn. I ate some ice-cream, which, like chop-suey, I find inflating at the moment of intake and lowering later. A little farther along the road I was hungry again and stopped at one of the string of ice-cream palaces which you encounter all over America; in mid-desert and on rocky mountainside alike these excellent resorts offer 'twenty-eight kinds of ice-cream'.

I could not believe, until I made this test, that ice-cream could be made in twenty-eight separate flavours. Now I counted them and they added up to thirty-three, all with names as fine as those of jewels or apples: Orange Pineapple, Peppermint Stick, Butterscotch, Butter Crunch, Black Raspberry, Walnut Brittle, Pistachio, Butter Pecan, Chocolate Chip, Grapenut, Fruit Salad and so on. Yet though this be heresy I found (or imagined) a sameness in flavour and texture. In Vienna formerly, and I suppose nevermore, Italians came from Italy each summer and opened ice-cream shops. One such was beneath my lodging there and each morning, even before shaving, I visited it. I can still taste that confection of *Hazelnuss und Citron*, which cost but fifteen groeschen. Never since have I looked on its like.

As you come southward the roadside life thickens again, so that the coastal country of New England disappears, or the senses cannot comprehend it. Everybody appears to sell something. Scarcely a house but is ready to receive Overnite Guests, Nite Crawlers or Tourists, or to sell eggs, fruit, puppies, Persian kittens, curios, antiques, maple candy, cider, icecold pop or sizzling steaks. All around and between the townships are the Dew Drop Inn and Dusty's Clams, Joe's Place and Aunt Martha's Home Cooking, the Dine-a-Mite Diner and the Hot Dog Shack. Any spaces that remain are filled with filling-stations and cabin-courts, and between them the combustion engine ceaselessly roars.

The traveller who is not native to this furious pace may yearn for a little bucolic quiet and I found it for a few miles when I left the clamant highway to seek a little seaport called Gloucester. In green lanes signposts pointed to Essex, Andover or Newbury, and here still beat the heart of the folk who colonized New England. I came over an old stone bridge that spanned a dreamy stream into Ipswich; Elizabethan houses, built of wood and untouched, stood around a village green where militiamen once trained to fight King Philip long before their grandsons threw off the English king. Here the names of the earliest settlers survive and some families still inhabit houses built by their forebears three centuries ago.

Ipswich was a cloistered survival, aside from the life of U.S. Route 1 and Main Street. Gloucester proved as pretty as Polperro, but was invaded by the mechanized times and by new colonists, those of Art. Its old-world streets were full of Art Shops, Art Schools, Art Training Institutes, Lessons in Watercolour, Painting Lessons, Art Exhibitions, and in many windows were the results of this activity; pictures of Ships In The Harbour. Regretfully I abandoned thoughts of a sleepy inn and of a peaceful hour leaning on a quayside wall by lapping tidewater. I turned about and drove to Salem.

CHAPTER 14

OF WITCHCRAFT AND DELUSIONS

SALEM, whatever it may be to its inhabitants, was to this wanderer a place of repose and revelation. The roots of the Republic's story are in it and Salem remains small enough for them to be studied in peace. It resisted or was shunned by the industrial age and thus retains much of urbanity and charm. It is of the towns that grow quickly and stop abruptly. In 1650 it was hardly begun; by 1750 it was a thriving seaport; by 1850, when the great sailing-ships came no more and the trade went to Boston and New York, it was arrested and sleepy. It has stayed much like that and seems unlikely to change.

By the water, near to its busiest streets and yet strangely remote, is the most fascinating memorial in America. This is the Pioneers' Village, a faithful reconstruction, not a bogus one, of the first habitations of the colonists from England. The site is genuine, for Salem was one of the earliest settlements, preceded only by those of Jamestown in Virginia and of the Pilgrim Fathers from Plymouth who landed from the *Mayflower* to found Plymouth, Massachusetts (not far away) in 1621.

Here in the twentieth century you may see what it meant to land on a rocky shore in 1626 and set about to colonize a wilderness. The ocean lay behind and England three months away; in front was a barren shore and something, boundless, hostile and savage, which had to be made into New England. The settlers were fifty men with a handful of tools. Here are the bark-covered wigwams and sod-roofed dugouts in which they first sheltered, while they felled and hewed timber for something better; the thatched pine cottages, with catted chimneys of logs and clay and deep fireplaces, which they next built in the shape of humble homesteads remembered in England; the first rough-hewn stools and tables and the cleared patches where they grew only edible or medicinal plants. Here is the first crude Governor's House (the governor's lady, however, soon died in it), and, moored alongside, a scale model of the wooden ship, the *Lady Arabella*, which the settlers watched sail over the horizon after it landed them. From such hard and tiny beginnings grew all the rest. Today's beholder feels the huge and oppressive isolation still.

In New England and in the South the struggle and achievement were the same and the men who performed them were of the same blood. How came the violent breach? The antagonism, skilfully exploited by third parties in 1861, was the projection into new lands of the one which caused a king's beheading and a brief dictatorship in England. The colonists of the South and of New England may in fact be roughly divided into Roundheads and Cavaliers. They were men of all classes, from labourers to squires, but of different minds. The Puritans and Pilgrims founded New England. The Southern settlers were men of more conservative feeling. Differences of soil and climate may have sharpened innate differences. The South with its cotton and tobacco became a land of big estates and plantations. The colder and less fertile North was a place for merchants and manufacturers.

'For the most part the New England immigrants' (says the *Epic*) 'came from the extreme Left Wing and were Puritans of the Puritans, as far as their leaders were concerned. A large part of the general mass was not, but from the first the colony, with a good bit of rebelling now and then, was forced to take the impress of the clerical and lay Left Wing leaders . . . The type of life which evolved in the South was in many ways the most delightful America has known and that section has become in retrospect our land of romance.'

In terms of today, then, the North was Leftist and the South Conservative. In the North the Puritan spirit kept much of its cold, hard shape, self-righteous and abhorrent of sin in others. At Salem this distinctive spirit led to events which the New Englanders of today like to call the Witchcraft Delusion. The suggestion of a passing error, now realized, might be another error. The age of delusions does not seem dead. People in the mass love their terrors; they hug themselves in a titillating fear of sorcerers one day and of flying saucers the next. Between the last wars American radio-listeners turned out in masses to repel a Martian attack; after the second war an Ecuadorean mob, similarly panicked, burned seventeen people alive in a broadcasting headquarters.

Thus Salem's outburst of 1692 was not so old-fashioned as New England now likes to think. It began when a clergyman saw children performing 'strange antics' and, in consultation with a colleague, diagnosed witchcraft, so that twenty persons, men, women and a clergyman, were executed (and also two dogs, which gave passing folk nasty looks, an error to which dogs still are prone).

Witchcraft in Salem ended suddenly when the townsfolk, excessively zealous, put word about that the Governor's wife was a witch. At that the thing was declared A Delusion. The witch-destroying judge in time publicly confessed his error and became Chief Justice; confession was good for Judge Sewall. The times, and their delusions, do not change much.

Salem was Nathanial Hawthorne's town. In life it did not like him, or he it; now he has the proverbial statue and other commemorations. The old colonial Custom House where he worked stands exactly as he described it in *The Scarlet Letter*. He claims to have found in an unused room there the papers of a long-dead official and the scarlet emblem of an adulteress which Hester Prynne was made to wear. That symbol, 'A', is equally typical of the New England conscience and of the parts of Old England whence its roots sprang.

Treading his haunts, I became deeply interested in Hawthorne's writing life. He wrote for years before he came by his Surveyor's post in the Custom House. Presumably he desired it, but it killed the creative impulse in him; he could not write. The decision to cast away a sure livelihood, as many later writers know, was hard. He was helped to it by a political custom of his country. A president died, a new one was elected, and offices throughout the land were redistributed to the friends of the new president's party. Hawthorne, already contemplating resignation, was dismissed and wrote that he was thus like a man who, having decided he ought to commit suicide, was fortunate enough to be murdered. This started him writing again and he became famous. It also led him to quit Salem. Before that he felt it 'almost as a destiny' to remain where his folks settled and lived for two hundred years. Afterwards he realized that 'human nature will not flourish, any more than a potato, if it be planted and replanted, for too long a series of generations, in the same worn-out soil'.

Hawthorne is part of an American conundrum: why did a group of great writers, Emerson, Whittier, Hawthorne, Longfellow, Thoreau and others, spring up at one time in this neighbourhood, in or around Boston? For a few decades a prolific literary growth flowered in America, only then and only there. These writers all believed in God, life and their country. At the same time, and also in New England, appeared the first prophets of the Civil War and of the pessimism which was to supplant the immense optimism of that day: William Lloyd Garrison and Mrs. Beecher Stowe. When the literary descent reached Mark Twain that writer saw the American Republic perishing, like republics before it, through baseness and corruption.

From then until today the literary inheritance has gone through a rake's progress towards an all-denying pessimism. Writers must exist in America today who see positive values in life, faith, tradition, the family and art. They are drowned in the clamour of the literary slummers. Jack London seems unwittingly to have given impetus to the trend. His earlier writing was virile and he wrote of slums because he grew up in them; personal experience is the raw material of any writer's trade. He then suffered the mischance of becoming typed, which sometimes befalls actors. He grew into a slum-writer and *sought* slums; he was invited to write a book about the London ones and dressed as a slumsman for the task. The approach may contain the seeds of degeneration in itself; towards the end he came to glorify suicide.

His countless imitators saw that dirt was pay-dirt. They were seldom of his type, hard-hitting buckos of the waterside, forecastle and gold-fields, but sedentary men who exploited a vogue. For them America became one great slum, from Main Street to Tobacco Road in the South and the San Joaquin Valley in the Far West. They descended from physical slums to the slums of the soul. The First World War brought in America (as in England and Germany) a large literature of incoherent disillusionment, like the mouthings of a drunken man sprawled on a bar-room floor. On the stage life as pictured by Mr. Eugene O'Neill appeared (one American journal said), 'a Freudian nightmare', while the Hemingway heroes (wrote another), 'wallowed in self-pity'. Jack London, jailed for vagrancy at Niagara Falls in 1894, wrote that the things he saw in prison were 'unprintable, unthinkable to me until I saw them, and I was no spring chicken in the ways of the world and the awful abysses of human degradation'. In the American fiction of the nineteen-thirties and forties no degradation seemed too abysmal for print, and the abysses were often depicted as the common level.

The thing became a literary infection. The Second War produced many books even more anarchic than those which followed the first one (in England, for some reason, this repetition did not occur; balance returned). In America some of the Boys Who Went Through Hell burst into the wildest fulminations. To judge by such books (said an American newspaper), 'Americans have only two diversions, liquor and sex. And when they aren't a-drinkin' and a-hellin' around they are talking about it with an obscenity that is utterly and hopelessly unimaginative and monotonous.' These books surprised me when I read them. In former times a man who fought in a war took that as part of his life and described his experience soberly, if he wrote about it. Such books remain good to read, from Sergeant Bourgogne's account of the retreat from Moscow, through Colonel Denys Reitz's story of the South African War, to Colonel Spencer Chapman's *The Jungle is Neutral*. If young men wrote of war before they reached it, they just said, 'If I should die, think only this of me . . .' or, had they the gift of a Julian Grenfell, in simplicity of spirit composed an 'Into Battle'. There was no whining, before or after. But at this mid-century the episode of war unaccountably brought back youngsters who saw only pollution and depravity in life.

When I was in America fiction fell into three main groups. The writers of the first, abandoning the present, pursued full-bosomed heroines in period costume from bed to worse through seven hundred pages. The second group contained the son-of-a-bitchin' G.I.s, discussing fornication from fortification to fortification. The third comprised the race-problem novels, in which villainous mobs persecuted harmless Jews or negroes; in translation to stage or screen the Jewish hero often became a negro or the reverse. Of ten novels discussed in one week by a leading New York literary review seven were on this theme; it was the fission-propaganda of the Civil War, renewed.

I sometimes seek a novel about any strange city where I may be, for these often give a quicker insight to its nature than any handbook. In one such city I bought such a book, which, if it was at all a picture of American life, was horrific. On page 1 the hero 'called for a drink'; on page 2 he said 'fix me a drink'; on page 5 he said 'I want a drink, would you like a drink?'; on page 6 'drinks came in'; on page 7 he 'poured himself a bourbon with trembling hand'; on page 8 he told his negro servant, 'pour yourself a drink'. This went on for three hundred pages, during which his friend married a prostitute, 'queers' betrayed each other with other 'queers' and alcoholic lechery ran riot. In its middle the story was interrupted for a page or two by the reflections of the hero, on a high moral tone, about his sister. He hated her; she had an aversion to Jews and an aloofness from negroes; she was unclean, undemocratic and anti-social.

I sometimes wondered about the sum effect of a mass of writing of this kind, over forty or fifty years, on successive generations. It might not be so great as its producers would like, for the thing in time breeds a revulsion. I read in 1950 that American book-sales steeply declined, and this may be a reason. Turning from such thoughts, I went to see Hawthorne's House of the Seven Gables.

I shall promptly revisit it if ever I go to America again. The house was delightful, with a secret staircase most suitable for escape when witch-hunters were at the door. True, I wondered vaguely if it could be so old; however, it was there. So were Hawthorne's picture, his desk and chair. Above all, the house *had* seven gables.

The American attitude to historical things is sometimes unusual, by our reckoning. They are used for what the traffic will carry, as Mark Twain said. Thus when I bought a copy of the book at the very house, I was slightly shaken to read, in the erudite introduction, that no such house authentically existed. Subsequently I heard rumour that a gable or two might have been added, for verisimilitude.

I later decided that this was of no importance. The house was undeniably lovely, whether it was the one Hawthorne wrote of or not. It lay by the waterside, in a pleasant garden. It was not run commercially in a narrow sense. Having been acquired by a woman of good works, the proceeds from visitors and the sale of this or that were devoted to some worthy purpose. I surmised, therefore, that the young women who guided me around and then served my meal were performing voluntary duty. This meal, eaten in the garden, made me feel that the loss was Hawthorne's, if this was not *his* House of Seven Gables. I could not recall one like it since a dinner at Le Perouse in Paris just before the Germans broke through. Salmon mousse with cucumber mayonnaise, a salad of the crispest lettuce and a subtle dressing, pear-jelly mould, grape-jam and succotash, muffins and butter, pôt-au-chocolat with whipped cream, and coffee; we eat so many meals in a lifetime and so few are perfect. I shall never forget that one.

CHAPTER 15

A BOAT IN BOSTON

BOSTON is but a corkpop from Salem and in its harbour lay a friend's boat, with cook and steward aboard. This was a brief haven for me from the motor-roads and cities, the harried search for food and lodgings, and the moving finger of the parking-machine, hastening to name me 'Violator!' while I looked for these things. The hardest thing to do in America is to sit back and look at it, to collect thoughts in peace. Now, suddenly, haste and distraction ceased. Boston lay spread before me and islands behind me. I lay on a sheltered after-deck and listened to wavelets lapping the boat's sides, or watched, in the pale-green paint of the awning, the reflection of moving water, like a grey curtain, softly stirred by the wind. The boat swayed soothingly; although I do not like rocking-chairs I think I would build a rocking-house, if I could. When I went into Boston I had no cares of bed or board and returned to peace; it was the perfect respite for a way-worn traveller.

It is the capital city of New England, and to the North what Richmond is to the South. Here the Republic began, for the Boston riots of 1770 and 1773 were the first thunder of the War of Independence and the first battle was fought at Bunker Hill. From my deck-chair I could see Bunker Hill and the spire of the Old North Church, where the sexton flashed signals to Paul Revere below that the British were moving to attack, so that Revere galloped round the countryside rousing the farmers to resist.

Today Boston and New England have been much invaded by the new immigration. In that the North is different from the South, which has remained homogeneous; Mr. Gunther mentions this, approvingly of the North and reprovingly of the South. The explanation lies in the different character. Puritans and friends, in all countries, ever saw virtue in a stranger and sin in a friend. Nevertheless, much of the earlier spirit and stock remain. To the political columnists and

98

comedians of New York, driving the wedge ever deeper, Boston's Backbay is a target for derision (rather as 'Bayswater' once was in London).

Boston grew up before the chequerboard pattern became general for American cities, and its streets are mazy, winding and narrow. They would be delightful, too, but for the press of traffic; to that problem the wit of men can perceive no outcome. It is a good-humoured place, where the large Irish population rids itself of native gall on those days of the year when some redcoat defeat is remembered; then uproarious festival is held. Once, needing to separate myself from a car, I was told by an Irish policeman, 'Sure, leave it there. Nobody will bother you if it's an out-of-State car. Even if they do fine you, they don't fine you the first time.' This fine Irish distinction pleased me as much as the spirit in which it was made.

Boston also has large Italian and Eastern European communities. I asked a stranger the way to the post office and he affably said he was going that way. As we went along he asked what I was and I said 'a foreigner'. 'Well, aren't we all!' he said. 'I mean that I don't live here, I'm a visitor,' I explained, 'where are you from?' 'I'm from the other side of Germany — Jewish,' he said. 'That would be Poland, wouldn't it?' I said. 'Yes,' he said, 'but I've been a long time here.' 'And how do you find it?' I asked.

'Oh, there's nothing like it, but I'm afraid they're going to spoil it,' he said. 'How so?' I asked. 'By a new war,' he said, 'none of us will gain from a new war.' 'I see,' I said, 'and who is going to make the new war?' 'Well,' he said, 'it's the Catholics and their feud against Communism. People have got so worked up about it you don't dare to talk about Communism or they call you a Red. But you can't keep it down like that.' 'But who is going to *make* this new war?' I repeated gently. 'It's the Catholics,' he said again, 'now in Boston there are 75,000 Irish. They came here to escape English persecution, but it's funny, people who have been persecuted, once they're free they want to start persecuting other people.' 'I've noticed that,' I said, 'in Palestine particularly, it's very odd.'

He ignored that. 'Well,' he went on, 'if we have a new war that's the end. If the atomic bomb is used we can kiss the world goodbye.

What we want is a world government.' 'I differ there,' I said, 'the world government would persecute somebody, and with the latest firework. But I don't think even a world government could destroy all mankind. Some would remain and start again and build something new, possibly better. That's happened before on this planet.' 'Say,' he said, 'where you from?' 'I came here from Africa,' I said. 'But . . . but . . . we're all in this,' he said, 'you don't think you'll be out of it in Africa.' 'I don't expect to be out of it anywhere,' I said, 'I'm just not worried. I think it's all going to be for the good in the long run. I don't suppose you or I will see the turn for the better, but if some people are going to make another war in order to set up a world government we'd better see who they are . . .' He sputtered in some agitation. 'That's not what I said,' he said, 'say, I just remembered, I gotta call on a friend here,' and he was gone, leaving me to find the post office.

The historical places of Boston seem to show the new time to even more disadvantage than those of the South, possibly because there is more of the new to accentuate the contrast. King's Chapel and the Old South Meeting House, where the Tea Party was organized, still stand. The Old State House, with the balcony from which the Declaration of Independence was read, survives among towering office buildings, and the Lion and Unicorn still support its pediment. The Old North Church and Paul Revere's wooden house are quiet islands, almost lost in a seething Italian quarter lively with the sounds and smells of Italy.

In the delightful little garden outside I found a tablet to one 'John Childs, who here on September 13, 1757 had given public notice of his intention to fly from the steeple and performed it to the satisfaction of a great number of spectators.' That, I thought, must have been even before the Flying Tailor of Ulm on his bench-sewn wings floundered into the Danube. If in 1757 a man truly flew from this steeple, surely everyone would want to know how he did it! But I met incuriosity and could only learn from an old record that 'as his performance led many people from their Business, he is forbid flying any more in this town'. I wondered what our times might have been, had such a ban been made universal for human flight, or even for the combustion engine. In South Africa there is an ancient Xosa tribesman who believes all the world's woes derive from it and he might be largely right. Where lies truth, between the man who deliberately chooses to remain primitive, if he is allowed, and the one who devises, first a metal blade for his plough, then a wheel, and so on . . . and on . . . ?

I spent pleasant days in old Boston, among friendly folk, and deeply contented ones afloat, watching the sun rise or go down, the lights wax or wane, and the water gently heave. There was only one distraction, a peculiarly American one which might have surprised Mrs. Thirkell's Aubrey. At the harbour-mouth was an automatic foghorn, in its sound exactly like a London air-raid warning. It apparently responded to a certain degree of moisture in the air, not to visible fog, and continued without cease for three days and two nights, during most of which time the weather to my landsman's eye seemed perfectly clear.

Too soon the respite ended. I packed my bags, was rowed ashore and went my way, through Rhode Island, the smallest but most crowded state, to the Connecticut coast. One day soon after that I was on the grandiose Merritt Parkway, running through enchanting country towards. . . .

The name need not be said. As it is approached a hypnotic spell comes down and you become a leg of a human centipede. You are part of a machine which moves, like a horizontal escalator, into New York. You watch the back of the car in front and the front of the car behind and become possessed by the shimmer of light on their enamel, the whoosh-whoosh of cars passing, overhauling, approaching. The speed-limit signs drop by degrees from fifty to fifteen and at forty miles you whoosh-whoosh into New York while other cars still pass at sixty. Over a bridge this time, and whoosh-whoosh along Riverside Drive until you can dive into a side-street, pause, take breath and begin the battle anew.

I made a badly planned entry, after dark, when I was very tired. To find a lodging at such an hour is no easy thing, and I was more than jaded when I secured one. An elderly lift-girl took me and my bags to a high floor and a most uncomfortable room. I heard a familiar accent. 'Yes, Ah'm from Man-chester', she said. 'You must have been here a long time,' I said. 'Forty-faive years,' she said, 'boot Ah've never lost mah accent. They all think Ah'm Scotch here. Ah was over theer last year. Mah son's theer.' 'How did you find it?' I asked. 'Ee, awful,' she said, 'woorse than ever. Ah wish he'd coom hoam. Ee, England's 'ad its daay. It's finished now.' 'It always is,' I said, 'but it doesn't lie down, does it?' 'No, it doosn't, doos it,' she said, 'it's foonny, izzntit?'

I left this gloomy New Yorker to her calling, went to bed and read Jack London's life. I came on a letter of his written to a friend in 1899: 'You say, "This is the beginning of the end — you'll see, within ten years the British Empire will have followed its predecessors, the Greek, Roman, French." Well, well, well! I'd like to talk with you for a few moments. It's simply impossible to take it up on paper. The day England goes under, that day sees sealed the doom of the United States. . . . When England falls the United States will be shaken to its foundations, and the chances are one hundred to one that it never recovers again . . . But England is not going to fall. It is not possible. To court such a possibility is to court destruction for the English-speaking people.'

Among thinking Americans I found a lively awareness that their Republic and the British island are in fact in the same boat, threatened by the same forces of destruction. I never found there, or in England, anyone who wanted the two countries 'mixed up', as Mr. Churchill said in one of his curious war-time speeches. Their whole genius is separate, if their destiny is linked. The disappearance of the separate outline, in fact, is desired only by the super-national planners of today, who aspire to be the World Governors of tomorrow. Jack London divined that fifty years ago. 'You mistake,' he added, 'I do not believe in the universal brotherhood of man. I believe my race' (he meant the Anglo-Saxon one) 'the salt of the earth. I am a scientific socialist, not a utopian.' Had he lived another thirty years he would by now have discarded 'socialist', I fancy. He was conservative to his marrow, and wanted to improve, not to destroy, which is the difference. He felt heavy on him the prescience of the perils now gathering round his country.

I was tired enough that night to be irritated by a gossip in an elevator. In the next room a man coughed and rasped incessantly. Mine was airless and dingy. I thought longingly of Boston Harbour.

CHAPTER 16

ON GOING WEST

I WAS going West, and spent a farewell evening with friends 'whose apartment overlooked the Hudson River. They were young people, friendly as Americans are when you come to them introduced; then you are passed pleasantly along from helping hand to helping hand. The nicest member of their circle was Joan Brent, whose loveliness and charm needed to be seen; but somehow we never reached her.

They were filled with the unquiet of New York. I enjoyed myself and wondered why the question so oft recurred, 'What shall we do now?' What we were doing seemed good enough, but 'We mustn't let Joan Brent down,' said Anne, 'I know she'll expect us. She's so lovely.' I expected a move, but the talk returned to the pace of life in America. Ben said he could only take one week's vacation this year and he would spend it at a Yogi camp, that way he'd get a week with peace and if he went to friends he'd get a week with drink, and he really needed a rest; at the present tension of business he wouldn't be any good in five years. We must go on to Joan Brent, said Betty, she was perfectly lovely. Anne said John was always telling her she'd better make the most of him for another five years and then find somebody else. Well, said John, it was true enough, look how young men were dying these days; the obituary pages showed that they were dying younger and younger and the dental decay rate in the United States was the highest in the world.

'Are things that bad?' I asked Betty. Well, she said, you've seen New York and you know what life is here, and I said, yes, but I supposed that was New York, I meant, it wouldn't be like that all over America. Ben said he guessed we ought to go on to Joan Brent, she was lovely. Well, I don't know, said Betty, you see our men have to work so hard to keep ahead of other men and of course their wives keep prodding them to get ahead and make more money. What should we do now, said Anne. John said he hoped I'd have an interesting trip but I'd find America much the same everywhere, it was all small-townish now. 'Something's gone out of this country,' said Ben, 'in the old days a man could say, I don't like this place and I don't like my neighbours, I'm going to move on somewheres else.' 'Now you see American life, this is how it is,' said Betty. 'What do you say we go over to Joan Brent?' said Ben. 'I'm hungry,' said John, 'what do we have in the ice-box, Anne?' Anne said she would soon fix something and quickly produced an excellent meal. 'What shall we do after?' said Betty while we ate it. Ten dollars a day for an odd job man, said John, and forty dollars a week for the least little bit of a girl to do your letters, it was murder. 'Shall we make ourselves fancy and go over to Joan Brent?' said Anne. 'Yes, do that,' said John. But we did not.

These glimpses of the American mind were much in my mind when I started westward next day. I had seen old America from the deep South to New England, with New York thrust into it like the later comers' bridgehead; now everything that lay before me was new. In the original seaboard, about three hundred miles broad, between the Atlantic and the Alleghanies, something that seemed permanent was begun in 1607 and by 1750 was a strong and vigorous civilization. Beyond those westward mountains lay a huge wilderness, claimed by France but containing only a fistful of French priests, trappers and *voyageurs*. Then in 1763 France ceded to England all the land between those mountains and the Mississippi, but simultaneously England forbade the colonists to cross the mountain barrier; the Indians were to be left their forests, plains and buffalo. After the War of Independence the Americans cancelled the Royal Proclamation of 1763 and began to move over the mountains to the Mississippi. Then in 1803 Napoleon, hoping to embarrass the English, sold the rest of the huge valley, westward from the Mississippi to the Rockies, to the Republic for 15 million dollars. 'Happy Austria, while others make war, you marry!' America grew in a different manner, acquiring Old Man River's huge domains for the price of songs.

Thus began that overland migration which history cannot match. At the start, around 1750, eighty thousand Germans and fifty thousand Scottish-Irish added themselves to the English population, so that, although they were smoothly absorbed, a distinctively 'American' personality began to form. It continued in that shape for a hundred years, until the westward-moving frontier halted in 1890. Into the subdued half-continent then poured the masses of the new immigration, quite different in character, and the future of the Republic, not its population, was cast into the melting-pot.

That is the shape of the American enigma today. There is no more escape to open spaces. Escape, from social, economic or religious barriers, was always a motive in all emigrations, to America, or across America. The first colonists resented the King and the Church and built up a fine civilization with a powerful upper class. Then, within it, groups took shape which resented those successful ones and simply moved out, seeking freedom in the West. That vent is closed now. The social and political conflict is a static one. Later newcomers press against men who cannot any longer say, 'I don't like this place or my neighbours, I'll go somewheres else.'

The young American today has to stand and fight, or stand and yield, in New York or Los Angeles, Saint Louis or Detroit. If he is of the older stock he is hard pressed by the later claimants to the American inheritance. A new America is rising round him, nowhere much more than a hundred years old. Eager to see it, I went West.

CHAPTER 17

CHASING THE SUN

I S E T out on the road to Baltimore, turned westward across the Blue Ridge Mountains of Virginia, and even saw a lonesome pine; the musical ride continued. This range is part of the high wall which was the inland limit of Colonial America for 150 years. Like the Pioneers' Village at Salem, it plainly tells the tale of immense obstacles overcome; the transmontane adventure must have been nearly as hard as the initial coastal landing. It is a country of wild grandeur now tamed; wooded mountainside, rolling downland and splendid farmland; streams cascading into green or steel-blue lakes; rivers muddy, sandy or red as rust. The swelling green breakers of the forests stretch endlessly and the soil looks good enough to eat.

Even today, in a car, the endless ups-and-downs and hairpin-bends are exhausting. To pioneers afoot this trail through almost impenetrable forests, where only wild men and beasts lived, must have been hard indeed. Beyond these mountains French and Indian names appear among the English ones, for the Jesuits and the French earlier penetrated these fastnesses by water from the north. Like the Spanish, they interbred cheerfully, and the Indians later mourned the French: 'They called us children and we found them fathers. We lived like brethren in the same lodge, and we had always wherewithal to clothe us. Seven generations of men have passed away, and we have not forgotten it. Just, very just, were they towards us.'

The Anglo-Saxons when they came did not, and still do not interbreed in the rule. These deep instincts in peoples are beyond easy understanding, and interbreeding and aloofness alike should be above criticism by any who have not lived with such matters. A curious thing in America is that, although the 'squaw man' was despised, Indian blood today is proudly owned by its possessors, whereas negro blood is not, any more than white man's blood is by the prouder negroes.

In these lands the stranger begins to feel the immensity of America, and never again loses the accompanying sense of it. By way of complete contrast, between America of the wilderness and America tamed, I listened as I went along to soap-opera in the car-radio. Soap-opera (to which the housewife listens while she works, unless she can find a coloured girl to come in daily for twenty dollars a week) is in the line of Lyceum melodrama and continues like *The Perils of Pauline*; all seems lost at the end of each instalment, but the next instalment brings salvation and if the story ever ends it ends well, after true love has run through a haunted house of mishap, where villains, heroes, spies and jealous rivals pop up incessantly.

In this episode Gloria, in a motor car, confided her troubles to a sympathetic girl friend. She was to have been married the day before to Jim when a telegram announced the arrival of Jim's wife Helen, thought to be dead, and daughter Jane. The sympathetic friend said, 'All will come right for Jim loves you,' and Gloria said, 'No, no, it cannot be, I cannot come between a man and his wife and child'; tears. Then, as the car drove on, Gloria suddenly said, 'Molly, you didn't . . . you didn't bring me here on purpose?' Molly, all unwitting, had driven past the Home where Gloria now would be honeymooning with Jim, but for yesterday's mischance. Then the microphone switched to Jim, at an airport, awaiting lost Helen. He, too, had a sympathetic friend, who said, 'All will come right, Jim,' but Jim said, 'No, no, Will, it cannot be, I love Gloria but Helen will never set me free.' The scene switched again to the incoming aeroplane, where Helen sat in front of a Mysterious Male Passenger, who had The Papers; Helen, clearly, was a grand girl after all and only pretended to be dead in order to trail this spy and get The Papers. The machine landed, Helen rose, the Mysterious Male Passenger produced a revolver, and this thrilling serial, which comes to you by courtesy of Consolidated Popcorn, will be continued tomorrow. . . .

Absorbed, I ran into Columbus, Ohio, while I listened and was so much intimidated by the mass of life, lights and traffic that I went on through, hoping to find a tourist-camp. The traveller on this road continually outruns the sun and has to adjust his watch, and I was glad of these gained hours in the nightly struggle for a lodging. The road-side was thick with pretty settlements of one-room cabins, cottages and chalets, and innumerable bright signs beckoned me to this Motel or that Tourist Park. My reception at each, however, was cool. I soon learned another lesson of the American highway. These comfortable little places are usually made for two; the price is 'per person'; and the proprietors do not like single guests unless they will pay the double price. Americans told me later that their function is primarily romantic, if that is the word. Thus the lot of the lone traveller is hard and only at a rather inferior camp far out of town could I get a cabin.

Then, needing food, I walked back some distance between the luminous encampments, looking for a place with chairs and tables. I found one called La Rumba, which sparklingly advertised cheap meals. Inside two mature ladies leaned against a long bar and chatted to an elderly barman whom they called Pop. Another man in shirt-sleeves wandered about and I asked him if I could eat. He seemed taken aback but a negress, aged but with skirts above her knees and frizzed hair, scampered up and said, 'Oh, yas, yas, yas, oh shoh you kin eat, oh yas, die gempmun kin eat' and vanished, whereon the shirt-sleeved man said, 'I guess she's crazy', and vanished too. I asked Pop for some fried chicken, which seemed to perplex him, and then saw that one of the ladies at the bar, fiftyish and buxom, looked at me with a curious, leery, half-compassionate smile. 'I'll get it for you,' she suddenly said and also disappeared.

I sat down to wait, wondering whether I ought to stick some of the drinking-straws in my hair. A really enormous woman in red sweater and red slacks passed through, followed by the negress carrying a waste-paper basket, and called to Pop, 'Give Mary a bottle of beer'. Then she turned, saw the negress, and cried furiously: 'Gorn out of it, Mary, follering me round with that dirdy old basket, gorn out of it, will yer, gorn,' whereon Mary scampered crazily out to regions unknown and Pop tried to climb into the cash register. Then the buxom woman brought my meal, calling into empty space, 'Mary, go and find the show girl, her dinner's ready'; she put it on my table with a strange, significant simper.

I felt an uneasy curiosity invade me, as in a troubled dream, about what might happen next; it all reminded me of the *Cabinet of Dr. Caligari*. Then, as at a wand's touch, the empty place filled with buxom, bustling waitresses, all of the forty-fifty generation, who busied themselves with the vacant tables as if these were crowded with guests. At the next table appeared a beautiful woman in a backless and strapless gown, and then Mary re-emerged from some depths, leading a massive creature whom I supposed to be the show girl; I could not guess what she was to show but if by chance it were herself, it would be much. She joined the other beauty and they talked volubly in some tongue unknown to me while they ate quantities of spring onions. Meanwhile my plump attendant watched me from a doorway, still with a meaning smile, as if she knew something unknown to me.

I may have been overtired; I could not get the feel of the place and my hair showed a tendency to rise. Why were all the waitresses like retired *Floradora* girls? Who were the two women next to me? Had I been in Berlin in 1930 I should have said *Animierdamen*, ladies whose duty is to remind gentlemen guests of their duty to the house. But all those spring onions!

It was unaccountable. What high revelry would follow in this strange place? I asked the motherly but enigmatic woman as she took my plate. 'What goes on here?' I said, in the vernacular, 'do you have a floor show or somep'n?' 'Sure,' she said, again with that odd look, 'it gets pretty busy here later. Stick around!' She went away and at the door turned with the most baffling leer of all. 'Stick around!' she said.

Who knows what I might have seen had I stuck around! I never knew a more unusual start to a night's entertainment. But I went, while mysterious glances followed me, and paused only at the door to watch a newcomer drop many coins in a gaming-machine. I have sometimes found profit in inserting just one coin after such an optimist has filled the machine. He achieved three pineapples, or something stated to pay a good return. The machine welshed. He called Pop, who came over and said, 'Oh, izzatso, h'm, well if that ain't the darndest thing, I guess that's funny too, because these machines had a card on 'em last night saying they wuz for amusement only.' Without demur the guest humbly departed.

Evidently life went new ways on these highways, I thought. I strolled back to my cabin and bed. 'R.R. noises' woke me several times, but between them I slept soundly and woke fresh as the lark.

CHAPTER 18

MIDDLE EMPIRE

IRAN with the sun deep into the Middle West, the third section of the Republic. First were the South and the North; then the white men conquered the Middle West; and last of all the Far West. This green central empire includes Ohio, Indiana, Illinois, Missouri, Iowa, Wisconsin and Michigan, and its verdant tide laps also into the eastern parts of Kansas, Nebraska and the Dakotas; then the arid lands begin. Through it, north to south, goes Ol' Man River, who knows at least one thing; that he makes these the most abundant foodlands of the earth.

Behind me lay places called Winchester, Romney, London, Brighton and Richmond. I came to other names: Athens, Troy, South Vienna, New Lisbon. Here the mellow civilization of the South and New England dwindled away. All the towns were new, and only in their residential quarters was the older influence still visible. The white wooden houses, and the farms, retained the English shape of the earlier coastal ones. The people of the countryside, too, kept the character of the earlier Americans, for their forefathers, who tamed this land, were of the old stock. The cities belonged to New York; the new immigration concentrated in these rising industrial centres and gave them its imprint. In 1920 three-fourths of the Americans born outside America lived in the cities, and these great population-centres, stretching westward from New York, now dominate American politics.

On this road were no more villages or slowly-ripened towns, only the small town, repetitive and alike, set in country that awed me by its sheer vegetable gusto. I never saw anything like it in size or fertility, an endless expanse of superb farm country with the young corn growing like a green velvet carpet in thirty- and forty-acre and bigger fields, fringes of great trees around, and fine farm-buildings, freshly-painted and well maintained. Through it all went the massive transcontinental highway, which from end to end spans a distance nearly as

great as that which separated the original settlers from America itself.
The going is easy now; the worst remaining peril is engine trouble, not
Injun trouble; the high road of Manifest Destiny is clear, though not
yet its destination.

From this great food-bowl half the planet might be fed, but for
governments. The whole story of the human race seems to be that of
the continuing struggle of men to arrest the disease of power in those
who govern them. The constant tendency, always and everywhere, is
towards more government, or despotism. The founders of the
Republic knew that. Jefferson was 'not a friend to a very energetic
government'; he favoured 'a wise and frugal government' which
should preserve order among the inhabitants 'but shall otherwise leave
them free to regulate their own pursuits of industry and improvement
and shall not take from the mouth of labour the bread it has earned'.
In 1950, in America as in England, this prudent principle was being
forgotten. For eighteen years, since President Roosevelt's inception,
the steady trend was towards more government, higher taxes, less
freedom. The first colonists fled from and the early Republic abhorred
that process; Englishmen in England fought it until it was dressed in
the sheepskin of 'Social security', when they forgot its wolfish
inhabitant.

This farm belt was heavy with riches, natural and acquired. The
corn was the real gold of America, a lode which cannot peter out while
the Mississippi flows. The wealth of two wars also flowed into it and
its farmers must be the richest in the world. They have fine homesteads, silos and fences, the best cars, the latest farm equipment, and
fortunes in the banks. Many of them were 'busted' in 1913 and deserve
good times.

They are at present protected against bad ones; seasons, markets,
crop failures, glut are all one to them. Though they naturally make
hay while the sun shines they distrust this unique security. It began
with President Roosevelt, whose advisers discovered the theory of
deficit-spending. Public debt, they said, was owed by the public to
itself; the length of the string of noughts was immaterial because they
all amounted to nothing. The theory has yet to be tested to the sweet
or bitter end. The political motive for it is to anchor the farm and

labour vote to one party, leaving only a decisive floating vote, which is to be had by anyone who declaims against racial discrimination. The cost of government now takes about a quarter of all income (in England, about forty per cent).

For the present the Middle West farmers live in an Alician wonderland. The government buys all products at a guaranteed price. If the farmer can get a better one he merely returns the public money, on which he pays no interest. One farmer sold the government 160,000 pounds of potatoes at $1.46 a hundredweight; it had already accumulated fifty million bushels of potatoes which it could not sell or give away and he bought back the same quantity, for cattle feed, at one cent a hundredweight. A governmental order to reduce the potato acreage merely moved farmers to shift the rows closer together. Meanwhile brokers imported millions of bushels of Canadian potatoes which, after paying duty, were still cheaper than the subsidized homegrown ones, which continued to pour into government stores. Billions of dried eggs were laid away in caves and warehouses until the government was forced to give them away, with twenty-one million dollars' worth of dried milk, to schools and welfare institutions. Twenty-five million pounds of cheese and a million pounds of butter, which the law forbade from cheap sale, remained to be got rid of. The problem of storing all this food became greater than that of producing it. The government announced that if its hoard were divided among a million people each would receive a daily egg for seven years, two pounds of potatoes a day for over three years, and a quart of skim milk every day for more than two years. The bill for all this was contained in the string of noughts, said to be worthless. However, the consumer paid, twice over, once in taxation and once in high prices.

When I was in America the government was spending about one million dollars daily to keep dairy products off the market and their prices up.

This was Socialist planning on horseback, paradoxically pursued by a president who was a Mid-Westerner and bred to dislike the very word, Socialism. The Middle West farmer did not complain, but flew to the beaches of Hawaii or transported his Cadillac to Europe for a tour there. Nevertheless, 'I don't think this is good business for the government', said one, 'but a man's foolish not to take advantage of it. My advice to the people in Washington is to stop spending so much money. They don't spend it; they squander it. The farmers figure if they squander for everybody we might as well get our share because we'll all have to make it up one of these days. I've been looking for something to happen before. It won't happen this year but it will come — it always has.'

I went through Indianapolis, chaotic with railroad tracks, and came at dusk into Saint Louis. Here, in the heart of the green empire, was the new America of the new cities and the new immigration. Presumably Lord Bryce, in his *American Commonwealth*, meant these new cities when he said the city was the one conspicuous failure of American democracy (for the older ones of the South and New England hardly deserve the criticism). In these later cities, says the *Short History*, 'corruption was most unashamed', 'rings' and 'halls' 'fattened on the public treasury, selling public franchises, exploiting crime and vice. Here the saloon and the house of ill-fame were protected and encouraged by the politician and the interests who profited by them, while criminal gangs went their way undisturbed by police interference'. That referred to the turn of the century but is still apt.

I came into Saint Louis by a long skyway, a stilted road which marched over slums, allotments, rivers and factories. All around cars beetled or choo-choos puffed along other skyways. The mass of signs alone had the effect of constant noise; they clamoured at the traveller 'No parking at any time', '15 minutes parking during the day', 'No left turn', 'No right turn', 'No U-turn', 'Stop-sign ahead', and innumerable other orders, one or more to each lamp-post. Rush-hour seems to continue all day, but if you come or go in the morning or evening you find that even this pace can be doubled and trebled. At night all the flickering, winking, jig-a-jigging, zig-zagging signs spring out.

Many people say they can gain no picture of America unless they go there. I found that these new cities made no clear impression on my mind which I could transfer to paper, partly because they are so much alike in their criss-cross design, and partly because their physical shape swims and their chief trait is a frenetic human unease, something unportrayable.

Yet with all this hurrying they repeatedly put me in mind of a slower movement, the old lockstep, which men once performed in prison yards, each man's arm on the shoulder of him in front. They reminded me, too, of a German film of the nineteen-twenties, called *Metropolis*. It was (I then thought) a morbid and stupid glimpse of some future world, where beings in the shape of men were brought up from dungeons to perform their toil and brought back when it was done; and these masses of faceless serfs moved, hundreds together, with a slow tramp-tramp, shoulders bent and heads bowed, to and from their task. For some unaccountable reason free men hastening about their business now recalled to me those pictured companies of slaves in the toils, dragging their feet towards a labour without reward or end.

Even Ol' Man River, the tireless and bountiful, looked weary and drab at Saint Louis, as if he were tired of living and scared of dying. I sought another cabin for the night. This is a strangely impersonal business. A neon sign in the darkness says 'Office'. Through a window you make payment, receive a key, and learn which little cottage is yours. That is your only meeting with your host. You sleep, usually, in a clean and comfortable little house; linen and towels are spotless; the water in the shower is hot. On the wall may be a notice saying the proprietor 'reserves the right to have the State Police take you off the highway' if anything is missing after you depart. When you go you leave the key in the door and the transaction is complete; you drive away, a shadow following earlier shadows, preceding later ones. The calling of mine host has changed.

Once more I looked for food, up and down the glittering road, and found a filling-station with a café. The pleasant attendant had served a year with the occupation army in Germany. When I said I knew Germany his eyes filled with reminiscent affection. 'I wish I could see Germany again,' he said, 'I wish I could live there. It's the prettiest little country in the world.'

He only knew two countries, and America has, somewhere or other, every conceivable beauty of nature, but I thought I understood him. He felt some lack in his own land. In Germany, and other European countries, men built up during a thousand years and more a culture that cannot be mass-produced or quickly reproduced. It is like wood or marble; put them in the hands of fine craftsmen and let the centuries mellow their work, and beauty emerges. Europe was like that; the American South and New England saw the beginnings of the same process; everywhere else in America are the raw materials but they are still raw. The secret which was brought to the coastal colonies was mislaid and has not until now been found again. This young man, I judge, missed that inheritance, and I met several like him.

He was from California. Though no open spaces remain to conquer, America is full of people moving around, to try something new somewhere else. I said I thought people lucky enough to be born in California stayed there. Oh, he said, his wife was from this small place near Saint Louis and pined for it, so he sold his place in California, rented his 'veteran's house', and bought this place. Did he like it? Oh, well enough; anyways, he'd give it a chance. He told me of his 'kid sister'. She was in films, a child star. Oh, I said, would I know her? He guessed not; she had outgrown childhood and with it stardom, but she was going to get back in. At that she came in. I thought her about eighteen.

She was a lovely girl, very much in command of herself, and her every movement and gesture were clearly studied for 'angle' and effect. As her only film experience was in babyhood, I guessed that she kept in training for the come-back. She liked talking about herself; she said she was in love and was being thwarted by the young man's mother, who was rich and a Quaker. 'She won't have me because I'm not a Quaker and I haven't a million dollars,' she said, but 'I'm going to get what I want, anyway.' 'What do you mainly want?' I said. 'I want a contract, a swell house, a convertible and a million bucks,' she said, 'I'll make it, I've plenty time.'

'How old are you?' I said. 'Thirteen,' she said. She had the dawn freshness of the *jeune fille en fleur* and the spirit of the time.

CHAPTER 19

ON OIL AND TWISTERS

THE flint-coloured skies opened and hurled thunder, lightning and rain on the land. This early-morning storm was of American dimensions and I drove through it for two hours. The road was like a river and the huge trans-continental trucks sped along it like seagoing craft, throwing up great wings of water. American motor car manufacturers deliver their vehicles by road, four to a truck, two on the engine-level and two on an upper story. These monsters commonly travel at fifty or sixty miles an hour and a wreck of one of them, or of a Greyhound bus, is a formidable affair.

I was nearly half-way across the continent and until now the busy roadside life accompanied me; I was never long out of sight of filling-stations, cabin-camps and trailer-camps. Some Americans dislike both the cabin-camps, which are built to stay, and the trailer-camps, which are on wheels. They think rootless communities are growing in them. The trailer-camps (England has nothing more comparable than the caravan-camps of transient holiday-makers) tend to become fixed settlements of homeless folk. For young people about to found a family the life may be easy, but has disadvantages. It appeals to retired couples, of whom about a hundred thousand live in these wheeled homes. They take them to the mountains in the summer heat and to Florida in the winter; at the journey's end they merely drive into a trailer-camp, plug in to water and electricity and are at home. If a cottage and garden have peculiar joys, they seem not to miss these.

Along the road, so far, continued the countless signs of something for sale, especially 'Antiques', 'Curios' and 'Hookwork rugs'. The American adores antiques. In the nature of things they are not plentiful, and those chiefly displayed are old cartwheels, sledded baby-carriages, wheelback chairs. As for hookwork, this was something genuine when the farmer's wife occupied herself with various kinds of work during long winter evenings. Today the bedspreads and rugs are everywhere alike and similarly priced, to the odd cent, so that some enterprising mass-production factory in New York may have moved into the business.

The conventions of courtesy changed as I went along. In the South I liked 'Mah frend' and 'You bet', and hereabouts I liked 'Hullo' as a greeting and 'Sure' in reply to 'Thank you'. 'You're welcome' rang rather bogus, like 'Don't mention it'. 'Come again' and 'Hurry back', at leavetaking, depended on the way they were said. They can be somewhat hollow forms. I stopped at a lonely roadside shack for a cold drink. It was served by a young girl who seemed to have lost the power of speech; some sorrow weighed on her. However, as I went out a mournful voice behind me said, 'Hurry back!'

I travelled across Missouri, along roads where masses of small tortoises stood bewildered, their heads thrust out as who should say, 'What next?' I wondered if this were the origin of the phrase 'sticking your neck out'; anyway, many of them did not live to learn why a tortoise crosses a road. I avoided them tenderly, but the highway was littered with the remains of unluckier ones, over which the crows fought. The population began to thin out and the land to deteriorate. I ran into Kansas, and for the first time in America came to a stretch of inferior country. There was a place called Joplin that looked like a half-ruined film-set, originally put up for a Western. In the background were pithead machinery and dumps that reminded me of Durham, and in the forlorn Main Street I breakfasted among tired and taciturn truckers slumped over their food; their lives seem hard and wearing for all the high pay.

In Oklahoma at last the roadside life ceased, and the green belt fell behind. Oklahoma has little farmland. It is part of the High Plains, wide and flat. If you raise your arms they touch the sky and if you spread them they reach the ends of the earth; I love this kind of country. As I ran into Oklahoma the clouds cleared, too; it was a beautiful morning. I was glad of that because twisters were about. I saw great trees overthrown, fields gashed as if by a gigantic bulldozer, and townships where wooden houses were flattened or unroofed.

I was coming at last to spaces still open, where whirlwinds (here called twisters) are at home. They seem to need great, flat expanses like these to develop their full force. It is like swinging a cat by its tail; you must have room. Hills and mountains frustrate the wind, so that it cannot get into its swing. But if it finds a place which is high and flat for several hundred miles it whips itself into a mad, swirling frenzy, like a dancing dervish, and pirouettes along until it falls in a foaming fit. At the height of its madness it twists the clouds into the shape of a top and spins along with tremendous power, destroying or sucking up what lies in its path.

After a little while, when I saw heavy, low-lying clouds beginning to curl into ominous tails, I wondered what steps a lonely traveller might take if he met a twister. I decided the best ones would be towards the nearest ditch. In one a man would be least likely to be plucked up and dropped several miles away (and the twister probably would not even be going in my direction). I drove along with dotted lines leading from my eyes to the roadside. I realized that relatively few roads have ditches; also the vastness and want of cover of Oklahoma were borne in on me.

Happily the twisting-tailed clouds dispersed. I ran into dingy country where the fields were weedy, bethistled and fallow, and among sorry-looking houses, shacks and shanties beings of the Pore Jed type listlessly glanced at a passing car. This was the kind of rural slum which recent writers have presented as typical of America. Not far beyond it was a delightful little city, crisp, clean and bright beside a broad blue river and beneath a wide blue sky: Tulsa. Here, at the end of the green empire, were the beginnings of another one. Oil: seldom have three letters said so much, in mundane things. If this land is poor, greater wealth lies beneath it than any farmer could grow or breed. Here the derricks went marching over the land and thrust aside all that stood in their way; at their feet the pumps, with a slow, rhythmic movement that again reminded me of the dehumanized masses in that nightmare Metropolis, sucked up the oil for all the cars, locomotives, ships and aircraft.

Fifty miles farther on my way a woman stood at the wayside by a dilapidated, heavily-laden and broken down car, and signalled to me. The wise rule in America is not to stop; the wayfarer who needs help suffers for many hold-up men who have used this ruse. However, she was not young and I stopped; an elderly man crawled out from under the car and asked me to drive his wife to town for a tire.

'Haven't you a spare wheel?' I asked as I drove her off. 'Oh yes,' she said, 'but we're moving and we have the car fully loaded and the spare is so old it just collapsed when we put it on and I told him before we started to get a good spare but he always knows best and said it will hold until we make Las Vegas and now we're stuck.' She paused for breath. 'Ah, husbands!' I said. 'Are you from Boston or England?' she said immediately. 'England,' I said, 'where are you from?' 'From Michigan,' she said, 'we heard Las Vegas was good so we just packed everything and came away.' 'You have everything in that car?' I said. 'Yes,' she said, 'and aren't these roads awful?' (they seemed excellent to me). 'And aren't the people dumb I asked a man on the road how far the next town was and he said he didn't know and I found a signpost with the mileage just round the next corner there seems to be a find-out-for-yourself spirit in these parts I hope New Mexico will be better I guess we'll have to go back to Michigan here's a filling-station perhaps they have a tire.'

They had. Afterwards I met many people moving in this sudden, casual way. The reason is apparently the vastness of the country; it offers changes of scene, climate and existence, at a road journey's end, comparable with those which an Englishman could only find oversea.

I came to Oklahoma City, sounded my horn outside a window marked 'Office' and arranged with a male head which emerged from it to inhabit a cabin. I carried my bags across, took a shower and was draped in a towel when an equally pleasant woman put her head in the door and said, 'Are you all right?' 'Fine,' I said. 'That's good,' she said, 'did you take the cabin from my husband?' 'Well, from some-one male,' I said. 'That's him,' she said with a friendly smile, 'I wonder where that bugger is now,' and she withdrew.

I wandered into the thickening habitations until I found a restaurant which was separated only by a roadway from the State Capitol, the typical domed building of a State parliament. All round the restaurant King Oil held court; his derricks and pumps invaded the gardens of small houses, the yards of filling-stations and cabin-camps — every-thing. Outside the window where I ate men were actually drilling; I could have leaned out and touched the great steel needle as it revolved, and I learned from them that they were already a mile deep. No oil-towers stood in the actual roadway, but they were in the lawns of the Capitol building and right up to its walls; at one more stride these long-legged monsters would mount its very steps. I tried to picture oil-derricks on Parliament Green and pumps at work in the courtyard of the House of Commons. The supremacy of oil was made vividly clear here. I watched the pumps slowly see-sawing in the garden, perhaps an eighth of an acre, of a little house. Its owner counted as a lucky man, for to strike oil, or have it found under your lawn, is about the only honest way remaining to a great fortune, by American standards.

In the dusk I sat on a bench outside my cabin, on a high bank by the high road. The roaring trucks dashed by, each with its array of red and yellow lights. This traffic never ceases, night or day. During a lull in it a single tiny light flitted round me and came to rest on the seat. I thought of a garden in Durban and fireflies there; it was fun to catch them and put them in the children's hands.

CHAPTER 20

THE ROAD TO SANTA FÉ

O N my way out of Oklahoma City one morning I stopped at a super-market by a bridge emblazoned with the name 'Santa Fé', and as I bought my daily carton of milk and packet of biscuits pictured cuirassed and helmeted Spanish conquerors making this trail, 350 years ago, as they sought to fortify their far-stretched northern frontier line. The Spaniards honoured God where they encamped, and bequeathed to the American Republic a host of names, Las Cruces, San Antonio, Los Angeles, San Francisco, Santa Fé and others, which chime down the centuries like mission bells.

I went on through Oklahoma, once Indian land. American friends, when they heard I was going that way (my route was chosen by chance) seemed puzzled and almost disapproving, as if they thought I could do better. Their picture of Oklahoma was not the golden one of the musical comedy and I thought it weighed on them a little. In these Oklahoman lands was written what seemed, but that God finally dis- poses, to be the end of the Red Man's story. Pressed back ever farther westward and crowded ever closer together, after the young Republic revoked the King's protective order of 1763, the Red Indians seemed to find a last place which they could call their own here, between Texas and Kansas. In 1835 President Jackson said a barrier had at length been raised behind which the Indian would be protected and that 'the pledge of the United States has been given by Congress that the country destined for the residence of this people shall be for ever "secured and guaranteed to them"'. Time showed that the white rancher or home- steader could no more be stopped from taking the whole country, from coast to coast, than today's oil-man can be prevented from drilling where he thinks profitable. In 1899 the last safeguards collapsed; the whole territory was opened for settlement and the flood poured in, over all Indian claims or rights.

The Americans, as they completed a unique piece of empire-making, retained a fierce dislike of 'imperialism', especially 'British Imperialism' (which would have protected the Indian). Through the whole process, too, continued 'the American dream', of which Americans frequently speak. The *Epic* explains it in the words of Samuel Adams: 'The natural liberty of man is to be set free from any superior power on earth, and not to be under the will of any superior power on earth, and not to be under the will or legislative authority of man, but only to have the law of nature for his rule.' Yet part of 'the dream', the *Epic* also says, is 'a remarkable feeling of sympathy for the "underdog" of any sort, economic, political, social'. It is an emotional thing 'which cannot be counted upon when in conflict with other emotions or desires, as has been exemplified in the case of our treatment of our own Indians; the plight of the Red Man, for instance, left the Slavery Abolitionists cold, though they were willing to pull down the whole fabric of America, if need be, to free the black man'.

These contrarieties (which continue in the Republic today) are not peculiar to Americans. History appears to be a crazy mosaic of such paradoxes, of which the Palestine Arabs are the latest victims. However, Manifest Destiny has not yet had the last word. For nearly three centuries the Red Indian was driven out or herded together in lands too small or arid to support him, and his numbers dwindled. He appeared to have chosen the primitive way of life he knew, and extinction, rather than the white man's civilization. Could he have argued the matter, he might have claimed that the real values of civilization may be as well upheld in a primitive system as in an advanced one, and that a mechanical civilization which abandoned those values would be as barbaric as any primitive one; today, he might adduce the Nuremberg Trials and the atom bomb in support. Anyway, he would not yield, and was dying out. Then, as this century began, he started to multiply again and now his numbers, in his cramped and barren lands, are increasing, while he has kept intact his tribal languages, rites and customs. Meanwhile, the white man's overgrazing and overcropping have weakened the prairie the Indian left behind, and the land might be desolate now but for the discovery of oil; the vanished herds of buffalo may have taken with them much fertility. These are the lands of the 'dust-bowl', where the swirling wind wolfishly tears away earth's flesh, the topsoil, and drives it along in a gritty storm that darkens the sky, thus intimating that, as in the South African Karoo, the desert is not far away and is ready to invade, if allowed.

The road ran through a countryside different from any I had met. Sometimes I saw no human being or habitation for fifty miles and drove that far without changing gear, speed or steering. I was often surprised by the flowerlessness of America until I read, in the *Epic*, 'The first few years of any settlement are years of grinding toil, and while the very foundations are being laid there is no thought or energy to be devoted to such amenities as flower gardens, trees, or even mere neatness and cleanliness out of doors. Such things have to come later; and little by little, as people got used to moving on, to devoting themselves to the quickest exploitation of every settlement and neighbourhood, they came to care less and less about general appearances. Like intellectual culture, such things came to be considered foolish ornament for those who were effeminate in taste and not up to a real man's work.'

Now, as I approached Texas, I saw a great mass of roadside flowers, all craning their necks towards me as if to say, 'Look who's coming!' In fact they saluted the rising sun, over my shoulder, but I liked to think of them as a dainty reception committee, for I recognized these old friends at once, though I never saw them before. My musical education overtook me again; I could not mistake that dark, intent glance. I remembered the leave days in London in 1918 when I first heard of them (I think Beatrice Lillie sang the song). More vividly I recalled evenings in 1940 and a girl at my side in the blue car who, as we turned towards London in time to beat the first air-raid warning, sang 'I'm going back to the shack where the black-eyed Susans grow'. I stopped and picked one for her. Then, suddenly, a roadside notice said 'Texas'; it brought a sudden interlude of brilliant green pastures and wheatlands, and then wide prairie again, with the road clear to see for a dozen miles ahead. It was like riding on the roof of the world. I saw hardly any cattle, no cowhands and no man on a horse, though a lad or two in high-heeled boots and, about the lonely homesteads, women in scuttle-bonnets.

I came at length to Amarillo, a little shambles of a place, half-way between a Wild West township and the typical American small town, with quantities of the old one-storied saloons, stores and shacks. No horses were tethered there, but the men, as they drove their cars, looked like cowpunchers, lean, lithe and lanky. They moved with a slow, equine grace, and their legs, in tight blue jeans, were like used drinking-straws.

The twister just beat me to Amarillo. Twenty great box-cars lay where they were blown from the railroad tracks and some fifty houses were destroyed or damaged. I posted my Black-eyed Susan to my companion of those London evenings in 1940, then found a cabin and tilted myself on a chair outside it to watch night fall over this little town in the heart of Texas. A red-golden flame burned upward into the still air, and lent its ragged silhouette beauty at this hour. It commemorated no unknown warrior. The townsfolk had been complaining of the smell given off by the waste-gases from oil refineries; now these were pumped into a slender vertical rod and burned off in it, so that from its tip a spearlike beacon flamed into the Texan night.

CHAPTER 21

WHITE SANDS

O N a grey and chilly morning I drove towards the Old South West, once wild and perhaps not much tamed now; for here twentieth-century man has done wilder things than the Wild West ever imagined; and despite the superb roads and stupendous Boulder Dam nature gives out an oppressive feeling of stored reserves of wrath. When the American Republic acquired this enormous region, where little grew, it was like a gambler who cannot fail at any throw; hence the immense optimism of last century. In the 1840s Mexico was invaded, President Polk using words later to become celebrated: 'Our patience is exhausted.' In 1848 Texas to the Rio Grande, New Mexico, Nevada, Utah, Arizona, California and much of Colorado were gained for fifteen million dollars! 'Even the plunder of Cortez paled in comparison,' says the *Epic*; and almost at once the arid soil of the third empire yielded a crop of gold that dazzled the world.

To the coastal civilization and the fertile Middle West was added this new realm of gold, silver and, later, oil.

The rising road ran on through sandy soil and scrub. What would the story of this new empire have been, but for gold and oil? It looked good for little that grows or grazes, but had the especial beauty of vastness below a great sweep of sky; in such places the earth is merely background, a flat platter on which the blue mould of heaven lies heaped, with a few dabs of white cloud for cream. The free and boundless prairie no longer exists; somebody owns or has enclosed it all and beside the road runs the inescapable wire. Neither man nor beast moved until I came suddenly on a little post-office-filling-station on the top of nowhere. A big, genial man conducted it, a former State Trooper from green and populous Illinois. This was the life, he said; he loved this high solitude.

Then vegetation and soil ceased and I rode up bare mountains, not expecting to see green things again until I reached California. Surprisingly, when I topped the range I came down into an enchanted bowl between the mountains, verdant, thick with orchards and fields. Here were Mexican Indians in adobe houses, who grew fruit, and all along the winding valley road their booths offered Cherry Cider or Mountain Apple Cider. As I climbed out of the green bowl again orchards gave way to fir-forests, which reached to the topmost peak of the enclosing wall; between the firs I saw a jagged snowcap. This was like Austria, and was a reservation of the Apache Indians, a tribe once so noted for ferocity that the criminals of Paris took their name. Now the remnant of them lived in their 400,000-acre reservation, hidden in mountains, with their dreams of bygone freedom. A few moved about between the firs and looked like kraalsmen in Africa.

I came to the top of the green wall and another startling transformation: suddenly everything that lay beyond was bare and lifeless again. The mountains fell to a plain and beyond it rose more mountains, with huge snowdrifts, glistening in the sun, at their feet. I drove towards them; they looked about five miles away. Ninety minutes later I still drove towards them. Slowly I came towards that gleaming, undulating sea of what seemed to be the purest driven snow. I knew it could not be that. When I reached it I found it was an enormous stretch of crystallized gypsum, called White Sands.

I realized where I was. Hereabouts the first atom bomb was exploded; a hundred years after acquiring these wild wastes the Republic found a use for them. Here the scientists continued their mole-like burrowing into the mountain of God's mysteries, and threw up a small hump. (Arizona, next door, contains the enormous crater made by a meteor in dark ages past and Russia is said to contain a much bigger one, made in 1916. Until now the universe, in its desultory bombardment of the planet earth, has chosen waste places for targets. Should it ever select a populous one, that might restore proportion to the current debate about atomic annihilation.)

These wastes are 'the most important spot in the world today', according to a Mr. David Lilienthal, who supervised atomic affairs when I was in America. The statement is debatable (Rome, Canterbury or Mecca might yet prove important) but is typical of the day in America, where public men for many years have tended to discount the notion of any power higher than man's, whereas the Founding Fathers of the Republic emphatically acknowledged another authority. Benjamin Franklin urged at an early Convention of the Republic that each session begin with prayer: 'I have lived, Sir, a long time, and the longer I live the more convincing proofs I see of this truth — that God governs in the affairs of man. And if a sparrow cannot fall to the ground without His notice, is it possible that an empire can rise without His aid?'

The first atomic bombs, dropped on the Japanese, were made here in New Mexico. The military leaders vindicated the calling of arms by opposing the deed, which was ordered by political leaders surrounded by mysterious advisers. Admiral William D. Leahy (who was personal Chief of Staff to the two presidents concerned, Messrs. Roosevelt and Truman) said in his book published in 1950 that when the bomb was used against Japanese civilians the Japanese armies were already defeated and ready to surrender (the British commander, Lord Louis Mountbatten, earlier said the same), and declared that by using it in that way the Republic adopted the ethical standard common to barbarians of the dark ages. The bomb in truth harmed the Americans and British more than the Japanese, for it robbed them of their heritage, their hitherto valid faith that they were peoples on a higher level of humanity, which they fought to preserve.

The true reason for its use emerged when that war ended; it was intended to blackmail the peoples who produced it into surrender. An organized clamour was raised in America (and England) that the atom bomb was demonstrably the unanswerable weapon (in military use, it was but one more explosive projectile); that America and the remnant of Europe were only safe while America alone 'had it'; and that when 'the others had it' annihilation awaited all. Salvation could only be had through 'a world government'; in other words, national survival, gained through two wars, must at once be surrendered.

This intimidation-to-an-end was carried to great lengths. Ten, twenty, a hundred million Americans would be killed at one blow! American public resistance to such incitements and excitements is weakened by long immunity from explosives on American soil (the unknown devil is always worse than the known one) and by the native tendency towards violent emotional extremes. Commercial concerns began to build atom-bomb retreats, provendered for siege; uneasy folk sought homes in Arizona; small-town boosters sold shelter in the Ozarks or caves in the Dakotas. One young man, proudly calling himself the first atom-bomb refugee, built a stone house in a Rocky mountainside, which he called Atom Haven.

All this was foolish for three reasons. First, the Republic remained militarily invulnerable between two oceans, save conceivably for an odd bomb or two. Second, the danger to it was from within, not without; from underground, not from overhead. Thirdly, 'the others' (that is in effect, the Communist Empire) already 'had' the bomb.

Clear heads knew that if the Republic were destroyed it would not be by atom-bombing; that kind of destruction was more likely to fall on what remained of Europe and on the British Island. General Leslie Groves (who was in charge of atomic development until it was entrusted to civilian hands) said, 'As far as the two larger antagonists would be concerned, I cannot see that they would come to grips . . . Both sides would probably avoid it of necessity. It would be difficult, anyway, and more effort than it would be worth for us. We should have to rely on heavy bombing, or the atomic bomb, for our defences.'

This forecast, of a war in which 'the two larger antagonists' (General Groves means America and the Communist Empire) would 'not come to grips' might prove the true one. It would mean that they would compete against each other with atom or other bombs in that part of Europe still relatively free and relatively undestroyed. That the Third War, or more accurately the third instalment of the Twentieth-Century War, would take this shape was certain, saving some intervention by God, from the moment President Roosevelt unaccountably agreed that the Communist Empire should advance to the middle of Europe and the American and British armies in the other half of it were dispersed. It would continue what plainly emerges as the secret pattern of the First and Second Wars: that of destroying Christian Europe, reducing it to serfdom, and setting up a pagan World State on its ruins. It is impossible to believe that a Third War would reverse that process; the change for the better can only come when a new and different generation of political leaders grows up and of that no sign yet offers.

Final salvation only lies in such different leaders, for ones of the present stamp could continue to convert military victory into defeat. England's physical survival in such a third conflict would again depend more on a few men at the Admiralty, War Office and Air Ministry than on any politicians, and if it were achieved could be endangered again at the fighting's end by the political leaders. However, it is the first thing to work and hope for. A heroic figure of the Second War who did not deeply impinge on the public mind was Lord Dowding. If he had yielded to enormous pressure and sent the last twenty-five British fighter squadrons to France in May 1940 the British island would have been lost without a Battle of Britain. This saving act (Mr. Churchill calls it 'an example of genius in the art of war') was the culminating one of patient, unknown labour spread over many years; the quality of the surviving British fighters proved as decisive as their disposition. On such men in the Services future survival would again turn; the atom bomb is not unanswerable.

In America, although the facts were known in competent places, the oracles of annihilation for years continued the cult of doom in their efforts to install a world directorate. That the Communist Empire already 'had the bomb' can hardly have been in doubt from the moment of the Canadian Prime Minister's disclosures to Mr. Truman (and Mr. Attlee) in 1945. In America recurrent, though episodic, exposures revealed the delivery of atomic materials to the Communist Empire, or the theft of such by its agents, planted in these New Mexican establishments, and the presence of its spies in all public departments. As in England, the whole process was never revealed to the public; each separate disclosure was the work of individuals who delved into a morass.

Then, in 1949, the seismographs recorded an atomic explosion in inner Russia, and President Truman announced that the Communist Empire 'had the bomb'. Mr. Molotoff and Marshal Voroshiloff publicly confirmed this, remarking contemptuously that they were not alarmed by others' atomic weapons. The 'secrets', thus lost, were American and British. The initial research work was British; after

America entered the war Mr. Churchill agreed that its results should be passed to America and further development of the bomb be left to it. From that point (at which the wastes through which I now travelled became, in the opinion I have quoted, 'the most important spot in the world') the 'secrets' seem to have been more accessible to the Soviet Empire than to their British initiators. British observers were not allowed to visit the newer American plants, but these, as events have shown, were permeated by Communist agents, so that the 'secrets' began to travel towards the Soviet State and behind the Urals another 'important spot' took shape. For years all warnings about this state of affairs were ignored. General Groves, the first military chief of atomic development, testified that espionage was conducted on a great scale, but said a presidential order debarred him from particularizing about it. Thus some doubt seemed to attach to Mr. Churchill's continued opinion (in March 1950) that 'We have no other overall effective shield at the present time from mortal danger than the atom bomb in the possession, thank God, of the United States of America'. Many American writers refer to the 'strange power' which constantly hindered investigation and exposure; whatever it is, it continues powerful today.

Mr. Churchill's statement was made some months after President Truman's announcement that the Communist Empire 'had the bomb'. Americans in the mass still had no true idea of the extent of Communist penetration in their affairs. That began with the changes made in established usage by highly-powered politicians during wartime. In America, as in England, the wartime status of 'enemy alien' was cancelled by stroke of pen, and all safeguards with it. Any who claimed to be 'friendly aliens' or 'refugees from Hitlerist oppression' could, on that mere assertion, be admitted to any place at all. The whole apparatus of security was riddled like a target by a sudden burst of machine-gun fire. In America, a still more perilous sequel was the transference of all atomic matters from military to civilian control.

After the belated announcement that the Communist Empire 'had the bomb', the prophets of extermination in America were left voiceless for an instant, but quickly discovered an even more unanswerable weapon. The hydrogen bomb would not only destroy mankind but the very planet — unless the planet submitted to universal government. Professor Einstein appeared on a television screen to declare that this bomb would bring 'annihilation of any life on earth within the range of technical possibilities'; an American scientist told Americans that it would be twenty thousand times more destructive than any atom bomb so far exploded; and a Canadian authority announced that it might cause the world to disintegrate in less than one minute. At this flying-saucers were seen on all hands and one American observer saw one land, and begoggled hobgoblins get out of it, Martian dwarfs two feet high.

A soberer evaluation, broadcast by a leading British scientist, was that the hydrogen bomb might make the world uninhabitable by creating a radio-active cloud covering the whole surface of the world. I find a certain charm in the picture of Martians asking each other what the cloud around Earth might be (as we do about 'canals' on Mars) and never guessing that it was just the end of man. However, I doubt if our brief human experiment of trial and error is ended. Wars have never annihilated yet; during the decade which included the last one the earth's population increased by about 150 million people.

I noticed in America a certain revulsion against the oracles of doom. The scare technique is only effective up to a point; then horror palls and the delusion gives way to questions. Americans began to see that their Republic was threatened more from within than from above. Not a great foreign war, but a great domestic disintegration, was their chief danger. However, many still confused the issues, which Daniel Webster separated in his eulogy of George Washington: 'If disastrous wars should sweep our commerce from the ocean, another generation may renew it; if it should exhaust our treasury, future industry may replenish it; if it desolate and lay waste our fields, still, under a new cultivation, they will grow green again and ripen to future harvests. It were but a trifle even if the walls of yonder Capitol were to crumble, if its lofty pillars should fall . . . All these may be rebuilt. But who shall reconstruct the fabric of demolished government? Who shall rear again the well-proportioned columns of constitutional liberty?'

Had he lived in 1950 he would have included the atom and hydro-gen bombs among the lesser dangers, and again have pointed to the greater one. In the last twenty years no American leader has spoken thus. They have put the threat of physical damage first, and have attacked 'the fabric of government' and 'constitutional liberties' in the plea that this would bring salvation.

Not far away from White Sands, at Los Alamos to the north, the atomic experimentation went on, then under Mr. Lilienthal. He was earlier in charge of an enterprise known as the Tennessee Valley Authority, begun under President Roosevelt. It was depicted as a grandiose scheme for enriching poor lands and poor farmers through the control of irrigating waters and the production of cheap power. Its actual achievements are vehemently contested. It has, however, an aspect of *political* power which was not publicly perceived when it was begun. It is an undertaking of the central government, but cuts across the territory of seven separate States. The American States always had a large measure of self-governing authority. While they retain that, a political coup in Washington would leave forty-eight organized State governments capable of opposition or resistance.

The Tennessee Valley Authority overrode State power in various ways. Schemes for nine other similar 'Authorities', covering other areas, lie on Washington desks. The picture of the future, if they were completed, would be one of political power passing from the elected parliaments and officers of the various States to regional 'Authorities', transcending State boundaries, superseding State authority, administered by directors appointed by the president. Mr. Lilienthal described this process as 'democracy on the march'; it might also be called democracy in retreat. His association with the Tennessee Valley Authority caused many Americans to dislike his entrustment with atomic affairs.

No atomic explosions attended my journey through this important spot, but White Sands were the testing-grounds for rocket-weapons, and a day or two before an improved example of the German rocket which London knew, fired from here, rose 100 miles at a speed of about 5000 miles an hour; or so the newspapers said. Obeying warning notices not to tarry, I sped on my way, came to the Rocky Mountains and began another stiff climb until at last I reached the summit and ran downhill into Las Cruces.

It was a lively little town, just north of the border but unmistakably down Mexico way, where dark-skinned policemen and postmen spoke broken English and folk of many colours strolled about between pleasant Spanish-type houses or adobe ones. Behind it mountains reached sharklike teeth into a brilliant sky. I wanted to see some cliff-dwellings in these parts but found the boosting habit an impediment. I went, in search of information about their whereabouts, to a Tourist Information Office, where a handsome executive spoke into a telephone. Why yes, he said, didn't his listener know the tourist industry was the second biggest in the country? Last year it grossed five (or fifty) billion dollars and we hadn't skimmed the cream yet; why, in Las Cruces alone last year it grossed ten (or twenty) million dollars and this year it would gross fifty (or a hundred) million dollars and next year two (or three) hundred million dollars, it was the biggest thing ever if it was organized properly, why in three or four years. . . .

This went on a long time and then he turned to me. He was startled that, with fine hotels and motels all around, I should inquire about cliff-dwellings and could not bring his mind to such trifles, so that I had to find my own way, and well worth while it was.

In Old Mexico, to the south, the Indians built a civilization of a barbaric magnificence. The king's palace was too big for one man to explore; the nobles wore golden cuirasses, jewels and feathered robes; in one grave 480 ounces of gold were found buried with their owner; those people read, wrote, and left manuscripts behind them. Away to the north, on the Great Plains, the Indians remained utterly primitive; they grew only what they needed to eat; and for the rest went hunting and fishing just like the highly civilized white folk. In the space between, in these arid lands of New Mexico and Arizona, a third community took shape which was neither primitive nor advanced, and vanished when it was in the midway-stage. These people learned to build houses of several stories containing many rooms; they knew the secrets of pottery and weaving. What was peculiar to them, they built their settlements in pockets made by weather erosion in the precipitous walls of the canyons. There, between heaven and earth, they were safe from hell, high water, weather and foe.

These cliffside townships are fascinating relics of a civilization, begun and gone. Looking at one, I felt the same startled amazement which seized two old-timers, one day in 1888. They were searching for stray cattle on the mesa when they came to the rim of a canyon and saw, a hundred yards across it, under an overhanging cliff, what looked to them like a miniature city, with many ruined towers and castles. An American scholar, Dr. Andrew E. Douglass, later reconstructed the brief story of these cliff-dwellers from the rings of trees used in their buildings. They were erected between 1066 and 1274 and were in use for some two hundred years. No man surely knows why the vanished townsfolk abandoned them.

Just out of Las Cruces I passed a filling-station with the sign, 'Last stop before the desert'. It was eroded, rock-desert, scrub-covered and bleak enough. The road was flat and blistering and when I reached more mountains the heat-needle began to move towards the red. I coaxed the car up torrid slopes, with several stops, and thought all trouble over when I passed 'The Continental Divide', for I assumed that would be the highest point. It marks the line by which you might walk dryfoot from Mexico to Canada; on the eastern side of it all rivers drain to the Atlantic and on the western to the Pacific. However, more mountains loomed ahead and at high noon the car stopped in a desolate region where the barren rock was covered with great boulders and a notice said, 'National Park: defacing or writing on the rocks forbidden'. In that deserted, unparklike place of a million boulders, I thought, the white man might have been left to indulge his love of scribbling.

The blazing sun would not let the engine cool and I spent an hour in that shadeless place before the car would start, but then the road ran downhill at last. Driving into the declining sun that evening, I was still ten miles from my day's destination when I passed a man lying by the roadside, with a bowler hat beside him. As I went on conscience troubled me. This was desert country and he must be far from any home. What was he doing there? Was he perhaps dead? Above all, why the crowning derby? You never see them in America.

After a mile I turned back and looked at him. He breathed, but might be ill. I wondered what to do. He might be drunk, but then, how came he so far from human habitation? I did not want to meddle if he were drunk, having learned a lesson in that matter. Once I lived near Paddington Station and in those purlieus plied a lady known to all as Marie. One day, chancing along, I saw her seated on the pavement, propped against the wall of the underground station. Her eyes were closed as in sleep and all around knew why. A young man, a stranger, came springing lithely up the stairs and into the street. His eyes fell on her and filled with indignation, for people passed her incompassionately by. He ran and lifted her tenderly in his arms; that is, he tried to. Marie was not light and he could not raise her to her feet (on which she could not have remained anyway). Thus burdened, he looked about, and saw a policeman, watching, chewing his chinstrap. He detached one arm from Marie and beckoned imperiously. The policeman, who knew Marie, continued to chew his chinstrap like a Muslim playing with his amber beads. The young man beckoned again, and called. Life went its way, a stream that divided around him, rejoined and flowed on. Anger gave way to perplexity in his eyes, and that to despair. He looked round like a hunted animal, then dumped Marie and fled back into the station, never again to succour damsel in distress.

I watched the man by the roadside, with the unaccountable derby. 'Be British, Reed,' I told myself, 'he *might* be ill.' A fly settled on his nose. Without opening his eyes he brushed it off, addressing it in terms that plainly proved his condition. I went on, and as the Arizona dusk came down ran into bejewelled Tucson.

CHAPTER 22

WHERE BAD MEN WERE

ARIZONA, in the arid but invigorating West, is better known to distant peoples than their native lands; an American episode which lasted fifty years is often more familiar to them than their own history and inheritance. The mind's eye of all mankind contains a sharper image than any books could give of the mountains, canyons and prairie; the stage-coach with its sacks of gold-dust, the waiting outlaws and the galloping posse; the saloons, boardwalks and hitchracks; the prospectors, cowhands, cattle rustlers and bad men. The reasons are simple: the moving-picture was invented as the Wild West episode ended, the story offered abundant material for good melodramatic entertainment, and the climate is ideal for photography. The picture which emerged was in part genuine, not wholly falsified by the spurious glamour which the dictates of 'box office', the cushioned seat, the amatory handclasp and the crunch of popcorn combine to add.

This country was to have been New Castile, a Spanish colonial empire of great ranches in the gift of the Spanish crown. That short-lived dream left behind a few relics, notably the lovely white missions where peace seems to have taken sanctuary. When Manifest Destiny swept over it, rootin', shootin', tootin', the gold, silver and copper were found and any fertile land was taken by homesteaders. Also, men who formerly exterminated the buffalo turned to stealing cattle and gold; the bad men had their day. Law and order could not be im-provised in lands where the frontier continually shifted westward and new townships sprang up overnight, fifty or a hundred miles apart. For nearly fifty years men were a law unto themselves, and then an episode ended.

What is it all now? The answer varies. I wandered about the bad men's citadels, Tombstone, Bisbee, Cochise and other places, where the names of Jesse James and Billy the Kid still ring, like the echo of gunshots. Some are ghost towns now, crumbling away. Tumbleweed blows through the deserted streets and in the graveyards the stones lie scattered, among them one to a Tom Smith 'hanged by mistake' and another to '269 unknown victims' of the gunplay days. Others of these places have taken new root in modern America and the bones of their wild past lie buried beneath Main Street's banks and stores.

Of these is Tucson, as likeable a little city as you will find in a desert. It was as tough a place as its neighbours, not long ago, and a surviving old-timer or two there can still tell many tales. It is white, bright and lively, full of big hotels, banks, fine shops, pleasant homes. Its roofline is low, which gives blessed relief in America; a man's head is in the air, and instead of canyonesque cliffs it has the wide desert sky for roof and dark, distant mountains for background. In the lemon-coloured dusk and velvet night its myriad twinkling lights, in pink and violet and mauve and rose, take on a quality of enchantment which the same hues quite lack in the sombre abysses of Broadway or Madison Street. It is a little Montmartre in the desert, with its night-clubs, open-air dancing restaurants, filling-stations, cabin-camps and used-car lots, all strung with vari-coloured illuminations.

I found it abundantly prosperous and wondered, why do some places become ghost towns and others bloom like this? Tucson is remote; all around is desert; the gold and silver days are waning or gone; people I met thought little of a current project to grow cotton in those infertile parts. I deduced that Tucson's wellbeing, and that of other places in Arizona, derived from boosting, which up to a point is only making the most of assets. The climate makes you feel you could walk on eggshells without breaking them. Its fame has been spread abroad and I soon found that the family man I met near White Sands, with his household in a truck, was but one of many trekkers to Arizona. Tucson's very remoteness recommended it, also, to people who sought immunity from the illusory atom bomb menace. Thus it has become a town of wealthy people who can go where they list and chose it for such reasons; retired folk with a modest but assured income; and confirmed invalids. The prosperity attendant on this immigration also brought masses of people seeking work.

The drawback of boosting is that 'the place everybody is making for' is not always what they hope. From my cabin I saw in the desert distance a long, curious shape and asked a man, who mowed the grass, what it might be. He said it was 'eight hundred big bombers being serviced for dispatch to the European Democracies under the Marshall Plan' (he had the patter pat; later I saw in other parts great fleets of laid-up war-vessels or wartime freighters, and hoped they would come to a better end than the American and British equipment which was lavished on the Communist Empire during the Second War). This man then told me he had followed the 'Come to Arizona, State of Enchantment' signs from New Jersey, but 'this place isn't what they say; I'm only paid twenty-five dollars a week for doing all the work of the camp and I'm going to Pennsylvania next week'.

This rich country, like poorer and more harassed ones, seemed full of people just arrived from, or anxious to be somewhere else. That is in America partly a survival of a tradition. The old-time prospectors were ever restless to seek gold in new hills, but when they reached them yarned affectionately about the *last* place they were in, just as old sailors commonly say the last ship they were in was wonderful, curse their present one and dream of a better. However, indiscriminate boosting seemed sometimes at fault. I talked to a filling-station lad who said the health-giving properties of 'this place' were, in his case, seriously misadvertised. 'I sold everything to come here,' he said, 'on account of asthma in my family, but the children are all ill. It's a bad spot for respiratory troubles because of the fine, invisible desert dust. Of course, the dry heat is good for rheumatism or arthritis, but me, I'm off next week.'

To me Tucson was friendly and delightful. The dark-skinned folk, Mexicans or Mexican Indians, pleasantly slowed down the American pace; they lounged or sat around in shady corners, dreamily gazing into space. Tucson was all ringed about with cabin-courts and trailer-camps and the settled community disliked these, as dens of loose-mating or unanchored folk. Plenty of houses stood empty, they said, but their owners would not let them because of rent-control (a pro-fessedly benevolent thing which in fact keeps people homeless), and the young folk could or would not buy houses, so that they drifted into trailer-camps. I found much misgiving about the future among sober heads, generally on the ground that 'this is not a united country'.

They feared the ceaseless incitement which, cloaked as a campaign against racial discrimination, divided the 150 million Americans into sections and boosted the claims of the smallest sections to be paramount in American affairs.

I met a significant example of what they meant. I took a cabin and found its proprietor unusually talkative. Recognizing a foreigner, he began to speak about America, saying he, too, was not American-born. 'I came here from Russia with my parents in 1906', he said, 'without a cent, when I was eighteen.' 'Oh, then if you now own this place you have done well,' I said. He shrugged; 'Oh, all right,' he said, 'my son is a State Attorney now.' I thought of the Statue of Liberty and the lines about 'send me your poor'; this was clearly a good American story. 'You *have* done well,' I said, 'that's no small thing, for your son to have risen to such a post.' He made no comment but began to 'sell' Communism to me, little guessing how much I knew about it. 'I've still got relatives in Russia,' he said, 'they've asked me not to send them any more money because they have enough. I wish I could say that here.' 'Hey!' I said, 'I know why people in Russia ask friends abroad not to send them money; they are not allowed to receive it.' He looked at me sharply and said, 'Well, yes, I guess perhaps that's so. What they want me to send is clothing.' 'I know, they're allowed to have that,' I said. He grinned, sized me up and strolled away. He, and the man at Boston, personified America's great problem, and the world's.

Still trying to beat the heat, and hot engine, I left Tucson one day before dawn. At its outskirts pale roadside statues loomed in my head-lights, with thumbs pointing towards California. The thumbers are now so distrusted in America that I wondered to see such numbers of them. (Once I saw two young men with a suitcase thumbing by the roadside in the early morning; when I returned eight hours later they were still there, sitting each at one end of the suitcase and playing cards on it.) I drove on while the great golden sun climbed over the moun-tains behind me and fell on other spectral shapes in the desert: the great Sahuaro cactus. It is like a giant cucumber propped on end, sometimes with arms, and recalls a Bushman painting of a human being. It puts forth a little posy of white flowers which it wears at an angle atop, like an Easter bonnet copied from Fifth Avenue. I reached Yuma before the sun was full and breakfasted beside a trucker from Los Angeles. His truck was a refrigerating one and carried ice-cream to Tucson and beyond, five hundred miles and more. In America that is a cat's jump, but the picture of these great overland vehicles, carrying ice-cream to roadside cafés deep in the desert, seemed most typical of this energetic country.

Yuma was a different place again, neither ghost town nor boom town. Its Main Street was true to type save at one end, where it reverted to Wild West mining-camp. Dark-skinned men, who only needed tomahawks and a few scalps to step straight into a Western, lounged against the old wooden saloons. Then, at the next turn of the road, was the old prison of the bad-man days. It looked like a Moroccan fortress, though less white, with its huge barred doors, and was set on a hillock overlooking town, desert and the Colorado River. In its graveyard many notorious gunmen found their six feet of earth. I waited for a long freight train to rumble past between me and it; out of a box-car popped the heads of two hoboes who looked like illustrations to *Huckleberry Finn*; unkempt, unshaven and red-eyed, they looked shiftily at Yuma and bobbed down again.

Yuma, too, seemed to have survived by devising new attractions, fitted to the times. It appeared to specialize in elopements; perhaps the proximity of the California State line and variations in State laws made it especially suitable for them. Anyway, the traveller from California was greeted with huge placards: 'Welcome to Yuma; Gretna Green Marriages; Marriages performed at any hour of the day or night in Special Wedding Chapel; Minister in Attendance.' The number and size of these signs suggested that the elopement industry flourished.

My cabin at Yuma faced a drive-in theatre. This is a new mushroom growth among the clustering encampments of food, drink, rest, fuel and entertainment which surround American towns. The first drive-in theatres were cheap and simple things, merely a large screen set in fenced, open ground. Now over a thousand of them exist and they are becoming ever larger enterprises, with their own by-products of swings, roundabouts, skittle alleys, dance floors, cafés, night-clubs and floodlit golf-practice ranges. The traffic seems able to carry all that and more; either the air or the romantic atmosphere whets appetites, so that four times as many hot-dogs, hamburgers and packets of pop-corn are eaten in them as in the indoor theatres. They claim, too, to have produced quite new classes of picturegoers: parents who bring the baby in the car, old and infirm folk, heavy labourers who do not want to change from work-a-day clothes. Rain does not matter, and soon spectators are to be supplied with heaters or coolers, according to the night. In these Western expanses the devotees often drive a hundred miles or more to see a new film.

This theatre showed *Bad Men of Tombstone* and was the perfect place to watch a Western, for this was the very country of the miners, bandits, rustlers and the two-fisted gunmen. The scene of the picture, Tombstone, was genuine, not a film-set, and I knew that now ghostly town. The people around me watched their own recent past, in a present vastly different. Tilted in their limousines beneath the Western sky, they ate candy and looked at the shadows of yesterday; they were hitched to a loud-speaker post as their fathers' horses were hitched to a rail. I loved *Bad Men of Tombstone*, in this setting, but forgot to un-hitch myself as I made to drive out, so that a loud wailing and screech-ing accompanied me. When I found the cause I restored the loud-speaker to its post, cautiously made my way among the guests' cars scattered on the ground, and went to bed.

CHAPTER 23

ON DATES AND DESERTS

OUTSIDE Yuma the last State boundary confronted me and
I changed my tune from Ragtime Cowboy Joe, that son of a
gun from Arizona, to California, here I come! A unique fron-
tier-post stands here; the boosters once enticed so many people to
California that the State tried to regulate the torrent by requiring that
incomers should show a sum of money. Public protest reduced that
barrier and the fruit-pickers rolled in again, also the political novelists
who were to depict their life in tones of sexual promiscuity and
squalor unrelieved. The sole remaining ban is on vegetable pests;
travellers must show bags innocent of diseased potato plants and the
like.

I was myself the boosters' victim for I thought California a blessedly
abundant land where fruits grew huge from sheer joy of the soil and
sun (in fact the southern part of it is desert and only constant irrigation
can produce those luscious harvests). Thus I thought the name, Desert
Edge, of the first place I came to meant the end of the desert I came from
and indeed it seemed a green paradise after the thousand arid miles
behind me, for the road ran between citrus groves, orchards, vineyards
and grainlands. Then masses of date-palms appeared, rearing tall
stems from thick old-leaf bases towards green pinnate crowns. I was
hungry and stopped at a delightful oasis where the date was sold in a
hundred different confections, date-jam, date-candy, date-cake and so
on, and the tallest palm was marked, 'Old Father Solomon, imported
from Arabia in 1912; it weighs five tons and gives enough pollen to
pollinate 400 female date-palms'. What a palm, I thought! I ate a
large date-ice-cream and a pound of dates in the shade of Old Father
Solomon and for the rest of the day felt strangely gloomy, as if iron
had entered into my soul. Arab tribesmen fortify themselves with
dates, just as the Chinese work and fight on rice and the African native
thrives on bread or mealies. Those who come of meat-eating stock

142

must be differently made. All my life I loved dates, after the Christmas crackers. Now I shall never eat one again, and for my part Old Father Solomon may rest from his labours.

This Eden continued for fifty miles and then reverted to desert. This was no longer the stony desert of the high lands behind me, but the picturegoer's sandy desert, where Beau Geste fought his battles over again before a movie-camera. A cold wind blew sand-drifts on to the road and notices warned of sand-storms; not long ago this was a bitter place but now the shining road insulated travellers, in their enamelled capsules, against hunger, thirst or loss of way. I saw a distant opalescent gleam and, I thought, the shimmer of mirages, and drove towards them. I was right; this was a dead sea fifty miles long.

The Salton Sea seems to be a huge saltpan, left inland at some incalculable time by the receding waters of the Gulf of California and recently flooded by the Colorado River. It lies well below sea-level and the hush of utter lifelessness encloses it. The earthmen wonder whether other worlds are peopled; here in California was a specimen of an uninhabited world, where nothing walked, ran, crept, crawled, flew or grew, where the spark of life had gone out or never been lit.

The geography of America is a morality play in itself, a graphic natural symbolization of the cross-roads to which man seems ever to come afresh, at which the white man now stands. On the eastern sea-board is the civilization so painfully built up, now arrested and imperilled; that was a God-fearing conquest of the wilderness. Then comes the reward for that first venture, the bountiful central valley, eternal abundance. Then again comes the arid West, the picture of what might lie at the end of any false road: emptiness and death. North of Salton Sea lies the terrible place called Death Valley, which the map-makers have marked 'National Monument'.

Here the traveller feels, not the youth of the Republic, but the age of America. The little roadside habitations and the signs, 'Gas', 'Eats' or 'Mixed Drinks' lend emphasis to it. Here antiquity is recent; you are thrust hard against the savage mien of nature in times now hardly imaginable and feel acutely the presence of monstrous forces held in leash. This picture of pent vengefulness makes the current babble about governing the earth seem petty nonsense. The words about wrath to come were meant, I suppose, to apply to human error, not to promise a senseless retribution for all human effort, good or bad. Here, however, you may see what the wrath might be like if it were called down. The wildness of the Wild West, in the sense of short human incident, was nothing compared with the natural wildness of these lands. In this bloodless earth, in the gaping wounds which drained off its life, in the writhing rock, you may see the picture of a past immeasurably distant and a future not lightly to be challenged by the fool who said ... Such places are not so much National Monuments as natural monuments, and warnings to man.

The desert continued for a hundred miles and then gave way to the groves and orchards, and soon to Los Angeles, the presence of which made itself felt afar off, like New York. Forty or fifty miles were filled with an indescribable human activity. The come-and-go spirit quickened the air. Everywhere houses, bungalows and shops were being built or offered for sale. A substantial home lay on its side in a ditch; it was on wheels and suffered this mishap in transit. A large green gap contained only a placard, 'A City in the Building', and a shack, where the real-estate man sold lots for yet another city, which I expected to find standing if I returned that way next day.

Once more a fly on the wheel, I was drawn into Los Angeles and after Houdini-like exertions extricated myself, found a cabin, and set out afoot in search of food. I lost myself in a Chinese quarter where young men played pool in front rooms and others probably smoked opium in back ones; so I thought, anyway, from the look of the elderly, mandarin-like Chinese who stood guard between. One of them, though he could not pronounce the letter 's', directed me in English towards a good meal. When it was inside me my date-born melancholy suddenly disappeared and I went happily to see the town.

CHAPTER 24

...AND MINISTERS OF GRACE...

LOS ANGELES stands on the opposite coast from the first settlements and is the opposite of all the earlier American Republic meant. Thirty-five years ago it was but a name on the map, and now it is of the world's biggest cities. What it yet may become, the mid-century traveller might ask in borrowed words:

Be thou a spirit of health or goblin damn'd,
Bring with thee airs from heaven or blasts from hell,
Be thy intents wicked or charitable?
Thou com'st in such a questionable shape.

It is a sprawling mass of loosely-rooted townships grown together without form. It is New York's suburb and Hollywood is its suburb, unless it is a suburb of Hollywood: that might be truer. It is more polyglot than New York, having additional Chinese, Japanese, Mexican and other infusions. By day it is deafening and by night dazzling. Nowhere else will the beholder see so many lights of so many colours. Surveying it from the enclosing hills he feels, or imagines, a tinselled impermanence in this city built on the irrigated sands. It has the all-denying spiritual desolation of New York.

I drove round and about it looking for the sea, the breath of which my being needed after the long land journey. My map seemed to show Los Angeles-on-Sea but I could not find the Pacific. Following the sun, I drove and drove through crowded districts served by street cars. The overhead cables were strung from tall, black poles with cross-pieces atop; it was an endless vista of calvaries against the sunset, with three thousand times three crosses. I saw distant hills and thought the sea must lie beyond them. I made for them and found Martian regiments marching over them, with the oil-pumps sucking away between their feet, but no way across the hills offered and I was about to give the Pacific up for lost when I saw a signpost pointing to

'Venice'. This, as night approached, brought me to a seething place which combined features of Margate, Blackpool and Peacehaven. I caught glimpses of dark waves between houses and then a young man asked for a lift to Los Angeles. I was glad to give him one for I doubted if I would find my way back through the maze.

'I thought Los Angeles was by the sea,' I said. 'Oh no, fourteen miles away,' he said. 'I guess you're an Englishman?' 'Yes,' I said. 'My people came from Birmingham,' he said, 'I'm from New York, I like L.A., it's fine and healthy for my daughter, I'm going to work now.' 'At this hour!' I said, 'have I met another writer?' 'No, a barman,' he said. 'Ah, then you can tell me something,' I said. 'What are these All-Nite Theatres I see, one even advertising "two dazzling features"? Who would want to be dazzled at dawn?' 'Oh, L.A. has a lot of them,' he said, 'you'd be surprised how many people throw down a quarter because they haven't anywheres to sleep; they get drunk and don't want to go home, so they sleep in the all-nite theatres.' 'But your two reasons are contradictory,' I said, 'which is it: they haven't enough money for a lodging, or they are so drunk they don't want to go home?' 'About haff-and-haff,' he said, 'you'd be surprised how many bums there are in this city without the money for a bed.'

I pondered this new type of dosshouse, where the homeless snored among plush while Gloria Glamor wasted her insubstantial charms on them. 'Yes, L.A. will be the biggest city in the world in a few years,' he said reverently. 'As it isn't a seaport and hasn't much industry,' I said, 'how did it get so big?' 'Oh, lots of rich farmers like to move into a city,' he said, 'and then there are the films, and thousands of veterans who were stationed here in the war stayed on, and industry is moving in now, and this is where I get out, I appreciate the ride.'

I found, however, that these causes did not wholly explain the growth of population in Los Angeles, and California generally. The earlier inflow, from the gold rush to the Goldwyn rush, was spontaneous, but the recent immigration has to some extent been politically instigated. Growing population means growing political power, in the capitol at Washington, in the United Nations building at New York, and thus in the world. A careful study of the American electoral system has clearly been made by interested parties, and the points found where power may be obtained. Of the 150 million Americans in forty-nine states, about 60 millions live in seven states, the thickly-populated industrial ones of New York, Pennsylvania, Illinois, Michigan, Ohio, Massachusetts and California. Each state, large or small, sends two senators to Congress, but the number of Representatives (in the lower house) rises or falls according to state-population. The concentration of population in these seven states gives them the balance of power in presidential elections. The political control of these states, therefore, is a major prize in the contest for power. Into these states the new immigration from Eastern and Southern Europe, after the Civil War, mainly flowed. It is fairly clear today that this movement was largely directed, in the case of the Jewish immigration, by the Political Zionists. In 1940, according to Jewish reference books, more than half of all Jewish immigrants went to California.

  Simultaneously an increasing number of negroes is being drawn from the South into these seven states by Communist-dominated unions. The powerful waterside union in California chiefly instigates this movement. It has long been a state within the Californian State (the flag of which, curiously, carries a Bear and a Star, both of suggestive implication). These unions are under the control of leaders of Eastern European origins. The polyglot population, which would get along well enough if the impact of the races were left to regulate itself in amity, is subjected to an unremitting propaganda of racial antagonism. Newspapers, literature, radio-programmes and plays constantly harp on the theme. The words 'white man' or 'gentile' are never used but the insinuation is that the white gentile population consists of bigots, baiters, mongers and 'Fascists', and that any decent ones must prove themselves by voting the way the propagandists wish. For such token of moral virtue the material rewards of the Welfare State are offered; the Republic, like England, if it is to go down, will go down with free dentures gleaming and half-price toupets waving in the breeze.

  By these means the vote of the seven key states has been mobilized for Democratic or Communist candidates, as a recent rule. At the last presidential election the only one of these states lost by the Democratic nominee was New York, where the large Communist vote split the Leftist block, and let in a Republican. By then, however, the Republicans were so intimidated by the bigot-and-baiter campaign that (like the Conservatives in England), they were leaning over backward to appease Political Zionism and Communism, so that their supporters would have been little cheered had their man won.

This is one reason, then, for the increase in California's population, which, with the number of its seats in Congress, is growing fast, while those of the older, non-industrialized states decline or remain stationary. Mr. John Gunther records that California's vote tipped the scale for President Wilson in 1916, and that in 1932 'a series of delicate and intricate manœuvres within the California delegation enabled Franklyn D. Roosevelt to win the Democratic nomination for President'. Without those two events the Communist Empire might not have risen, first, and spread second, or the Zionist State been set up.

Thus L.A. and California are important. Los Angeles is growing into a political stronghold of the new immigration on the Pacific, as New York is already its chief one on the Atlantic and in the world.

CHAPTER 25

VALLEY OF LIGHTS AND SHADOWS

I DID not tarry in central Los Angeles but took a cabin off the Hollywood Boulevard, where the road strikes uphill towards the Hollywood Bowl and the hills, and contemplated the metropolis of the moving-picture. If the whole human conglomeration called Los Angeles seems like an incandescent bubble, reflecting shapes and lights and tints but with only frail substance of its own, Hollywood is its glittering inner filament. The place seemed as shadowy and impermanent as its own plays. Hollywood was built in a day, as Holyrood (say Scotsmen of that ancient abbey) was not; the two places are symbols of opposed philosophies, the faith that endures and the temporal schemes that fade. Hollywood peculiarly belongs to the group of consanguineous cities, New York, Chicago, Johannesburg, Tel Aviv. Once, in a visitors' book at Johannesburg, I found above a Hollywood signature the comment: 'Magnificent; only equalled by Hollywood.' The remark was apt: like draws to like the whole world o'er.

The encampments which cluster beneath the name Los Angeles, Hollywood, Beverly Hills, Bel Air, Pacific Palisades and the rest, sprawl over countryside of great natural beauty which reminded me of the Valley of a Thousand Hills in Natal, save that the ocean lay on one side, whereas that valley is landlocked. From my cabin I could see these humps, hillocks and hills rising to mountains, their sides covered with houses, or half-settled, or yet unbuilt. Among them, clamant with placards by day and neon by night, rose Tap-Dancing Schools, Hearing Improvement Institutes, Song-Writing Studios, Music-Teaching Institutes, Ballet Schools, Eye-Education Institutes, Reducing Institutes, Psycho-Analysis Institutes; it was like the Charing Cross Road and the quack quarter of Soho, deified. On all hands guides waited to show the traveller the way, not to the stars, but to the Homes of the Stars. A great placard on a vacant lot announced that 'an extraordinary hotel' was to be built there. The greenest places were the domains of the Burial Parks (the notice outside, 'Free Parking', refers to motor cars; interment is expensive); though these will never move a Gray to compose an Elegy, they prompted Mr. Evelyn Waugh to his 'tragedy of Anglo-American manners' and I met many Americans who see an alarming symptom of the times in their frankly pagan and commercial approach to the disposal of human remains.

Against this evanescent background the human beings I met, too, seemed shadowy, fleeting figures. Alone among them my host seemed glad to be in Hollywood; he sought relief from a muscular atrophy and the sun benefited it. My neighbour and his wife, come two months before from far away in search of the good life, had both found good jobs but were going back to the firm soil, the green dampness and the hard winters of Connecticut. This being a populous place, I sometimes took thumbers aboard. One was a young man of exceptional good looks whom I guessed to be a film aspirant. He resolutely kept a remarkable profile turned to me until he found that I could be of no help in that ambition, when he relaxed and said he guessed he was through with Hollywood, he was going back to bit parts on Broadway. Another was an Englishman, originally of the North Country comic type, who was also stranded and asked for a small loan, and he was hardly gone before a negro appeared at my car window, saying he was a good cook-butler from the British West Indies, could I help him to a job?

I spent my most pleasant hours with film folk, chatting and looking down on the Aladdin's Cave which is Hollywood by night. They were some of the nicest people I met anywhere and a newspaper candidly written by them would be an exceptionally interesting publication. They complained that in Hollywood you 'died intellectually', though I thought they meant spiritually. About this time an English actor left Hollywood with audible distaste, saying it was 'an awful place, run by a few moronic old columnists'. He survived to win great success on Broadway, but most of the performers do submit to the thrall of some elderly ladies who enjoy the confidence of the rajahs of film-making and hold the choice between 'good' or 'bad' publicity over the players. When I passed through the studios one of the tragi-comic star-and-studio tiffs was in progress. A row of mobile make-up vans, used 'on location', bore each the name of a star, among them that of the one who had 'walked off the set', a Miss Garland. Some rival or small-part player had scribbled with chalk across her name, as who should say, 'You're out, see!' That tiff was composed, the star returned, and the columnist aunts pronounced a blessing (but it broke out again later).

Hollywood, built on the irrigated sands, looks and feels as unsubstantial as a house of cards, but that is not the truth of its importance in the world today. It contains the most potent machine, of this or any time, for forming or warping the mass-mind. No temporal power of emperors or popes ever reached areas or multitudes so great. Its industry is in name one of entertainment. In fact it gives huge opportunities for propaganda, that is, the implanting of a certain set of ideas in the mass-mind by suggestion. This has become a major aspect of its activity. Hollywood has become a projector of subversive suggestion. It acts as the agent of New York in this. 'Hollywood is nothing more than a suburb of the Bronx, both financially and from the point of view of talent,' says Mr. John Gunther, '. . . to be accepted in this nation, New York acceptance must come first. I do not assert that this is necessarily a good thing, I say merely that it is true.'

The Americans I met agreed that it was true, and thought it bad. The picturegoer who sees a Hollywood film generally sees something that has passed the tests of acceptance by New York; the exceptions are rare and producers who rebel against the thrall meet much antagonism in many ways. The propagandist insinuation which runs through most pictures, in varying degree, is roughly on these lines: that the English-speaking peoples and white gentiles generally are an inferior mass, prone to base dislikes which must be combated; that their own faith, history and tradition are unimportant; that their womenfolk are in the main shallow or worse; that they cruelly oppress beings of different hue or belief. It is the fission-propaganda, for dividing Christian or white folk among themselves, which proved effective before the Civil War. That incitement (says Mr. Dale Carnegie in his biography of Lincoln) raged for thirty years, and poisoned the minds of people who know nothing of the South or of slaves with tales of boiling water, red-hot irons, burnings at the stake, blood hounds and licentiousness ('the South,' said Wendell Phillips, 'is one great brothel where half a million women are flogged to prostitution').

The suggestion of Hollywood films today follows a similar line but is devised on a broader front for a worldwide audience. It is that the white folk in the mass, not now merely the American Southerners, are innate haters and baiters, who can only be reformed, or prove conversion, by embracing Communism and Political Zionism. The permeation of the film-output by this subtle suggestion takes two forms, one positive and the other negative. A few films are wholly devoted to the propagandist purpose. These, which give the point to the whole, revive Mrs. Beecher Stowe's attack on 'racial prejudice' and in them Simon Legree is reborn as the oppressor of Jews (or still of negroes if audiences tire of the first version). The remaining films conform to the negative rule that they should contain nothing *contrary* to the suggestion of the positive ones. Thus three-fourths of a 'production programme' may consist of Westerns, gangster or thriller pictures, and musicals. The Westerns are 'good box office', and as Indian voters are few redskins may be freely hated or baited in them. The gunman-pictures are also remunerative and follow the slumming tradition of recent American literature. The musicals draw well and their prevalent tendency was described by Mr. Jay Nock as 'the filthy vulgarization of woman's beauty'.

The broad inference of the whole 'production programme' is that people as evil as those of the gangster films or as empty as those of the musicals would naturally be given to the foul aversions depicted in the 'racial prejudice' pictures. The finer aspects of American life, history or tradition are almost completely ignored in the Hollywood output. It is an illusion that 'box office' is Hollywood's only and golden rule; the purpose of political suggestion overrides all else. I found players and lesser production specialists aware of this paramount policy and repelled by it. It is the true reason why the great pictures have so seldom come from Hollywood; art cannot thrive among such inhibitions. Once leading performers and other prominent people in the industry gave evidence before a parliamentary committee which tried to trace the thing to its subversive roots. They received 'the treatment' in press and radio and found work hard to obtain thereafter. The actor, like other artists, acts to live and does not live to act and the majority knuckle under; but they are not happy in Hollywood. Foreign players who arrive with a great reputation, particularly, often blur into oblivion like a fading negative after a few years there. When I talked with great players of the past or present I was often reminded of my own experiences in journalism, which underlies a similar thrall today. As good Americans, they feared the corrupting influence which they felt around them.

The extent of the bondage was much greater than I realized before I went to America. In earlier days each new mining-camp or rising township built a theatre, and the greatest players and singers of the world came to those remote places. Today 'theatre' means picture-theatre and outside New York, with a few exceptions, the living theatre has been destroyed. That means more than is at first apparent; it means that the play, as well as the players, must pass the over-riding test before Americans can see it. In former days none could tell Irving or Booth or Otis Skinner what to accept or reject and they made their choice by the old canons; playwrights all over the English-speaking world wrote plays and actor-managers or producers selected from them; the best came to the top. Now all the world's a screen and the plays are 'screened' before they are screened, by the central authority. Scripts for film-plays must measure to the supreme standard of acceptance; if a book or stage-play is selected it usually undergoes revision, often beyond recognition, before it is filmed.

Good films from other countries, or ones which conflict with the Hollywood tenets, are excluded by the same machine, which controls the theatres as well as production. Americans are cut off from the best of the world's pictures, almost as if they lived on a desert island. *Oliver Twist* was long banned, in the American zone of Germany as well as in the Republic, because the lesser of two villains is a Jew. *Hamlet* was in effect long excluded, save for the Little Theatre Round the Corner in one or two big cities. One of the few American producers outside the occult circle said such a film as the Italian *Bicycle Thieves* 'would not stand a chance of being shown in the average American small town theatre; Hollywood would not permit it'.

This mental air-conditioning covers the whole territory of the Republic. Having studied mass-mind-control in Communist Moscow and Nazi Berlin, I felt in Hollywood that I had seen everything. Oddly, the most reassuring spot I found in this ephemeral but despotic place was the one which I might have expected to be the most impermanent of all. In a corner of the littered grounds of one big picture-making concern was a little pleasance, come into being by the accident of this industry. Where all else vanished with the end of a picture, here a few relics of famous shadow plays remained, and by some chance the living truth of people and events survived among the debris of makebelieve. On one side was Tara, the white Southern house where Scarlett O'Hara flirted with her beaux, and on another the millstream cottage and old stone bridge where Mrs. Miniver composedly battled with the war. Around were other survivals, and in between were fragments of lawns and gardens; overhead, birds sang. This was all plaster front and façade, propped up behind by planks and beams, and yet the story of the South and of England was real and poignant in this unfrequented patch, where only a gardener worked or a studio hand came to eat his sandwiches. These deserted sets were genuine in the metropolis of the bogus; somehow, enduring values and verities flowered in a green corner between white pillars and a lichened roof.

The time came to go and I drove out to Santa Monica to prospect the route. It lay in a bay as wide and lovely as Durban's, with mountains running sheer to the sand's edge. In the distance, ahead of me, I saw the coastal road running below the mountains and eagerly imagined that stage of the long journey to which I looked forward with particular zest: the run northward, beside the Pacific, to San Francisco.

CHAPTER 26

CASTLE OF DREAMS

I LEFT Hollywood early and half-awake and only after twenty miles realized that I had missed the coastal road and was travelling inland, though in the right direction. Grass and vegetation were brown, and I recalled what a famous woman player in Hollywood said to me: 'This is really desert, and if we didn't keep on watering it, it would go back to desert.' The feeling of living in a place innately hostile to man combines with the spiritual oppression to make people uneasy and restless. Southern California lies on the latitude of the Sahara, fruit-growing and other farming is really oasis-cultivation, and in the background lurks unfriendly nature.

I turned towards the coastal road, through the old Spanish country, never truly settled but dotted with small settlements and missions, and came to one of the loveliest of these, Saint Bonaventura, founded in 1770. Now the typical small town has grown up around it and it stands on the main highway, with filling-stations, five-and-ten-cent stores and all the commotion of Main Street for neighbours. Yet the church and its cool garden were filled with a deep tranquillity; the peace that passeth understanding indeed, for I could think of no mortal explanation for the sudden hush that lay beyond a white wall. It sent me on my way refreshed, and I came at length to the ocean road and, after a small place or two, to a long, unpeopled stretch and a lonely roadside signpost with a name. No habitation was to be seen, and a few days before the name would have meant nothing to me; I should have run past it. Now it attached itself in my mind to fragments of a story heard in Hollywood. It was one peculiarly American.

I turned off the highway and in a few moments a place came into view, unlike anything I saw anywhere else in America. It was less than a village and lay asleep, or dying, by a blue lagoon, with the ocean in the distance. A few houses hid themselves among trees and birds sang. There was a church, closed, and a post office, open but deserted. Only one thing moved; a girl in a glittering, kingfisher-blue swimsuit came out of a house, drove away and was gone. No shops, stores, filling-stations or any of the usual things; either they were kept out or stayed away. Then, where the road curved towards the lagoon, I found a big warehouse, shut, and a pier leading to the water; a notice said, 'Wharfage operations discontinued, trespassing strictly forbidden'. As I looked round this abandoned place I pictured a busy wharf and warehouse, cargoes landing, people bustling about; and now, this. . . .

There was a man of wealth and renown. He married, unhappily. Then he met a woman whom he loved. Divorce was precluded, and they began an unwedded partnership which became too permanent for the world to begrudge them it, even if the world were wont to reproach rich men. Yet rich men may find happiness especially hard to reach, and perhaps this one was aggrieved that he could not have the one thing he wanted.

I invented this explanation, anyway, for the palace he built at the loneliest part of this Pacific coast, and filled with fantastic treasures from the ends of the earth. To this wharf they came and were carried to the high mansion where he thought to capture peace and cage love in a castle among the clouds. The marble halls were packed with costly things, the great grounds stocked with strange beasts, and from high solitude he looked down on the vast Pacific. He owned the little village, too, and its decline or demise was part of the natural end of the story.

He was not only rich but powerful. Had the cards of chance fallen a little differently he might have become president. But he commited a cardinal sin. He opposed American entry into the Second War and thus crossed the path of those forces which stood to gain by it. He was vulnerable. Barely disguised, a moving-picture was made of his life, love and citadel.

He had thought to enclose his love and his disappointment in a place where no eye could reach. The picture tore down every wall, curtain and veil. I recalled that film, seen many years before; only now did I understand all the circumstances.

I drove back to the main road and on, and soon passed a drive, where great gates stood wide open but a notice said, 'Trespassing strictly forbidden; no sightseeing allowed; please do not ask for passes, because they will not be given'. A mile farther on I stopped and looked back. There it was on the tallest mountain-top, a huge white place of turrets, towers and terraces, wings and countless windows. Now, when it all did not matter much any more, someone still tried by 'No sightseeing' notices to shut out the prying world, which from a million picture-theatres had long since looked into every corner of this high fastness.

Only when I went on my way did I realize how lonely was the spot chosen for that astonishing mansion. All at once the entire roadside apparatus of food, drink, fuel and lodging, which followed me from New York, even through the desert, faded away. I ran through splendid country which changed from aridity into one of grassland and grainland, apparently devoid of human life. I saw that if any mishap should befall me I should spend a lonely night. The road returned to the sea and suddenly became a narrow shelf running along mountainsides, which fell steeply down to it and as steeply again to the ocean. Notices said, 'Curves and gradients for the next 64 miles'; hairpin bends for such a distance were new even in my experience. Other notices repeatedly warned, 'Slide area; watch for rocks on pavement' (that is, boulders on the roadway); I pondered the chances of dodging a descending boulder and divided my eyes anxiously between road and mountainside.

I doubt if the world can surpass the beauty of this road. It ran across innumerable great bridges, thrown over gulches and canyons. Each must have cost a fortune; in such American undertakings cost seems of no account. The road twined and twisted up and down the rock face for about a hundred miles, and at every yard the huge vista of ocean and mountain changed its shape. It was exhausting driving and I saw I should have to go much farther than I expected before I could hope to find a lodging. The whole cabin-camp organization, on which by now I relied, suddenly fell away.

I came to a deep, dark cleft in the rocky walls where huge sentinels stood: 'The first of the famous Redwood Trees, which are only to be found in one narrow belt of California.' Some of these trees reach 350 feet and are 2000 years old; they were there 'when they crucified my Lord'. Among them I had again the feeling, which followed me through the West, that America is old in a way no other great populated country can be called old. Nowhere else does man hurtle in such sublime, or vainglorious, indifference along peerless roads through such grim places, dark with the anger of nature disturbed for the first time since time began. The road turned inland, ran through fragrant mimosa banks and carpets of purple hedgehog, and suddenly fell down dark, precipitous declines, thickly clad with the huge redwood trees. The bare rock, above the vegetation line, looked as if it were the place where creation began in agony; in the contorted, writhing groins and loins of those mountainsides you could see the pains of that primeval labour.

Midnight struck before I reached Monterey and found a cabin. As I fell into bed a pandemonium of sirens and alarms broke out and I went to sleep expecting the next morning to find the place ruined by earthquake or fire. Instead I found it unscathed and wonder to this day what event can have caused that appalling clamour.

CHAPTER 27

'...ENJOYMENT OF PARADISE'

SIGNIFICANTLY, the pleasantest parts of the twentieth-century Republic are often those where colonial memories linger on; English ones in the East, French and Spanish in the deep South and South-West, and here in the far West Spanish ones again. These traces are few, for the Spanish, and later the Mexican, occupation only amounted to a few missions and military posts, scattered over a huge area, but their influence still pervades the air. Monterey was such a fragment, in a great blue bay. It has a few surviving houses built by Don This and Don That, and even one made from the timbers of the *Natalia*, in which Napoleon escaped from Elba to begin his Hundred Days and meet his Waterloo; the ship was wrecked at Monterey in 1834.

I began the last leg of the Pacific run and soon came again to oil derricks. The irrepressible search for oil is impressive. The day before, not far north of Los Angeles, I saw derricks marching out into the very sea, where the water was shallow. The oil-men had drilled down through sea and sand and on the end of little piers the strangely human pumps worked away by themselves, in their slow, unpausing rhythm. I sometimes wondered what would happen if the prospectors one day learned that oil lay below the lost continent of Atlantis, or in the stratosphere; no doubt they would get at it, somehow.

The marvellous road climbed along the sides of mountains high above the sea and after fifty miles I came, suddenly, into San Francisco. It is a fabulous city, the finest new one I saw in America; though it is polyglot it does not bear the Babylonian stamp of the new immigration, but is recognizably and attractively American. Its situation is exquisite. New York shows that a fine natural setting is not enough, and may be spoiled; San Francisco has improved on its native advantages. It is built on hills around a great, islet-studded bay, which is shaped like a 'C' reversed and facing the ocean. Across the gap in the

'C' runs the Golden Gate Bridge, the middle span of which, over a mile in length, is suspended in air by cables; the weight of the bridge, and the mass of traffic which uses it, makes this even today a marvel. Far below, great liners look like small craft and sailing-boats like tiny birds.

On the slopes around rises the white city. I do not know if the lesson of the earthquake preserved it from the fate of New York; anyway, the highest building is not much more than twenty stories. It is full of green parks and squares, of streets with little, clipped trees, and pleasant homes, all as bright as new paint. A hundred years ago all that stood here was a Franciscan Mission, a Mexican fortified post, and a few primitive habitations containing less than a thousand people. Then, as the Americans took over, gold was found in California, and the last stage of the American conquest was a two-way, tidal surge which flooded the remaining empty lands. The miners, 'Forty-Niners, rushed overland from the East, but many more came round by sea to this remote bay, landed and pushed eastward to meet the others. Behind them San Francisco rose from the ground like a conjuror's tree.

The gold was found, of which Columbus, seeking the new route to the Indies, wrote, 'It is the most precious of all commodities; it constitutes treasure, and he who possesses it has all he needs in this world, as also the means of securing souls from purgatory, and restoring them to the enjoyment of paradise.' His Most Catholic Majesty's opinion about this pronouncement is not on record, but it throws light on the being called Columbus, who appears to have been of a pagan nature. Gold never yet bought health or happiness and its story until today, when most of it is buried in Kentucky or Russia, might rather suggest that it carries some inherent malison.

It would not stay with those who found it. The first was one Captain John Sutter, who ten years earlier swore fealty to the Mexican government and was granted huge lands in the Sacramento Valley, some sixty miles from San Francisco. He called his realm New Helvetia, in the tradition of New England, New Netherland, New France and New Spain. In 1848 he and his partner found the gold and before the year's end the gold-rush was on. Sutter's claims, like the Indians', were brushed aside by the swarming gold-seekers and he ended his days in Washington, vainly seeking to assert his title. Most of the miners fared no better. Many were seamen who deserted the gold-rush ships in San Francisco and rowed upriver to the goldfields, leaving the hulks to rot, sink, or be used as saloons and boarding-houses; at one time five hundred derelict vessels were stranded there.

Almost overnight a city appeared. The wily ones did not go to the goldfields, but waited in San Francisco for the miners to bring the gold to them, and soon the nuggets and gold-dust accumulated on the gaming-tables, the saloon-counters and in the bordels. San Francisco passed through a phase of lawlessness hardly equalled in the history of white men. It was ruled by gangs of escaped convicts or ticket-of-leave men, many of them from the British penal settlement at Sydney, so that they were called Sydney Coves and their quarter Sydney Town (later, the Barbary Coast). In two years the town was six times fired for pillage, but the culprits, if brought to trial at all, were freed by venal judges prompted by purchasable politicians. The contemporary *Annals of San Francisco* remark, 'The police were few in number and poorly as well as irregularly paid. Some of them were in league with the criminals themselves and assisted these at all times to elude justice. ... Seldom could a conviction be obtained ... Not one criminal had been executed. Yet it was notorious that, at this period, at least one hundred murders had been committed within the space of a few months.'

This was the beginning of something which remains today a major problem in American cities; the corruption of justice. One authority, Mr. Herbert Asbury, wrote of the passage quoted, 'It is interesting to note how aptly this describes present-day conditions in many American cities', and this is a typical American comment. The period of lawlessness in San Francisco was, if not ended, at least checked by two remarkable interventions, of a kind which have occurred only in America, as far as I know. They were uprisings of exasperated townsfolk, who took the law into their hands to establish some sort of law.

The student of the Republic's story very soon finds that 'lynching' was not a form of infamous racial prejudice. It was nearly always the desperate performance of a duty which police, public prosecutors and judges refused to do, and was aimed against white malefactors. This is the reason why Communist propaganda today incessantly attacks the memory of something that happened many yesterdays ago; the new wreckers fear its reappearance tomorrow. In San Francisco the Vigilance Committee spontaneously took shape and stamped out the worst dangers to individual life and property by public executions, dissolving when order was established. While highway violence thus decreased, the subversion of public officials by criminals became rife again later and is as serious as it has ever been in Los Angeles today. When I was in America a leading journal, speaking of that city, wrote, 'California politics is shot through with graft, bribery and corruption; the dividing line between the underworld and those sworn to defend society against gangsters and murderers has been worn tissue-thin.'

San Francisco gradually struggled clear of the worst of these things. In 1920 the Barbary Coast was at last subdued, and when I saw it it survived as a night-life district rather similar to Sankt Pauli, in Hamburg. Chinatown, risen from the ashes of the fire which destroyed its fetid dens, was a placid place of narrow streets and shops full of jade, ivory, embroideries and Chinese food. Either dead or dormant were the bloody tong wars between the Hop Sings and Suey Sings, Sum Yops and Suey Yops; a demure respectability prevailed where once Chinese girls, brought across the ocean, were put to prostitution; however, if Chinese girls were no longer 'sold down the river' at this mid-century, China itself could be, and was. The tong wars were ended by the last Manchu Emperor, Kwang Hsu. Appealed to from San Francisco, he called in his statesman, Li Hung-chang, who said, 'The matter has been attended to; I have cast into prison all relatives of the Suey Yops in China and have cabled to California that their heads will be chopped off if another Sum Yop is killed in San Francisco.' At that time no man foresaw that the oriental torture of holding relatives as hostages would be introduced into Europe by the Communist Empire.

Life in San Franciso, I thought, should be good. I liked to dine at leisure in the restaurants of Fisherman's Wharf and then drive to my distant cabin across the Golden Gate Bridge, looking for the dazzling night picture of the city. I seldom saw it because the bridge was often wrapped in a black fog, so that only the next two or three lights along the bridge itself were visible. This ride through a black tunnel, hundreds of feet above the bay, was at first an experience as startling as the under-river one in New York. The town behind was hot; up here the air was chilly and dank and the fog swirled and eddied round like black cotton wool, through which vehicles suddenly loomed, whoosh-whooshed past and were gone. I found that fog on this bridge is a habitual and unwelcome visitor. The townsfolk were clearly used to it, for all traffic continued at unabated speed. I was glad to clear it and the hill beyond and run downhill into a crystal-clear night, sparkling with lights.

One Sunday night I sat outside my cabin and watched the weekend traffic, returning to the city by a road which ran before my eyes straight for many miles into the country. I could see the headlights of thousands, perhaps tens of thousands, of cars, all pressing hard on each other's wheels and racing for bridge and city. That unbroken stream must have stretched for twenty, thirty, perhaps fifty miles, and did not cease or slacken; it was as if a gigantic horde of beetles, three abreast, came thronging out of the night with blazing eyes.

I can picture almost any earthly event or calamity, and even a trip to the moon. My mind could not envisage the day when America has twice as many motor vehicles. Would the whole land become one great conveyor-belt, filled with things on wheels? Would they all take wings and fly? The stray wayfarer may wonder, but such problems bother no American; he will fix that, or it will fix itself.

CHAPTER 28

SNAKE-TEMPO IN SACRAMENTO

TURNING my back to the ocean and my face towards the long
overland journey again, I drove round the shores of San Francisco
Bay. Behind me the fog-blanket still lay over the mountains but
I rode beneath clear skies into a great fertile plain that stretched far
inland. Sparkling creeks invaded it and once, when I thought deep
water far behind, I came to one where half the American Navy
seemed moored or laid up. Between commercial announcements and
soap opera the car radio called on young men to volunteer for various
services. Thinking of Western arms supplied to the Communist
Empire and the Zionist State, I reflected that ample weapons should
be at hand, in all camps, to begin any new affray, and that 'private
arms manufacturers' could never again be blamed for this. If it happened, American and British fighting-men would again find themselves
opposed by arms bearing the marks of their own factories, or made by
their own machines, 'lease-lent'; much of the gold, too, which the
'Forty-Niners wrested from this Californian soil, had gone that way.

I ran through these historical gold-rush lands to Sacramento, which
contains all that remains of 'New Helvetia': the fort John Sutter built
in 1839 against the Indians; it is now a quiet and lovely place of lawns
and hedges and loopholed walls hung with wisteria. Sacramento,
beneath the curious bear-and-star flag, is the State capital of California,
an enchanting white town of flowers and blossom, parks and fountains,
trees and palms, set beside a broad blue river in a verdant plain. It has
the charm which some cities seem to be given at birth and others never
acquire. I went to its post office and was arrested by the sight of a
young man who stood statuesquely at its door.

His hair fell to his waist and his beard to his chest. He wore a square
of green material draped over his shoulders and fastened at the neck,
and two other squares joined to make breeches, so that his chest, lower
legs and feet were bare. He held a staff and a toy snake, of the kind

sold in the five-and-ten-cent stores, and a rough leather satchel with a sheet of paper protruding from it, on which I read, 'Sundog'. People stopped, stared, murmured and giggled. A man said audibly, 'Why is that guy standing there? Who does he think he is, John the Baptist?' A woman sniggered.

I disliked the mockers. Clearly he served his faith, whatever it might be, in this strange way; if this was his manner of upholding his God, he might at least be left alone. But of what religion, old or new, could he be the prophet, this lonely man of Sacramento? I went towards him and saw he might be blind. 'Why are you here?' I said. 'This is part of a publicity campaign to popularize my new dance-music,' he said. Illusions fell from me. I should have known, I thought.

'Oh, is this music, and are you selling it?' I said, drawing out the sheet marked 'Sundog'. 'Yes,' he said, 'anything from a penny.' 'So you are doing this for publicity,' I said, 'is that why you are dressed so? Your appearance suggested a religious motive.' 'I always dress like this,' he said, 'it isn't much of a compliment to compare me with John the Baptist, I'm not a Christian.' 'I didn't compare you with John the Baptist,' I said, 'that was a compatriot of yours.' 'But I've been expecting you to, everybody does,' he said. 'Not everybody,' I said. 'No doubt you observe,' he said changing the subject, 'that all my clothing and appurtenances are in the form of squares?' I saw that a small leather-pouch, for money, was also square. 'Ah, yes, so they are,' I said, 'is that good?' 'My ear-rings, too,' he said, proudly touching leather pendants from his lobes, 'I had them made by Indians.'

I looked at the music. 'What does Sundog mean?' I said. 'I am Sundog,' he said simply, as if that told all. 'And is this really dance-music,' I said, looking at the sheet, 'has it a dance-rhythm?' 'Well, I don't know what you understand by dance-rhythm,' he said. 'I'm just quoting Sundog,' I said, 'it says here, "a new song in a new dance-rhythm".' 'Well, I call it snake-time,' he said and then I saw that, to clinch the matter, he carried two five-and-ten-cent snakes, 'as a matter of fact my ambition is to conduct, like Toscanini.' 'How is your sight?' I said, gently. 'There isn't any,' he said. 'But then, how would you conduct?' I said. 'Oh, I would not attempt to conduct any music but my own, which I know by heart.' 'Are you always here?' I said. 'No, I arrived last night and go on tomorrow,' he said. 'How do you travel?' I asked. 'By overland bus,' he said, 'I'm going to Denver from here.'

I felt I had started something I could not finish. There ought to be a graceful way of ending this, I thought; perhaps a sinuous *pas-de-deux* performed by Sundog and myself on the steps of Sacramento post office; but I could not find the right note and somewhat abruptly left him, a half-naked man draped in green, blind and with hair to his waist, to popularize his snake-rhythm in the sun. I drove away and on the road was puzzled by the presence of new thumbers, many of them, in couples, male and female, with suit cases. Then I remembered that this was the road to Reno, to quick divorce and immediate re-marriage. As nearly everybody in America owns at least one car I wondered why they did not transport themselves. I could only guess an answer: they thought it more romantic to thumb a ride. However, I gave them none, but put green Sacramento behind me and continued along towards the arid lands again.

CHAPTER 29

WIDE OPEN TOWN

LEAVING cornfields, ricefields and orchards behind, I began to climb the Sierra Nevada, through sweet-smelling firs; I was not to see much else that grew green for many hundreds of miles. Suddenly a roadside sign said, 'Snow conditions on this route'. I disbelieved it and thought it must remain there from winter to winter; I was sweating and the engine showed familiar signs of overheating. Then, peering ahead, I saw a great blanket of greyblack cloud, immobile, which looked like the permanent cloud-cap of snow mountains, and wondered. I passed altitude signs that said three, four and five thousand feet and before I reached six thousand the car just struggled over a crest and stopped; the map showed two thousand feet yet to climb. So much for smartypants in Hollywood, I thought, who blew a pound or two of winged insects out of the radiator and said I should have no more hot engine.

Cars seem even more sensitive than human beings to changes of temperature and altitude. This excellent one (a friend's) disliked heat and height and I wondered how I should surmount the pass. While I waited lightning jaggedly cleft the black mass of motionless cloud ahead; clearly storms raged there. At last the engine cooled and I went on. To my surprise the heat-needle went back and back; the car, recognizing familiar New England temperatures, was enjoying itself. I passed log cabins and lumber camps among the firs, and clearings where the grass was of a green I never saw before, and ran into the sleety storm. 'Slippery when wet', said the roadside notices; round a bend were a great truck, wrecked, and a car wrapped round a tree, and skidmarks everywhere, and men gazing lugubriously at the mess; mountainside crashes in America are awe-inspiring affairs. I went on again, now shivering, a few miles from the wilting heat of the plain. Suddenly I came to snow and a high road where I seemed to ride along the tips of fir trees. Then, all at once, I was over the summit and far below a great turquoise lake lay among silent conifers. I had climbed eight thousand feet in fifty miles; now I lost two thousand feet in a few moments, serpentining down a nearly vertical corkscrew road with the gear in first, towards lonely, unfriendly country, the Nevada State line, and Reno.

Nevada, between the Sierra Nevada and the Rockies, is the least habitable and least inhabited State. The settlers shunned its cold barrenness. The miners rushed to it for gold, silver and copper, but the lodes grew weary and gave out. It might have reverted to wilderness, but the American spirit does not brook that. Substitutes for natural fertility and mineral wealth were devised. Nevada calls itself 'The Cyclone Cellar of the Tax-Weary'. Notices at the State boundary offer new inducements to settlers; the State levies no taxes on income, inheritance, death, sales, gift or anything else. Nevada is solvent, for revenue is gained in other ways. One famous one is simplified divorce and marriage. Another is company-formation; directors and shareholders need not live in, ever see or own any initial capital in Nevada, to form a company there. A third is the wide-open regime for drinking and gaming.

'Wide open' is a term of the first importance in America. It means the saloon that never shuts, the swing-doors that only remain closed until they are pushed. Nevada is wide open and if it were bigger and more populous the bonanza kings of the underworld might all retire to it. They need a bigger field and operate all over the Republic, especially in the great cities, which have populations many times that of the whole of Nevada. Great untaxed fortunes are today only to be made through drink, drugs, gambling and prostitution (or a lucky oil-strike) and in the main centres of population the vice-rings concentrate all energy on getting and keeping all those doors 'wide open', through the bribery of officials. The rewards they can offer are large, for the sky (and the openness of the doors) seem the only limits to the traffic. The clutch of the underworld thus closes round party-machines and reaches high into the control of politics. It is a tumour in the body politic and civic of which all are aware but which none dares to remove.

Reno is a small fish in that murky pond. The big prizes, of money and political control, are in such places as Chicago and Saint Louis.

Reno gives, in miniature, the picture of what a *lawfully* wide-open city would be. Most of the big ones pretend to forbid or regulate drink, gaming and prostitution, then tacitly tolerating them through subverted officials. In Reno wide-openness is the law; all is open as the day and open all night. No need exists to build a saloon athwart the county line and shift all the tables across it until a new sheriff has been 'taken care of' (this happens elsewhere). In Reno the thing is a tourist-attraction and source of revenue, in an infertile land.

In glittering streets the saloons stand side by side as they stood in the wild days, the trophies and relics of which cover their walls. They are filled, night and day, with newlyweds and newly-unweds, tourists, and a few persistent natives, drinking and gaming. The calling of gambler is a lawful one. These eye-shaded men, who operate the tables of roulette, poker, faro and many other games, still wear the tight-lipped, expressionless face of their trade. Some of the gamblers are women, dressed as dude-ranch cowgirls, who carry their names on brooches: Bessie, Anne or Jean. Many women play, too, among a unique, continuous noise like the clicking of countless typewriters. It is that of the slot-machines; I counted three hundred in one saloon. The gamblers no longer carry guns; they do not need to, for the players only too eagerly stand and deliver to the one-armed bandits. That delightful cartwheel, the silver dollar, is now illegal in America, I believe, but in Nevada is the common currency; Nevada has silver-mines still and no gaming-machine will respond to the insertion of a paper note.

The profits of the traffic are beyond accountancy. An institution which surveyed it reported that fifty million Americans (one in three) gamble regularly. Each year they pay eight milliard dollars to bookmakers, another milliard to the gaming-machines, and one more milliard to the 'numbers racket' (similar in essentials to the English football pools, which similarly appeared not long ago in an affair involving the subversion of officials). A substantial share of the proceeds goes to undermine the law.

A New York judge who collaborated in this investigation saw no clear remedy, saying that the root of the trouble lay in the people themselves. Few knew that the dice were loaded against them, he said, but even if they knew did not care; they were like the man who was warned that a game was crooked and replied, 'I know, but it's the only game in town'. That is another way of saying 'There's nothing else to do', and, to be understood, needs to be considered against the whole background of American life as it has come to be shaped by the aversion from literature and music, the disappearance of the theatre, the lack of small gardens and private domains, and the common feeling that the cultivation of the mind is effeminate. In Nevada you may come at midnight to some tiny, remote place and find the dealers shuffling and the machines click-clacking in a dozen saloons. To reach the only game in town Americans will come from towns very far away. In the Nevada desert is a place of twenty-five thousand people, Las Vegas. In 1950 a new 'gambling joint' was opened there which had a large swimming-pool, a coloured fountain thirty-five feet high, a floor-show costing several thousand pounds weekly, the kind of chef who uses a sword and a super doll's-house for guests' babies. It cost about a million pounds to build and on the opening night about £250,000, at current rates, changed hands.

Reno, glittering beneath wild mountains, was an experience indeed. My evenings there, however, were spent more profitably than with the one-armed bandits. My cabin-proprietor's daughter was a Western film star, a remarkable girl who carried on a regular broadcast programme; in this way her father had come by a collection of sound-effect records, used in radio work, with which he entertained and instructed me. The old sound-effects man (glass of water, peas in a tray, coco-nut shells) has clearly passed on. There seemed no imaginable noise which was not somewhere on these disks, from a cat having its tail twisted to a dogfight, a baby crying, the screech of brakes, horses snickering, whinnying and neighing. Applause there was, too, in every possible degree. I already knew how the cheers in the Red Square at Moscow are made; but now I shall never again believe even in the plaudits of a twentieth-century studio audience.

CHAPTER 30

THE GHOST OF GOLD

IN another dawn I set out from Reno across mountain meadows and climbed to six thousand feet in the Sierras, bound for Virginia City. Not long ago this road was a rough track down which the swaying, four-horsed stage-coaches came, bullion bars beneath the seats, sparks flashing from the tortured tires, drivers straining on the great brakes, passengers clinging to the sides; here, sometimes, one rolled over the edge into the canyon below, or masked bandits waited. Now, when Virginia City was dead, it was a superb modern highway and the changing picture of the angry ranges was magnificent in the early light.

I came over a summit and into the gold camp. Half-ruined, lifeless, it lay in the rising sun. My footsteps rang loud and hollow on the plank sidewalks, like those of some spectral visitant to a haunted manse. The boards were worn by departed miners' boots so that knots in the wood stuck up like thumbs. Behind their awnings the sagging saloons leaned against each other; the Bucket of Blood, the Bonanza, the Brass Rail, the Gold Nugget and many more. It was as if miners, sheriffs, saloon-keepers and sporting girls had been spirited away not long before. In the dusty, broken windows of tumbledown shops lay odds and ends of old stock, women's hats of the 1890s and the like. From decaying walls peeled brave posters of the Christy Minstrels marching into town.

The impatient American spirit marches roughly over the past. What do you do with an old automobile, or a played-out mining-camp? Why, junk them! Ghost towns are numerous in the West. Some have vanished, some are deserted ruins, some are 'coming back'. Always a few people remained who would not or could not leave. In those which have not 'come back' their lot is as lonely as that of hermits. Others discovered the sightseers' value of their townships, collected the relics, cleaned the place a little, reopened the bars, and created a simulacrum of the Old West. The tourists came agape and roads were made to help them. A little life returned, of a new kind.

Virginia City is one of the most successful in making the best of its abandonment. Here, in 1864, the Comstock Lode was struck, and the news went round the earth. The Californian miners flocked to Nevada when they heard it, and San Francisco grew faster still. The Bonanza Kings were the lords of this 'good earth' ('borrasca', the Spanish-Mexicans called the goldless kind). In Virginia City and adjoining camps were sixty thousand people. It was another windfall for the North, though the Virginia Citizens were deeply divided about the Civil War far away and hung opposing flags from poles which now bear bullet marks; one woman saloon-keeper, who climbed a mast to lower the Union and hoist the Confederate flag, was shot as she came down.

Here Mark Twain edited the *Territorial Enterprise*. Virginia City, like all new towns of that American day, built a theatre, Piper's Opera House, which still stands. When Ghost Town was Gold Town the best singers and players and the great professional beauties came to this remote place; Edwin Booth, Caruso, Lily Langtry, Maxine Elliott, Harry Lauder, Charles Wyndham, Patti, Paderewski, Lottie Collins and Dion Boucicault with his *Lights of London*. The theatre still has the window where gentlemen parked their guns, and the playbills of *Uncle Tom's Cabin* (those yellowing posters remain more exciting than the most lurid placards of today's picturemakers). As the auditorium was flat the stage was tilted upward from footlights to backcloth, so that the rearmost miner could see all of Lily in a long gown or Lottie in a short skirt. A temperamental barnstormer or emotional actress would have needed to avoid any over-impetuous movement (hands uplifted to heaven and eyes upturned to the gallery) on this stage, or they might have broken into a trot and been unable to pull up before they fell among the musicians.

While I wandered round Virginia City awoke. The saloons opened and men strewed sawdust on their floors. Once this absorbed more than dregs; in one saloon Suicide Table is preserved, where three successive proprietors shot themselves after losing all at a dice-throw. The miners are gone and minors are not served; at breakfast-time, however, I saw a man reel through a swing-door who looked as if he stepped out of the 1890s. Possibly he too was there for verisimilitude; if he was, he seemed happy in his work for later, when I imagined him snoring in bed, I saw him stagger through another swing-door.

Lost in the mountains, Virginia City too has the stuff of a morality play (a picture-play was made about it once, but elsewhere, though the place itself is a perfect Western film-set, ready-made). Here the gold-seekers impoverished the earth. In California gold was got by washing gravel, but the Comstock Lode wove its glittering way deep through mountains, and underground-timbering began, six hundred miles of workings. For sixty miles around every tree was taken and now the mountainsides are bare. Perhaps £200,000,000 worth of gold and silver were taken, then the lode ran out, the miners dispersed, fires and weather ruined the town, until it struggled back to its present ghostly state. The morality play ends with a riddle: what purpose is the gold serving now?

I drove back through Reno, past 'Desert ahead' signs, towards more arduous journeys. At long intervals in the stony, scrubby desert fingerposts pointed to remote, invisible habitations, This Ranch or That Ranch. The loneliness of the open range survives, without its freedom, for the wire was everywhere. I came to the first of the salt lakes. From one the wind swirled the salt-dust into a constant, vertical shape; until I drew near I thought it was a geyser blowing. The Bible says that Lot's wife, when she turned to look at the ruin of Sodom, was turned into 'a pillar of salt'. I wondered if this eerie white column in the desert was that which the words meant. Did Lot's wife vanish in a salt-storm, pillar-like in shape? Much might be clearer in the Bible if we comprehended its allusions better.

Here small places were fifty or a hundred miles between. This is a trap for the solitary traveller, who is ever tempted to try and reach one more township and may find himself struggling through the night in fading hope of bed or food. I passed glittering, miniature Reno's, called Winnemucca and Elko, where the cabin-camps were full, and at midnight was still pressing on through a black, empty land where the rare names on the map proved to be but filling-stations (each full of gaming-machines). I was resigned to a cold night in the car when I came suddenly on a place called Wells, which I found next day to have but 1400 inhabitants. It blazed with light in the desert and at one o'clock in the morning twenty saloons were wide open. None had more than three or four guests, but in each the banker dealt cards to these few inveterates, and clearly no establishment would close while one player or tippler remained in it.

I found a room, but not sleep. In the next one a curious company, a man, woman and dog, kept up a weird chorus of talk, laughter and yelping through the night, so that I needed no alarm to start again before dawn. At four the sun, like a light suddenly switched on, burst over a mountaintop and not long afterwards I came over another one and saw an amazing sight: the Great Salt Lake, lifeless, unwrinkled and opalescent, about a hundred miles of it. The mountains mirrored in it were duplicates more than reflections; it had a dazzling shimmer and sheen. The road ran straight into and across its few inches of water, with a railway beside it laid on banked earth. Then the water ceased and only the hard, glittering salt remained, where the speed-contestants have driven racing cars at three hundred miles an hour. A river, named the Jordan, flows into the Great Salt Lake and disappears, in theory by evaporation. No living thing, save a little shrimp, can exist in it.

In the middle of it I had my first flat tire. The night before I shivered and saw the faint luminosity of snowcaps in the darkness; now I was drenched with sweat before I changed the wheel. In the West you alternate between Saharan and Alpine conditions suddenly and recurrently. At last the job was done and I ran on into Salt Lake City, in time for breakfast.

CHAPTER 31

IN HONEYBEELAND

SALT LAKE CITY, the capital of 'Friendly Utah' (as the State-line notices truly say), differed astonishingly from all else in America. In spirit, this seemed another world.

Utah lies deep in the barren West, with gold-rush or cattle States on all sides. The pioneers who founded those neighbouring States went there to get gold or land. Another motive drew the pioneers to Utah; the one which brought many of the first settlers to America. The Puritans and Pilgrims called it flight from religious persecution. To Utah, when it was wilderness, men came for religious freedom, and for its sake settled in the bleakest place they could find. When a Mormon leader, dazzled by California, hurried back from San Francisco to entice the main body of Mormons thither, his superior, Brigham Young, refused to move. The Mormons, he said, would decline in a competitive community and perish in trying to colonize a seaport. These pioneers alone resisted the lure of gold or rich lands and stayed to struggle with a desert. From that beginning grew a State dissimilar from today's forty-seven others. Were it surrounded by deep water it might now be the independent State of Deseret (Mormon for 'Honeybeeland'); fantastic realms grew in these parts a century ago.

The story is amazing. On September 21st, 1823, Joseph Smith, an obscure 17-year old youth, at his village home in New York State was visited by an angel of the Lord, Moroni, who told him of a book, written on golden plates, that was buried in a hill there. It contained 'the fulness of the everlasting Gospel', and two stones were buried with it which contained the keys to its translation 'from the ancient Egyptian'. Four years later the same heavenly messenger delivered these to Joseph Smith, and received them back when the translation was done. It was 'The Book of Mormon', on which The Church of Jesus Christ of Latter-Day Saints was founded. Its lesson was to the effect, among much more, that the North American Indians were a lost people of Israel and that the American lands would see a Second Coming.

Who would believe that? The time was one when men and women, in a new country, eagerly flocked to new sects; these were often profitable to the leaders; Shakers and Holy Rollers flourished. However, all religions were born in happenings inexplicable by scientific analysis, and their prophets all claimed to have received revelations and tables of laws. The Mormons believe in the message to Joseph Smith as others believe in the visions of Buddha, the appearance of God to Abraham, the visions of Saul on the road to Damascus and the revelations made to Mohammed.

Anyway, Joseph Smith was martyred for his faith or killed for his presumption, whichever may fit. He founded his church in New York State; was driven into Ohio (where the first temple was built); driven out again to Illinois, where the Mormons built a city, Nauvoo, and their numbers grew. Then Joseph Smith and his brother were imprisoned and, while awaiting trial, taken out by an armed mob and shot. Once more the Mormons, under their new leader, Brigham Young, trekked; this time over the Rockies to Utah. They stopped where Salt Lake City now is, built a city, temple and State, and made a desert blossom like the rose.

Joseph Smith was hated because he introduced plural marriage, claiming that this too was a divine command. Moral opinions about polygamy vary in different religions and countries. In America, where Mrs. Beecher Stowe and the Abolitionists were whipping up hatred of the South by depicting Simon Legree surrounded by black concubines, polygamy in the West was politically embarrassing to New England and the North. Mormon records say it was popular with Mormon women; however, the dead cannot testify. In the 1890s the Mormons repudiated polygamy, not from conviction but to gain membership of the United States, as a State. It is outlawed today and a small obdurate group, which tries to persist, is sternly repressed; however, Mormons are not deeply persuaded against it.

The story of Utah under Brigham Young is as remarkable as the man. A Christian potentate with many wives, he truly kinged it over Honeybeeland. His official residence, the Beehive House, and his private residence, the Lion House, remain, the one with the beehive atop and the other with the lion over the door, and both emblems are apt to this strong and busy man, for the two houses are connected by a passage and each of the gables of the Lion House marks a wife's bedroom. In the roadway near them stands his statue; Mormons and non-Mormons both like to point out with a smile that his back is turned towards the Mormon Temple while his face, and outstretched arm with open hand upturned, are directed towards the Zion Savings Bank (a Mormon institution).

The persecuted often become persecutors and Brigham Young followed precedent. His gunmen, the 'Destroying Angels', were feared by rebels and apostates. They could not subdue the exile leader in far San Francisco, Samuel Brannan (who kept his own bodyguard and left the Church) but they dealt harshly with a small dissident group which broke away in 1862, declaring that Brigham Young was not the divinity he claimed to be. Their leader, one Joseph Morris, said *he* had seen visions, conversed with God and was the Lord's annointed. These Morrisites did what the Mormons had done; they packed, trekked and settled some forty miles away. Brigham Young sent five hundred men with artillery after them and mowed them down.

However Joseph Smith and Brigham Young may appear at the final balance, the fact emerges that Mormonism has achieved something exceptional in this place, since 1847. Possibly God bestows His blessing on those who seek, whatever their leaders, the merit being in the search; the Mormon faith is *Christian*. Many parts of the West speak of the malevolence of nature or the decay of human schemes; in this desert spot is peace, confidence, sober living and the feeling of civilization.

Salt Lake City, though small, is more of a city than many bigger ones; it has urbanity, a gentler way of life, and the belief that God is more than gold. These things show themselves in the kindlier manner of people, the unhurried traffic, the drinking fountains at every corner and the rills of clear mountain water that constantly freshen the gutters, in the appearance of streets and homes, and in temperate habits. The Mormons control Utah, though they are not in the majority. Accordingly the State is not 'wide open'; drinking and gaming are restricted; across the State's borders stand 'Last Chance' saloons for those who wish to pay a last forfeit to the one-armed bandit before entering Utah, or to provide against thirstiness inside it. The Mormons do not drink liquor, eat moderately, and pay a tithe of their earnings to their church; Utah heads the health and longevity tables.

Mormon legend says that Brigham Young, when he emerged from the mountains with his first exhausted band after their long trek and saw this dead land between him and a dead sea, struck his staff on it like the prophet and said, 'Here we will build a temple to our Lord!' That is legend; but anyway, the solitary place was glad, the desert has blossomed, and the temple was built within forty years. It is to this city what another temple was to Jerusalem; all streets are built to and from it; 'First South' and 'Fifteenth West' mean 'from the Temple' (which only Mormon initiates may enter). The Tabernacle, behind it, is a huge oval building with a dome twelve feet thick entirely supported by great buttresses around its sides; that might not be a simple architectural problem today, but the Mormon pioneers built it with their own hands soon after they reached this barren spot. Legend, again, says that the Salt Lake City seagulls came in answer to Mormon prayer and ate the locusts which destroyed their first efforts at cultivation. The seagulls are certainly there, and unexpected to see by the dead sea into which a river called the Jordan vanishes. It is all very strange.

Whatever its past or future, Salt Lake City today is a pleasantly reposeful island in America's unease. What has been built here was built on faith and is strong. In the gentler spirit of the place the traffic frenzy and the parking terror fall away. People move in measured time and the air is not rent with clamour. Prices are lower, and hands do not grasp. A spacious place has been set aside for 'out of State' cars, so that the traveller comes to a haven.

What Utah may become, who knows? The stranger soon meets the resident who dislikes the Mormons, and the man who says 'The only good thing about this place is the climate'. The critics complain that the poor man cannot buy beer by the glass but the rich one can drink what he likes in the great, Mormon-owned hotel. The non-Mormon population is growing and might in time swamp Salt Lake City as it has swamped other places. Nevertheless, the organization founded by Joseph Smith and Brigham Young has proved very strong and supple and has kept civic control for a hundred years. I doubt if the world has anything quite like it.

I went to bathe in the Great Salt Lake, where dawn and sunset paint lurid hues on a lustrous ivory palette. You cannot sink, but cannot swim with comfort; notices warn you not to get the briny water in eyes, nose or throat. Also, in this one place where depth does not matter, you can hardly get out of your depth; after a mile of plodding the water only reached my waist. It was wonderful for sun-bathing, and oddly, the sun did not burn. The first Spanish explorers were told by Indians, 'It is a very harmful lake; any part of the body bathed in it becomes inflamed at once'. Expecting to be quickly scorched, I emerged, not even pink, but covered with white salt, which brushed off in masses. Medicinally, this bathing might be fine; after it, and some days in and around pleasant Salt Lake City, I was more than restored from a long and wearing journey, and went on to Colorado fighting fit.

CHAPTER 32

COLORADO: EL DORADO

C OLORADO was bleak. As in Nevada, the soil here is hostile to man; Utah stands between the two as a human victory unique in these parts, one of faith. In Colorado the ranchers and home-steaders often had to give up after their flocks and herds had eaten the soil dry so that it reverted to sagebrush, thirty-five acres of which will feed but one cow. What brought it fame and population lay beneath the soil. At the period when the Republic drew an ace every time it cut the pack, Colorado saw a third strike like those of Sutter in California and the Comstock Lode in Nevada. In those days, when Pizarro's mythical City of Gold between the Amazon and Orinoco still gleamed brightly in the legends of Spanish-speaking men, it was El Dorado come true. In 1859 the gold-seekers rushed towards the Rockies and the gold, chalking 'Pike's Peak or bust' on their covered wagons or hand-carts. The westward-moving frontier jumped 700 miles at a bound towards the glitter of gold in those bitter ranges.

The day was very hot when I reached the Rockies. The engine stalled again and before me lay a pass 11,500 feet high. I longed to be over the great north-south spine and on my way towards green lands. Soon after I started afresh, however, I was more in danger of frostbite than heatstroke. I went up and up, through alpine water-meadows where streams and rivulets bubbled, through the deep and sorrowful silence of forests on high slopes, up to bare rock blanketed with snow where ski-ers sported and into mournful grey cloud; then down through a long ravine, describing the letter 'S' until I was dizzy, into desert-heat again and Denver. I stopped at the first place I saw to have a broken cable repaired, and while I waited was kept in talk by an old gentleman who stood around.

Age may be solitary, amid the pace that passeth understanding. Wherever I went I saw these old folk. The vestibules of cheap hotels, particularly, were always full of them, big-hatted, shirt-sleeved, suspendered; waiting, watching, thinking. They were there from dawn to dusk, seldom speaking save to ask a stranger whence he came, whither he was bound, what he did. They seemed cast on some sand-bank of life's estuary where they awaited its submerging tide with passive rancour. Mr. Somerset Maugham observed them: 'When I have travelled through America I have often asked myself what sort of men those were whom I saw in the parlour-cars of trains or in the lounge of an hotel, in rocking-chairs, a spittoon by their sides, looking out of a large plate-glass window at the street. I have wondered what their lives were, what they thought of and how they looked upon existence . . . With a soft hat on the back of their heads, chewing a cigar, they were as strange to me as the Chinese and more impenetrable. Often I have tried to speak with them, but I have found no common language in which I could converse with them. They have filled me with timidity.'

Inscrutable they are, and they have a fixed place in the hurried American scene. The absence of seats in public places might be part of this mystery of the old folk, as of the hard lot of the bums. (I once asked a man about this and he said, 'If you put seats in the parks bums sit on them'. I said that seemed the natural destiny of seats and bums. He said you couldn't encourage bums. I said I didn't see how they could be discouraged and what should we do without them? He looked worried, as if he thought me a subversive.) In a small Western town, in 1922, a druggist put a bench outside his store. At once it became 'a loafing headquarters for the local gaffers', men between sixty and a hundred who sat there year in, year out, 'looking like a jury of irritable terrapins, whittling, spitting and passing judgment on everything that passed' (an American newspaper description; these old gentlemen do load the air with a verdict of censorious spite). By 1949, after a quarter-century of this daily condemnation, the housewives were so unnerved that they asked the druggist to remove the bench, saying, 'Why, they must spit two or three gallons a day! They ain't died fast enough, these old men.' The bench was removed, but the aged men made such a fuss that it was soon put back, and they are on it now.

This old gentleman of Denver was loquacious, and gave me an acid commentary on the times. Aw hell, he said, when he was married before the Spanish-American war (1898) he and his wife lived a year in a box-car; he was 'on the railroad and she was game'. Then she found a one-room apartment and wanted her own furniture. Hell, she got it all for 42 dollars, secondhand; 'after all, once you got furniture it's secondhand anyway, ain't it?' He let that apartment, furnished, for 59 dollars a month in 1918; ten years later he was glad to get 15 dollars for it. He paid 399 dollars for his first automobile; now 399 dollars was just the down-payment. Hell, the young folks today thought the down-payment was the end; they didn't trouble to think about the payments to come. When they bought furniture they had to have everything of the best, hell, 400 dollars for the bedroom suite, 300 for the dining-room suite, hell, they'd do better putting 3000 or 4000 dollars away for the hard times ahead. Business was slowing down but, hell, the punks who drew big money from the government thought it ought to go on like that for ever. What would happen to all the production in a few years time when money was tight and the European countries were recovering and sending their goods across? The punks would see, aw hell.

He gave me some insight into the minds of these old folks who sit around. I drove on into Denver, settled myself and looked about me. Denver, like Reno and all the mining-camps, sprang up overnight, but it has taken firm root, flourished, and is now the biggest city of the West, until you reach the Pacific. Like Haw Tabor, who chiefly built it, many bonanza kings died in penury, but others reached Pike's Peak and were not later 'busted'; they founded families still wealthy and powerful in Denver today. Around the real-gold-leafed dome of its Capitol spreads a town of great contrasts; its main streets are as fine and its mean ones as squalid as any in America.

My lodging was in the poorer part, among tumbledown brick and adobe houses, intersected with dark alleyways and inhabited by a diversified breed, of many colours. Larimer Street was near and gave me my first close view of a thoroughfare as distinctively American, at its level, as Main Street. Here, where the varigated throng surges to and fro, slop-shops, pop-shops and junk-shops, bars, saloons and snooker-pool rooms neighbour each other, with the neon cross of an occasional Rescue Mission between, and the whole pot boils day and night; the hard-drinkers perch on their stools before breakfast and at almost every hour.

With memories of Edna May, I went into one mission room, where seven little coloured children, seven elderly men (two of whom slept), and two young men confronted a preacher and a young woman who told the seven children the parable of the Lost Sheep. Mission work must be hard in these wide-open surroundings. The traveller who talks with Americans soon comes to some understanding of the Prohibition experiment. It failed because moral attitudes cannot be enforced by legislation. Not much effort has been made, by taxation or other means, to temper the abundance or potency of liquor, and possibly none is feasible (in ghostly Virginia City, when I was there, the few citizens voted unanimously against reducing the number of saloons on the ground that this was an attack on the American Constitution). Thus the trade, and any effects it may have, continue almost un-regulated, with local exceptions. Many Americans dislike this unrestrictedness.

In Larimer Street every third establishment seemed to be a pawnshop. Once it was the centre of fashion in growing Denver; now Denver has moved away from it and the elegance of the large hotel there, which was once 'the last word in luxury', is hard to picture today. I found its entrance hall full of the usual veterans, waiting in judgment, and its bar empty save for one woman, who sang. She might have weighed seventeen stone and had the remains either of beauty or of what Wilde called really remarkable ugliness. She had a very strong stage person-ality and a more powerful voice than I ever heard in a woman. In London, perhaps, she might not have needed to spend her days serenading bygone triumphs at a decaying bar, for London loves its Kate Carneys and Florrie Fordes to the end. None but myself heeded her or her song, which shook the rafters, and also dated her; it was, 'Teasing, teasing, I was only teasing you'.

I went back to my hotel and tarried among the ancients who sat there because one, in loud tones, told a strange tale. Things overheard often defy explanation and, as I missed the beginning, I was left without the clue to an astonishing human experience. What I heard was, oft-repeated in accents of reverent emphasis, 'The doctor made me drink a pint of whisky a day for ninety days to drive the stuff out of my system. A pint of whisky a day for ninety days! I was drunk for ninety days! And I don't drink! I don't touch whisky. I told him I'd never taste it again. But he made me drink a pint of whisky a day for ninety days!'

I wonder still what ailment was cured by this treatment. The evening of this man's days was plainly to be cheered by the recounting of his ninety days and life had left him little else to tell; that was made clear when, having exhausted even this theme, he buttonholed a new-comer and urged him to see this or that picture, then showing in town. The stranger, disappointing man, was a commercial traveller who spent every evening watching pictures and had already seen them all. To that the elderly man replied, 'Then you cain't do nuthin' here. There's nuthin' else to do. I go to 'em all. The pictures is my only pleasure.'

At that I went upstairs, pondering the consolations of age.

CHAPTER 33

MYSTERIOUS WAY

I SAW another aspect of the American scene in Denver: revivalism. Apparently Denver is a centre of it and it has several permanent 'revival churches'. Their advertisements stirred my curiosity. These offered faith-healing to the music of accordions and steel guitars, and an evangelist who was to take a piano apart and play upon the strings of a piano with accompaniment of another piano. I wondered if that added up to two pianos or three, and went to see.

I found a large, barnlike building in a humble district. Strange sounds, as of sorrow or illness, came from it and inside I discovered about a thousand men, women and children, who emitted them. On the platform a man made various announcements and between them threw up his arms and cried 'Praise the Lord!'; then the people threw up their arms too, and waved them, while the men groaned, the women keened, and all puckered their faces, while many wept. The sounds and gestures were familiar to me. Around Durban is a sect of Christianized Natives who wear long blue robes with a white cross on the back. They have mingled Christian with pagan things and drive out devils in the manner of a tribal war-dance, prancing round the possessed ones, trampling and kicking them, with movements and noises akin to those I now heard.

Between the groaning and keening men and women stood up and held forth in incoherent words, sometimes in gibberish. Then the folk on the platform stood with bowed heads and when it ended they said 'That is marvellous, praise the Lord!' and the oohs and aahs began again. At the announcement of a hymn-tune the tempo abruptly changed; the puckered faces cleared, the lamentations ceased, and the people sang with terrific gusto. Next a handsome young man with a strong personality spoke; I could not judge if he genuinely wished to spread the Gospel but he could have sold snowshoes in the Congo. By turns he took off his coat, undid his tie, unbuttoned his collar, wiped his brow and spoke of the strain of his work. The church, he said, needed *men*; unfortunately (he tried to skate back over that 'unfortunately') two-thirds of its members were women. I looked about me; four-fifths of the congregation were women, all sharing a mien of unfulfilment, and usually women were the ones who sprang up and babbled. Next the young man spoke of miracles. A gentleman ('present today, I believe') had been cured of cancer by attending these meetings and had the X-ray plate to prove it.

Then he played a banjo and sang a song, 'Baby Gloves', about an old dad and mum left all alone with these tiny mementoes of children grown and gone away. After that an older man said that Brother Jones had often been offered 'thousands of dollars without charge' but had 'just brushed the money aside', and he admired Brother Jones for that. However, he implied, Brother Jones would like some money and he would now take 'a love offering for Brother Jones'. Thereon women sprang up to 'bear witness' in jumbled words to Brother Jones's merit; 'Give till it hurts!' cried one. With great clamour of brass, wind and rub-a-dub the collection was taken and brought in much money, the figure being greeted with the loudest groans of all.

Next I went to a finer hall in a better district. I could not tell whether these revival churches belonged to some parent body having the form of a properly constituted church; I rather guessed that anybody could open a revival church, anywhere. The second one was packed, too, but with sober folk of the middle-class, lads and girls, young couples with babies in carry-cots, substantial people of mature age. They looked as good a section of the community as any body of selectors would choose, and were of the quiet, prudent type which usually rejects a spurious emotionalism, especially in religion. The drill, however, was the same; a frenzy was whipped up, culminating in a deft collection. A song-leader with a squeeze-box led a hymn (which a young man next to me whistled piercingly and melodiously) and mentioned casually that he had been miraculously cured of warts. Then The Gospel Four sang 'I wanna be God's friend 'n a liddle bit more' in swing-time. Prayers followed, with the moaning and shrilling and tears, the shimmying and shaking; then more talk of miracles, and the collection. To thwart the reluctant giver and small gift, the plate was put below the preacher and men and women were made separately to march up to it. Thus the human ambition to keep up with the Jones's was exploited and large sums were gathered (apparently several times a week).

The people obviously liked the giving, the fluorescent crosses, the pretty girls at the electric organs, the two xylophones and the piano, the personable Gospel Four, the lusty singing and the frenetic self-abasement. All this satisfied some spiritual void in them and they were not people in whom an easy response to the bogus might have been expected. Clearly the yearning to attach faith to something is a motive; this is a form of reaction against the life of 'materialistic gusto', though it may be exploited by materialists. I thought of the man who joined the crooked game because it was the only one in town, and the other whose only pleasure was going to the pictures.

Revivalism clearly has a continuing market value, and American susceptibility to it goes back to the beginning of the Republic's story. This is a native form of emotionalism, not the imported, exotic one of New York. It was there before the admixture of blood began. The records show that people of unmixed Anglo-Saxon stock behaved differently, in America, from the way they would have behaved at home. Revivalism today is the old Camp Meeting in a new form.

Ralph Waldo Emerson spoke of the 'monstrous absurdities of the Methodists at their Camp Meetings', having been told of an instance 'of several of these fanatics jumping about on all fours, imitating the barking of dogs and surrounding a tree in which they pretended they had "treed Jesus" '. Prince Achille Murat was an eye-witness and left fantastic pictures of orgies in the woods. Mr. James Truslow Adams's *Epic* says that one, in 1801, was attended by some thirty thousand people, while seventeen preachers and many volunteer orators preached continuously from a Friday to the following Thursday. At one time three thousand people lay unconscious, while hundreds 'jerked' and 'barked' in unison. 'Just as human nature, dammed in one direction, finds outlets in another, so the emptiness of life on the frontier led the emotions to find relief in wild orgies . . . The almost incredible Camp Meetings catered both to the settler's desire for company and to his need for expression in emotional life. The inhibitions of his starved

social and emotional life were suddenly removed by the mass psychology of these vast gatherings, at which thousands would exhibit
pathological symptoms in unison.'

That is a fair description of revivalism one hundred and fifty years
later. The land is no longer so empty in the physical sense, and places
like Denver are full, but a spiritual emptiness has remained, or returned,
and the emotions find relief in these modern Camp Meetings, the
revival churches. Of the earlier times, Mr. Adams wrote: 'Man craves
an outlet for his emotions and these had been completely starved in the
monotonous, hard-working, lonely, drab existence of the outer
settlements and frontier.'

In today's America of the one hundred and fifty millions, the movies,
radio, television and the ball-game, man apparently still craves an outlet for emotions which all these do not satisfy. In the Republic of
forty-nine States there seems still one empty state; that of the spirit and
the mind. Clearly there *is* something different, incalculable, in the
American soil and air; or so I thought, in the revival churches.

CHAPTER 34

SILVER SPOON

ENVER has two or three theatres, that is, places which were
built for living players. Hollywood has long since driven out
the flesh and blood performers, and of them and their plays
remain only a few photographs, programmes and playbills. Yet the
largest of them, the Tabor Grand Opera House, still contains the living
stuff of the eternal human comedy in such measure that the shadow-
plays there seem more than usually unsubstantial; the reality of life is
in the place itself. It saw the start and end of a farcical-tragical-melo-
drama of sin and retribution, so much overdone that the very boards
of the Lyceum might have groaned in protest against it. Nevertheless,
it all truly happened; this theatre was the scene of a play stranger than
any its footlights ever lit.

Even the names of the characters ring as if they were chosen to burlesque Lyceum melodrama, but are genuine: Haw (H. A. W.) Tabor,
the moustachioed gallant; Baby Doe, the golden-haired; and Silver
Dollar, the innocent cheeild. Tabor came with the gold-rushers to
these parts a hundred years ago. He was an unsuccessful miner, and
opened a store at Oro (which he later renamed Leadville). There, in
1875, the gold-miners' discarded dirt was found to be silver-bearing
lead carbonate of high value, and another rush began, the silver-rush.
Tabor's store prospered and in 1878 he let two penniless Germans have
sixty-five dollars' worth of food against a one-third share in anything
they might strike. A few months later he sold his share for a million
dollars and within a few years could no longer count his millions. He
became king of Leadville (which he hoped to make the capital of
Colorado), formed his own Tabor Fire Brigade and Tabor Light
Cavalry to fight flames or disorder, and built an hotel and theatre.
When Denver was chosen for capital he plunged into great schemes
there.

At Central City, another mining-camp some seventy miles away,

189

was a Mrs. Elizabeth Doe, brought from afar by a gold-seeking husband. The miners called her Baby Doe: what melodramatist could contrive a name more expressive of gentle and helpless femininity? She was young, pretty, unhappy. The fabulous mining-camps then had the same appeal for ambitious young ladies that Hollywood holds today. Tabor's name rang over the mountains. Baby Doe went over the Rockies to Leadville and caught his eye. Divorces were obtained and they married. Tabor's renown was so great that the President attended the wedding in Washington, and Tabor was enabled by political wirepulling to achieve his supreme ambition, a United States Senatorship (albeit, only for thirty days). He took with him for this brief senatorship a silk nightshirt with flounces and inserts of rose-point lace, and four inches of lace at the wrists of the episcopal sleeves.

During this time he built, among other edifices in Denver, the Tabor Grand Opera House, sending architects to study the theatres of London, Paris, Berlin and Vienna, and emissaries to Brussels, Paris and Japan for carpets, tapestries and timber. From his box hung a two-foot block of silver with 'Tabor' on it in letters of gold. Above the proscenium arch was a painting of Shakespeare; Tabor, inquiring who it might depict, said 'What did he ever do for Denver?' and supplanted it with his own portrait. In this theatre (and the one at Leadville) appeared Sir Henry Irving, Ellen Terry, Duse, Bernhardt and many other famous ones.

I saw the curtain which fell on the grand opening. It shows the sun setting on the ruins of some fanciful temple, where wild beasts roam among broken pillars and crumbling pomp; the obscure German artist, whom Tabor paid fifteen thousand dollars for it, added at the foot two lines by Charles Kingsley:

> So fleet the works of man, back to the earth again
> Ancient and holy things fade like a dream.

Presumably this pointed allegory held no personal warning for Tabor, who for a few years looked down on this splendid house from his flower-filled box, with Baby Doe and her two baby daughters at his side. The invisible god-mothers of morality attended the second daughter's christening. She was named Rosemary Silver Dollar Echo Honeymoon

Tabor (the sins of the parents!) but was ever known as Silver Dollar, Tabor's favourite symbol. This period was the peak of what today's picturemakers would call The Tabor Story. A hundred peacocks stalked the lawns of his Denver mansion. He was a rajah; at his wedding he sent agents to Spain and Portugal to search for the legendary crown jewels of Queen Isabella, so that Baby Doe might wear them. The men returned with some jewels, of whatever authenticity, and a rope of pearls, which she wore.

In 1893 all fell into the ruin pictured on the dropcloth. Silver was too abundant. The twentieth century, and the closing grip of gold on the world, lay ahead; Tabor may have been an early victim of that process. The gold-kings forced the repeal of the act which authorized the purchase of silver bullion and its coinage into dollars. Silver was suddenly not much more valuable than nickel. Almost overnight Tabor's fortune dissolved; the mansions, theatres and hotels went, the furnishings and Baby Doe's jewels; Silver Dollar's inheritance vanished. Tabor, who had given the land on which Denver post office stood, was saved from utter destitution by the gift of the postmastership and died in 1899, leaving Baby Doe, now forty-five years old, with her two daughters. He bequeathed one worthless silver-mine in Leadville, telling her 'Whatever happens, hold on to the Matchless; it will give you back all I have lost'.

Baby Doe, strange woman, held on to the Matchless Mine. I went to Leadville, a hard journey even in good weather, and saw the wooden shack, only habitable at the last extremity, where for thirty-six years she held off all comers with a shotgun. A more desolate spot is hardly to be imagined outside Arctic regions. Leadville, where she had found the famous Tabor, died around her (of late years a little life has returned there) but she stayed on, a ghost in a ghost-camp. Few mortals since Saint Simeon Stylites can have imposed on themselves a more horrific self-martyrdom. The elder daughter soon went away. Silver Dollar stayed on until she was nearly twenty, when she too fled; she became a salesgirl, danced in night clubs, drifted around. The mother thought her in a Chicago convent until, after ten years, Silver Dollar died. She was in the Chicago depths by then and died by boiling water poured or spilt over her. She left a photograph with the message, 'If I am killed arrest this man'. A coroner's jury was 'unable to determine whether said occurrence was accidental or otherwise'.

The elder sister, being informed, said 'I never approved of my sister; she looked at life so differently. I can see no more reason now why she should be more to me than just a dead woman down in Chicago. Why should I, who have pride and position, and like only quiet and nice things, have to claim her now in this kind of death?'

Baby Doe lived ten more years in the shack, utterly alone, and then was found frozen, wearing newspapers for warmth and with sacking round her feet. She was eighty-one; when she died Hitler was dictator of Germany. That seemed strange to me, as if the melodrama covered. centuries. She puzzled me. Was this Baby Doe a cornered tigress, defending in her own way the memory of a man, against all comers? One detail made me think she tenderly loved her Haw. Among his relics at Denver are some pyjamas from the great days. Pyjamas in 1885 were not elegant and Haw, who in his portrait looks like Groucho Marx half-eaten by wolves, must have cut as odd a figure in them as in the rose-pink nightshirt and golden sleeping-cap. But Baby Doe's hand worked an intricate pattern of silken white flowers on these pyjamas; the task must have taken months.

There was yet a sequel; a picture was made of Silver Dollar's story, and the world première was at the Tabor Grand Opera House, where Baby Doe, blazing with jewels, and her babies once sat in the Tabor box. A Miss Daniels played Silver Dollar. From Baby Doe to Bebe Daniels; such was the story of this theatre.

I went also to Baby Doe's Central City, a ghost-town now half-rematerialized (Colorado has seventeen official ghost-towns; others, not much less spectral, vigorously repudiate ghosthood and remain officially mortal). I drove for nine miles along an alarming ledge of mountainside, and understood why an earlier English traveller, the Rev. F. Barham Zincke in 1868, asked at Central City if anyone had been killed lately on the approaches to the town. No, replied the landlord, he was glad to say no one had been killed for two or three years, but every year several persons had died of accidents on the hill.

As I reached Central City I saw that the more tumbledown places had been boarded up and freshened; the inhabited houses were cared for; and a deserted mine, with its buildings, shone silver in a new coat of aluminium paint. All this was background to the Opera House, which has been made the scene of an annual play festival; it is a forced growth in this remote place, but so is opera at Glyndebourne, and it has been successful. Americans are in the mood for such things at present and come in thousands for the three summer weeks of drama or opera, leaving revenues behind which ensure ghostly Central City mortal life for another year.

When I was there the festival was at hand. There was a gentle fragrance of show-business in the air and in the street strolled sopranos and contraltos, tenors and baritones who, but for Hitler, might have been wearing dirndls or leather shorts and drinking coffee in the Café Bazar at Salzburg. In a few weeks they would all vanish and wraith-like Central City would await the next year's annual migration of Art to the Rockies.

CHAPTER 35

FROM WYOMING TO ARMAGEDDON

ON my way to Wyoming I drove across a plain, running parallel with the Rockies; stopped to look at a stockaded fort of the Indian days; and as I started again switched on the car radio. In America this instrument is a valuable guide to the nature of the countryside. Within the radius of such places as New York, Chicago or Los Angeles it fills the air with the alien dirges of a spunkless miserabilism, 'I'm so blue, boo-hoo boo-hoo . . .' In New Mexico or Southern California it gives out Spanish songs and music. In Kentucky, Tennessee and the Middle West you often hear the pleasant hillbilly numbers, which are like musical soliloquies of a man who leans against a barn-door and whittles a stick. In Texas, Arizona, Wyoming and other states of the horse-and-cattle tradition come the entrancing jingle-jangle, clip-clop, yippee-i-ay melodies which contain the very swing and rhythm of a horse's shoulders and haunches.

This day was Sunday and, by way of complete contrast, a radio preacher spoke of Armageddon to any who listened on the wide plains. That is to say, he examined the prophecy of Revelation and tried soberly to interpret it in the light of today. Wisely, he said that he gave only 'the best explanations known to us and ones that do no violence to any other parts of the Bible'. The matter deeply interested me, because if any prophecy of the Bible has a clear reference to this time it is the one about Armageddon. So many prophecies are vague or capable of interpretation by any man who fathers a wish on to a thought; this one seems to be proving itself day by day now and ought to be completely tested soon.

The radio preacher examined the famous allusion to the great battle of the lords of the earth, and their gathering in 'a place called in the Hebrew tongue Armageddon'; the great destruction which follows, and 'the cup of the wine of the fierceness of his wrath' then given to 'great Babylon'. He thought this battle of Armageddon would be or already was an earthly one, but not 'a battle' in our sense of one clash of arms of limited duration and immediate, visible result. He interpreted it as a gigantic ideological conflict which might include several wars of arms and the periods between them. He believed that both the twentieth-century wars might be contained in that continuing struggle, but neither they nor another was in itself and alone 'Armageddon'. They were parts of the whole, yet to be completed.

As to that outcome, he turned to the second great prophecy of Revelation, which tells of the binding of 'that old serpent, which is the devil' for a thousand years, so that he 'shall deceive the nations no more' until the thousand years be fulfilled. That, said the radio preacher, in his judgment meant that Armageddon would be followed by a spiritual resurrection, a renascence, lasting a thousand years. After that, once more but only for a brief while, 'Satan shall be loosed out of his prison and shall go out to deceive the nations which are in the four corners of the earth . . . to gather them to battle'.

If his interpretations are right, we are in Armageddon now and have been for at least thirty-seven years, probably much longer. We might continue in it for another five or fifty. I look at these things with a trained journalist's eye, which fastens on any major fact, or anything, non-factual but evidential enough to enforce belief. In this matter of the prophecies of Revelation two points are formidable enough to impress any man, believer or unbeliever.

The first is that the two twentieth-century wars have both, at their ends, proved to be mainly concerned with 'the place called in the Hebrew tongue Armageddon', that is, with the Palestinian land containing the valley of Megiddo, though this place was not mentioned at their beginning. I feel sure, and hope I may see proof or confutation of this, that any third war will at its end similarly prove to be mainly concerned with the conquest and ownership of that territory, wherever or under whatsoever pretext it starts.

To my mind that is almost conclusive proof that this is Armageddon, and the final evidence is not far off. The second arresting piece of evidence that those prophecies do relate to this time is the repeated reference to 'the deception of nations' and 'that old serpent, the devil'. 'The deception of nations' describes better than any other four words could do, written so many centuries ago, the methods by which the Christian nations have been brought today, unseeingly, to fight each other for a cause of conquest in Arabia which they neither perceived nor could understand. As to that old serpent, the devil, I see him in Soviet Communism and Political Zionism, the two-headed serpent hatched in a Russian lair which now holds the masses of Gentiles and Jews alike in its coils.

Thus I was glad to hear that a man who studied the thing with the eye of faith came to the same conclusion as one who looks at it with that of a political observer. He, too, saw the old devil defeated at the end, according to prophecy, though after many more tribulations for the Christian nations, and that also was my belief. In this matter to-day's journalist has a hard task. Living in the time of the old serpent's success, and seeing more of his victories ahead before he is enchained, he pictures the world as it goes and foretells the tale of new deceptions. But 'By a divine instinct men's minds mistrust ensuing danger', and

> The first bringer of unwelcome news
> Hath but a losing office; and his tongue
> Sounds ever after as a sullen bell,
> Remembered knolling a departed friend.

Yet Shakespeare had the golden rule for a journalist in the 1950s, as for all others and all else:

> There is some soul of goodness in things evil,
> Would men observingly distil it out,

and that applies to Armageddon and the prophecies of Revelation. The old serpent and the deception of nations *will* yet be chained and defeated, and the Christian nations, if by way of further suffering, *will* come to the spiritual resurrection they need. If our time is the long, dark one of Armageddon, the bright upward road nevertheless resumes at the end of it.

That was my own belief as a political writer and seemed to agree with a cleric's reading of the most renowned prophecy of all. Glad to have switched on my radio by chance, I ran across another state line and came to Cheyenne.

CHAPTER 36

ON DUDE RANCHES AND DINOSAURS

CHEYENNE shone like a new pin by day and shimmered in neon by night, in the midst of nowhere. It was once the capital of the cattle kingdom; the round-up, the branding and the long drive led to Cheyenne, or Abilene. It lives largely on the memory of the Cattle West (as Gallup, in New Mexico, on that of the Indian West, and Central City, in Colorado, on that of the Golden West), and capitalizes the legend in its annual Frontier Days Show. Buffalo Bill was the State's benefactor, for he invented the Wild West Show, which has now become the rodeo or stampede. The dude-ranch thrives in Wyoming, and Cheyenne is full of dude-Western clothing-stores, from which obvious New Yorkers totter out on the cowman's high heels (even the Garment Centre cannot provide bow legs) and beneath ten-gallon hats; they reminded me of the good Viennese who wore the Viennese garment centre's idea of Styrian peasant's dress to drink coffee in Bad Ischl. The genuine cowman may still be seen. The great days of the cattle kings are gone, leaving a few relics like the perforated painting of a cow in the Cheyenne Museum. It was originally presented to the Cattlemen's Club and promptly received the contents of a six-shooter; art was outcast in communities where 'Anyone who dressed better than his neighbours, who put on airs, who flaunted domestic help, was looked on with suspicion.'

Wyoming, on the High Plains, is the size of England and contains as many people as Leicester. This population may not grow much as the State's resources of farmland, pasture, oil, dude-ranches and tourists cannot greatly increase. Substantial areas are uninhabitable, the fertile parts are small, and the sheep and cattle that followed the buffalo thinned down the grazing. Wyoming's people do not claim any summer, saying that spring lasts just long enough to merge into autumn, and in winter it knows blizzards in which nothing can live. It is the state of storms and even in the clement season I was often caught in these, as they prowled around the vast plains. As no natural obstacles impede them there they swell and rage and you see monstrous, many-uddered shapes with pouring teats many miles away. In these great spaces you perceive the entire size and form of such a storm; its central core of deluge, its trailing, weeping fringe and its dark envelope.

Thinking the open range vanished everywhere, I came unexpectedly on roadside notices, 'Open range; be careful of stock', and sometimes passed antelope standing with big, benignant eyes by the highway. 'Home, home on the range, where the deer and the antelope play'; the musical ride continued. Once, while the car radio played 'Tumbling along like the tumbling tumbleweed', I saw masses of this rootless plant, like stacked cannonballs among the sagebrush. I thought I would leave Wyoming quickly because the green lands called me urgently and I had far to go, but found myself repeatedly delayed by marvels which it made no effort to display, but of which I learned. Quite near Cheyenne was Como Bluff, where in 1876 the bones of the incredible dinosaurs were found.

I found a lonely, sullen hump beside the great road, with nothing but a small house, privately built and containing some fossils and literature, to mark the place of so great an event. Here lived the monstrous reptiles, Brontosaurus, Diplodocus and the rest, the skeletons of which were reassembled and set up in various museums of the world; some were eighty feet long, seventeen feet high and weighed several tons. They may have lived 150 million years and have died 60 million years ago, and none knows why they died. Once great herds of buffalo roamed these lands and we know why they disappeared, though future excavators might wonder; but the times of the dinosaurs knew no men or bullets. Their decaying carcases, if theory is right, formed the earth's oil deposits.

But why did those enormous brutes die out? Were tiny mammals, on four legs, too clever for them? I often thought, in such parts, that America is a place to study the ends of worlds rather than the beginnings of new ones. Nowhere else that I know does present time seem so small or past time so huge, like a dark wall so high that you cannot see its top. I looked at Como Bluff and pictured stupendous scaly things creeping, crawling and hopping about, then lying down to die in caves, or being buried by some convulsive eruption, here where the great motor highway runs. Behind the Bluff lurked a storm, black and scowling; golden beanstalks of lightning climbed up tall black cliffs of rain. A yellow light fell on Como Bluff so that it stood out, above the grey land and beneath the stormclouds, like one of those monsters, with long, spiked and curving back.

I drove through the storm and, turning aside at a signpost, came again on something typical of this great restless country. Wyoming has, not ghost towns, but ghosts of towns. It knew yet another kind of rush, the coal-rush. The railway, as it spanned the continent, needed coal; here coal was found and a town grew up in 1868, called Carbon. In 1900, when the best coal was exhausted, the railroad company just took up the rails and went away. 'The majority of the population were unable to sell their houses and were compelled to leave them standing; they were destroyed by thieves and vandals.' That was forty years ago, and all I found of Carbon was a cemetery. The same thing happened at Cambria quite recently, in 1928. The town, which even had the traditional Opera House, died overnight when the tracks were taken up. I read that it was a 'ghost town' but in fact every vestige of it has disappeared in twenty years! Thus the urgent American spirit moves on. The Indians and the bison were driven from their fertile plains; the plains grew bare and the newcomers could not do much with them; it is all a puzzle of time, man, beast and soil, yet to be resolved.

This emptiest-but-one of the states, where the wind rode on a broomstick over flat blcakness or lurid, sweltering canyons, fit settings for the gorgeous Indian sun-dance, held a spell for me. I found its empty landscape often more dramatic than any animated human scene. It is a place to visit with a self-supporting expedition, or at least a caravan, so that you may be freed from all preoccupations of time, food or weather, for it is full of wonders. One of these caused me, when I was impatient to press on to green country, to make a detour of many hundred miles back to the north-west. Having no great interest in scenic beauties or tourists I did not intend to go to the Yellowstone Park, but could not resist when I heard of the petrified forests there.

These are different from the petrified forests of Arizona, which many playgoers know. There the logs of great trees, turned to stone, lie about the stony desert, a thing remarkable enough. But in the Yellowstone whole forests of these trees, still standing, rise above each other in the heart of a mountain, each one buried by lava which in time has become fertile enough to grow another forest, then similarly submerged. The Yellowstone River, like a knife cutting through cheese, made a gorge two thousand feet deep through this region and exposed the standing stumps at successive levels, among them those of giant redwoods. That I had to see.

It meant another start at dawn and a long and lonely ride, first through green plains, then across prairie drying into desert. It went, also, through a place called Rawlins, notable only, in this age of the human-lampshade stories, because a man was authentically skinned there. He was one Big Nose George, who incurred dislike in the 1880s and was lynched. A local doctor (later governor of the state) sawed off the top of his skull for a gift to a girl medical student (the bones and truncated skull were recently disinterred and placed in the local museum), and then skinned the body, tanned the hide and made a medicine case and some shoes from it. The shoes are still to be seen at the bank. The Wild West *was* wild.

Where the country looked too arid for human life I saw the Indian reservation; the Indians made their last stand in Wyoming and a small remnant of Shoshoni and Arapahoe Indians now exist here. Then I came to one of those Western regions where the agony of creation shows in the contorted and distorted land. At some time the earth, visibly, had moved like the sea in storm, tossing and rolling, and been petrified in its last convulsion; you could see the breakers. Mounds and hummocks of volcanic rock lay where they were spewed; the lips of dead volcanoes were still pursed, as if they might yet emit fire and brimstone again one day. Through all this, in superb disdain, ran the splendid American road, and brought me suddenly into a narrow gorge between high, rocky walls through which a leaden river flowed towards a blood-red mountain, which at the last moment it and the road encircled, so that I came to a dun-coloured desert where blood-red hills and hummocks diminished into flatness.

After this menacing place little Cody, on the edge of the Yellow-stone, was reassuring; bright, busy and typically American. It is named after the great showman who was called Buffalo Bill because he killed five thousand buffalo in eighteen months to feed the men who laid the trans-continental railroad, and lives on his legend, on the Cody Museum, and on its annual, lifegiving Cody Stampede. The show goes on, under its new name. I wandered round Cody with memories of a bright arena at Southend-on-Sea, about 1900, I think. I can still see magnificent Buffalo Bill firing at glass balls thrown into the air by another horseman. How marvellous that was! I know now that concussion or small shot will shiver a glass ball, but have learned also that good showmanship is made up of pardonable deceptions and remain for ever grateful to Buffalo Bill. The Cody Stampede was in progress, but *without Indians*! To me that was a sinister sign of a bogus time. Buffalo Bill might have faked marksmanship or even palmed an ace, for all I cared; he would never have omitted real Indians from the Wild West Show. This was a stampede from Cody! I could not learn why the Indians were excluded. Great debate went on about it in the little town, but all behind the glove; strangers were not welcome to these secrets and even familiars watched their words. I felt that truth was lost to the world if Indians were lost to Buffalo Bill's show; this was a blow at the roots of my being.

In another fifty miles I entered the Yellowstone and once more climbed the Rockies, up and up and up, through sad and silent fir forests, beneath heavy clouds, in cold, driving rain. Then I burst out of the firtops upon a lake, almost an inland sea. On its shores campers huddled in tents and trailers beneath weeping trees; dry weather may be needed for a successful holiday here. I went on for another hundred miles, through fantastic places, enormous canyons with swift little rivers hurrying through them far below and their upper faces made by nature in the shape of cathedrals or fortresses. At nightfall I came to a most genteel, Cheltenham-like hotel and fell into bed, exhausted.

Next morning, as I could not hope to find the fossil forests unaided, I went with an impressive letter of recommendation to seek the Rangers' help. The Rangers, who are knights of woodcraft, do not ecstatically admire tourists. The tourists like to photograph themselves feeding the bears and if they get a quick cuff on the ear the Rangers have to shoot that bear, which they dislike. The tourists also cause forest fires, which break woodsmen's hearts. I was not that kind of traveller, but the Rangers did not know; my cordial missive found no ready response. However, I persisted and at length a Ranger was detailed to guide me. In his company I spent a memorable day, which I had earned, too, by that arduous journey.

But for him I would have needed a week to find the fossil forests. They are not marked on the tourists' maps, probably because the tourists, as they would say, could not care less. We set off in his truck and came at once on three bears, mother and two cubs, standing like hitch-hikers at the roadside; they wanted cake, however, not transport. The bears are very kind to human beings and sometimes, when these seem in playful mood and put children on their backs or dangle buns before them, join in the fun with a little pat or short-arm jab (these are the little black bears; the few surviving grizzlies are seldom seen).

My Ranger ran his truck off the road and drove it about half a mile, over rough, rising ground towards the firbelt of the mountains. Then we left it and I saw before me a climb of some fifteen hundred feet, through the trees, to bare summits. I guessed that my companion might expect a little entertainment. My back contained, unknown to him, a cracked spine and this was hard going over places evidently avoided by man as a rule, for we clambered round a shoulder of rock and saw before us a mountain sheep with two lambs, tranquilly sunning themselves on a ledge. We were quite near before they winded us and then they went off in amazingly sure-footed bounds, from crag to crag, into the forest below. They looked like small antelopes and moved with superb grace.

I survived to the top of Specimen Hill, where there was the stump of a huge tree, enmarbled. The lava covering must have been gradually worn or washed away by wind or melting snow until it reappeared, after inconceivable ages. Then, slipping and sliding down the loose mountainside, we came again and again to the trunks of standing trees at lower levels, which once grew in earlier and ever earlier forests, each in turn buried by lava. The place gave a man a sense of proportion about time, life and space. From the forests around rose the vapours of the boiling, bubbling, steaming, spouting geysers and mudholes in which the Yellowstone abounds. Far below, beneath the tourist-camps, the curio shops, the ice-cream and hot-cake cafés, the machinery which caused this tremendous process still worked away.

Going down was quicker but harder than going up. I achieved some thirty feet of the descent in one slide on my back, among the slipping debris of petrified trees, and was glad to stand again with only a bruise or two. As we drove back the Ranger asked me about Socialism in England. I said I thought it was of that old serpent, the devil, any-where at all, Liberalism, Socialism and Communism being the succes-sive coils; however, I thought England might yet extricate itself from this embrace. He said he felt that way too (men who live with wood-craft are seldom far from truth) but he guessed the thing was coming in America and he didn't know how to stop it. I often met this feeling of helplessness in America, and elsewhere. It is produced by 'the decep-tion of nations', but I fancy that another mood, of self-saving action, follows at a later stage.

I spent an evening with the Ranger, his wife and four children, in one of the pleasantest homes I saw in America; it contained a happy and united family. Then I boiled my bruises in a hot bath and prepared, once more, to resume the overland journey.

CHAPTER 37

ART AND THE MOUNTAIN

ITURNED eastward again from the Yellowstone, with its obsidian fortresses and silent mystery, its boiling mudholes and pent wrath. The fine roads and tourist camps convince no reflective traveller that man has yet arrived to stay in this volcanic place, where the last few buffalo graze in immunity. Even vegetable life seems to shrink from his coming for here the firs die in masses of some unaccountable blight, which is strange, because the fir is the hardiest of trees and seeks out high places, where nothing else can live, serenely to fulfil its lonely destiny.

Fantastic climatic changes awaited me. The Yellowstone, at nine thousand feet, was chilly. Four thousand feet below I ran through Cody into stifling desert-heat again, and soon after that into the Big Horn National Park, an exquisite place of flower-carpeted Alpine meadows, little blue lakes and dancing mountain streams, with none of the menace of the Yellowstone. Then came arid ranchland again, a cold night in the car on the edge of Wyoming, and a dawn ride into South Dakota, where a filling-station lad once more undid my plans. He told me of another marvel near at hand, the sculptured mountain, and I made one more detour, to see it. It took me through another lovely National Park, the Mount Rushmore one, up an almost vertical spiral road through the firbelt, to the peak itself.

It is impressively American. If a mountain is to be sculptured, the sculptor must go to it, and mountains usually stand in inaccessible places. South Dakota is one of the emptiest and remotest states, if anything can be called remote in a land of such unrivalled highways. The brow of lonely Mount Rushmore has been fashioned into the likeness of four American presidents. This is described as 'the greatest sculptural feat ever attempted by mankind'. The late Mr. Gutzon Borglum used a steeplejack's cradle and a roadmender's electric drill, or something like it. I could not imagine how he kept the sense of line and proportion, suspended in space and carving the mountainside with something less than a high-precision tool. Unkind falls of rock may have forced him to rearrange the group of the four huge granite heads, six thousand feet above sea-level. They have a somewhat compressed appearance and Theodore Roosevelt looks rather like a man who tries to see what goes on between the heads of Washington, Jefferson and Lincoln.

Mr. Borglum thought the American philosophy was too much obsessed with 'business and bellies' and that 'the creative longing' was starved. Thus he ardently approved President Franklyn Roosevelt's programme of public spending, which began in 1933 as one of welfare projects and soon expanded to include Art. The 'Federal Arts Projects' became the subject of much controversy, but Mr. Borglum thought they 'opened the door to the world of creative impulse, without which people perish . . . All there is of God in creation is what man has in lonely martyrdom wrung from nowhere and everywhere . . . Have we in gold, the worship of Aaron's calf, made our final bow in the hall of world fame, to be remembered with Rome for our abuse of wealth?' He complained of the indifference of earlier presidents to such matters of art and welcomed the better Rooseveltian time. During many years, in lonely elevation, he wrung the four imperishable heads from the hard mountainside; when he died his son completed the work.

From this unique mountain top spectacle I drove downhill again towards the hottest wilderness of all; the Badlands. Along the roadside signs began to tell me of the remarkable things I might see, learn, eat, drink or buy at 'Wall Drug'. I was not at first interested but with the passing leagues these invitations to gaze on rare beasts, be photographed with a grizzly, study Indians, buy Mexican jewellery, obtain a free history of The Badlands, and much more, began to exercise a compulsion on me. What *was* 'Wall Drug'? I found myself driving faster and more eagerly as the signs flashed by.

As I sped into Rapid City I guessed the answer; Wall Drug must mean Wall's Drugstore in this town. I raced round looking for the ever-helpful Chamber of Commerce, but this was still early and it was not open, so I went to see the plaster dinosaurs in its park (possibly a Federal Arts Project?) and returned later, breathless, to ask where

Wall's Drugstore might be. The pleasant girl was puzzled; then a light dawned and she said, 'Oh, you mean *the* drugstore *at* Wall, two hours away, on the edge of the Badlands.'

By now I only wanted to get to Wall Drug. I left Rapid City (no slow place; it was quick to boost its advantages as an atom-bomb retreat) and, ever faster, followed the signs, some five hundred miles of which already lay behind me. I realized that I was in the grip of a sales-machine of hypnotic appeal, which I ought to resist, but I could not stop. At last, with screech of brakes and sigh of anticipation relieved, I came to Wall, a tiny place which in winter is sometimes buried in snow; now it was buried in tourists, all allured from the several points of the compass by those signs. How easily might a druggist, in so minute a township, fall into the rut of merely running a drugstore! The owner of this one was a genius. That radial array of signs must have cost a small fortune, but I saw that the outlay was all worth while.

Having seen all wonders I went on with mind at rest but apparently still clouded, for ten miles farther on I realized that I was on the wrong road, going away from The Badlands. I was then flat on my back, striving with a flat tire. Once in my life I owned a car with a hydraulic jack; you just worked a small lever, beer-handlewise, and it dropped four small legs which lifted all four wheels from the ground. That was the only truly happy time I have known with cars. Ever since I have had jacks which refused to jack, or let the car suddenly down on the toe of my shoe, happily missing the toe inside. I was in that hopeless plight when a voice said, 'Got a flat?' Crawling out I saw a friendly road-patrolman and said, 'Yes, got a jack?' Not only had he, but this friend in need did the job.

So I drove back to the Badlands, which look as you might expect the moon to look, if it were hot, a parched picture of the earth in eroding wrath. It is as if it were the devil's own bit of the planet and he had stabbed and slashed with some great knife until all fertility drained away from yawning wounds. South Dakota, finding the unwelcome name of 'Badlands' wished on the place by the early French Canadian trapper who saw it first of white men, has skilfully turned it into a tourist attraction, thus making the best of a badlands job. It is another 'National Monument'; the boosters call attention to it strange beauty (it has a rancorous grandeur), and built a fine road through it for the tourists.

When I emerged from the Badlands the arid West at last lay behind me and I ran right across Nebraska to its capital, Omaha, on the fringe of the prolific Middle West. At two the next morning, after the hardest day's journey I ever made, I was picking my way carefully through the dead, dark streets of Fremont, still fifty miles from Omaha, when furious clamour sounded behind me. It should have awakened every sleeper in Fremont, but Americans seem inured to sirens at any hour (I sometimes saw bridal processions of twenty or thirty cars circulating slowly in town streets with every driver's finger pressed hard on the horn; this form of wedding celebration is common).

As no other was abroad at that hour I guessed the pandemonium to be directed at me, and stopped. Two threatening blue figures appeared from another car, halted behind me. 'You was swaying about all over the road,' they said, 'get out, will yer!' The tone was that of films I had seen, and until then supposed to be overdone. I got out and was told I was drunk. The next move, in the film tradition, would have been for me to reply: 'You can't do this to me,' and then to be led away crying, 'It's a frame-up, I tell yer, it's a frame-up.' Instead, as a night in jail, though in later retrospect it might be amusing, looked disagreeable now, I temporized.

American friends advised me before I began these travels to beware of small-town traps, set for out-of-state drivers. These are good for municipal revenues and also for policemen, who need seldom fear that a stray motorist will enjoy the protection in superior places that local lawbreakers sometimes invoke. I think this was such a case. My good interlocutors were distinctly hostile; moreover, what they said was untrue and they knew it; I had been driving with especial care because I was very tired. I said so, with an air of smiling English surprise. They brushed the objection aside, but less certainly; something about me puzzled them. They rattled off catch-questions and then said suddenly, 'Where have you been drinking?' 'Gentlemen,' I said, 'I never touch it' (I do not, when driving). They calmed down and, scratching their heads, looked at me with the air of anglers contemplating the one that got away, and decided to lay off. However, they did a curious thing. They said I was on the wrong road for Omaha and put me on a false one, so that it was past four in the morning and dawn was breaking again when, after twenty-five hours of mountain, desert, plain, cold and heat, I drove into sleeping Omaha. It seemed packed to the seams and by the time I found a room sleep was wasteful; I scrubbed the thick dust of travel out of my pores, breakfasted in an early cafeteria, and set out to see life in Nebraska.

CHAPTER 38

ON MEALS AND MEALIES

THE return to populous places and fertile lands was a relief. In the arid West I often thought of Mr. Patrick MacGill's lines, 'The nearer you are to nature, the further you are from God', especially in those empty parts where once the monstrous reptiles moved and volcanoes spewed. The name Great American Desert, if unpopular now, is still true. Omaha, on the edge of the green belt, was reassuring, for here the real and eternal wealth of America began; there can never be ghost-towns in the Middle West, for people must eat, the corn-standard cannot be abolished, and the vein is inexhaustible.

It was a small city much like others of the later Republic, with its domed capitol, its Main Street all neon-and-nylon, farmers ruminating in the hotel vestibules, workmen driving their cars towards pork-packing factories, and the Missouri running through. In it I first met a problem which continued to plague me; that of the heat. As I came from Africa, where it never incommoded me much, I had given it no thought; now I found it a major encumbrance. Not all American hotels are air-conditioned; indeed, of the kind I used few were. The humid temperature achieved something which nothing but physical mishap ever did before; it immobilized me. I could not go about, drenched, among happier beings whose dryness I envied. When I pondered the thing I realized that in African heat I was never confined between concrete cliffs; this immurement changed life into a ludicrous conundrum, to me insoluble.

This comic predicament made even the search for food a hardship. It is often a problem for the stranger in America and his experiences vary greatly. In Salt Lake City I ate well and cheaply, in other places poorly. In Omaha the wish to avoid exertion drove me to the cafeteria nearest my lodging and it proved a haven. To the industry of meals applies the golden rule of an American song: It ain't what you do, it's the way that you do it. In principle the cafeteria seemed to me all wrong, for good service is essentially part of a good meal. I remembered a chophouse in London where the old waiter once brought potatoes in their jackets and, holding them in a spotless napkin, crumbled them flourily on the plate; I knew little *Wirtschaften* on the Rhine where the serving-girl's smile added zest to appetite. By contrast, it seemed a disconsolate thing to take a tray, shuffle along a counter, collect your food and utensils and carry them to a table. I tested this theory in New York and other places and thought I was right; self-service reduced eating to a gloomy occasion, the orphaned child of bodily necessity.

This place in Omaha (and sister-houses later found in Des Moines, Mobile and New Orleans) showed me that at the highest level the cafeteria may have some advantages even over good restaurants. For one thing it saves the buying of pork in a poke ('I'll have the gammon if it's good'); you see what you choose, and if the food is good that is important. In this establishment it was excellent, and the march past the dishes was exciting; deft young men advised as you went along and pleasant girls kept your coffee cup filled when you were seated. The process was well thought out and run, and I would have liked to open just such a place in England.

Near my lodging was a street of bars, dingy shops and missions, similar to Larimer Street in Denver (and I met its like again in other cities). The biggest and toughest-looking bar was a brick building painted blood-red. Within it, bodies went through the rye; outside it usually stood a young man with an off-note cornet, an elderly man with a big drum, and three women, who sang 'I was glad when Jesus entered my heart' in different keys. A few habitués of the bar always stopped to listen, either on the way in or out. Then the young man said, 'If you gentlemen will take off your hats Mrs. Smith will say a prayer', and the tipplers uncovered. One of them, finding the vertical tiresome, propped himself obliquely against a parking-machine-post, sometimes looked at his hat as if he wondered why it was in his hand, and sank back into his devotions. When the prayer ended the habitués paid money (a kind of forfeit, I supposed) and entered the bar, while the youngest woman, following them to its threshold, fervently addressed their backs about the evil of drink; the face at the bar-room door. It seemed a well-organized proceeding.

I packed once more and went on to Des Moines in Iowa, happy in green, domesticated country, neither arid nothingness nor mountain wild, but a land of good growing crops and farmhouses. This was the Fourth of July, when the mealies should be knee-high; in many places they were nearly shoulder high. Next to sugar I know no crop so splendid to watch as healthy maize. It grows in great green banks on strong stems with big, shining leaves that look as if they were polished with dew each morning early. Des Moines stands in the heart of this green and gold empire. It is a town of trees, but the sun was so vertical that they only cast a little puddle of shade around their feet. The humidity, I was told, was ninety-seven. A draught through a car window seemed more desirable than anything else in life and after two days I went on, for the sake of that breeze, through a rural countryside more prosperous, I suppose, than any in the world. Here the towns became more frequent and bigger and the population denser as the road returned towards the teeming states of Illinois, Indiana, Ohio and Pennsylvania; the world was one of green avenues converging on the great industrial regions.

For a few miles I travelled with a passenger, an old lady who thumbed me with appealing smile. She lived in a village eight miles from Iowa City and went there each day to work, she said. She was a kitchen-worker at an hotel, and until a few months earlier was a dormi-tory-maid at Iowa City University, at 125 dollars a month, 'but after seventy the State won't employ you, they reckon you ought to go on benefit'. Here, in the lengthening shadow of the Welfare State, was a woman who would rather work until she dropped than go on benefit; until she said this I thought her nearer eighty than seventy for, though vigorous, her face was gnarled and wrinkled. 'You like to work?' I asked. Oh yes, she said, she liked to have something to do and the doctors said it was the best thing for you, so she took the kitchen job 'at 100 dollars, but I get my food'. I thought it must be pleasant, even at seventy, to be fit for a good day's work, to travel eight miles daily to and from it, and to earn a hundred dollars and your food.

After I set her down I stayed awhile in Iowa City, which was as unexpected in its nature and atmosphere as Salt Lake City. For some reason the turbulent waters of American life divide and flow around it, leaving a quiet and reassuring islet in their midst. Then I went on into Illinois, which looked even richer and more abundant than Iowa and there I found again what I had almost forgotten in the West: the quick succession of busy small towns, with humming Main Street in the middle and pleasant residential quarters around, where wide streets ran between great shady trees that overhung cool, white houses. This was the thickly-populated central region of the Republic once more. For forty miles I drove through a countryside which surpassed anything yet in its look of wealth. Yet its air contained a restless something, and suddenly I was in the grip of a maelstrom I knew. Through tunnels, over bridges, beneath the straddled legs of elevated railways, I was whizzed and whirled along, dived into a parking-lot, climbed dizzily out of the car and gazed around, blinking.

This was Chicago!

CHAPTER 39

OF BACON AND A BEACON

I LOOKED down from another lodging on a riotous and chaotic city, the cousin of New York. On one side lay some traces of a quieter Old Chicago, where trees grew in the little gardens of declining town mansions. On another was a mass and mess of slums and empty lots left by slum-demolishers. From a dingy wall a large notice asked, 'Are you buggy? Fumigate yourself for $1.50 a room'. In the background rose the Babylonian towers of office buildings, one of which contained twenty-five thousand people by day; on top of another, twenty-storied one was a spired church. In narrow streets between, street-cars ran below elevated and above underground railways, and beneath these last, again, ran a merchandise-subway. Accidents, when they occurred, were bigger than anywhere else. Behind the mountainous buildings lay a lake like a small ocean, Lake Michigan.

Chicago has often meant hogs to visiting writers, American or foreign. The city's proud insistence on the annually rising figures of mortality in the stock-pens has largely caused this. A man who enjoys a rasher should not blench at the thought of pigs dying (Mr. Rabindranath Tagore averred that vegetables feel pain but no tears were ever shed for the agony of countless onions); yet the subject has a macabre appeal to literary minds. In 1882 in Chicago Oscar Wilde, reclining on a buffalo robe in velvet doublet, knee-breeches and silk stockings, 'closed his eyes at the mention of the stockyards and looked sick'. In 1906 Mr. Upton Sinclair stirred the Republic with *The Jungle*, an *Uncle Tom's Cabin* of the hog-pens. In 1919 Mr. Somerset Maugham, though not critical, was gruesomely impressed by the struggling, squealing, knives and gore of what he saw as 'a caricature of the Dance of Death'.

I saw no bacon, but looked long at a beacon, flashing from a Babylonian tower, which seemed more significant. Newspapers may be read by its light in ships or aircraft miles away. What piqued my curiosity more than that (I once read print in Saint John's Wood by the light of burning Saint Paul's Churchyard) was its name. It was originally called 'The Lindbergh Beacon'. I suppose people who are now thirty years old do not remember that fantastic furore of 1927. No young man ever sprang at one bound to such peaks of fame. No mortal rewards need have been beyond Lindbergh. He could certainly have aspired to the presidency, had he accepted certain bonds, for the mass-newspapers frenziedly played M'Bongo to him (M'Bongo is the African praisemaker who stalks before a chief calling him Great Elephant, Earth Shaker, Stabber of Heaven and the like).

His humiliation was as complete as that of T. E. Lawrence a decade earlier. The condition of M'Bongo's praise was submission to M'Bongo's dogmas. Lindbergh became suspect before the Second War began and intolerable when he opposed American part in it. He seems to have been, not so much against American recourse to arms in any case at all, as against the shape he saw behind that particular war (the use of American and British arms to expand the Communist Empire and set up the Zionist State proved him right in the event). This opposition was mortal sin and brought on him a vengeance recognizably tribal. He was 'smeared' into oblivion, the trappings of adulation were torn off, and, among many other things, the beacon was given another name.

Thus Chicago's re-named beacon is a symbol of something supremely important in the Republic: 'smearing', which is M'Bongo's alternative weapon. 'Smearing' is known in England but is deadlier in America. It is an organized thing, with long experience behind it, and its effects are great. It springs into action there against any who genuinely oppose Soviet Communism, Political Zionism or The World State.

The might of this hidden machine is fascinating to study on the spot. I know an American writer who was nationally famous and earned some forty thousand dollars a year until 1941; he then expressed doubts about the outcome of America's entry into the war and his income collapsed overnight, to nothing. He is now slowly fighting his way back. Against an army of newspaper-writers and broadcasters who serve the three causes I have enumerated, a handful stubbornly fight for native American interests, defying the smears and threats and succeeding by sheer strength of conviction in forcing their views into print. One of them, whom I also know, has a lonely house, the grounds of which he has to keep floodlit at night, for protection.

Thus the former 'Lindbergh Beacon' seemed to me possibly more significant than anything which incoming passengers might read by its light five miles away; that literature was more likely to darken them. It shines over a city that boils and bubbles with the yet unanswered riddles of America. One hundred and seventy years ago Chicago was a log-fort. Today it is a towered and turreted enigma, of many millions. Behind its grandiose lake front, it is a crammed, seething place, like a building of an early Western mining-camp; all barn behind and pretentious 'front' opposed to the street. The 'native-born American', in the old sense, is greatly outnumbered in its population. The Germans and Irish predominate and from motives of circulation among them its newspapers are lustily anti-British.

I found that one newspaper building contained an atom-bomb shelter provisioned for three thousand people. I said to my friend there, 'What, you expect atom-bombs on *Chicago*!' (the thing seemed somewhat fanciful to me). 'Not on Chicago,' he said, 'on *this institution*!' Yet he was an enlightened man, and had every reason to know that his institution was more in danger of subtle permeation than of destruction from above. However, the Cult of Doom has had amazing effects of delusion. In 1950 an explosion of some dynamite at a small port in New Jersey sent panic-stricken mobs rushing through the streets with the cry of 'Atom bomb!' and a few months later, at Devonport in England, the same cry arose when barges of explosives blew up in the harbour. In the second case what should have been generally clear (and could have been prevented) was soon admitted; that this was sabotage; and that probably applied to the American incident too.

The population of Chicago is probably as mixed as that of any place on earth. In Halstead Street, which is twenty-five miles along, almost every nation in the world seems to have its little colony, Italians, Mexicans, Greeks, Swedes and others, and mixed-breeds of every variety. Maxwell Street, which appeared to be a mixed Jewish and gypsy quarter, contained more and noisier folk than I ever saw in one place before, all pushing, shouting, quarrelling, laughing, buying and selling in the narrow roadway between lines of booths. Chinatown was sedate and tranquil by comparison. The Chinese today succeed in living as a closed community among other peoples without harsh impact. Chicago's seven thousand Chinese have their own proper quarter and small, self-called Town Hall, with a Chinese court where they try minor Chinese malefactors, sometimes sending the judgments to be rubber-stamped by American magistrates round the corner.

Wandering in these places I came by chance on West Madison Street, which might have been designed, built and peopled, as I saw it, by Hogarth. It is but the prolongation of Madison Street, which is a great central thoroughfare, and at first I thought it just a mean quarter, filled with dirt, din, joy, misery, darkness and light like any other. Then I saw men lying in the street, and said to my companion, 'That's a funny place to sleep'. 'Yeah,' he said, 'they're asleep all right; knock-out drops.' He nodded towards lines of men who leaned against walls. 'Those men haven't a dime,' he said, 'if they had they'd be inside.'

In bright daylight, I needed a few seconds to comprehend. Then I saw what he meant. The prostrate men were unconscious, those sitting on the kerbside were only half so, and the ones on their feet presumably waited to borrow that dime. They leaned against the walls of liquor-shops which displayed large notices, 'Whisky, full ounce, 20 cents; double-shot, 35 cents'. The results were plain to see, stretched on the pavements. At all hours of the day, I found, the scene was similar, and recumbent forms lay in the refuse-filled alleyways. In the early morning, when thirst needed encouragement, the double-shot ('Our Morning Special') cost but 18 cents!

I remembered hard drinking in London forty years ago but professional drinking on this scale (for these men had no other professions) was new to me. A hundred years ago London may have known something comparable; the Borough High Street then was described as 'a continued ale-house, not a shop to be seen between red-lattice and red-lattice; no workers but all drinkers.' What I now saw seemed a great waste of lovers, husbands, fathers, homes, crafts and careers. Prohibition is vain and appears wrong. Regulation of quantity by taxation and of quality by supervision might be an answer.

Chicago, however, is a wide-open city in the broadest sense, by order of the vice-syndicates, and this is one aspect of the effects. The city took brief cognisance of West Madison Street just after I discovered it. One morning a newspaper-editor 'picked his way to work through Skid Row's reeking garbage and broken bottles, stepping past the bodies of sleeping derelicts on the sidewalks', and thought this would 'make a good story'. In his sense, it did; his newspaper's circulation rose by twenty thousand copies daily while it continued. He sent two reporters to live as bums in Skid Row for a week; one became violently ill from the double-shot but the narrative was produced. There were eighty-two saloons in three-quarters of a mile of street, all openly breaking the liquor and health laws, and forty-six doss-houses with a nightly population of twelve thousand men, formerly of all classes from the managerial and professional to the manual-labour.

The report for a time closed down fifty-six saloons. However, even during this brief alarm thirty-two unconscious men were counted on the sidewalk during a ten-minute walk. The interests engaged in keeping the city wide-open are the most powerful in Chicago and the Police Commissioner 'threw up his hands', asking, 'what can we do?' Soon the good story was forgotten. Chicago has always been so.

Yet Chicago was also the scene of a scintillating glimpse of that beautiful and elusive thing, the American Dream. The oft-used words denote a genuine and admirable longing for something noble if unclear; visions are commonly vague in outline but contain great power to inspire. The World Fair of 1893, white and shining, was a sudden, brief realization of that peculiarly American yearning; in 1925 Sir Charles Cochran remembered it as 'the most impressive thing of its kind that I have seen'. Its swift creation and abrupt dissolution reveal two sides of the American character, which between them make up the whole enigma.

The idea of a World Fair to commemorate the four-hundredth anniversary of Columbus's discovery of America took shape in 1890. In a land where the cities vie for live conventions as Roman ones fought for Homer dead, this was a glittering prize, and Chicago won it. In January 1891, with opening-day but two years ahead, a few architects gathered on a lake shore then not much less desolate than the Atlantic coast where the first settlers landed in 1600. In May 1893 the Fair was opened.

In those two years seven hundred acres of sand or waterlogged ground were reclaimed and a dozen palaces built, together with hundreds of smaller buildings, canals, basins, lagoons and islets. For once 'American architects were freed from the demon of rent-values and the building-envelope'. All the buildings were white and of a uniform cornice-height. Meanwhile Chicago itself was still paved with cobble-stones or cedar blocks, the uneven sidewalks were largely of wood, the slums were far-spread and foul. Mr. Walter Crane wrote of it, 'Long straight roads break off short on the prairie, to be continued when this pays. Along these straight roads are planted at regular intervals excessively irregular houses, the genius of the American architect breaking out in weird, conical towers, vast verandas, mansard roofs; the main roads are bordered with huge telegraph poles.'

That is still a picture of large areas of Chicago today. In 1893 something entirely different sprang up on the lake-shore, almost in a night. 'For the first time in American history a complete city, equipped with all the public utilities caring for a temporary population of thousands, was built as a unit on a single architectural scale. Unique in being an epitome of what we had done and a prophecy of what we could do if content with nothing but the best, it was a miniature of an ideal city; a symbol of regeneration. A new epoch began in American architecture, the epoch of the classical. It endured for a few months. A vision was ordered to appear and then ordered to disappear.'

The huge, swift achievement; the warning touch of disintegrating doom; these two familiar apparitions of the American landscape reappear in the story of the World Fair. It was scarcely open when a Chicago bank, with a branch in its grounds, failed; wealthy Chicagoans indemnified foreign exhibitors. A warehouse caught fire and seventeen firemen were killed. As the Exhibition closed the Mayor of Chicago was assassinated. The white city remained, silent and deserted, as winter approached, and businessmen spoke of white elephants. What to do with a white city, its purpose served? Why, junk it! Fire solved the problem. The great palaces were burned down. Only the Art Palace survived and stands today, as the Field Museum, a monument to an astonishing feat.

The World Fair left Chicago with what it might otherwise have missed, the splendid lake front which is its one beauty, with fine parks and buildings, Planetarium and fountain. Only there, in Chicago, may you hope to find a quiet spot or restful moment, particularly in the Planetarium, where the most marvellous of all man-made machines projects on to a domed roof the entire picture of the day or night sky at any moment of the past or future; the contemplation of time and space is spiritually reinvigorating in a place so given to the passing instant. The fountain too is a joy. All cities ought to have fountains, constantly playing. They had them when drinking-water had to be fetched from fountains, but these should not be stilled now that water is laid on, for beauty contains a utility, and perhaps the greatest.

When I have forgotten much else I shall remember the fountains of the Schwarzenberg Place in Vienna. Hidden lights of many colours played on them, and shafts and plumes and columns of water, ever-changing in shape and hue and lovely as flowers, rose and fell in the summer night while I sat with my coffee and watched. Men knew how to live, once. This fountain in Chicago recalled that other in the city now in pawn to doom; it was a soft and delightful thing in the hard, angular brightness of Chicago at night.

CHAPTER 40

CITIES FULL OF VIOLENCE

CHICAGO is full of the showplaces of gangsterdom; something pestilential surrounds them still, as if their doors bore a red cross. The tourist guides lead their flocks to the café where Big Jim Colosimo was shot (whose throne passed to Johnny Torrio, who faded out so that Al Capone succeeded, who went to prison so that it descended to other, present kinsmen); another café once owned by Diamond Joe Esposito, who was shot between his bodyguards; the garage where seven Moran gangsters were machine-gunned by rivals, two dressed as policemen; the spot where a 'hanging prosecutor' was killed; the night-club of one Ginsberg who died of fright while awaiting electrocution (he was a pessimist; in the last 639 gang murders thirteen persons were convicted, but not all executed); and other X-marked spots.

I went to America believing that the gangster days began and ended with Prohibition, which gave a galvanic impetus to illicit brewing, distillation and purvey. This was a major error, born in the perusal of the mass-newspapers; in truth, gangsterdom is more powerful than ever before, because organized crime is now firmly allied with politics. The masses of American people seem held in a clutch from which they cannot break free. The general attitude towards organized crime is (as Mark Twain said about the weather), 'Everybody complains of it but nobody does anything about it'.

Mr. James Kem, a Senator from Missouri, expressed common public feeling in scriptural words: 'Mr. President, the land is full of bloody crimes and the city is full of violence.' Organized subversion of law today is a quite different thing from the Wild Western lawlessness of earlier times. That was a hot-blooded condition of the open spaces where the forces of law were weak, some men took what they wanted, and other men lynched them to enforce some security. This is a cold-blooded thing of the teeming cities, the systematic corruption of an established order of law and justice for gain and power. It is of the snake, not the man-eater. It is (wrote Mr. Priestley) 'not a tropical underworld of hot blood and passion, of people too barbaric for the bourgeois virtues; it is a chilly, grey, cellar-like, fungus world, of greed, calculated violence and a cold sensuality'.

Gangsterdom in the 1920s and 1930s seemed just a sudden outbreak of violent crime. Rival gangs fought merely for spoils, hijacked each other's liquor, muscled-in on each other's precincts, killed each other, and that was that. The kidnapping of Colonel Lindbergh's son in 1932 (when the father was a national idol yet unsmeared) forced Congress to act. The gunmen publicly most notorious were hunted down and by 1938 Mr. Edgar Hoover of the Federal Bureau of Investigation (America's Scotland Yard) thought the gangsters' day was over. Now the hidden organization proves stronger than ever. Organized crime is one of the three most powerful forces in the Republic and its coils reach round the entire edifice of political and civic administration.

The centres of the organization are the great polyglot cities, New York, Chicago, Los Angeles, Detroit, Cleveland, Saint Louis, Miami and New Orleans. From these its tentacles spread over the land into small and smaller towns (in 1950 a quiet place of 15,000 people in Kentucky had its entire police force and 160 other people under indictment for vote frauds, illicit gambling and neglect of duty). The aim is to make the whole Republic 'wide open' for gambling, drinking (against which regulative laws exist in nearly all States), drugs and prostitution. The method used is the purchase of politicians and officials at all levels; it is facilitated by the American system of redistributing public offices after elections. The following quotations (a few from a large mass) show how the matter is constantly discussed, though as yet without any effect:

In Kansas City the alliance between politics and crime exploded in the killing of Charley Binnaggio and his gunman Charley Gargotta . . . It is the duty and responsibility of the President to enforce the laws but obviously this is not being done . . . It is little wonder that respect and confidence of the people for the laws have dropped to an all-time low; the unholy alliance between politics and crime is responsible for this . . . No gambler can operate without crooked friends at city hall and in police headquarters.

The real crime menace is the huge gambling syndicate which has a grip on politics ... The Mafia is the super-government of a nation-wide and world-wide crime organization which now has tentacles reaching into the Cabinet and White House itself and almost every State capital ... The link between the new-style gangster and the shady politician is the biggest story in America today and its surface has only been pricked by the reporters' pens ... A share of the gangster's profits, as crime investigation committees during the last few years have revealed in Detroit, Chicago and elsewhere, is laid aside to buy local politicians who have the power to select police, prosecutors, judges and legislators ... The syndicate operates by subterfuge in every big city except Chicago, where an open alliance between politics and the underworld has brought about conditions that are a disgrace to civilization.

Politicians need money, racketeers need immunity (a Police Chief from Ohio).

The reason the Police Department takes things on the side is because they don't make enough to live on. If you offer them a gift they don't take it; they grab it and tear your arm off with it (a gangster).

The recurrent allusion, in all such complaints, is to the 'alliance between crime and politics'. This is universally known and individual Americans speak of it with detestation, fear and impotence. They overlook its larger aspect, which students of recent inquiries in England may also ignore. It is that officials, once suborned, must toe the line for ever, and the higher they are, the more important the line. Corruption may reach at last into major actions of State policy and endanger the life of a nation; more than gaming-machines, drinking-hours or numbers rackets are at stake. Forgetting that, many Americans tell themselves the Republic will in time, somehow, get the thing out of its system. A book about Chicago expresses this feeling: 'It is difficult to get indignant at Chicago. So much is so open and law-breaking is so obvious that it comes to appear normal.'

Organized crime in its present form is a product of the later immigration which started with the Civil War. The big names in it are Italian, with some Russian-Jewish ones, and it can only be understood by considering those origins. The great waves of immigration from Italy and

Eastern Europe came from places where the secret society was indigenous and membership descended from generation to generation of the same families. The tradition of enmity to law and long experience in conspiratorial methods were brought to the new land. Signs of connection between Soviet Communism, Political Zionism and the crime-syndicate have often shown. One leading operator was prominent in the money-raising campaign for the Zionist adventure in Palestine. Gangsters are frequently defended by lawyers representing the American Civil Liberties Union, which was described by a Californian Senatorial Committee as 'expending at least ninety per cent of its efforts on behalf of Communists who come into conflict with the law . . . Its main function is to protect Communists in their activities of force and violence in their programme to overthrow the government'.

The Italian organization is at least ninety years old and goes back to the Sicilian Mafia, which is centuries old. The Italian Government tried to root out the Mafia between 1860 and 1880, so that 'at least a hundred of its members' arrived illegally in New Orleans' (according to the Italian Consul there). These men committed some seventy murders in twenty years, most of them with the 'Mafia gun', a forerunner of the deadly weapon still preferred by gangsters in the 1930s (it was a shot gun with the barrels sawn off to about eighteen inches, the stock sawn through near the trigger and hollowed to fit the shoulder; the stock was also fitted with hinges so that the gun folded like a jack-knife).

About 1880 one Giuseppi Esposito (possibly a forebear of Chicago's Diamond Joe) fled to New Orleans from Sicily (where Italian troops sought him for cutting off the ears of an English clergyman, Mr. Rose, and sending these to the family to accelerate ransom) and organized the Mafia there. He was captured and sent back to Italy, but his men killed the detective who arrested him in New Orleans. Eleven Italians were charged with this murder but New Orleans saw that prosecutors, jurymen and judges could not be trusted; the Italians were acquitted and the Mafia held high festival. Then occurred one of those spontaneous American uprisings against the corruption of justice; some hundreds of townsmen went to the jail and shot the men.

This setback seemed final, but in fact the Mafia proved to have remained in being and grown stronger. Al Capone's cousin is a leader of the organization today and the Unione Siciliano is freely mentioned in the continuing, but impotent, public debate. The editor of a leading American newspaper in a current book states that the crime syndicate has drawn such revenues from gambling, drugs and prostitution that it has invested the proceeds in legitimate trading in a large way and now owns a chain of great hotels, hundreds of night-clubs, restaurants, stores, skyscraper buildings and a steamship line! The general staff has plainly suffered little from the loss of the Pretty Boy Floyds and the Baby Face Nelsons.

Of fifty 'public enemies' proclaimed by the Chicago Crime Commission in 1931 none was convicted and several operate happily there now. In New York Irving Bitz (once of the 'Lepke Mob') popped up for an instant in some new affair and proved to be employed in the office of a leading newspaper, where advance information useful to the bookmaking ring was to be had. Dandy Parisi, formerly of 'Murder, Inc.', long sought for the murder of one Irving Penn in 1939, was found in New York in 1950; he belched loud disdain as the judge dismissed the charge for lack of corroborating evidence (Irving Penn was unlucky; Big Albert Anastasia, Kid Twist Reles, Pittsburgh Phil Strauss and Mendy Weiss planned the death of one Philip Orlofsky, but Dandy Jack, working to a description, shot the wrong man!).

Those are the smaller men. The big ones bloom unseen, and each knowing writer puts a different name to the head of the octopus. Frankie Costello in New York is the great chief; Charlie Fischetti in Chicago is the biggest shot; Tony Goebels in Brooklyn is 'The King'; opinions vary, but nobody *knows*. The rival gangs no longer engage in pitched street-battles, or steal each other's liquor, or throw pineapple bombs into shops which have refused to pay for protection. The method has changed. Possibly there are no rival gangs now, but all have merged to besiege the politicians and through them to pursue bigger game: power in the land.

The killings which continue are picturesque, internecine and infinitely mysterious. Arrest, charge and conviction are at the moment obsolete words; enigmatic disputes are summarily settled between gentlemen who seem above all law but their own, and that's the end.

Benny the Meatball (supposedly 'the big shot around Los Angeles') 'runs screaming into the night with five bullet holes in him'. He is succeeded (they say) by Bugsy Siegel, also once of 'Murder, Inc.', who is then shot on a divan in a lady friend's home. He is followed (men think) by Micky Cohen, who formerly killed Maxie Shaman, but in self-defence, and was acquitted. Allen Smiley, who sat beside Bugsy on the fatal night, becomes Micky Cohen's colleague. Pauley Gibbons, a rival (so people guess), 'falls under a hail of bullets'. Hooky Rothman is shot in Micky Cohen's chair in Micky Cohen's clothing shop. Micky Cohen, emerging from a Los Angeles restaurant, is greeted by shotgun-fire from behind a hoarding opposite (bad luck for a man who rides in a bullet-proof motor car from which he can turn floodlights on to his whole domain while still afar off, and who, in his home, can watch all that approaches on a radar screen). Mr. Cohen is only scratched, but his bodyguard, Neddie Herbert, is killed, and a police companion badly wounded.

Nothing ever becomes known. The crime reporters each time produce a dozen theories. The dead man was shot by a rival for his place or because he had 'squealed'; the murderer was a 'squealer' and feared vengeance; the police killed him because they couldn't get him any other way, or because he had 'squealed' about payments to officials; or he was killed in revenge for another killing. The coils of conjecture are endless, but conjecture is the end. It is like peering into a nest of vipers where there are many hissing heads but apparently only one, writhing body. The crime syndicate does not extirpate itself in this way, but grows stronger. These casualties must amount merely to a fractional inconvenience within it; they resemble Stalinesque purges.

I was around those parts when the attempt on Mr. Cohen briefly excited public opinion. The story, which illustrates the subject as well as any, began with the arrest of seven men in a car for driving the wrong way in a one-way street (the prudent Los Angeles policeman devotes himself to traffic transgressions but even then may go wrong). The seven men had just finished beating a shopkeeper 'until he looked like the end-product of a meat-grinder', so that the policemen found on them revolvers, loaded canes, tire-irons and the like. At the police-station, however, the desk-sergeants, after one look at the captives, refused to charge them and restored their belongings. The matter would have ended there but that, by chance, an amateur photographer took a picture of the seven men, while they were being searched; he sold it to a newspaper-editor who recognized them as associates of Mr. Cohen and printed it with adverse comments about the police.

Public curiosity, thus stirred, was further stimulated when another colleague of Mr. Cohen was arrested for carrying firearms. Mr. Cohen complained that this was a false charge, only brought because he had refused a donation to the Mayor's electoral fund. He added that one of the police officers concerned took payments from a woman brothel-keeper and that this could be proved by the disks of tapped telephone conversations (apparently a local specialist was tapping such communications for Mr. Cohen, and also Mr. Cohen's for the police). The lady involved was in jail, having arrived there through another police officer, who sent a policewoman to gain incriminating evidence by offering her services in The Madam's establishment. At Mr. Cohen's intervention The Madam was brought from prison and testified that she had indeed paid money to the police officer who arrested Mr. Cohen's associate, and also to the one whose charges sent her to prison. At that the corroborative witness, the policewoman, said she had perjured herself for love of her superior. Thus The Madam made good her words to the officers who arrested her, 'I'll have your jobs, you're only a couple of peanuts in the bottom of the bag'.

Whatever the truth or untruth, the moral seems clear; that a policeman who interferes with the vice-trade incurs deadly risk. For the rest, a Police Chief resigned and another was appointed, and the newspapers closed the matter with allusions to 'the pattern of police bribery and police protection under which the rackets operate'.

The Federal Bureau of Investigation appears to labour in vain against these conditions. The case of Al Capone remains the proof of its difficulties; he was only brought to book, at last, for income-tax frauds! So it still is. A coroner's jury may say 'Murder', but the State or District Attorney's office may append, 'No evidence', 'Stricken off', or 'Dismissed for want of prosecution'. The devices of delay also are infinite in the hands of smart lawyers (an American judge once said 'Litigation at some point must come to an end', but that point is hard to reach), and the statute of limitations is short. One much-sought leader was arrested, as a last hope, for swearing at the police. Admitting to 'bastards', he said the President once called a reporter a son-of-a-bitch, and acquittal upheld his constitutional rights.

One peculiarly American factor also works against the repression of organized crime. 'The lynching mob exists in America in two forms' (writes Mr. Edmund Lester Pearson in *Studies in Murder*), 'the mob which hunts down and kills some wretch of a malefactor, or alleged malefactor; and the mob which rails against legal officers who are engaged in protecting the community against crime . . . Ten thousand tears are shed in America for persons accused of murder, and even for persons convicted of murder, to every word of regret spoken for the victims of the murders. And that, according to thoughtful investigators, is one of the reasons why America leads the world in its shameful record for the unlawful taking of human life.' Moral indignation about *organized* crime is difficult to match with an emotional sympathy towards *individual* crime, and this might explain the failure of general opinion to rise effectively against the gambling, drink, drugs and prostitution ring. The crime-ring killings very seldom come to court, but the scenes which sometimes attend individual murder-trials have something of the delirium of the Camp Meetings.

Individual crime exists everywhere and would not deserve especial notice in a book about America. Organized crime is different and appears in America in a degree unknown elsewhere. The alliance with politics lifts it from the size of a fungus to that of a redwood in the American scene, and its effects might be as great as those of a civil or foreign war. The crime-ring, through its agents all over the land, sets out to suborn officials and politicians with money or the promise of *votes*. The service demanded is the wide-open regime, in the form of tacit non-interference with the gambling, liquor, narcotics and prostitution traffic. Once a party organization has been so subverted, however, its political policies are bound to come under similar pressure. The ultimate aim appears to be the subversion of the Republic itself, not merely profit. If a State is to be ruined before it is taken over, this poisoning of its life at the source must be in the interest of political ambitions, not merely of dope-barons.

One of the ring's practices is to bribe revenue officials and then blackmail businessmen and others through the threat of high assessments. A grand jury reported that in President Truman's home county 'one arrogant racketeer, feeling that a prominent businessman had not been polite to him, had this man's real-estate assessment tripled. When the victim apologized and opened a credit account for the racketeer the original assessment was restored'. This jury was shocked into making an interim report which spoke of 'terrible lawlessness, utter disregard of our States as well as our municipal laws'.

The deepest root of the evil, however, is the crime-ring's delivery of votes, or forgery of them if they cannot otherwise be obtained. Because of this factor, the results of American elections cannot always be accepted as genuine. The hidden process was illumined by an event in President Truman's constituency in Kansas City in 1950, when two men were found shot in the headquarters of the First District Democratic Club in Truman Road. They were Charley Binnaggio, who claimed to be the 'boss of the Democratic Party machine' in that place, and his 'bodyguard and enforcer', Charley Gargotta. Every day (at the club where they were killed) 'boon-seekers ran a gauntlet of stony-faced hoodlums' ('gimlet-eyed gorillas' is another favourite description) who dispensed patronage to the purchasable. Binnaggio was 'a political big shot'; he had 'thirty thousand votes in his pocket' and 'boasted that he controlled thirty State legislators and had elected the current Governor'. Some of the votes he thus 'delivered' were the subject of inquiry by a grand jury, which indicted sixty-seven of his helpers for forging them. The evidence was put in a safe in the county courthouse; someone blew it open and made off with the incriminating ballot-papers. The inquiry then collapsed.

The public will never know why Binnaggio was killed. The picture was the familiar one; the two men seemed to have died before they knew that anything threatened, and thus did not suspect their visitors, whoever they were. They had squealed or might squeal; the usual theories were discussed. The leading newspapers remarked, without excitement, that 'the alliance continues between the underworld and many of the big-city Democratic machines that piled up the votes for the Fair Deal' (the Roosevelt-Truman regime), and that 'these bullets echoed in the White House'. The upshot of it all was that for a while a few Senators and Congressmen vainly sought to drag the matter into the open and 'the chances of effective action to enforce the law remained remote' (to quote one of many newspaper comments).

Chicago more than any other place makes the traveller wonder what America's future is to be. That is not to predict by dark insinuation that it will come to no good end; the huge latent strength of that great majority of Americans who want a Christian and decent life is obviously enough, if it can assert itself, to expel toxic matter from its system. It is merely a confession of ignorance. Today's traveller in Chicago simply has no past experience by which he can measure future possibilities, for the white man's world has never known anything like Chicago; I think that is plainly true and demonstrable. It is something quite new, at least in degree, and the results can only be judged when they appear. The second city of America is undeniably ruled by forces organized to stimulate and exploit the baser weaknesses of human nature, and to that end to subvert what white men have always in the mass held to be the Christian order of law and decency. Their law is today the only law in it. Such conspiracies have often been known in the European parentlands of America but never had more than local and temporary success. I feel sure modern history can show no other case of a great city being in effect conquered, occupied and ruled by them.

The only comparisons that can be made, as far as the conspiratorial method goes, are with the Mafia in Italy and the Communist and Political Zionist secret societies in Czarist Russia. As for the outer results, the Casbah of Casablanca, Port Said and the waterfront of Marseilles alone offer some possibility of comparison. Those were special cases, however; seaports and the sharpset appetites of seafaring men from the ends of the earth have always combined to produce small centres of human degradation. Chicago is not a seaport, so that those factors are absent, yet it far outdoes the Casbah, Port Said, Marseilles and all other such places put together in the open, commercialized display of prostitution, sexual perversion, the narcotics trade, drunkenness and gambling. Madison Street West offers but a small sample of its contents; the nude-show bars, the 'call girls', the dope-pedlars and the panders are innumerable. I thought Berlin between the wars was the ultimate in these things. Compared with Chicago today it was as a peanut to a pumpkin. The wayworn writer feels, or should feel, no call to moralize about such things. The more important aspect is that the whole is organized and operated by a single, central organization, The Big Mob, for purposes of political power and that now, according to all qualified observers, it has gained great power in the highest places.

A foremost authority in the subject, Mr. Jack Lait in *Chicago Confidential*, says this state of affairs has been brought about by 'our immigrant hordes' and study of it shows this to be the fact. The two traditional countries of the secret society, Russia and Italy, provided most of the immigrants of the last seventy years, and in the new country the secret societies were able to gain more power than even in their homelands; the masses of Jews and of Italians suffered under this equally with all others when the native-born American politician fell under the unaccustomed thrall. The Big Mob in America today is clearly the Sicilian Mafia of old, with organization intact, rules and methods unchanged. A current encyclopædia says it was in Sicily 'a secret society which in the latter part of the nineteenth century aimed at superseding the law and ruling the island. Its chief weapon was the boycott; violence was resorted to only for vengeance; funds were raised by blackmail. Popular support enabled it to control elections, avoid legal proceedings and influence industrial questions'.*

These are precisely the methods used by The Big Mob in America, on a grander scale than ever before, and the internecine killings in the average lead to an increasing predominance of the Italian over all other elements. Mr. Lait says that operations are still conducted from Italy, by Charles ('Lucky') Luciano, one of the few leading gangsters with whom American justice caught up, at least to the point of expulsion. He says that the American headquarters is in New York but that the real centre is Chicago, where The Big Mob under Colosimo, Capone and Torrio experienced its first great growth in strength and wealth

---

* It is a striking reflection that in its homeland, Italy, ever racked by revolution and war, the weak State authority has never yielded to the Mafia, but fought and fights it constantly down, whereas in the mighty American Republic it has achieved its present peak of power, as the Senatorial inquiry of 1950-51 fully and publicly confirmed.

during Prohibition, and where alone it completely controls affairs (twice during the last ten or fifteen years its sway was challenged even in New York!). Through the investment of its booty from narcotics, liquor and prostitution in open enterprises like real-estate, hotels and stores, and shipping it has become, he says, a kind of corporation or cartel equalling, or transcending, in wealth and power such licit concerns as the Standard Oil Company. One gangster, briefly held for murder, protested, 'I've got more cash than Rockefeller and there's twenty of us with more than I have; no one's going to push us around'. A Treasury Department official said this particular man was 'inclined to boast' but certainly had 'as much as $150,000,000 in currency in Chicago safe deposit vaults'.

The heyday of The Big Mob did not end with the ending of the thirteen-year period of Prohibition, during which the foundations of its empire were laid on the proceeds from boot-legging and hijacking. On the contrary, it began then. The dwindling news of gangsterdom from America gave the outer world the impression that it was in decline, but the real reason for this was, not that gangsterdom was broken, but exactly the opposite: that the prosecution of gangsters ceased! This started, like permeation by Communism and Political Zionism, in 1933, the year of President Roosevelt's inauguration. The president before him, Mr. Hoover, was a vigorous enemy of the racketeers and his efforts to crush them now look like a main reason for the vendetta since pursued against him.

Before 1933 The Big Mob operated in a relatively small way through the subversion of local bosses. After 1933, Mr. Lait says, it broke out from Chicago to take over 'the entire state and the entire nation, to break through directly to the top, by-passing the whole succession of intermediaries'. Mr. Lait says that a *quid pro quo* arrangement of 'votes for favours' was made directly with Washington. He repeats the statement in various forms several times and adduces what appears to be proof positive: since 1933 'there have been few Federal prosecutions of Syndicate gangsters — and in Chicago none'. This was why The Big Mob disappeared from the news, while its power increased; 'from that time on major prosecutions of important underworld leaders practically ceased'.

This state of affairs received an impressive mark of official approval in 1947. In that year two Chicago police officers of long service arrested one Jack Guzik (who made the statement I quoted earlier) in connection with the murder of a man who challenged the authority of The Big Mob, refusing to surrender his racing news service to it. Guzik was released within two hours. The two police officers were charged with depriving the arrested man of his civil rights (apparently by searching him for arms). Two eye-witnesses of the murder retracted their evidence and a third was killed. Charges, changed to 'conspiring to obtain a fraudulent indictment', were then laid against the two police officers, but dropped. They were next brought before a Civil Service Commission which dismissed them from the force. They appealed and two courts ordered their reinstatement. A third upheld 'the wholesome decision of the Civil Service Commission' (a Supreme Court appeal still pends) and, says Mr. Lait, 'That was notice to Chicago's seven thousand policemen that the racketeers and their assassins must not be disturbed; none has been since, not up to now'. In fact the warning was a clear one to police officers far beyond Chicago, in all cities where The Big Mob is strong.

The root reason for the strength of The Big Mob's hold on American politics is that it is successful in subverting both main parties. Although it promises 'votes for favours', it includes in its calculations the possibility that the opposition party *might* somehow come to power, and with forethought infests it too. In England the Conservative Party is prevented by some occult grip from truly opposing Soviet Communism or Political Zionism and therewith deprives its followers of genuine ability to choose. In America the Republican Party similarly submits to those two thralls and to the third one as well, that of The Big Mob. Mr. Lait says, 'The unique, baffling Chicago situation is that there is no "opposition". In every other machine-manipulated municipality there is an aggressive minority party, an active "reform" movement of some proportions. In Chicago there is none. The Republicans, who long owned the county and state, now depend for sustenance on reciprocal deals; mustn't offend our foes, because we'll need them, so we'll keep it peaceful; no mud now, boys, or we get nothing.'

I do not think that situation is 'unique' to Chicago, even in America.

In the larger picture it exists throughout America and England and the remaining Western countries. The whole shape of it has only been perceived and publicly exposed by Mr. Roosevelt's predecessor, the former President Hoover, who in 1950 said the issue in America was clear; the two major parties should become opposites, and the Republicans should become a frankly conservative party. He told the Republicans, 'There is no room for you on the left', and the Democrats, 'Your die is cast, you are the party of the left'. Then he said to some members of both parties, 'You are not in your proper spiritual homes . . . If there cannot be a reasonably cohesive body of opinion in each major party, you are on a blind road where there is no authority in the ballot box.' That is an exact description of the blurred and confused situation to which permeation has brought the Conservative party in England too, and England with it.

In addition to the corruption of politics and the bargain-counter display of human merchandise at its lowest levels of degradation, the rule of The Big Mob has produced a third effect in Chicago, the ultimate working of which is equally hard to foresee. The Negro population there is now by all appearance (trustworthy figures cannot be obtained) the biggest single group. Formerly, when it was much smaller, excellent relations existed between the white and coloured folk. Today there are large and growing Negro quarters through which white folk hurry by day, reluctantly stopping even at red traffic lights, and hardly venture at all by night, and white women should not go there unescorted ever. The figures for murder, rape and all other violence in Chicago's Fifth District are beyond anything ever known in white countries.

This great Negro influx was by no means wholly a spontaneous one. The novelist Anthony Trollope, as he travelled in South Africa about the time the American Negroes were being liberated, foretold the danger that 'unscrupulous white politicians' would make use of black men, given the vote before they were ready to understand it, and Chicago today is the picture of what he foresaw. Very many Negroes were induced to go to Chicago and Los Angeles (as the Puerto Ricans to New York) by cheap fares and other enticements. The object was to tip the voting-scale, and this was achieved; Chicago the city and

Illinois the State *were* by such means captured by the Roosevelt-Truman administrations from the Republicans.

In this way Negroes from the remoter parts of the South, who seldom handled five pounds at one time in their lives before, were in masses brought to Chicago, where during the war they could earn fifty pounds a week. If there was ever a true economic need for them there it passed with the war, but they were kept there after it, employers being moved by threats from the white politicians to employ them, and relief being lavishly distributed if they remained unemployed. Racial resentments were created where none existed before, as they always must be when large and sudden population-movements are instigated for political ends.

The result so far has been that a law-abiding, established, slowly-growing and amiable Negro community has been swamped by a great host of imported newcomers who have been dazed and dazzled by the entirely new way of life into which they were plunged. For The Big Mob, they are as clay to the potter, and Bronzeville (which contains the Fifth District) is the result, a place where drunkenness, drug addiction and all depravity run riot against a background of dirt and human congestion. This was once a better district of good houses and pleasant streets. The raw Afro-Americans brought their still semi-tribal way of life into it, turned mansions into antheaps and apartment buildings into tenements, and pushed out in all directions. In Chicago they are in fact driving out the white population from substantial areas. Friendly mingling of the races on the old level has almost stopped while the lowest of both races flock together, especially the degenerates. The state of affairs in the South during the Reconstruction years has been brought to Chicago and reproduced in large parts of it.

This is the work of The Big Mob and of the white politicians who have allied themselves with it. The city is firmly in its grip. Mr. Lait says, 'There just is no recourse against injustice. There is no place, no person to whom the helpless who would appeal can go. The blind alley of politics-gangdom-graft ends in a solid wall which none may crack or vault.'

In 1950 a Crime Committee of the U.S. Senate held an inquiry lasting a year into organized crime and political corruption. Its report, issued in May 1951, tallied in many conclusions with these observations of a casual outside observer.

CHAPTER 41

SMALL TOWN

ON my way out of Chicago I passed again through West Madison Street, where lay the men shot and doubly-shot. The tourist-buses go up and down there and the drivers tell their passengers through hand-microphones that this is 'The Land of Forgotten Men'; a misuse of words, for though these prostrate ones may for periods succeed in forgetting the world, by the sightseeing industry they are not forgotten. Then I toiled out of the city by the eastward road, a slow job, for Halstead Street does in a manner continue for the renowned twenty-five miles. When it ceases genuinely to be the name goes on and throws off ghostly side-streets, 125th, 150th, 175th and so on. The signs for 1000th and 10,000th Streets are not yet there but will come, in this country of 150 million people and 35 million motor cars.

At last I ran out of Chicago and Illinois and into Ohio and by way of complete change stayed awhile at Bryan, a small town of a few thousand souls. Readers of *Main Street* know Gopher Prairie, the raw small town of unlovely homes and stores sprung up in the fields where neighbours know no seclusion, private life is wide open to Mrs. Next-door's prurient curiosity, gentler souls yearn for Art and boosters cry Our City. The Gopher Prairies are numerous and account for the tone in which many Americans say the words, Small Town. A city-bred American friend of mine dreams of retreating to one from his exhausting surroundings. His wife, who grew up in a Gopher Prairie, merely answers, 'You don't know the small town; I do,' therewith saying a last word clearly unanswerable.

In these parts, however, I saw many small towns much pleasanter in appearance, whatever the real content of life in them, than Gopher Prairie, which was a farming-camp. They were like New England over again; outside Main Street, at all events, their homes were white in green aisles of elms and the white wooden churches abounded. In time I learned the reason for this transplantation. New England soil is poor and when the frontier began to move westward many Yankees flocked after it, lured by tales of better earth. Maine, Vermont and New Hampshire were to some extent depopulated, and those States of The Beginning are among the emptiest today; the ghost-school-house, ghost-farm and ghost-barn are not uncommon there. The New England spinster became a familiar figure and one man tried to meet two crying needs by transporting her in hundreds towards the lonely bachelor in the West.

Thus the mushrooming new towns often grew up like the old New England ones, with the white houses, gleaming Wren-style churches, and, sometimes, village greens. Bryan had a large open green place, a bandstand and a band. It reminded me in this of an old-time German garrison town; however, no visible sign of German population offered and such things are not quickly ascertained, in an American small town. It was all very pleasant, with children romping round the bandstand. In America such simple enjoyments as a band in a green place, cool with trees, are rare and a certain resentment against them is constant. I felt it even in Bryan. The band was good and obviously one of volunteer musicians. When I went to a drugstore, wishing to sit down while I listened, I found a gang of lads feeding nickels into a jukebox to drown the sound of music outside.

I went on from Bryan, through Sandusky, and ran along beside another great inland sea, Lake Erie, to Cleveland, where the car broke down for the first time, by what seemed happy chance outside a large sales-and-service branch of the firm which made it, in the middle of the city. I left it in the loudly protesting traffic stream and dashed across. They were sorry, but the entire mechanical staff of their huge organization had been on strike for three months! It is sad to be stranded in the midst of a central thoroughfare; all America becomes one great accusing face and anathematizing horn; I felt like a Lilliputian in Gulli-verland. At this crisis a complete stranger with a truck appeared, with-out a word wasted began pushing me through the traffic, and after a mile or two taciturnly steered me aside into a repair-workshop, then departing before I could even thank him.

For a day or two I idled among friends and explored Cleveland, a fine city by the lake, with an abundance of trees and parks, and many great industries. Here Mike Polopski, the best-paid artisan in history, earns one hundred dollars a week (sensibly diminished by his union dues), owns a limousine, and lives in a somewhat inferior house, with a wife, television set, large refrigerator and a machine which washes, rinses, wrings and dries. Save for the house itself, and what that might connote, he lives well. He already earns more than the $4000 a year which President Truman has foretold as the average income of an American family by 1966. The only cloud in his material sky, if it is one, is the unanswered question: will deficit-spending by his government lead to a 'bust' (as it does for private persons) and what is to be done with the apparently inexhaustible production of American industry?

As to the first, the currently unfashionable school of 'sound finance' holds that the ultimate 'bust' is inevitable. As to the second, only God, by the look of things, can provide the solution. When the small British island (which does not grow all the food or contain all the raw materials it needs) was wealthy, it bought food and raw materials abroad and largely paid for these with manufactures; and the world prospered with it. The Republic has all the food it needs and almost all the raw materials, and must somehow dispose of an apparently boundless surplus of manufactures. The conundrum is not now acute because a large proportion of these are in effect dumped in foreign countries in the benevolent manner known as Marshall Aid. If other countries recover and build up their industries again, their intake of American manufactures will decrease while American industry continues to grow. At the end it would be thrown on its own market, which is great but could hardly keep pace with such expansion. At that point the system of deficit-spending, to keep up prices and standards, might logically lead to cars, refrigerators and television-sets being stored in caves and warehouses, like grain and potatoes. Alternatively, the deficit-school of politics might declare another 'emergency', leading through the seizure of 'emergency powers' to 'control', impoverishment and the loss of individual liberty.

Thus Mike Polopski, at present flush, wanders along an enshadowed road trodden by the British working-man twenty years ahead of him.

If his house is inferior to its gadgets, that is only because he has never thought much about houses. If he wanted a better one he could today still have it, of any kind he chose and could pay for. The stage at which that may be denied him, in the name of an 'emergency', lies farther down the road, about where the British working-man now is.

Cleveland was suffering from an outbreak of robbery with violence and sexual assault, the effect of two current causes. The visible immunity of the great crime-rings has weakened public respect for the law, so that unorganized, individual ill-doers now set out to break it in their own way; and that is made easier for them because the love of mechanical things has led to the disappearance of the neighbourhood cop (or policeman on his beat). Modern cities all felt that their policemen ought to rush about in zone-cars with screaming sirens. Constabulary duty was mechanized and became a thing of loud exhausts, corners taken on one wheel, and microphones ('Calling all cars, calling all cars . . .'). This might be useful if the mobsters still fought each other in the streets, but today, for higher efficiency in the organization, they kill each other privately and without fuss. Thus the mechanized police have been left like an armoured division in guerrilla country, and the small local criminal gladly watches them whizz by before he goes to work. The man he feared has gone; that was the foot patrolman, who knew every honest citizen, bad character and doorway on his beat and was near at hand when anything went wrong. The man in the zone-car has no such local knowledge or eye for detail. Unorganized but violent crime has thus become a major problem of the day and the people of Cleveland were thinking of self-help in the form of Vigilance Committees.

Having come so far, I could not return to New York without saying at least good day to Canada; I followed the long lakeside road to Buffalo and crossed the frontier. It was as if the wind abruptly fell. The nervous tension which fills even the empty spaces in the Republic is suddenly relaxed, on the farther side of a river. This is an inexplicable thing, but palpable. The easier pace of life communicates itself to the very air, even of woods and fields.

I ran for ten miles along a picturesque riverside, towards a distant, stationary cloud in the clear sky: the spray from Niagara, suspended in air as eternally, I suppose, as the snow lies on high mountains. It was good to break the long journey for a little while at Niagara, and to spend the time planning the route for a future Canadian one. This was a long-cherished ambition, for I had good Canadian friends in both the wars. I remembered one of them, Eric Read, spinning down to death below me at Lens on Boxing Day of 1917 and, as I looked at Niagara, thought how little he and others of his Canadian generation could have suspected the strange things that would happen in the next thirty years. Their Canada, like the American Republic and the British island, was caught in the web of the grand design and, with the rest of us, would not know the shape of the future until Armageddon was complete. I went to Normandy in 1944 with Canadian troops and among Canadian press correspondents, as among British and American ones, saw some of those new figures of our time, men in khaki battledress who were not truly Canadians, or British or American, but quickly-naturalized Communists from Eastern Europe, thus enabled to obtain all manner of information. The Canadian spy affair of 1945-46 was but the partial exposure of something then obvious to any trained eye.

The temptation to go on to Toronto was strong but for that moment had to be resisted. I recrossed the frontier to Buffalo and began the long ride across New York State, breaking the journey only for a few days at another small town, Le Roy, one of the new-New England places. It had a little white church which, like many others, was the loveliest I ever saw, pretty white houses in the homes-section, green lawns and sidewalks, and trees that grew, in relation to the trees I grew up with, as if each was the apostle Jesus loved. The delightful, pedimented and porticoed houses closely rubbed porches and seemed to me to deserve more space between, but that, whether fault or virtue, is universal in America and belongs to the general fear of uppityness and stuffed-shirtiness. In comfortable, softly-lit interiors elderly men read newspapers or women played bridge; on stoops, mothers and fathers rocked themselves; at the Firemen's Fair the children ate ice-cream, or rode on the roundabouts and the firemen, in clownish dress, made lusty music. It was all as jolly as could be. On to this little white-and-green place red-and-gilt Main Street of the hot dogs and hamburgers was abruptly stitched, a discordant levantine bazaar where a village green would be harmonious.

I went on from Le Roy and found New York State, lush and long-settled, a demi-paradise. Marks of poverty are rare in this country of fine farmland, substantial homesteads and townships which grow ever closer together. There were many lakes, not great inland seas like those which accompanied me for many days, but little, blue, domestic ones, just big enough for fun in a small boat. The roads are good all over the Republic, but here the double- and treble-tracked highways, with their overpasses and underpasses and cleverly-contrived inter-sections, reach perfection. I turned southward at Albany and was going hard for New York, resolved to resist any new temptations to tarry, so that I might get there betimes, when I saw a sign, 'To Catskill, by ferry'. Who could withstand that? At once I turned aside.

I soon understood why that idle old Dutchman chose this country-side for his twenty-year sleep. Here, on the edge of turmoil, was a mysterious, empty land of rolling, wooded hills, lonely and slumbrous. A notice said, 'Live on the Rip Van Winkle Ridge, lots for sale', but few seemed to have come there to live, unless they were asleep in the meadows. I came to a crossroads where the trail vanished; no new fingerpost pointed to the Catskill Ferry and no human being stirred. I chose a road at random and plunged ever deeper into country from which life seemed gone. Then I passed an old, old man, and a little farther an old, old woman, both asleep under trees and both with baskets of cherries for sale. To whom could they hope to sell cherries on this unfrequented road, or had they perhaps been asleep for twenty years? It was an eerie place. At last I came to another unsignposted crossroads where another old man sat beneath a tree. I called to him, 'Which way to the ferry?'

'The ferry?' he said after some instants, sleepily, 'the ferry hasn't bin working for two years' (or did he say twenty?). 'But there's a sign, way back, pointing to it,' I said. 'The ferry,' he repeated dreamily, 'hasn't bin working for twenty years' (or perhaps he said two hundred). I felt as if I had passed from the mortal world into some dreamland peopled only by male and female Van Winkles. In America a sign that points to a long-vanished ferry is almost inconceivable; on the

brink of New York it is incredible. I looked at the old man and decided
he had just awakened after twenty years. I wondered if he found the
world greatly changed, and decided he would not. Here in Rip Van
Winkleland it looked as if it might not have altered since time began.
What did the other differences amount to, anyway? Wheels turned
faster, motor cars multiplied, the gadgets increased; but the world was
essentially the same, the grass and the oak grew, the Hudson River
flowed, faith, hope and charity contested eternally with envy, malice
and hatred. Why, there must still be even a road to New York!

I roused the old man (he was asleep again) and with shaking finger
he pointed the way and closed his eyes. I went off and once more, in
the late evening, was carried by the conveyor-band into New York.
I had a journey behind me which, as I looked back, seemed like one
round the earth, so varied was the alternation of sun and snow, farmland and desert, plain and sea, mountain and prairie, populousness and
emptiness, tumult and quiet.

CHAPTER 42

HOT SPOT

I CHOSE the hottest season on record to return to New York and but for arrears of reading and writing, which I could overtake indoors, should have added a completely wasted fortnight to the book of a life usually full, for I could not go out by day. I gained much respect for New Yorkers, who must have some especial reserve of endurance to support life during their midsummer heat. This steam-bath atmosphere puzzled me and I could only account for it by the structure of the city, with its tall canyons and lack of trees. It lies on the latitude of Madrid, but nowhere else along that line, or in Africa, have I met heat of this peculiar kind. Durban or Cape Town in January, when their inhabitants believe themselves sorely tried, are by comparison airy and cool.

The New York winter, though also renowned, must be relatively a minor affliction; clothing can be donned endlessly, but not so shed. The summer-tide heat adds one more element to the tensions of New York, from which large masses of the population can only escape to the unimaginably thronged beaches of Coney Island (where several *millions* of people gather on holidays!). The bus-drivers, who have to take fares and give tickets while they manhandle heavy vehicles along crowded streets, struggle with a loathing of their passengers, who have to suppress a seething resentment of surly answers or sudden, jerking starts which they think intentional. The jealousies of lovers, the quarrels of women, the rivalries of taxi-cabmen, the disputes of labourers flare into sudden outbursts and the newspapers are full of violent assaults, all plainly born of the heat. Everyone is a little mad, say the gossips, and they still add, as if this ancient commonplace were novel and remedial, that it isn't the heat, it's the humidity.

I think my big toe alone saved me from prostration. Only repeated shower-baths gave relief; my bathtub lacked a shower, and mere immersion in a tubful of tepid water refreshed not at all. I found by experiment that by lying in the empty tub, turning on the cold water full jet and sticking my toe up the tap I could produce a fair substitute for a shower. It was not easy for taps are not quite the shape of big toes, which fill them at the sides but leave gaps fore and aft, so that the jets come where the pressure is greatest, at the sides. This caused an excellent lateral shower, which drenched the walls and floor but left me dry. However, with practice I was able to regulate that and to direct a revivifying shower upon myself.

The only other relief was that given by a small swimming-bath beneath a club, of which I was hospitably made a temporary guest, and when I learned of it I hastened there. It was a place of cubicles, couches and well-muscled attendants in singlets and shorts, one of whom said, 'Do you want to take a swim, sir?' Yes, I said. 'That's fine,' he said, and pointed to a doorless cubicle towards which I started when, in the manner of a parliamentary custodian relieving visitors of their guns, he said, 'You won't need those, sir', and took my swimming-trunks. Evidently an old New York custom, I thought.

I felt September-mornish, but no doubt looked charming, when I came out of my cubicle. A pink gentleman stood on a weighing-machine, the hand of which registered 210 lbs; he looked so alarmed that I wanted to comfort him by telling him it might be fast. I sought the bath, keeping my eyes before me, and thus found that I repeatedly encountered myself; the place seemed to be a hall of mirrors, perhaps suitable for a gathering of goddesses. I never saw myself in the mass before and was about to dive away from the spectacle when another voice said firmly, 'The showers are in that corner, sir', and I had to make a long walk around the bath, accompanied by all my other selves, an unnerving promenade which caused me to hurry into the first shower-cubicle and turn on the first tap I saw, so that fierce jets of boiling water made me jump like a scalded cat. Then at last I plunged in. The water was warm and highly chlorinated. After that I kept to my room and made do with my big toe, only emerging at night to take the air along Riverside Drive or the Hudson Parkway, where the *Queen Elizabeth*, all lit, poked her nose over into the town.

I made one exception, when I went by day to see the funeral of Mr. Cohen's colleague, slain on the Sunset Strip in Hollywood. I was cautious about this, recalling the mishap suffered by Mr. Linklater's Don Juan, the Limey who was the only man shot at a gangster funeral. I cased the job (as the saying is, I believe) before I approached too close. However, the days of ten thousand dollar caskets, five thousand dollars' worth of flowers, and a dutiful procession of mayors, judges, prosecutors, politicians and aldermen following the hearse, seem to have gone. This was a decorous occasion, without display or gunfire. Numbers of citizens watched it non-committally from balconies, windows and street-corners. Among the mourners, for all I know, may have been many stony-eyed hoodlums or gimlet-eyed gorillas. They certainly looked grim, but were resplendent in clothes of the latest style and respectfully stood around the rabbis as the cortege formed and drove away.

I had one other experience in New York which I shall ever remember because it seemed somehow typical of that strange city. I went with a friend to his bank, where he presented a cheque, and the cashier, with swift, next-please efficiency, paid him five hundred dollars too much; no mean sum. He discovered this on the pavement outside, and said, 'I'm going to buy my wife a large diamond.' 'You wouldn't do that!' I said, awed. 'You watch me,' he said. 'But think of the principle of the thing,' I said. 'This is a matter of principle,' he said, 'I cannot bring myself to return money to a bank, banks are the natural enemy of man.' 'But,' I protested, 'the widows and children . . .' 'A bank,' he insisted, 'has no widows or children, it's just a great, big, beastly, soulless, grasping, impersonal bank, stuffed with money; it's morally wrong to give money back to a bank, it would be like compounding a felony.' He plainly felt strongly about the thing as he stood there in Wall Street, gazing at the Little Church Around The Corner. 'Think of that cashier,' I said, 'he'll be fired and he probably has two wives and twenty children.' 'He deserves to be fired,' he said, and went in and repaid the money. The cashier said casually, 'Ah yes, I remember now, I miscounted the serial numbers, thanks a lot.'

'He didn't seem much bothered,' I said as we came away. 'Of course not,' he said, 'five hundred dollars wouldn't have been noticed in that bank, it's cigar money.' 'How times have changed,' I said. 'How so?' he asked. 'I was thinking of my own early days as a bank clerk in London,' I said, 'once the half-yearly audit was held up dead by an errant penny. We juniors all longed to find that mistake of one penny piece, somewhere in the books; it would have meant a good mark for the young man who detected it.' 'Did you find it?' he asked. 'No,' I said, 'the Chief Cashier found it, he was already about as high up as he could get.' 'Tough!' he said.

I made ready to leave and went to Washington to say adieu to good friends there. Hitler's yacht lay in the river (its new owner was wondering why he bought it and what he should do with it). I leaned on a railing, looked at it and let my mind run back along the years to 1933. Odd, I thought; but for all that I might still be a newspaper correspondent in Berlin, it seems such worlds away. I wondered if a secure and placid life would have been better than the years full of roaming and danger, beneath a sky ever more uncertain. Well, for my part I was glad to have lived in this way and at this time; at least the lot of my generation never contained a dull moment, and I accepted it thankfully. I turned about, went to New York to collect two sacks of books and another crammed with papers, and began the last leg of an American journey, back to the South and a ship.

CHAPTER 43

LAST LAP

I LEFT New York a much more seasoned traveller than the awed and dazed one who was whirled into it one spring morning months before. I now knew its measure and meaning, and its true place in the great country I had explored. As to the remaining journey, I had picked up many tricks of the road, of food and lodging, and no longer felt a learner, lost among knowing initiates. After I crossed the Hudson River by bridge only two thousand road-miles and three large pieces of water (the Delaware River, Chesapeake Bay and Atlantic Ocean) lay between me and relaxation; it was a cinch.

I came southward through New Jersey and at pleasant New Castle crossed the Delaware (if the famous family whose name it bears earlier brought that name with it from Normandy, in William's conquering army, it has indeed travelled far and wide). On the farther shore I was once more in the land of American beginnings; placards announced 'The Kent and Sussex Fair' and the next town ahead was Dover. My road by-passed Dover, but for old time's sake I turned aside to pay homage to its name and memory. In 1940 the other Dover was the chin of England, sturdily stuck out against a threatening knockout blow. A good companion of mine was booked to sing there (a little-sought engagement then) and in the blue car, with some last dregs of petrol, I drove her to Dover. We should have had various permits, but in the heat of that day such things were still unorganized; Dover liked us and let us in. That gay adventure among the shells, bombs and dog-fights returned to me vividly now.

This Dover was a country place, a small town of the earlier Republic. Its earlier village green was now a broad, verdant expanse surrounded by fine public buildings, schools and the like. The modern American school-building is the apotheosis of the humble schoolhouse of old. Expense appears not to count and good models are followed, so that even in tiny, remote places a great edifice stands apart that looks like a

246

small university for a thousand scholars. The actual content of education in these places, however, is a matter of controversy often bitter among Americans.

Mr. Albert Jay Nock, a great authority, says the theory of education in America has been turned upside down. Formerly it was that of teaching people how to live, and now it is that of training them to do things. He traces the revolution to the visit of a Harvard president to Germany, where he discovered and brought back the elective system of subjects. From that beginning it spread from universities to colleges, secondary schools, primary schools and even (says Mr. Nock) to *Kindergaerten*. The ruling idea was that everybody should go to school, college and university and there study what he, not a pedagogic elite, thought best for him.

Subsidies and endowments were inexhaustible and thus the American educational system 'took on the aspect of a huge bargain-counter or modern drugstore', whence begowned and behooded graduates emerged carrying academicians' diplomas for 'business administration, retail shoe-merchandising, bricklaying and the like' (the mortuary heroine of Mr. Waugh's tragedy of Anglo-American manners graduated in 'Beauticraft', having briefly studied Art, Psychology and Chinese as ancillary subjects). This revolution, Mr. Nock writes, 'began with a drastic purge, a thorough guillotining of the classical curriculum, wherever found; such Greek and Latin as escaᵖᵉᵈ the Reign of Terror was left to die of inanition in dens and caves oᵥ earth', that is, in the rare schools or colleges which by some chance survived it.

Mr. Nock thought American education deteriorated greatly through this unheaval, and I heard constant complaint about it. One of the currently fashionable polls was held in 1949 and announced that the percentage of people who read books (for what that may be worth) is 21 in America, 33 in Sweden, 35 in Australia, 40 in Canada, 43 in Norway and 55 in Britain. The survey stated that in America 53 per cent of people continue schoolgoing beyond elementary school and in Britain only 13 per cent, but that the group of highest-educated Americans, nevertheless, was well below the British average. Another matter which disquietens American parents is the permeation of State education, through prescribed text books, by Communist doctrine. In New York State, in 1949, the Regents' examinations in all schools were based on a list of pamphlets, about half of which were issued by Communist 'front' organizations. Thus, while the American school-house of today might be the envy of teachers and scholars in less wealthy lands, what goes on inside it is a matter of much concern to large masses of the population.

Dover was a pleasant place, and so was Salisbury, the next township. Though New York and Philadelphia were not far behind, this Del-Mar-Va Peninsula (so-called because the State-lines of Delaware, Maryland and Virginia all cut across it) already said, 'This is the South'; it was once plantation country and here the negro population began. I came to Cape Charles, ran the car into a fat-bellied Chesapeake Bay ferrysteamer, and after an hour was set ashore near Cape Henry, where those very first settlers of all landed on a shore as bleak as that which the Pilgrim Fathers named Plymouth Rock in 1621.

A few miles later I ran into the happy, squalorous negro quarter of Norfolk, Virginia. When I first reached America I did not much notice this contented slovenry of the coloured districts, probably because I came from Africa and was familiar with it. Now that I had seen the rest of America, where the white folk on the whole maintain their own standards of improving hygiene and cleanliness, it caught my eye more. I saw that American negroes in the mass tend to live not very differently from negroes in the white man's cities of Africa.

The American negro has been a freeman for seventy years, votes in increasing numbers, can earn sums which might make many palefaces paler with envy, and may aspire to a house. Those things are beyond most natives in Johannesburg or Cape Town. Yet the American negro does not live on a much higher scale; apparently his instinct is not to improve his abiding-place.

That might or might not come in time; the real puzzle is whether he wants the white man's way of life. He was prised away from a quite diverse one, where a man was warrior, hunter and idler, under his chief, and his wives did what fieldwork was necessary to support life. He believed in that theory of existence, and any debating society might argue its merits. His tribe made war on other tribes for women, cattle or land, but he did not know the notion of free men freely competing, acquiring goods, improving their lot. Does he like it now that he has seen it, in America? That is all uncertain, though it is the claim which white inciters make for him in their feuds with other white men; he is a pawn in this game.

The spiritual family of Mrs. Beecher Stowe never consider what the negro *wants*. What he truly yearns for, as far as I know him, is a separate life from the white man, even if the twain must live side by side. If there is a 'colour bar' it is God's, and he believes devoutly in it. While I was in America a thing happened which is much to the point. Four schoolboys (from white New England, inevitably) were sent 'to see the South' and find out the facts of 'racial discrimination'; clearly they were expected to return full of the usual virtuous indignation. They were primed at the start and polished at the finish by leading foes of 'racial discrimination' in New York. In the South they talked to as many negroes as they could find, particularly at a coloured university in Tennessee.

On their return to the furious, negroless North they reported 'what constituted, perhaps, our greatest surprise', namely, 'that the Southern Negroes did not always seem to desire the abolition of racial segregation' (this might indeed be a shock to anyone bred in the atmosphere of New England, Manchester or Bloomsbury). They found this view prevalent among negro students at the Fisk University. Their report produced an uproar of reproach from *white* expostulants, a Dean and others. Eighty years after *Uncle Tom's Cabin* it is still heresy to speak truth about the negro (and has become so to say it about Political Zionism). My own observation in the American South was that the negro's lot there slowly but steadily improves (as in Africa) by white men's standards, but I remained as uncertain in America as in Africa whether that is the way the negro wants it to go. His loud friends, the Liberals, Socialists and Communists, are his real enemies, for they would deny him his true ambition: a separate being within the white man's kraals. They wish to bring him to a darker bourne, from which no fellow-traveller returns.

Norfolk was a rip-roaring dockyard town such as Plymouth or Portsmouth may earlier have been (there *is* a Portsmouth here, too, which seems virtually part of Norfolk), and if not wide open, then much more than ajar. The men, establishments and ships of the American Navy abounded; at sea America seemed armed to the teeth, as England now, one gathers, to the dentures; however, its barques might still bite and Devon outlast Bevan. I found a room next to one booked the moment before by two jolly sailormen who sent up a bottle of whisky to occupy it while they went out. I foresaw revelry by night next door. My window looked on the flat roof of an adjacent building and when I glanced at it my expectations increased; it bore some hundreds of bottles, clearly tossed overboard by earlier jolly sailormen in my hotel, who forgot they were not at sea.

Mysteriously, hardly one of these bottles was broken, though they clearly had travelled twenty or thirty yards. I saw that I should not be awakened by the noise of *breaking* glass, and wondered if some enterprising manufacturer could have produced an unbreakable sort for this especial purpose. That cannot have been the explanation, however, for among the bottles lay many jugs, toothwater-decanters and tumblers, the duplicates of those in my own room, which surely could not have been made of fortified glass by even the most thoughtful hotel keeper. Resisting the temptation to try a decanter or two, I gave up the puzzle. Perhaps we approach a time when the recognizable qualities of glass will be that it is unbreakable, non-transparent and will cut diamonds? The trim little shoregoing launch of the boat in Boston Harbour was made of glass, but looked like anything else.

With a curiosity stimulated by those bottles I went out to look at Main Street; Norfolk promised to be lively. It was thronged with sailors in neat white suits, this Sunday evening. Nickelodeons, juke-boxes and radios clamoured against each other from bars, restaurants, cafés, movie-theatres and pin-table rooms, all glittering and click-clacking. The sailors rolled in and out of them and of the shops which sailors love, the windows of which were full of especially smart uniforms, badges, medal-ribbons, trinkets, gifts and much more. Between them, equally bright and busy, were the tattooists' shops, which showed pictures of ladies tattooed in intimate places and men illustrated from head to foot. There was one of a man with a tattooed face, like an African witch-doctor's mask. I wondered what sort of life he had.

Not every woman would love that face on a pillow beside her (though I suppose the odd one might, if she were odd enough). If he made a livelihood by displaying this frightful face, in booths or circuses, how did he set about buying a meal or a shirt? There are weak hearts in the world. I wondered (as Noel Coward might say) what happened to him.

The tattooists prospered, this Sabbath eve. Their overheads are small; they only need a needle, ink and bright shop-window and the sailorman, vaingloriously offering himself for patterning in it, provides the free advertisement and custom-attracting display. These lads were well-developed and clearly liked to show it. One was being tattooed by a woman, happily only on a bicep; a male artist in the next window was busy on a thigh.

I slept well, being wakened but once by the crash of old-fashioned, breakable glass, and went my way, pausing to seek out Old Saint Paul's Church, the wall of which still contains an indignant cannon-ball fired at the rebellious colonists by the last English governor, Lord Dunmore, from a ship in the river. Having become used to the parallelograms of American cities I lost myself in Norfolk, which is a pleasantly rambling place, and long drove round districts of naval homes, attractive white ones embowered in masses of a pink-flowering shrub, welcome to the eye. At last I emerged and went on from Norfolk to Suffolk, from Williamston to Windsor and a lesser Washington. Now that I knew the populous central region where the farmland, the industry and the newer immigration are concentrated, I realized how sparsely peopled the South is. These were lonely roads; the wayside life of the car-and-tourist industry fell away and townships were far between. The great farmhouses of the Middle West are unknown here, for their counterparts, the plantation houses, are gone and the country is one of small farms and smallholders. The places where crops grow look like forest-clearings and as you go along the clearings become fewer and the forests greater.

Sometimes marsh and swamp mark the approach to tropic climes. Immensely long bridges go over broad rivers swelling to the sea; the water looks oily and ancient and the trees and undergrowth grow right down into it, a sure sign of jungle. The bridges are not the great, disdainful, stone-and-metal structures of the newer parts but low, wooden ones with drawbridges in the middle for any craft that might wish to pass, and they bear notices, 'Don't use when in operation' (I thought that any man who tried to cross an open drawbridge would hardly be in a condition to read the notice). Here were great tracts of land, either never cleared by man or reverted to nature after the ruin of the plantations, yet even there the lonely road bore the signs, 'Encroachments are strictly prohibited', which are the American equivalent of 'Trespassers will be prosecuted'.

Suddenly, running down this deeply-indented coast, I came to Albemarle Sound and tiny, lovely, astonishing Edenton in North Carolina. This is a lonely and formidable countryside now and the reader's eye, moving back, perhaps can picture what it was three hundred years ago. Yet here the colonists settled and built as if they had six hundred years of island security behind them, the English Channel and British Navy all around, and nothing to fear ahead. Here is a perfect Georgian courthouse, facing the Sound across a broad greensward that runs between fine white mansions and huge, spreading trees.

In the 1770s the ladies of Edenton held a famous tea-party in the Boston sense (though they did not throw the tea in the sea but drank it). The time was come to show King George who was who, and the Edenton ladies were violently belligerent. They were as warlike then as the ladies of New England were later. In both cases, colonists against king, or North against South, the ladies' cry was 'Up boys and at 'em'. The idea that men tear themselves from gentle, restraining arms when they take up arms seems an ancient fallacy; often their womenfolk are as martial as themselves. For that mattter, in the most recent war women were nearer to the fighting than ever since Boadicea and apparently will be in the thick of any next one. At the foot of Court House Green in Edenton now the iron cannon still point sturdily across the Sound at ghostly British ships and around the sculptured teapot on the greensward, perhaps, gather the shades of pretty ladies who may discuss the unforeseen sequel to the war they knew.

I spent a few lazy days in Wilmington and felt again the lingering fragrance of the Old South, the much-mocked one of magnolia and moonlight. From Wilmington Rhett Butler ran cargoes of Southern cotton through the Northern blockade to Liverpool, to earn a little money for the impoverished South and more for himself; and to Wilmington he returned, through the blockade, with things the South needed. Here a few old planation houses still stand and the beards of the Spanish Moss hang grey and sad from the live oaks around them; it is as if Don Quixote passed that way, collided with a bough, and escaped with his head but left his beard, which then took root and multiplied.

In the South such relics of the dead past impressed me less than living differences which endure. They are intangible yet positive things which derive from the old days and the distinctive way of life in the South then. The comparison first forced itself on me in Wilmington because by that time I had seen the North, Middle West and West. I felt a gentler spirit; people were courteous and unhurried and gave smile for smile; the noise and pace of traffic were less. Food was good and pleasantly served; there I found the best and cheapest lodging I had in America. There was no wide-openness. By ten o'clock nearly everything was closed and I doubt, but am not sure, if even an all-night drugstore was open; evening was a quiet hour in Wilmington. The term, 'a civilized way of life', may convey too much or too little, but I believe most travellers from afar would concur that the civilized way of life in America is now chiefly to be found in the South, which is speciously presented to the outer world as the enemy of civilized ways.

The feeling of jungle increased as I went on to Charleston in South Carolina (it was easy to picture alligators farther south, in the Floridan Everglades, a name graphically expressive of dark, swampy, secretive, impenetrable, eternal haunts). The men, apparently anarchist in motive, who destroyed the plantations without preparing something better to take their place, dealt an almost mortal blow at this part of the Republic. Here the shack-and-share-cropper country began. Listless-looking white folk, caught between their own and the dark man's philosophy of life, hung about or rocked themselves on the porches of dilapidated homesteads, and idle darkies lolled around the rare filling-stations and stores ('Lazy-bones, lyin' in the hay, you'll never earn a dime that way, lyin' in the new mown hay'; the musical ride continued).

Charleston seemed half dead (because, I found, its people were fled to the beaches from the overpowering heat). This welcome emptiness enabled me to find a good, cheap room at an hotel where a fountain plashed in a green courtyard and to wander round the lovely streets at leisure. They retain something of the charm and elegance of the Old South, which Manhattan derides, and life in them is on the softer note which I previously met only in Wilmington, Salem and Salt Lake City. Had the South won (which was never possible) Charleston would be a leading port and city. Instead it is small and quiet and Northerners call the elderly Southern ladies who seclude themselves in it 'Charleston freaks'. With Cemetery Ridge at Gettysburg, it is a monument to the war of brothers and the sadness of calamity is still in its air, for here the war began, when the Southerners fired on Fort Sumter, occupied by Union troops.

Several old plantation houses survive round Charleston. Near one was a thicket of trees killed by the hanging moss, so that only bare, rotting bones remained, with the pendant beards. The decay of the roots had rotted the soil too, and slimy, stagnant, scum-covered water had gathered, so that the bearded skeletons rose from a fetid, primeval swamp. I remembered the stone forests and spouting vapours of the Yellowstone, with their constant hint of volcanic action, and the feeling of desert-held-in-check that fills Southern California. Looking at these murdered trees, behung with the assassin's beards, and the green mire at their feet, I thought how quickly it might all revert to creeping, steaming jungle if man lost his hold.

Between Charleston and Savannah, in Georgia, was more forest and share-cropper country, haunted by the ghosts of tobacco- and cotton-crops once abundant. Broadway playgoers for seven years thronged to see the human desolation of this countryside, depicted on the basest level of degradation. I turned aside to see two places of the earliest settlement, Beaufort and Port Royal. Beaufort was delightful and contained the usual house from which the Marquis de Lafayette harangued the colonists about the evils of aristocratic rule. Port Royal, sleeping by a sound beneath the multitudinous beards, was like world's end. A railroad track ended at a wooden shed where a forlorn porter sat and gazed into nothing; behind mosquito-netting on the porches of wooden houses elderly people sat as if turned to stone. I seldom saw a place so remote from the pulsations of life and to revive myself had my hair cut in Beaufort.

'Good morning, sir,' said the barber, 'I've just been having a word with a friend who's father just died from a stroke; he's better gone.' From that beginning he talked of many things. He did not like Beaufort at first, he said, thirty years ago, but his son was born there and so he stayed. 'It was good for him?' I said. 'Oh, he's done well,' he said, 'I sent him to a military school.' I never clearly understood the function of those schools, the announcements of which, showing boys in uniform, fill the advertisement pages of the better periodicals, so I encouraged him to expand. I gathered they appeal chiefly to parents who distrust the State-education system. 'Boys usually get sent to the military academies to get disciplint,' he said, 'my boy, he wasn't attending to anything but foolishness while he was at school there so I sent him to the Wilston Military Academy to get disciplint. They get disciplint there and they never lose it. The boys there always call you Sir when they talk to you, the others never do. They put 'em in the bullring if they don't do what they're told. That means they have to keep walking round and round, for two or three hours sometimes. They'll do anything to keep out of the bullring. That gives 'em disciplint. It cost me four or five hundred dollars a year for him, with board, but it was worth it and if I'd another boy I'd send him there.'

I left him, a contented man who had found the answer to that mortal danger, social security, and came soon to Savannah. It was a sudden surprise, as delightful as the rainbow you meet at sea, without any rain to account for it, for it was the best-favoured and proportioned place I saw in America, remarkable for having developed so much grace and charm in a very short time. The colonists under General James Oglethorpe only landed here in 1733, to fortify the King's other colonies against the Spanish threat from the South; by 1865 the South was prostrate. Thus in 130 years a mellow little city grew, with all the lineaments of taste that its kind, in Europe, acquired only in the course of centuries.

Like Washington, Savannah proves the curious proposition that a city laid out for defence gains a long start towards civic beauty.

Savannah shows, too, that the parallelogram-plan, of straight streets intersecting straight streets, need not be ugly; all depends on the excution. General Oglethorpe and a Colonel Bull worked to a good plan. Each settler was given a town lot, or plot, separated by broad streets which at their intersections, however, widened into large squares, where stockades were built so that they made a series of forts in which the townsfolk could quickly assemble and command all approaches from successive vantage points. The result today is that at every corner a vista opens of wide, shady streets leading into shady, open places, from which other leafy streets lead again into other leafy squares. This pleasant setting produced buildings equally delightful. The churches follow Wren, and many houses are of English Georgian style, designed by architects who crossed the Atlantic for the purpose; among them was William Jay, whose native taste, acquired in Bath, has left several fine legacies.

The successive squares of Bull Street relate the paradoxical story of the Republic in their monuments. First comes the statue of the King's governor himself, Oglethorpe. Then follow the memorials to the colonists who threw off the kingly yoke and the proletarians who helped; the Marquis de Lafayette, the Comte d'Estaing, the Polish Count Pulaski (the German Baron von Steuben's statue is somewhere else). The last one is to the liberated republicans who then fought each other; Bull Street tells in stone the tale of history's little jokes.

As I went farther south the heat became a daily torment. These temperatures are something for a white man to reckon with, and I wondered about his life in Florida as I entered its gates (other State-lines have mere notice-boards, but the State of Flowers, characteristically has Gates).

Florida awaited the traveller with the beaming 'front' of a real-estate man. An especially trim and shining stretch of road, with a manicured look, ran between 'Welcome to Florida' signs, through The Gates and past a palatial Information Pavilion ('We are here to help you; nothing to sell') which was padlocked and empty. The outstretched glad hand took the apt shape of an avenue of extended palms. At Chesapeake Bay, far behind, roadside notices told me I was going 'From Pines to Palms', that is, leaving the chilly North for the exotic South, but I saw no abundance of palms thereafter. Now Florida resolutely made good this boosters' boast. The palms looked wistful, as if they knew their place but did not really want to be there, and where they ended great pinewoods began and accompanied me for two days; not even in Pomerania have I seen pines in such profusion. The soil of Northern Florida is poor and sandy and pines, almost alone among growing things, like that kind of earth. However, the booster can do no wrong and 'From Pines to Palms' was the alluring slogan. Where the brief display of palms ended human beings awaited me and thrust into the car handfuls of leaflets offering me suites in the finest hotels, all down the coast, at prices so low that I would have liked to settle there, until I remembered that this was the off-season (people like to go to Florida in winter).

I came to Jacksonville, a bustling, sweltering little New York packed with people, noise, traffic and merchandise beneath the blazing sun. Florida, the southernmost State, is not truly of The South. It was never really colonized by the English or Spanish, though Spanish forts, here and there implanted in it, marked the northernmost reach of the Spanish conquest. Rather as a territorial claim than an actual possession, it was bandied between England and Spain during the century of the American War of Independence and passed to the rising Republic in 1821, but it remained empty and played no great part in the Civil War. Its development and inhabitation began with this century and the boosters. During the 1920s the real-estate men proclaimed it an earthly paradise, and fantastic cities, like Miami, grew on the edge of primeval swamps through which fine roads were driven. Like Southern California, Florida is very much a colony of New York. The spirit of Manhattan jumped over the distasteful Old South, with its courtly tradition, and landed in these sub-tropical parts. In Floridan cities life reassumes the tone of New York and Chicago; muted motor-horns and after-you drivers give way to the pressing throng and the loud, imperative toot. Miami is a stronghold of the organized gambling-ring, with its associated trades. Life in Florida has a forced, transplanted air, as in Southern California; again the traveller wonders, how enduring and deep are these roots?

Jacksonville, glitteringly new, was in sharp contrast with Saint

257

Augustine not far away, the first white man's town ever founded in what is now the United States. The Spaniards built a fort there in 1565, forty years before the English colonists set up Jamestown, and this fort remains, a thing of age, strength and beauty (preserved in it is a letter written to George Washington by his friend Chris Gadsden, who was held prisoner there by the British during the War of Independence; he wrote: 'All of them behaved with decency to me and I have not had the least insult offered to me.' The chivalry of war two hundred years ago shames the barbaric vengeances of today).

This fort and a shrine near to it are the earliest monuments the Republic has, and possibly significant, because the acknowledgment of God remains tangible in the air, and is absent from more recent encampments. The first colonists, English, French or Spanish, all came with faith in their hearts. The Spaniards here, when they first anchored off a shore then savage, waited for the Feast of the Nativity of the Virgin to go ashore and begin their work, and called the fort they then made the Citadel of Saint Mark. They named the town that was to be built for the saint whose feast-day was nearest, Saint Augustine. The chaplain of their fleet at once founded the first Mission (the Name of God Mission) and on its site the little shrine of Our Lady of Milk and Happy Delivery stands today. In the mirage-like scene of Florida these two places, the formidable fort and the tiny shrine, equally give out an effluence of enduring strength and peace.

By way of another American contrast, Saint Augustine has a curious museum of ephemera, apparently brought together by someone who collected other men's collections of odds and ends; matchboxes, souvenir buttons ('Good old Dewey' or 'Vote for Franklyn D. Roosevelt'), the heraldic spoons beloved of holidaymakers ('A Gift from Gopher Prairie'), glass pickle-jars, old watches, tintypes, dance-programmes, alabaster busts of last-century ladies and the like. The disposal of such a miscellany, once amassed, must be a major problem, unless you buy land for a great bonfire or charter a ship to sink it at sea. By some means, this one found its way to Saint Augustine, of all places!

However, it included a pleasing thing, a painting of one Pero, cast into prison by the Spaniards when they conquered the Netherland, centuries ago. He was starved into making confession of heresy, but was allowed the visits of his daughter who, being with milk, was the means of his happy delivery. The picture shows him receiving that life-giving nourishment. The Spaniards thought his continued health and rosiness a sign that God was in him, as may have been the case indeed, and set him free. The legend was then new to me but since that day, in the manner of these things, I have come across it in various other forms; de Maupassant uses it in his own fashion.

I turned eastwards across Florida, towards the Mexican Gulf, and passed through enormous pine forests (I read in the newspapers, without surprise, that forestry officers from all over America came to Florida to study, not the palm, but pineology). I lazed awhile by a slow, sleepy, brown stream called the Swanee River. Its dreamy, unhurried movement is more in tune with the negro's soul, as far as I can judge it, than the dizzy rush of Main Street is. A white man wrote the song, but it seems to catch the dark man's philosophy. Then I took refuge from the heat for a day at a cool, shady and friendly little place called Madison, went on and came out at last on the Gulf Coast at Panama City.

All was arranged (unless the programme is constant) for me to observe the extremes of human and natural activity in America, and at this moment a hurricane was prowling about the Gulf Coast. It was a rogue-hurricane, or as Americans expressively say, 'a bad actor hurricane', on the exits and entrances of which the stage-manager (or weather-forecaster) cannot count. It blew where it listed and none knew, though all wondered, where it might pop up next. In Saint Augustine, two days before, I thought the bad actor was about to do his turn, for black clouds suddenly gathered out of the blue and blazing sky, the trees on the bar at the mouth of the bay became agitated, as if they wrang anxious hands, and I heard the distant soughing of a big wind; but it passed.

I sneakingly hoped to meet the hurricane, because I read that the great hurricanes of 1926 and 1927 brought sudden tumblings of the barometer to 27 or 28 degrees. I did not know just what the temperature now was, but it felt like 127, and I would have settled without haggling for 30 or even 35. When I left Madison the morning was much cooler, as if the bad actor were not far away. There were sudden gusts and the beginnings of rotary movements in the clouds; it was as if a rabid dog, tied by a fraying rope, yelped and strained to break loose. I made some speed through the remaining pine stems, which hurricanes use like matchsticks, and gladly emerged on the open Gulf coast. About here, the morning papers said, the hurricane might strike during the day, unless it were an even worse actor than any supposed. Safe now from pulverization by tree-trunks, and not caring much about burial by sand in my hopes of icy blasts, I went happily along the unsheltered coastal road, now melting in the heat again.

I came to a lovely place where sands purely white and firm stretched, unpeopled, as far as I could see. The sky held a kind of frown, not enough wholly to obscure the sun, and the water lay still and unbreathing, like a great cat about to pounce, lapping the sands without creamy edge or murmur. It was of a strange, luminous pale-green inshore, of a leaden grey a little way out, and of an irridescent, butterfly-wing-like blue beyond, where a little sun filtered through the frown. I could not resist it; only once, at Lake Erie, had I used those swimming-trunks; two or three miles ahead dunes rose beside the road and if the bad actor appeared I might quickly reach that cover, for what it was worth. I drove off the road on to the firm-looking sands; promptly the wheels sank to the axles.

I thought I would not after all welcome a hurricane. In the far distance I saw something fluttering from a lonely mast and remembered newspaper allusions to hurricane-signals. The sky's frown contained a hint of rotation and sudden gusts came. I noticed, without gladness, that it was *much* cooler. I wondered if I would be better inside a car bowling along like tumbleweed or lying flat on the ground, or trying to. I scooped out sand from under the wheels and scrabbled about for pieces of jetsam. I found nothing bigger than kindling, but forced bunches of this under the wheels which, when I started, ground them to powder and into the sand.

Then my guardian angel appeared, who wears skins of different hues but never failed me yet. A car came at speed along the empty road. I did not try to stop it; drivers are reluctant to stop in America, and I thought I could not fairly ask this one to delay, as he might dislike hurricanes. However, he stopped unasked and was a young man of strength and ingenuity. Like beachcombers we ranged those sandy plains for tindery twigs and twiglets, jammed them all round the wheels, and he rocked the car forward, backward and sideways while I accelerated and the smell of scorching rubber rose and at last one wheel was on the road and then another, and with a final, convulsive, screeching and malodorous heave the rear ones followed and I was free. May blessings attend him ever.

The devil was ill, the devil a saint would be. I drove fast; more speed, less hurricane, I thought; but a few miles beyond the hurricane-signal I came to a silver strand lonelier and lovelier yet, and fell into error again. Thinking sand the only peril, I carefully pulled well into the side of the hard road by a high dune, and undressed in the car. Then I found I had left my trunks where I stuck before. I looked around. For miles either way road, sands and sea lay empty, as before life's creation. I jumped out, ran round the high dune and to the water. It was the most glorious bathe of my life. However, the sky grew uneasier, so I came out, ran lightly up the sands and round the dune to the car; parked behind it was another in which two elderly ladies ate sandwiches.

Like Lord Tom Noddy, I felt that nought was to be said, but, unlike him, that something must be done, and quickly. I leaped like a gazelle at one bound into the driving seat and on to the accelerator and pulled up, still breathless, about three miles away to get into shirt, trousers and shoes. A good actor would have handled the episode with more aplomb, perhaps. Cured now of all interest in hurricanes I went on and came at nightfall to my starting-point, Mobile, an innocent in America returning as a fairly seasoned explorer. Little time remained; I continued through Mississippi to New Orleans in Louisiana and to my homeward ship.

CHAPTER 44

WAITIN' ON THE LEVEE

THE vessel, however, was late and I thus gained welcome days
in New Orleans, where Old Man River runs broad-mouthed and
many-tongued into the Gulf after his long journey between banks
which have seen more startling changes in a century than most rivers
know in five hundred years or more. The countryside far around New
Orleans is estuary and the city's soil is so permeable that the cemeteries
stand above ground and the dead are put in storied vaults built on it.
Given this marshy character and the temperature of those latitudes at
the season when I was there, the moist heat of New Orleans was a new
chapter in a book I thought to have read to the end.

The contrast between the beginnings and the continuation of the
Republic is sharply shown on either side of Canal Street, a thoroughfare (so broad that four parallel street-car tracks are hardly noticed in
the middle) which runs through the city to the curving Mississippi like
an arrow to a stretched bow. On one side is old New Orleans, the
square mile called the Vieux Carré, and on the other new New
Orleans, the American city. The Vieux Carré was first French, then
for a space Spanish, then briefly French again, a colonial city of
Imperial France and Imperial Spain. Its physiognomy is Spanish
because the older French town was burned down; its nature is predominantly French. In 1803 Napoleon held title to the million square
miles then known as Louisiana, and President Jefferson said that if
Napoleon took actual possession of it 'we must marry ourselves to
the British fleet and nation'. Napoleon averted that by selling Louisiana
for fifteen million dollars. The New Orleans French liked this new
bequeathment no more than their earlier abandonment to the King of
Spain and, entrenched in the Vieux Carré, indignantly watched the
'foreign invaders' arrive and encamp across the moat where Canal
Street now runs. They refused social mingling and the street urchins
followed the newcomers about, crying:

'Méricain coquin,
'billé en nanquin,
voleur di pain. . . .

The urgent American spirit soon marched over all that and racial
outlines have been obliterated, or new ones superimposed, in New
Orleans now. Italians are most numerous among the population; next
come the Germans and then the French. The Negro and mixed-breed
element is large. The city is now more kin of New York than of the
Old South, save in some of its residential parts. It is a citadel of the
gaming-syndicate and is wide-open; drinking is hard and dubious
entertainments are prolific. New Orleans, too, produces a good deal
of the drama and literature of depravity which mar the American
scene at this passing moment. Even hard-bitten New York reviewers
sometimes recoil from these emanations 'righteously indignant in one
breath and droolingly prurient in the next, like the notes of a small-
town peeper on the broom closet of hell'.

The new way of life has flowed over old town and new alike, but
the Vieux Carré in its physical shape remains the monument of a
different one. Its narrow streets are blocked with tourist-buses and
loud with the cries of guides, but on either side are graceful houses with
balconies and galleries of delicately-wrought ironwork and open door-
ways which reveal pleasant inner courtyards, with trees and flowers,
where family privacy once ruled; the change in note and tempo is that
between a bebop band and a spinet. Here people lived who went at
nights to the opera, theatre or ball, things which Hollywood denies to
the mass of Americans today. They lived so when the country was a
wilderness of beast and forest; now that the wilderness has been tamed
the graceful way of urbane life has been almost lost; it is as if the wild
took revenge on the city.

The people who lived in this pleasant place, built round a cathedral,
called themselves Creoles, thus claiming to be of pure white blood,
chiefly French and partly Spanish, and hoped to found a new nation.
The first shipload of Frenchwomen brought to the lonely bachelors
of New Orleans seems to have carried ladies who, though white, were
more readily wedded then than they were later included in family-

trees, but the next one contained girls escorted by Ursuline nuns whose blood later Creoles gladly claimed. Even so, however, bachelors far outnumbered marriageable girls and this disproportion produced a new, brief-lived race, the famed Quadroons of New Orleans.

The Quadroons must obviously have been of both sexes, but survive in history only as lovely females (the offspring of half-breed women and white men). All travellers of that day, including Harriet Martineau, agree about the great beauty of the Quadroons; a puzzling thing because, in my observation of today, the mere mingling of colour by no means infallibly produces beauty. Anyway, the young Creole gentlemen traditionally chose a mate at one of the Quadroon Balls and installed her in a tiny house on the Ramparts until he should marry. Her ambition was to be so selected, and her dream, to be wed. That seldom happened, but she was cared for while the alliance lasted and when it ended retained the little house; she preferred this lot to marriage with a Quadroon. The Creole ladies detested the Quadroon girls.

Of all that, remains only the Quadroon Ballroom, now the home of an order of negro nuns. Above the stairway where the Creole gallants and the Quadroon beauties went to chose and be chosen, and the foreign visitors to marvel, is the inscription, 'I have chosen rather to be an abject in the house of the Lord than to dwell in the temple with the sinners'. New Orleans must have Quadroons still, for it has folk of every imaginable hue and countenance, but as a delineated group the Quadroons have vanished, and so have the Creoles. The girl who sells you a tie or handles your telegram may be a Creole or may not. The American way of life has dispersed them or impressed them into the mass and they may only be studied still in such books as Mr. George W. Cable's *Old Creole Days*, where 'Tite Poulette, Jean-ah Poquelin and Madame Delphine live shadow-like again while they wait for destiny to absorb them.

The Vieux Carré remains a pleasant place at a quiet hour and it shows how drastically the trappings of life there have changed in a short time. I liked an inscription on a marble slab in the cathedral which, like a troubadour out of his century, lyrically commemorates 'Don Andres Almonaster y Roxas, native of Mayrena in the Kingdom of Andalusia, Chevalier of the Royal and Distinguished Spanish Order of Charles III,

Royal Regidor and Alferez of the Cabildo . . .', and much more. (It reminded me of a noble Spaniard once portrayed by Charles Hawtrey, who at each new introduction recited all his grandeeships and ever ended with, 'I 'ave ze right to wear my 'at in ze presence of ze King — but as 'e is not 'ere I take it off!')

The Place d'Armes (now called Jackson Square, a topical and typical renaming) by contrast contains the rusty remnant of what must surely be the first submarine (unless another, recovered from the Yellowstone Lake, was earlier; I never could learn by what fantastic means it came there). No man who has seen this one will ever marvel again at the midget submarines of today. It was built to contain two men who propelled it just beneath the surface by turning a handle; if they wished to reverse they turned the handle the other way. It carried a spear with a detachable point, to which a time-fused explosive float was attached. The theory of its use was to run the spear into the side of a wooden ship and then withdraw, leaving the spearhead in the hull and the charge near enough to blow a hole in it. I believe the Civil War ended before this Southern craft could be tested.

Lost or curious communities abound in the New Orleans country-side. There are backwoods communities of Holy Rollers, Sabines said to have come first as sailors from the Barbary Coast, Walloons whose ancestors served in Napoleon's armies and emigrated to America after his fall, and Acadians. The 'Cajuns (the name has been shortened, like soldier to sojer) are as mysterious as any. Their legends give them Armenian origins; they are supposed to have been a dispersed Christian sect which wandered over Europe, settled in Normandy in the Middle Ages, and migrated about 1750 to Nova Scotia. Their expulsion from there by the British and their flight to New Orleans is the theme of Longfellow's poem, 'Evangeline'.

Voodooism, with its attendant spells, charms, evil-eyeing and smelling-out, survives among the negroes, who brought it from Africa. In Durban once I knew a woman who could not keep native servants and found they fled from some chalk marks which her little boy had scribbled on the door of their quarters; they thought themselves 'tigati'd'. This same thing continues in darker corners of New Orleans today. The countryside around is that of the bayous, well suited to superstitions. It is a mysterious, secretive region, half land and half water, where countless creeks, rivulets and streams wander tortuously through swamp and marsh, and a smuggler or slave-runner who knew his business could paddle his boat to New Orleans and back by a hundred different ways. Today great motor-roads run through it to the lair of the famous pirate Jean Lafitte, at Grand Isle.

Something strange and fierce still invests the Louisiana air. Here arose a politico named Huey Long who in the 1930s bade fair to out-Roosevelt Roosevelt in his promises of milk-and-honey. He gained a great following and did not vainly boast when, soon after President Roosevelt's election, he wrote a remarkable book called *My First Days in the White House*, the text and illustrations of which showed Mr. Roosevelt as his subordinate. He might well have reached that house; his 'Share Our Wealth' programme titillated mass-nostrils even more than the Roosevelt 'New Deal' and he held out such Socialist-Communist promises as Full Employment, the Redistribution of Wealth and Social Security. However, M'Bongo was in the other camp, and Mr. Long was an embarrassing rival. He was shot (presumably by 'a madman') in the midst of his bodyguards.

I thought I had organized my journey very well when I reached its end, New Orleans, hale and hearty. I knew I had gone too far and too fast, slept and rested too little in great heat, and neglected meals; I had to, having so much to do in a short time. I counted on the sea-trip to make good anything that needed restoration and thought I had calculated the matter to a fraction. I was wrong, for Nemesis beat me at the post. A few days before I was to sail the old malarial affliction smote me, and brought dysentery with it. I was not very well housed, having reached New Orleans at the same time as a convention of some befezzed organization, so that rooms were hard to get. However, I had a bed and took my fever into it, hoping I should be able to struggle to the ship later.

Whatever else I might waste, I thought, I would not waste time. Sweating and almost disembowelled, I propped myself against pillows and began in quavering notes to sum up what I had seen and learned in America. . . .

PART TWO

BEHIND THE SCENE

CHAPTER I

THREE SERVITUDES

My experience is that a man may have many countries and one
that he loves: his own. I found much to respect and admire
everywhere I have been: the diligence, thrift and virility of
Germans, the poetry and patriotism of Poles, the taste and urbanity of
Frenchmen, the charm and friendliness of Austrians, the happy energy
of Belgians, the dour industriousness of Hollanders, the mellow
peasant culture of Croats and Slovaks, the indomitable nationhood of
Serbs and Bulgars, the brilliant valour of Greeks. I felt all these things
as part of a common Christian inheritance in which I equally shared.
Cracow Cathedral, the Cologne Dom, Saint Stephen's at Vienna and
Saint Peter's at Rome all meant as much to me as Saint Paul's and
Canterbury, and they meant the same thing, like the Saxon and Nor-
man citadels of England, Carcassonne and Avignon, and the Baltic
castles of the Teutonic knights. Europe's many wars did not alter that;
out of the quarrels of kings, popes and barons emerged ever a clear
purpose and an improving way of life, commonly Christian. The
century of Armageddon, I believe, is to show whether all that is to be
destroyed, and the American Republic might have the greatest part in
deciding the issue.

In America, again, I felt this underlying kinship of Christian purpose,
but overlain now by much confusion. Its huge strength and energy
are as admirable as the good nature of the masses of its people, once
reached, and the beauty (and especially in the South, the charm) of its
women. Americans are filled with an urgent longing to fulfil the
American Dream and a deep perplexity about its shape. A great quantity of idealism, faith, hope and charity is stored up in a younger
generation, particularly, which feels spiritually lost and is the easy prey
of misleaders. The great question, which may decide the outcome of
Armageddon, is whether this stored energy will be put to continuing
the 2000-year process, the splendid results of which are clear to see in
Europe, or to destroying it, and therewith the American Republic too.

The sharp visible contrast between the earlier Republic of Richmond, Washington and Boston and the later one of New York, Chicago and Los Angeles shows that the decision may be balanced on a razor edge.

In America a period of spiritual pessimism has followed on the century of optimism. This is not disproved by monetary wealth or the wearing of buttons with the words, 'I am proud to be an American'. It is not a native thing either, though the tendency towards violent emotional oscillations, which wise leadership could arrest, partly derives from the experience of the frontier period when 'mind and emotion became ingrowing and nature took its revenge in the form of occasional outbursts of violent excitement'; the *Epic*, speaking of a hundred years ago, says: 'The Camp Meeting is a key to much that we shall find even in present-day life, in a nation even yet emotionally starving.' This emotional unfulfilment, a product of the excessive concentration on material things, leaves a mass of unused spiritual energy drifting about in the Republic, like loose ballast in a ship. If the ballast can be moved to one side, the ship will list and possibly founder; for twenty years, at least, an organized effort has been made to achieve that effect. Two hundred and fifty years ago William Penn said, 'Either nations will be governed by God or they will be ruled by tyrants.' The Republic has been brought to the brink of that choice by the stealthy indoctrination of the unstable body of pent-up emotionalism with the teaching that it must destroy Christian nationhood and set up a pagan world tyranny, obliterating nations.

Thus the Manifest Destiny of 1850 has changed to a destiny nonmanifest in 1950. A hundred years ago the course seemed clear; westward the course of empire took its way. When the western limit was reached the vernacular question posed itself, 'Where do we go from here?' For some time past America has produced no William Penns to restate eternal truths. The leaderless mass stands irresolute, not yet quite a firmly welded nation, while many voices cry that America's manifest destiny now is to destroy all nations and Christianity with them; the thing is more subtly said but that is the purpose.

Hatreds, passions and prejudices are to some extent innate in man and may be reduced by wise leadership or inflamed by bad. As I have gone along I have seen that they are incited, in all countries, by organized forces from outside for the purpose of setting up the World State on the ruins of Christian nations. That key once found, the dark origins of our twentieth-century wars and the strange doublings their courses took are alike plain to understand. The parent organization goes back at least to the French Revolution; all European and American wars since then seem to some extent to have been deflected by it; the second war of this century clearly was brought almost completely under its control and so directed that its outcome left but one more stage of the grand design to be completed.

This is 'the deception of nations' mentioned in Revelation as an integral part of the process of Armageddon, if Biblical prophecy be true at all. The deception of the American nation was very great, despite the outer panoply of free nationhood which it retained for the nonce at the war's end. It was promised four freedoms, but in truth was surrendered to three servitudes.

The first of these is the now visible supremacy in its affairs of a new, foreign ambition: Political Zionism. No American politician of rank today dares challenge it, and this submission has apparently been brought about by what the founder of Political Zionism, Theodor Herzl, called 'the awful power of our purse'.

The second servitude is the permeation of American public life at all levels by a second foreign ambition, Soviet Communism. This is the other prong of the pincers described by Herzl: 'When we sink we become a revolutionary proletariat.' The edifice of State is weakened at the top by the power of the purse and at the middle by the infiltration of revolutionaries. This second process began in full force with the inauguration of President Roosevelt nearly twenty years ago. Demonstrably it led to the warping of major courses of State policy and has not yet been stopped, merely a little impeded. These two foreign ambitions, ostensibly separate but born in the same place, appear to meet in the central ambition of a World State, dominated by them. Plainly they intend, if they can, to bend the strength of America to that end.

The third servitude, which helps the other two by corrupting political life at its foundations, as distinct from the higher citadels and departmental levels of power, is organized crime. The grasp of these three forces on the body politic and civic of the Republic, and their influence over the leaderless mass of spiritually starved opinion, are great enough to make America's destiny doubtful, no longer manifest, today.

This three-coiled captivity is not merely an American plight. It occurs in all the remaining nations of the Christian West and caused the ruin of those now submerged. It is greatest in America because, by all evidential signs, the emigration from Eastern Europe was mainly and deliberately directed thither, for the purposes of power. In England the visible, though unadvertised, power of Political Zionism is as great; no leading politician of any party (with one possible exception) now resists it. The deflection of major acts of State policy has been clear to see since the Balfour Declaration. Permeation of public life by Soviet Communism is considerable and official resistance to exposure as constant as in America. Organized crime, in the gaming, liquor and prostitution sense, is much less, though Eastern European figures often appear in the occasional revelations of attempted political corruption.

Essentially, the mass of Americans and of British are in the same boat now. I never in either country found any mass of people, outside the immigrant sections involved and those natives whom they suborn, who wanted American or British nationhood destroyed, or even merged. The broad legions of people wanted to retain their own national identity under the government of God, not to disappear serf-like into a shapeless mass under an Asiatic supremacy. The question whether either nation will be able to keep its individuality, now that the occult servitudes are so strong, is the one which the rest of this century of Armageddon will answer. The course and outcome of the Second War were portents as ominous as they could be for the result of any third one. Nevertheless, I found in both countries that widening masses of opinion were becoming alert to the shape and purpose of the grand design, and as to the final upshot, Saint Mark has a word for it: 'And ye shall hear of wars and rumours of wars. See that ye be not troubled, for all these things must come to pass but the end is not yet.'

Clearly the revolution of destruction will go on awhile, like a danc-ing dervish pirouetting towards his foaming collapse. After seeing

America I felt sure that every effort would be made to use American and British strength a third time to complete the ruin of the Christian area, and even to set these peoples against each other if the purpose could be better served that way. I felt equally sure that the grand design would fail at the last and that the end of the Christian two thousand years is not yet.

CHAPTER 2

ZIONISM PARAMOUNT

THE three forces which weaken the whole structure of American public life in effect serve the strongest among themselves, Political Zionism, which stands behind the seats of the mighty while the others work in lesser places, if to similar ends of power-over-politicians. The proof of this supremacy is to be found by a simple test: the extent to which public discussion is permitted.

It is entirely free in the matter of organized crime. No day passes but this is publicly debated somewhere in the Republic, in the tone that it is loathsome but normal, and not to be put down. Huey Long once said he could buy politicians 'like sacks of potatoes' and the daily talk in America is always full of such allusions to purchaseable men. The great argument, however, overlooks possible effects on national policy and treats the matter merely as one of local 'wide-openness' and parochial effects; possibly for that reason it is so free. That wireworm at the roots may imperil the whole plant is an aspect ignored.

The case of Communist permeation at the middle level is different. Public discussion is nominally free, so much so that the outer world receives an impression of 'a witch hunt' in constant progress. In truth public anxiety to know what goes on is combated, and powerful opposition is offered, from the highest places down, to the general demand for knowledge and action. The chorus of 'hysteria', 'Red-baiting' and 'anti-Semitism' reaches a higher crescendo each time some startling disclosure is achieved by persistent investigators. The great bulk of Americans have in fact been thwarted for seventeen years in their wish to have the stables cleansed (this is the case in England, too).

At the topmost level, a virtual ban on public discussion of Political Zionism proves the paramountcy of its sway in American affairs. As in England, the open expression of doubt about this territorial ambition, and support for it, has been almost driven underground in recent years. An imperial thrall has been laid on America in this matter. Traditional

274

Americans, whose forebears detested laws of lese-majesty and the genuflections of courts, now find their leaders performing an even humbler obeisance in this direction; like foremost politicians in England, they thus emulate those Rumanian nobles who long bowed to the Sultan's rule, vainly hoping to keep rank and possessions. The Soviet ban on 'anti-Semitism' (which was in effect a veto on public discussion of the origins of Communism) has in practice been extended to the British island and the American Republic in the matter of Political Zionism. It is lese-majesty in a new form and because of it present-day Americans and Englishmen do not as a rule see the grave future courses and penalties to which support of Political Zionism has committed them.

The way in which this overlordship has been imposed on the Christian West is wonderful and fascinating to study. It has all been done so quickly and with such sure skill (and if it is evil, as I think, may be to the good in the end, for the catfish in the tank reinvigorates other fish grown lazy). Political Zionism and Soviet Communism both grew up side by side in the Jewish areas of Czarist Russia, within Jewish families living beneath the same rooftree. The golden age was then dawning for Jews everywhere. When Napoleon convened their Grand Sanhedrin in Paris in 1807 the Rabbis declared that Israel existed only as a religion and aspired to no national resurrection. All over the world even Orthodox Jews, clamant for civic equalities, strenuously denied that Israel was a nation within the nations; Reform Judaism echoed this avowal. In England Jewry vowed that if England should emancipate the Jew it would fill his heart with consciousness of country; he would think, feel, fear and hope as an Englishman. America was opening to Jews and the same pledge was made on their behalf there.

It was true, too. Jews in those countries did lose much of the sense of being different which accompanied them, like a curse, down the centuries and caused them (not the Gentiles) to build ghettoes for themselves. They became good and happy Germans, Englishmen, Frenchmen, Americans. They seemed to confound those opponents of the Jewish Disability Bill in the English Parliament who argued that the Jews looked forward to the coming of a great deliverer, to their return to Palestine, to the rebuilding of their temple, to the revival of their ancient faith in its tribal form, and therefore would always consider England not as their country, but merely as their place of exile. Similarly, those events disproved for ever the lie that men inherently hate Jews.

Yet the English objectors, and Americans who raised warning voices against the new immigration, were made true prophets by the event. All that was gained was swept away by one section of the community of Russian Jews. They revived and imposed on Jews everywhere the old teaching, 'Do not cultivate strange lands, soon you will cultivate your own; do not attach yourself to any land, for thus you will be unfaithful to the memory of your native land; do not submit to any king, for you have no master but the Lord of the Holy Land, Jehovah; do not scatter among the nations, you will forfeit your salvation and you will not see the light of the day of resurrection; remain such as you left your house; the hour will come and you will see again the hills of your ancestors, and those hills will then be the centre of the world, which will be subject to your power.'

The destructive achievement, in both the Zionist and Communist aspect, came from the Jews in the Russia of the Romanoffs; that is the key to understanding of the present and future. The Jews who made those two great movements were not Semites; on that point all qualified authorities agree; *their* ancestors never knew 'the hills of your ancestors'. They were the descendants of a Russian, Mongol-Tartar race converted to Judaism in the seventh century whose remote forebears never trod Palestinian soil. Their two destructive exploits are astounding, considered as feats, like those of weight-lifters, but still are less extraordinary than the submission to them of leading Gentile politicians in the Christian West during the last forty years.

The tale, more fantastic than any of the Arabian Nights, is most plainly told in Dr. Chaim Weizmann's *Trial and Error*. It shows the soil where the two destructive movements grew, to their present fiery bloom, in the last decades of the past century. There was a little White Russian village 'within the Pale', with 400 or 500 Russian families and under 200 Jewish ones. The Jews kept to their own streets of their own wish, so that Jews and Gentiles were strangers to each other's ways of thought, dreams, religions, festivals and even languages. All buildings were of wood save two of brick, the church and 'the house of the richest Jew'. The Pale of Settlement was 'a prison house for Jews'; yet the typical Jewish family depicted had a house of seven rooms and a garden and some acres of land, the father employed fifty or sixty Russians in the season. There was no starvation or any pogroms in the place though pogroms were heard of elsewhere (the student of these things will often come across such statements). Russian servants were employed and the matriarch of the family went each summer to distant Bohemia or Bavaria.

It does not look too dire a picture. Yet within this Jewish household, in the 1880s, was ferment. The 'Return' was in the air, 'a vague deep-rooted Messianism, a hope which would not die'. Such families were deeply divided among themselves, so that brothers and sisters often would not speak to each other. The line of dispute was between those young Jews who wanted to overthrow the Czardom and gain power inside Russia (the later Communists) and those who wanted to recreate a Jewish nation in Palestine (the later Zionists). The matriarch said, well, if the revolutionary son were right they would all be happy in Russia, and if the Zionist one were correct she would go to Palestine, so all would be well either way.

It is a vivid picture of the beginnings of the things we now experience. It is given as one of Jewish misery, but the Russians seem to have been much worse off. In *From Pharaoh to Hitler* Mr. Bernard J. Brown, writing as a Jew, says, 'When the Jews talk about oppression they are mistaken in assuming that they have been the only oppressed people on earth. As late as 1860 there were over 23,000,000 Christian peasants in Russia in abject slavery, while the Jews of that period in Russia followed their trades and professions, enjoying reasonable freedom and prosperity consistent with the form of government and general economic conditions prevalent at that time.' This Russia, nevertheless, the younger Jews, to judge from Dr. Weizmann, wished to destroy. True, a third body of Jewish opinion existed, that of the Jews who wished to 'assimilate' themselves, like Jews in the West. Throughout Dr. Weizmann's book these Jews appear as more detestable than Gentile 'anti-Semites'.

At that time the victory of those Jews, who wished to 'keep the peace of the city' in whatever land they dwelt, seemed certain. The whole history of the world for eighteen hundred years had been one of gradually improving humanity and enlightenment, broken only by what seemed the passing nightmare of the French Revolution, and in this upward process Czar Alexander II was a typical figure. It was he who in 1861 liberated the 23,000,000 Russian serfs, so that a new dawn broke for the innumerable races and faiths of Russia. A reconciler and unifier, he was killed at the decisive moment, like Lincoln, the Archduke Franz Ferdinand, Alexander of Yugoslavia and Count Bernadotte.

Repressive measures followed against the population generally, including Jews. The masses were resentful and, says Dr. Weizmann, 'among the Jews this first folk awakening had two facets, the revolutionary, mingling with the general Russian revolt, and the Zionist nationalist'. This, then, was the actual birth of twins long in gestation, Soviet Communism and Political Zionism. (At the Communist revolution of 1917, however, Jewish revolutionaries did not 'mingle with the general Russian revolt'; they led it exclusively, and from that day to this the leadership of Soviet Communism has continued to be predominantly Russian-Jewish, while that of Political Zionism has been almost exclusively so, though it is represented as a movement of *all* Jews throughout the world.)*

* The first Communist Government, according to the American Ambassador in Moscow in 1918, consisted of ninety per cent of Russian-Jewish revolutionaries returned from America, and the ban on anti-Semitism, with a death penalty, clearly identified the regime. In the following thirty years Russian-Jewish dominance in international Communism was repeatedly shown by sporadic disclosures in Canada and America, and this continues today. In Russia itself this dominance appears to have persisted up to the present time, though masked by the withdrawal of recognizably Russian-Jewish figures from the more visible places of power in the Soviet Union. In 1946 an American Jewish authority, Mr. Louis Levine, reported at Chicago after a visit to Moscow, that many of the high ranking government officials were Russian-Jewish: 'They did not look Jewish but they spoke to me privately in Hebrew or Yiddish.' Russian-Jews, or men of Russian-Jewish origins, predominated in the two short-lived Communist governments of 1918-19 in Hungary and Bavaria, which fell because the Red Army, on that occasion, was not present to enforce their survival; they reappeared in the Communist Government imposed on Hungary by the Red Army after 1945. The dominant Russian-Jewish influence in the Government foisted by the same means on Poland was remarked by an American Ambassador, Mr. Arthur Bliss Lane, and an English M.P., Major Tufton Beamish, in books published in 1948 and 1949 and many other observers. The same thing happened in Rumania. In Soviet-controlled Eastern Germany, according to a Zionist newspaper,

In the decade following Czar Alexander's murder Dr. Weizmann went to school at Pinsk. He did not personally experience pogroms but 'did not need to live in the midst of pogroms' to know that 'the Gentile world was poisoned'; indeed, he knew little of Gentiles but from the first they were to him 'the symbols of menacing forces'. The frame of mind seems clearly innate, not the result of thought or experience; it might fairly be called 'anti-Gentilism', an emotional antipathy and not a reasoned antagonism. It coloured his approach to school-going: 'The acquisition of knowledge was not for us so much a normal process of education as the storing up of weapons in an arsenal by means of which we hoped later to be able to hold our own in a hostile world.'

The world, however, was not hostile to Jews. All doors were open to them, and that seems to have disquietened Dr. Weizmann more than anything. At Pinsk (where he had 'no social contact with Gentiles', who were a minority of the population) he found many assimilationist Jews. The Zionists were becoming compact and began to fight 'assimilation'. Thus Dr. Weizmann locates the actual sources of the thing which overclouds the world today; he says the foundation layers of the Zionist State are Pinsk and Vilna, Odessa and Warsaw, and many lesser-known Jewish communities of those Eastern European stretches; that is Russian Jewry.

Dr. Weizmann disliked Czarist Russia so much that, graduated at Pinsk, he crossed the German frontier clandestinely and went to Pfungstadt. He found there something previously unrealized by him; that German Jewry was exerting itself to be German (he calls this 'a

'life has brought changes for the better; not a few Jews today occupy high positions in the Government and Administration, positions which no Jew had ever before held in Germany . . . The Supreme Judge in the Eastern Sector of Berlin is a Jew and so are several senior judges in the provinces outside Berlin.' Could the facts be ascertained, I think most of these men would prove to be Russian-Jews or of Russian-Jewish origins. The first Israeli Government consisted of eight members, all but one born in Russia or Russian-Poland. The Communist and Zionist movements, therefore, appear both to be still under the paramount control of one section of Jewry, the non-Semitic Russian-Jews or Jews of Russian antecedents, which now, in fact, rules over most of Asia and a large portion of Europe and extends a powerful influence through America and England. A clear picture of the whole process, however, cannot be gained without considering the fact that Gentile politicians in Christian lands have decisively helped it, and that anti-Zionist Jews have probably opposed it more strenuously, though as yet no more effectively, than non-Jewish leaders anywhere.

queer chapter in Jewish history'). He obtained a post at a Jewish boarding school and decided that its principal, who held such views, was an intellectual coward and a toady. The sight of Jews entirely free seems to have appalled him. He was 'lonely and desperately homesick' for Pinsk, for the little village in the prison-like Pale! 'It was better in Pinsk, though Pinsk was Russia.' He longed for the separate, ghetto-like life of the Jews there, and returned. Pinsk seems indeed to have been a good place for Jews, because his four years of military service were due 'but I managed to talk my way out of the army in a special interview with the local military commander, a decent and cultured Russian who thought it a pity to have my education interrupted!'

Later he went to Berlin, Freiburg, Geneva and other places, where he found Jewish students from Russia increasing in number and revolutionary fervour. They were militant cells engaged in fighting 'the assimilationist revolutionary movement, not on its revolutionary but on its assimilationist side'. This means that they worked *for* revolution and *against* the reconciliation of Jew and Gentile, which they saw as an obstacle to revolution. Nevertheless, the 'assimilationist' Jews remained aloof: 'I cannot say that anything resembling real intimacy ever grew up between the Russian-Jewish student colony and the Jewish community of Berlin; the gap between the two worlds was almost unbridgable.'

This great gulf was in time to be bridged by Mr. Lloyd George, Lord Balfour, later British leaders, President Wilson, President Roosevelt and President Truman, and the Jews who were happy in those Western countries were to be driven back across the bridge into the clutch of a tribal nationalism which they did not desire.

In the next ten years, as student and then teacher at those Christian universities, Dr. Weizmann learned 'the technique of propaganda and the approach to the masses'. Meanwhile a westernized Jew, Dr. Theodor Herzl, emerged as the visible leader of the conspiracy now grown into an open movement; by publishing *The Jewish State* he first proclaimed the *territorial* ambition. Not one Gentile in a million, probably, even noticed it. World Jewry, which knew what it would mean, was put in the condition of a dovecote invaded by a cat. This was the reversal of all that Orthodox and Reform Jewry alike had promised; in the end it would mean the ruin of the achievements of centuries.

In Dr. Herzl first appeared the phenomenon of this century, the Zionist operator on whose knee Gentile politicians sat as puppets. Rabbi Elmer Berger says, 'With Herzl that group of Jews which committed itself to Zionism and acknowledged him as its leader entered a peripatetic kind of diplomacy, which took it into many chancelleries and parliaments, exploring the labyrinthine and devious ways of international politics in a part of the world where political intrigue and secret deals were a byword.' Dr. Herzl began successfully to court what Mr. Bernard J. Brown describes as 'the false praise of those Christians who, for one reason or another, seek Jewish favour'.

Herzl used words which seemed of the most foolish pretension at the time, but were modest in comparison with what Political Zionism later achieved. When his first important Jewish backer died, Baron de Hirsch, Herzl wrote, 'Hirsch dies and I enter on negotiations with princes.'* He hoped to buy for twenty million pounds a charter for Palestine from the Sultan of Turkey, who ever needed money, but that fell through. Seeking an interview with the Kaiser, he promised 'the diminution of radical' (that is, revolutionary) 'propaganda in Europe, in proportion to the development of national effort among Jews', but when the Kaiser delayed in procuring Palestine for him Herzl wrote threateningly to him, 'If our work miscarries, hundreds of revolutionaries will at a single bound join the revolutionary parties'. He told one of the Rothschilds, who feared Political Zionism, 'I will start a great agitation in which it will be difficult to maintain order . . . You think it is a misfortune to operate with masses; consider well, would it not be a greater misfortune if I set the masses in motion by a tumultuous agitation?'

Herzl in such words precisely foretells, as if by divine or demoniac

*A bright sidelight on the methods used in the 'negotiations with princes' (and, after their disappearance, with politicians) which led to the rise of Zionism to its present status of a world power: Crown Prince Rudolf of Austria, heir to the doomed Habsburg throne, committed suicide on January 30th, 1887. A few weeks before, wishing to make provision for a favourite woman friend, Mitzi Kaspar, he obtained a loan of 100,000 gulden 'from the banker, Baron Hirsch, in return for an act of friendliness he had performed in December, when he invited the banker to meet the Prince of Wales' (the future King Edward VII). From documents in the secret archives of the Imperial Court at Vienna, quoted by Count Carl Lonyay in *Rudolf* (Hamish Hamilton, 1950).

revelation, the working of the machine he built; the crushing of Gentile nations between the power of the purse and the revolutionary masses, both controlled from the same source. He used the famous phrase about 'England being the point where the Archimedean lever must be applied', and England was so used (though not by him) to prise open the oyster. After Herzl's death his threats became realities. He failed, or did not succeed quickly enough for those whose passions he aroused; he seems at the end to have become terrified of the thing he began. When he called the First Zionist Congress he found he was no longer master of his machine. 'There rose before our eyes', he wrote, 'a Russian Jewry the strength of which we had not even suspected . . . They represented the views and sentiments of the five million Jews of that country . . . What a humiliation for us, who had taken our superiority for granted!'

Russian Jewry took over, as Russian Jewry took over Soviet Communism, and Russian Jewry remains the master-force today. Herzl became a discredited Messiah. In 1903 he produced at last an offer of Uganda, from the British Government. I cannot recall any comparable donation in history, but it was derisively rejected by the Russian Jews, who now controlled a project which was gathering momentum like a wheel rolling downhill. Herzl relieved his extremists of further annoyance by dying the next year, at forty-four, an opportune death, for by sponsoring the Uganda scheme he made himself, if not quite a reconciler and peacemaker, then a 'deviationist' (in the modern idiom). Much worse than that, during a visit to Moscow he warned the Political Zionists against harbouring revolutionaries in their ranks! His death occurred at the decisive moment.

At that time Dr. Weizmann, now thirty, poor, little known outside Zionist circles, was on his way to England, which he chose as a country in which 'at least theoretically' a Jew might be allowed to live and work without let or hindrance (the words 'at least theoretically', published in 1949, seem mildly amusing in the light of all he was able to achieve; in this case practice more than vindicated theory). He went to Manchester with but a letter of introduction to a professor at the University there. He was 'very warmly received', given the use of a laboratory at a nominal rent, access to 'the Holy of Holies' (the storeroom where fine chemicals were kept), 'consistent kindheartedness' from workmen 'who spared no effort to produce any piece of apparatus or furniture that I asked for'. Soon the services of two research men were added and, within the year, the offer of a research scholarship and a weekly lectureship. This seems fairly sympathetic treatment and was but the beginning of much warmer friendliness. However, in 1932 Dr. Weizmann, contemplating the wild beasts of the Kruger National Park in South Africa, observed, 'It must be a wonderful thing to be an animal in the South African game reserve; much better than being a Jew in Warsaw — or even in London.'

Manchester produces in its natives a moral outlook akin to the New England Conscience, or to the warm humanity of Bloomsbury and Greenwich Village. Its corporate soul responds like a harpstring to the cries of oppressed beings far away, and the farther away the better. In Manchester the newborn babe's first cry is not of pain, but already of righteous indignation about the lot of Thailanders, Vietnamese, Louisiana Negroes and Durban Indians; and the first words it says are probably 'Hands off Liberia'. If the world has a conscience (and *The Times* has said so), Manchester is its guardian. What Manchester thinks today the world thinks tomorrow and regrets the day after; the best way to foresee the tribulations of the future is to read a Manchester newspaper. Manchester adores strange causes and exotic visitors; they must be good, they've come so far, and the things they complain about are also delightfully distant. Manchester succumbs to such blandishments as charmingly as a mid-Western farmer's daughter of the 'nineties to a Chicago salesman.

Dr. Weizmann says he went to Manchester to keep out of Zionist politics for a time; but he landed in a most propitious place for their pursuit. He had what he himself calls an astounding experience of Manchester's illusions soon after he arrived. He shared his laboratory with a Japanese student and the two read with delight newspaper reports of Russian defeats in the war with Japan, then in progress; the Japanese because he was Japanese, Dr. Weizmann because he longed for his native Russia's defeat. Later he read in the Annual Report of the Director of Laboratories a proud eulogy of the international nature of the Manchester Chemical School and of the unifying influence of science, which made it possible for two mortal foes, 'a Japanese and a Russian, to work side by side there during the war!'

If the mere desire to do good in some vague way at someone else's expense qualifies for a place in heaven, the spirit of Manchester will one day be highly enthroned there; if the scrutiny of facts and right or wrong also belongs to the qualifying process, it will meet grave trouble at the turnstiles. At Manchester in 1906 the notion of transferring masses of East Europeans to Palestine made immediate appeal. The little matter of the Arabs there did not worry the Manchester Conscience, for the Arabs had not studied the technique of propaganda and the approach to masses or sent anyone to Manchester. The Chairman of the Conservative Party there was a Zionist (this is something which still bedevils both the large political parties in England and America). Before he was two years in England or had much command of English Dr. Weizmann found himself closeted with the lately defeated Prime Minister (and leader of the Conservative Opposition), Mr. Arthur Balfour, in an hotel room!

Does history show a more fateful meeting? A mysterious foreign ambition began to entwine itself round British policy. Dr. Weizmann, an obscure newcomer, found that Mr. Balfour had only 'the most naive and rudimentary notion of the movement' (a description which remained good twenty years later when Lord Balfour first saw the Arabian land where, in the meantime, he had undertaken to set up a National Home for the Zionists. Being warmly welcomed in Jewish parts of it, he said it reminded him of a general election tour, but with everybody on the same side. Against the wishes of his Zionist hosts, who wished 'to spare him as much as possible', he went on to Arab Damascus and had to be smuggled away from an infuriated mob and to a ship. He may thus at the last have suspected another side to the question; he had but a few years to live).

In 1911, after seven years, Dr. Weizmann's position at the university was worth £600 and his wife's, as medical officer for several city clinics, £350, so that the joint income, as he says, was considerable for those days and possibly vindicated England's comportment towards newcomers, Jewish or Gentile. On this account, perhaps, the German Jews in Manchester were contentedly assimilated. Dr. Weizmann,

however, felt most at home with the Russian Jews there; the old
English-Jewish families 'might just as well have belonged to another
world'. Russian Jews predominated in the Jewish community and a
strong Political Zionist group took shape around Dr. Weizmann in
Manchester. In 1907 he first saw the country of his ambitions; he
found it a dolorous one where 80,000 Jews lived, in poverty and amity,
with some 550,000 Arabs. All that was to be changed.

The First War began in 1914; long-memoried readers may recall
that it appeared to be concerned with such matters as the rape of
Belgium, ending Prussian Militarism, and making the world safe for
democracy. At its start Baron Edmond de Rothschild told Dr. Weizmann that it would spread to the Middle East, where things of great
significance to Political Zionism would occur. The first few months
saw another fateful meeting; Dr. Weizmann, by chance he says, was
presented to Mr. C. P. Scott, editor of the *Manchester Guardian*. Mr.
Scott, whose ideas about the matter may have been as rudimentary as
Mr. Balfour's, asked typically Mancunian questions ('Are you a
Pole?') and was told of Dr. Weizmann's hatred of Russia, then England's powerful ally. This did not deter him from immediate enthusiasm. Thereafter when he went to London Dr. Weizmann habitually
met him at the station, Mr. Scott's usual greeting being, 'Now, Dr.
Weizmann, tell me what you want me to do for you'.

This led to a third fateful meeting. When the war was still four
months young Mr. Scott took Dr. Weizmann to breakfast with Mr.
Lloyd George (Mr. Asquith was then Prime Minister and, learning of
a scheme to transplant Eastern Europeans to Palestine, said it was
fantastic). Mr. Lloyd George told Dr. Weizmann that a leading
English Jew, Mr. Edwin Montagu, would bitterly oppose the project.
Indeed, the mass of Jews everywhere, other than those from Russia,
were firmly against it. At this time the curious process began; wherever
established Jews resisted an enterprise which they thought perilous to
Jewry, Gentile leaders turned against them. The little-known Dr.
Weizmann from Russia was more kindly heard than the eminent
spokesmen of Jewish communities established in England for centuries.

Mr. Lloyd George sent Dr. Weizmann again to Mr. Balfour, who
apparently first asked an obvious question: how a friend of England

could be so anti-Russian when Russia fought on our side? Dr. Weizmann spoke of pogroms and expulsions which made 'every Russian victory a horror for the Jews' and this seems to have satisfied Mr. Balfour, who said, 'It is a great cause you are working for. You must come again and again'. Such are the things which secretly go on in war-time. This was in 1914, when the Russian offensive saved Paris. I remember the enormous casualties the Russians suffered; without that effort the Allies might have been lost.

Whilst Czarist Russia in the east took the brunt off bowed French and British shoulders in the west, Dr. Weizmann told British leaders of his hatred for Russia. The very name of Political Zionism was unknown to the fighting-men or the watching masses, but behind the scenes this new ambition took root and stem in London. Dr. Weizmann says his meetings with Mr. Scott, Mr. Lloyd George and Mr. Balfour were but 'the beginnings of our discoveries of friends'. The thing, unless one looks for baser motives, seems today only explicable as an infatuation among public men. Political Zionism in the next few years made immense strides, and if they were not even greater this was due to the opposition of Jews, the mass of whom stood everywhere as firm as they could behind Gentile politicians who went down like ninepins.

After two years of war English Jewry still refused to demand more than 'equal rights' with the Arabs and 'reasonable facilities for immigration and colonization' in the event that the war should put Palestine in the hands of England or France. At the Foreign Office Mr. Lucien Wolf (until then accepted as the secular spokesman of British Jewry) protested that Political Zionism was a purely East European movement. He and his kind fought vainly against Gentile politicians who seem to have been possessed. When Mr. Lloyd George became Prime Minister, and prepared for the fatal deed, he told Dr. Weizmann, 'I know that with the issuance of this Declaration I shall please one group of Jews and displease another. I have decided to please your group because you stand for a great idea.' These words will first be fully tested when the great idea reaches its full consummation and I think that may not now be long.

Dr. Weizmann, curiously, wrote: 'We hate equally anti-Semitism and philo-Semitism; both are degrading.' If he meant by this anti-Zionism and pro-Zionism he ought to have hated Messrs. Scott, Balfour and Lloyd George. The circle of these champions widened and its multiplying members remained 'completely baffled' by the opposition of British Jews. The then editor of *The Times*, says Dr. Weizmann, expressed intense annoyance because anti-Zionists wrote letters of protest to his paper (in later years such expostulations were rebuked as 'anti-Semitism'). Lord Milner publicly reproved those who thought Palestine should remain what it was, Arab. Mr. Philip Kerr (later Lord Lothian and an Ambassador to America), wrote contemptuously to Dr. Weizmann, from Russia, of 'so-called British Jewry' and said no amount of talk by Mr. Edwin Montagu 'or people like him' would stem the tide.

This gestation of the thing now accomplished is fantastic to contemplate. Dr. Weizmann went to the Admiralty and found that his Zionist work thrust itself insistently into his labours there. He converted Sir Mark Sykes (Chief Secretary to the War Cabinet), Mr. Leopold Amery (later to be Colonial Secretary; Mr. Amery was 'incensed when leading Jews attacked the scheme openly'), Mr. Ormsby-Gore, Lord Robert Cecil; the slip became a landslide. He found his work easy then because it was in the realm of the abstract; he says, in memorable words, that 'the great difficulties, like the Arab problem, had not yet come to the fore'. In the later events the Arabs, and pledges made to them, never came much to the fore.

America, too, was now being roped in. The Jewish Question having been solved by the centuries, a new Jewish Question was thrown up there, the Political Zionist one, and the Zionist leader, Mr. Brandeis, was appointed Adviser to President Wilson on the Jewish Question; the era of The Advisers began. Then General Smuts, from South Africa, appeared in London and heartily assured Dr. Weizmann that something would be done about Palestine and the Jewish people. By this time a growing family of powerful men, freed from the peace-time checks of public debate, accepted the Russian Jews, the Political Zionists from Eastern Europe, as 'the Jewish people'.

Thus Politican Zionism, which in 1880 was but a matter of violent inter-family dispute between Jewish-revolutionary and Jewish-nationalist sons in Jewish homes in Russia, by 1917 was imperiously presented to the British and American governments as the demand of the entire Jewish people. Still the great masses knew nothing of it and thought the war they fought was for the liberty of men and nations. They could not dream that one of its primary purposes was to drive a small, harmless and allied people out of its native land and instal East Europeans in their place.

They were never consulted about that, though their leaders secretly vied in fervour for this cause. Dr. Weizmann says, 'Our difficulties were not connected with the first rank statesmen. These had, for by far the greatest part, always understood our aspirations, and their statements in favour of the Jewish National Home really constitute a literature. It was always behind the scenes, and on the lower levels, that we encountered an obstinate, devious and secretive opposition.' The words 'behind the scenes' and 'secretive' are notable, for the masses knew very little of the methods by which 'first rank statesmen' were won. However, Dr. Weizmann did not invariably find first rank statesmen so admirable. In a much later connection (the Czechoslovak crisis of 1938) he refers to Mr. Neville Chamberlain's 'profound ignorance' and says he does not know if it was 'typical for the British ruling class, but judging from its behaviour at that time it either did not know, or else it did not wish to know because the knowledge was inconvenient, disturbing and dangerous'. The three adjectives might equally apply to the first rank statesmen in England and America who took up Political Zionism; either they did not know or did not wish to know whither that would lead, and their uninstructed peoples were dragged along with them.

Of those 'first rank statesmen' who in 1917 prepared the first triumph of Political Zionism Lord Robert Cecil (Assistant Secretary for Foreign Affairs) is exceptionally important because he alone (Dr. Weizmann says), 'saw it in its true perspective as an integral part of world stabilization. To him the re-establishment of a Jewish Homeland in Palestine and the organization of the world in a great federation were complementary features of the next step in the management of human affairs.'

I do not know, but doubt, if Lord Robert Cecil ever explained the matter to his own people like that, but in these words a much bigger nigger pops out of the woodpile. In them the 'National Home' no longer appears as an all-satisfying end in itself, as it was first presented to be; or even as the basis of a future Zionist State, which it was denied to be. The words contain the true shape of the whole ambition, as I believe it to be, for they speak of *world* stabilization, of a *world* federation, and of *managing mankind*. If this future world federation is to surmount nations, why had it to begin with the creation of a new nation, the Zionist one, unless the 'management of human affairs' is to be assumed by that one?

In 1917, with the First War in its fourth year and the masses still all oblivious of such large schemes for their future, the secret process suddenly accelerated and cleared, as if a developing fluid abruptly brought out the outlines of a negative. Either all the fates conspired, or the Political Zionists were then strong enough, to displace any front rank statesmen who still resisted and to supplant them with men obedient to their will. Mr. Asquith, the only important objector remaining, had been overthrown, and one may now doubt whether deficiencies of leadership were the cause. The real reason may have been certain secret Anglo-French treaties about Palestine which might have preserved the Arabs from their approaching fate. President Wilson was prompted sternly to denounce 'secret treaties' (Americans retained a holy horror of these two words until President Roosevelt, in 1944-45, made secret treaties on a really stupendous scale) and Mr. Asquith went. The new government was made up of men to whom, apparently, Political Zionism was by now a foremost issue of the war (I recall with humility the importance I then attached to the French front, above which I flew). Mr. Lloyd George was Prime Minister, Mr. Philip Kerr his secretary, Mr. Balfour Foreign Secretary, Lord Robert Cecil Assistant Foreign Secretary, and so on. Lord Robert Cecil had been assured that 'a Jewish Palestine would be a safeguard to Palestine, in particular in respect to the Suez Canal'. This put the matter on a plane below mere righteousness, but even at that the final test has yet to be made and might be interesting to watch.

Another significant thing happened while the fateful issue was in the balance. General Smuts, arrived in London, was acclaimed as the symbolic figure of Boer-British reconciliation. The public masses in South Africa and England knew nothing of his admiration for Political Zionism, and hardly its name. He was invited to join the British War Cabinet, a proceeding without precedent in the Commonwealth which his Boers greatly resented. He did join it, in a status never clearly defined, and was offered the command in Palestine by Mr. Lloyd George who (General Smuts says) 'was very anxious that a determined offensive should be made in Palestine ... He was strongly under the impression that *Palestine should be made a decisive feature of the war*' (my italics). Learning from the military authorities that they counted the enterprise of little *military* value General Smuts refused the command, but in the Cabinet presented his plan for such a campaign, which was eventually undertaken. Thus as the First War drew to its end Palestine was made 'a decisive feature' and British Commonwealth troops, not for military reasons, were used to conquer the territory of the future Zionist State.

The great moment thus approached. To the last British Jewry repudiated Political Zionism, to the 'downright annoyance' of the editor of *The Times*, who spent 'a good hour' discussing with Dr. Weizmann 'the kind of leader which was likely to make the best appeal to the British public' and produced 'a magnificent presentation of the Zionist case'. In such circumstances may leading articles about major issues sometimes be written. By August 1917 Dr. Weizmann was able to inform Mr. Felix Frankfurter (later esteemed as an adviser by Presidents Roosevelt and Truman) that the only remaining obstacle was 'outside interference — *entirely from Jews!*' (these delightful words about outside interference by Jews in Political Zionism are Dr. Weizmann's). Before the decisive Cabinet meeting Dr. Weizmann wrote to the Foreign Office to protest against the anti-Zionist view being urged at it by 'a prominent Englishman of the Jewish faith'. At the last moment President Wilson cabled support for the Zionist cause and the British and American Jews were finally undone.

The overt, fatal deed followed; the Balfour Declaration fathered a 'Jewish National Home' in Palestine and, as I think, tethered the British and American peoples to the ambition of a Zionist-controlled world federation which lay behind it. The Declaration hardly indented the consciousness of the British and American masses and they still do not see its full consequences for themselves. Its immediate meaning was only clear to the Arabs and to British officials and soldiers in Palestine. It led to thirty years of Arab risings and then to an Arab war against aggression, broken by overwhelming force. During that period Commissions were repeatedly sent to Palestine to find the reason for so much trouble and each in turn reported the blindingly obvious; that the native population objected to enforced displacement by Eastern European newcomers. Similarly (as Dr. Weizmann records) administrators who went to Palestine favourably inclined towards Political Zionism 'as an almost universal rule . . . turned against us in a few months'.

The front rank statesmen, who thus prepared their peoples' future tribulations, were happy. Lord Balfour thought the Declaration the great achievement of his life. Lord Robert Cecil (one of the founders of the League of Nations) thought the National Homeland of equal importance with the League (soon to die). President Wilson and Mr. Lloyd George announced that the National Home would be the foundation of a Jewish Commonwealth, so that, the war being over, the broad masses were at length able to perceive this object of it. General Smuts said, 'One of the great objects we fought for in the war was to provide a national home for the Jewish people'. The people concerned, however, were never told that this was an object, let alone a great object, of the war they went into. Nor was a similar objective ever announced as the aim of the Second War; but events show that this was the fact and the peoples might logically assume that a primary object of any third war, though cloaked at the start, would be the expansion of the Zionist State, and the imposition of a 'world federation' and a new 'management' on mankind. In the aftermath of the Second War such aims, earlier concealed, were much more openly admitted by leading politicians, and little room for doubt remains about their future attitude.

The last day of the First War saw Dr. Weizmann, the unknown immigrant of twelve years before, lunching with Mr. Lloyd George while delirious joy filled the streets outside. After lunch the Prime Minister (now almost forgotten) was borne from Number Ten on the crowd's shoulders, watched from the window by Dr. Weizmann, whom the crowd would not have recognized, if it saw him. That strange scene appears to me still to have topical significance. The leading men of the Christian West had identified Political Zionism, a movement of the revolutionary Russian Jews, with World Jewry everywhere and forced the rising generation of Jews into this grasp. They undid the work of centuries and renewed the ferment in Jewry just when it was allayed. In doing this they scouted and affronted their own established Jewish communities. If any statesmen survive, or are growing up now, their task will be to undo what was done, and they will need the help of God and the prayers of men for that.

In that first stage of the great plan leading British politicians, editors, soldiers seem to have succumbed as if to hypnosis, and lost even patriotic prudence during the greatest war in history. Vainly did the British Jews point out that the Political Zionists were 'an international organization which included different, even enemy, elements' and refuse all truck with them. No such objections, Dr. Weizmann recalls, 'ever occurred to the many Englishmen who were encouraging us so generously in those days'.

The explanations which leading men later gave for their submission to the Russian Zionists were casual or misleading. Mr. Lloyd George gave contradictory accounts of motive. One was that the promise of a National Home was expected to rally Jewish opinion throughout the world to the Allied cause; in fact the bulk of British, American and German Jews were opposed to Political Zionism, and this remains true today to an extent only lessened by the fact that new Jewish generations have been told by British and American leaders that they consider Political Zionism to be The Jewish People; their situation is analogous to that of the Eastern European countries which had Communist governments forced on them by the Christian West. Another Lloyd Georgian version is that he promised the National Home to Dr. Weizmann, in the manner of Napoleon bestowing a kingdom, in gratitude for a new method of producing acetone, a substance much needed during that war. Dr. Weizmann (who received the cash payment customary for such services, in this case ten thousand pounds) refers to this statement with gentle irony, saying that 'history does not deal in Aladdin's lamps'. He also mentions that Mr. Lloyd George, in memoirs designed for the masses, said he first met Dr. Weizmann and became interested in Political Zionism in 1917 (the year of the Declaration); whereas, says Dr. Weizmann, they met long before that and Mr. Lloyd George's 'advocacy of the Jewish Homeland long predated his accession to the Premiership'.

Slowly truth emerges, with the passing of the years. A vital, or lethal, twist was given to the declared aims and purposes of the First War and this distortion continued, with ever graver effects, through the intervening years and into the Second War. Even on the low level of material advantage the thing proved a curse to the British. The politicians and editors had been told, and so informed the masses, that, the National Home once established, 'England would have in the Jews the best possible friends'. Of Jews that might have been true, but the Political Zionists proved inveterate enemies, ever crying that England should enforce their rule in Palestine by arms and killing British soldiers and officials for twenty-five years because this was not done. No such murderer ever received the penalty for murder; in no land ever occupied by the British, for periods short or long, has that ever occurred before. During the twenty years of peace and six of war the authorities in London who sent men to do duty in Palestine intervened to protect their assailants if they were killed doing it. Nothing was allowed to stop the transplantation of Eastern Europeans to Palestine. The Arabs breed fast, however, and maintained superior numbers. Clearly a Zionist majority could never be achieved unless in the confusion of another world war (which the masses thought inconceivable). Hitler arrived opportunely.

When he began to do things obviously planned to make another great war certain the Palestine adventure had broken down. Without open war the National Home could not be converted into a Zionist State. One of the last administrators, Mr. Malcolm Macdonald (the son of a Socialist Prime Minister) inherited the illusions about Political Zionism fashionable in political quarters but as Colonial Secretary, when he had to handle the actual substance of this dream, was quickly undeceived, like all others. His term of office produced the White Paper in 1939 which was a British Government's confession, after twenty-one years, of an earlier one's error; it was to restrict Zionist immigration and set up an Arab State in Arab Palestine within five years. Thereon the Second War broke out.

Just before that Mr. Churchill first appears in Dr. Weizmann's narrative as a champion of Political Zionism (his predecessor, Mr. Chamberlain, is criticized by Dr. Weizmann for speaking of Czechoslovakia as 'a little country far away of which we know very little'; however, the British supporters of Political Zionism harshly handled a little country still farther away of which they knew even less). By this time Dr. Weizmann was in touch with a new generation of first rank statesmen, most of the earlier ones being dead. The day of the great debate in Parliament, for and against the White Paper, found him lunching with Mr. Churchill, who was to speak, 'of course', against it. Mr. Churchill read his speech to his guests and asked if Dr. Weizmann had any changes to suggest.

Then the Second War began. Initially it was supposed to be about Poland, Czechoslovakia and other countries, which in the event were treated as if they were the culprits, not the victims, with the connivance of the Western leaders. The British Island survived, and also the western half of Europe, which was left in such plight that it might at any time be overrun. In the Second War as in the First the twin causes born in Czarist Russia were served; the Communist Empire was aggrandized and the Zionist State set up, with the help of American and British arms. This phenomenon having appeared in two wars, its recurrence in larger form in any third one plainly could only be prevented by the exposure and disentanglement of Soviet Communist and Political Zionist influence from British and American State policy. Possibly this is not even feasible during the present generation of first rank statesmen, who seem to accept the thrall as a normal thing. However, new generations arise and tomorrow is also a day, as the Germans say.

During the Second War the weight of Political Zionist pressure gradually was transferred from London to Washington and applied there with practised skill, again at the decisive moment; America was drawn into the fatal coils. There was a sound reason for this. As Dr. Weizmann wrote, front rank politicians are easily won for Political

Zionism, but greater resistance is met on lower levels, where public servants seem to be of stouter timber and hold tenaciously to their conceptions of duty and principle. As the Second War began he met these hindrances in England.

He records that, very early in that war, he saw Mr. Churchill (not yet Prime Minister) at the Admiralty. He said he 'hoped Mr. Churchill would see the enterprise through' and the Political Zionists would want after the war to build up a State of three or four million Jews in Palestine; Mr. Churchill replied, 'Yes, indeed, I quite agree with that'. I do not think the British islanders, at that dire moment, ever knew that Mr. Churchill conceived this among the aims of the war; if he publicly said so I must have missed it. I knew he attacked the White Paper, but also recalled that in 1922, when he was Colonial Secretary, he officially announced that the National Home would *not* mean the 'imposition of a Jewish nationality upon the inhabitants of Palestine as a whole'; any expectations that it was to be made 'as Jewish as England is English' were impracticable and His Majesty's Government had no such aim, nor did they contemplate the disappearance or subordination of the Arabic population, language or culture in Palestine; the Balfour Declaration contained nothing that need cause alarm to the Arab population of Palestine.

Mr. Churchill became Prime Minister and in August 1940 (while the Battle of Britain yet impended) Dr. Weizmann wrote to him, urging that the Zionists in Palestine be accorded their 'elementary human right to bear arms' (a matter which involved the elementary human right of the Arabs to remain in Palestine). Much later the Zionists amassed many arms, in secret ways, and used them against the British to such effect that the responsible Minister recorded a serious interference with the British war effort. At this moment, however, authorities at lower levels proved resistant and Dr. Weizmann refers to 'the frustrations we encountered'.

Mr. Churchill's memoirs are unexpectedly illuminating at this point. Without much comment he reproduces his own documents which show that long before August 1940 he urgently wanted to arm the Zionists. These papers appear in the volume called *Their Finest Hour* and perusal of them made me wonder whose finest hour that was. Mr.

Churchill took office on May 10th, 1940, and says he was conscious of a profound sense of relief. At last he had the authority to give directions over the whole scene; 'I felt as if I were walking with Destiny, and that all my past life had been but a preparation for this hour and this trial.' I remember that hour very well and doubt if any of the cornered and almost defenceless British Islanders, save possibly a few initiates, thought the man who took on the burden could have room in his heart or mind for anything but the island's survival or fall. Nevertheless, Mr. Churchill, at such a moment, diligently strove to further the Political Zionist cause, so far away.

He acquired 'the chief power in the State' on May 10th, as France disintegrated. By May 23rd, as disasters accumulated, he was instructing his Colonial Secretary that 'The main and almost the sole aim in Palestine at the present time is to liberate the eleven battalions of excellent regular troops who are now tethered there; for this purpose the Jews should be armed in their own defence and properly organized as speedily as possible'. On May 29th, while the evacuation from Dunkirk was at its height, he repeated the order more urgently. That seemed fair enough at a moment when the British Army looked likely to be lost in France. He reiterated the order on June 2nd, by which time the salvation of the British Army had changed the situation. On June 6th he complained of military opposition to this order, saying eight battalions were needed to build up a new expeditionary force and he had only agreed to wait for eight Indian battalions to relieve them if these were sent at once. At the end of June he complained of 'difficulties' with two Ministers, particularly Lord Lloyd, the Colonial Secretary responsible, 'who was a convinced anti-Zionist and pro-Arab. I wished to arm the Jewish colonists'.

I may be odd, but when I look back on those tense days of Dunkirk I still find it hard to understand that, at such a moment, a British Government could find time to think about arming the Political Zionists in Palestine. On June 28th Mr. Churchill sent a memorandum to Lord Lloyd in terms which must be rare between a Prime Minister and a responsible colleague. He said the large number of troops in Palestine were 'the price we have to pay for the anti-Jewish policy which has been persisted in for some years' (the policy was that enunciated in the statement of a Colonial Secretary, Mr. Churchill, in 1922). If the Jews were properly armed, he said, those troops would become available 'and there would be no danger of the Jews attacking the Arabs' (in 1950 this observation appears sanguine). He thought it was 'little less than a scandal that a time when we are fighting for our lives these very large forces should be immobilized in support of a policy which commends itself only to a section of the Conservative Party'. He had hoped, added Mr. Churchill, that Lord Lloyd 'would take a broad view of the Palestine situation . . . I could certainly not associate myself with such an answer as you have drawn up for me' (presumably a Zionist spokesman in parliament had been prompted to put down a Question asking why the British troops were not withdrawn and the Zionists armed, or some such thing).

In Ju y again (while the British Islander thought presumably his lonely plight to be an all-exclusive preoccupation), Mr. Churchill 'wished to arm the Jews at Tel Aviv, who with proper weapons would have made a good fight against all comers. Here I encountered every kind of resistance.' Clearly, 'difficulties at lower levels' arose; men responsible or on the spot, with a sense of duty, are not easily to be convinced that such a course as the one now proposed is right. Apart from that, the reference to 'proper weapons' is striking. At that moment the weapons of the British Army had been lost in France and the British Island was almost unarmed (I well remember the long search I had to find a forty-year-old pistol, which none other would buy, in a second-hand shop in Exeter). Mr. Churchill records that our armies were unarmed except for rifles, that the whole country contained barely 500 field guns and 200 tanks of any type or condition. Even at the end of September he was urgently appealing to the American President for 250,000 rifles 'as I have 250,000 trained and uniformed men into whose hands they can be put'. In these circumstances the urgency shown in July to give arms to the Zionists in Palestine seems at least premature; no doubt the Arabs would have held it to offend against 'the hitherto accepted dictates of humanity', to quote a phrase fired by Mr. Churchill against one Hermann Goering.

In August and September, as England's ordeal began, Mr. Churchill repeated his exhortations, and later volumes of his memoirs than I have may continue the narrative. I feel sure the beleaguered British people at that time were unaware that the arming of the Zionists, which in effect would mean the transfer of Arab Palestine to new owners, was so important in their affairs; they fancied their own plight to be a total and paramount preoccupation. Anyway, Political Zionism did not at that moment succeed in its next objective. Responsible men at lower levels or at the scene delayed the downhill process for a while (the further services of Lord Lloyd might have been beneficial to all concerned, including the mass of Jews, but he died in 1941). By the war's end, however, the thrall was upon first rank politicians in America and the second fatal deed was perpetrated.

Dr. Weizmann went to America in 1940, 1941 and 1942. He found among 'the top political leaders' real sympathy for Political Zionism, but, once more, had trouble with 'the experts in the State Department' (professionals are often troublesome; they know something of the subject). Before his third visit, he says, Mr. Churchill told him, 'I would like to see Ibn Saud made lord of the Middle East — the boss of the bosses — provided he settles with you . . . You might talk it over with Roosevelt when you get to America. There's nothing he and I cannot do if we set our minds to it.' Dr. Weizmann found powerful friends for Zionism, including particularly Mr. Henry Morgenthau, Junior, whose name attaches to the Plan for Germany which, in effect, bisected Europe and made a third war as certain as any human event can be. President Roosevelt was (in 1942) 'completely affirmative' about the Zionist ambition in Palestine (though Dr. Weizmann does not clearly record whether he definitely accepted the proposition that 'the consent of the Arabs' should *not* be sought). By this time politicians everywhere were competing for Zionist favour like men struggling for the last seat on a band wagon and the British working man's Socialist Party issued its admirable pronunciamento: 'Let the Arabs be encouraged to move out as the Jews move in. Let them be handsomely compensated for their land, and their settlement elsewhere be carefully organized and generously financed' (seldom have a few words so precisely described the opposite of the subsequent event, when the Arabs were encouraged with bombs to move into destitution).

In September 1943 Mr. Churchill again gave 'friendly reassurances' to his visitor and in November 1944 was 'very specific', speaking of partition and of the inclusion of the invaluable Negev in the Zionist State now generally, though privily, proposed. Mr. Churchill also urged Dr. Weizmann, who was going to Palestine, to stop in Cairo and see Lord Moyne, one of Mr. Churchill's colleagues who was showing improved comprehension of Political Zionism (Dr. Weizmann was unable to comply because the news of Lord Moyne's better behaviour apparently was not known in Palestine, so that he was killed by Political Zionists in Cairo only two days later).

Then the Second War ended and the real trouble began. Just before it closed President Roosevelt, on his homeward way from Yalta, received Ibn Saud on his cruiser. What he said is astounding, if his words are rightly quoted by the *New York Times* of October 19th, 1945: 'No decision will be taken with regard to the basic situation in Palestine without full consultation with both Arabs and Jews' and 'I would take no action in my capacity as Chief of the Executive Branch of our government which might prove hostile to the Arab people'.

He died immediately after saying this. The fascinating question is, did he say it? If he did, it was in the nature of a deathbed conversion, return to grace, or perception of truth by revelation; the remainder of this century would look very different if 'top line politicians' habitually spoke so and acted accordingly. He died, but had he lived his political health might never have been the same again, those words once spoken. His confidant, Mr. Harry Hopkins, gives a different version, much more in keeping with the present pattern of politicianship. He says President Roosevelt demanded that Ibn Saud admit more Jews into Palestine and was 'wholly committed publicly and privately and by conviction' to his demand.

In the private commitments, at least, one may believe in these times, and whether Mr. Roosevelt underwent a last-moment illumination or not is but a collector's item, for his successor accepted those commitments. At the decisive moment American strength was used to set up the Zionist State, as British strength was used exactly thirty years before to proclaim the National Home. The war's last shot was scarcely fired before Mr. Truman requested Mr. Attlee to infuse another hundred thousand Zionists into Palestine (which thus became the first culprit to be punished for Hitler's acts!) The British Government recoiled like an executioner appalled. It was politically impossible for the first Socialist Government to begin its rule by an attack on Arabs, and thus blatantly to demonstrate that the war-against-aggression was one for aggression and against defenceless small peoples (even though support of Political Zionism and readiness to drive Arabs from Palestine was by this time the final test of a good British Socialist, too! In 1939 a Socialist leader, Mr. Herbert Morrison, wagged his finger at an errant Socialist, Mr. Malcom Macdonald, who sought in his responsible office to avert the catastrophe in Palestine, and mournfully reminded him that he was *once* a Socialist!)

The deed demanded was just too crude and in practice infeasible. Thereon, with the ease of a neat change of gear, the American Republic was used to supply the desired acceleration. In this matter the junior Mr. Henry Morgenthau was 'of particular assistance', Dr. Weizmann says (the father was resolutely anti-Zionist; this is an instance of the way in which Political Zionism, once fathered on all Jews by Gentile politicians, widened its influence among Jews of the rising generation). The son gave his name to the disastrous Plan for Germany which both Mr. Roosevelt and Mr. Churchill initialled and then publicly regretted; however, Mr. Truman followed his counsel in this matter. In Palestine the Political Zionists increased their attacks on the British until only two alternatives remained; to suppress them or get out. The British Government got out.

In New York the body called The United Nations was set up. As individual politicians nearly all had shown submission to Political Zionism, equal subservience was to be expected from any corporate body. On November 19th, 1947, just thirty years after the issuance of the Balfour Declaration (when Dr. Weizmann waited at the Prime Minister's Secretary's office in case the British Cabinet at its decisive meeting should need him), President Truman received Dr. Weizmann 'with the utmost cordiality'.* That same afternoon the American

* Dr. Weizmann told Mr. Truman that the Zionist State, as Egypt might deny it the use of the Suez Canal, ought to have its own canal from Haifa or Tel Aviv to Akaba; two years later, as part of his programme of global expenditure, Mr. Truman announced a 'Fourth Point' for 'capital investment in areas needing development'. This enterprise, which was earlier recommended in Communist publications, might prove to include the new canal.

delegation at the United Nations received telephonic instructions from the President to support Political Zionist claims.

Ten days later the United Nations, at American insistence but on legal or moral authority unknown, announced that a Zionist State would be set up in Palestine after the British withdrawal. At the last the American and British Foreign Ministers sought to avert the deed. The resignation of Mr. George Marshall (who told American Senators it would be like touching off the powder keg of a new world war) was not long delayed. Mr. Bevin as I write still politically survives a fierce campaign of vengeance, waged in newspapers throughout the world as well as the couloirs of politics. (He has since died.)

This event gave the lie to every moral principle ever stated by Western politicians as the issue of the two wars. The Arabs were in-offensive people who harmed none, had no part in causing either war, were not connected with the events in Europe which were supposed to have caused those wars, were themselves oppressed, and as the direct result of each war had their land thrown open to an invasion, mock-ingly sanctified in the second case by a self-elected body claiming to represent The World. The Arabs may be as good or bad as most or worse than any; that is not the point. The moral principle was publicly derided and crowned with thorns on each occasion and the lesson for the future is plain. If it is not clear enough, the utterances of top line politicians unmistakably point to a continuance of the process. They were even more enthusiastic than those of the First War about the National Home.

Mr. Truman (whose presidency was undreamed of by Americans when the Second War began), said in 1949 that the day when he recognized the Zionist State, in reality his creation, was the proudest of his life; how many Americans could have imagined that in 1941? Mr. Churchill, having accused Mr. Bevin of 'prejudice against the Jews in Palestine', described himself in 1950, in a message to the Friends of the Hebrew University of Jerusalem, as 'an unfaltering Zionist who always had the interest of the Jewish people at heart'; how many British Islanders realized that in 1939 or 1940 or understood what it implied? Mr. Anthony Eden (in whom Mr. Churchill sees the next Conservative leader in England) told Jewish ex-service men (according to the Jewish

Agency) that the emergence of the Jewish State was the most memorable event in the recent history of the world; what would British folk have thought had the matter been foretold to them in that form in 1939? General Smuts told a Zionist gathering in 1950, 'I bracket the Battle of Britain and the resurrection of Israel as among the human highlights of our epoch'; yet the one was resistance to invasion, the other invasion of a small and helpless land.

Obviously the future will not improve while this exotic ambition keeps its hold on leading men in Western countries. Only increasing public alertness and a new breed of politicians could bring a change for the better. The affairs of nations are passing out of the hands of nations and entering (as Rabbi Elmer Berger wrote) 'the labyrinthine and devious ways of international politics in a part of the world where political intrigue and secret deals are a byword'. One has the feeling of being in a dark room where tentacles delicately wave and grope, and with sure grasp fix on a man, another man, and another man. . . .

General Smuts seems to me especially representative of a type now universal in all English-speaking countries. He, Mr. Churchill and Dr. Weizmann were all born about the same time. His life shows a line undeviatingly Christian, patriotic, conservative and reasonable save for the inexplicable championship of Political Zionism. He fought with his South African Boers against the British (Mr. Churchill was in the opposing ranks) and afterwards led the cause of Anglo-Boer reconciliation. The Boers did not want so quick a friendship with England and resented him; the British South Africans were glad to live under Boer leadership if the great family were preserved. Neither group knew that the Zionist cause (then unknown to the masses) was deep in his heart. His purpose in entering Mr. Lloyd George's Cabinet in the First War was to plan a campaign in Palestine and, if he could, to command it! His approved biography says he later regretted refusing it and wonders 'whether he would not prefer, to the memories he has, the thought that he entered Jerusalem'. In 1948 he said the Zionist triumph had been the one highlight in an era of tragedy and failure and 'I am proud of the fact that the last important act while I was Prime Minister was the recognition of the State of Israel'. In 1949, to a Zionist audience, he said 'I am happy to have been associated with at least one thing in my life which has been successful, and I am glad that South Africa has had a small share in the realization of the great vision'.

South Africans, like the Americans and British, never knew that *this* was 'the great vision'. General Smuts, like American presidents and British prime ministers, became caught up in paradoxes. He told his obdurate Boers that 'hankering after the past can lead in the wrong direction' but supported Political Zionism, which invoked a past two thousand years older and beyond all proof. A Boer politician, when General Smuts visited London for a Zionist gathering, said, 'He flew six thousand miles for the purpose of honouring Jewish nationalism and then he flew back six thousand miles to continue undermining South African nationalism'; this applied equally to almost any leading American or British politician. (Nor was General Smuts always so good a counsellor as British people thought; during the collapse of France he urged that those last few fighter squadrons should be sent there, which in the event saved the British Island and what else was saved by the Second War.)

When all has been examined the workings of General Smuts's mind, and that of all such leaders, remain in this matter incomprehensible. He said, 'There never was such nonsense as this idea the Jews have that they are an exclusive, pure race. They are the most impure race on earth. I doubt if they are even Semites.' Yet he joined in the clamour against 'anti-Semitism' and called it 'the manifestation of a canker which eats into the very heart of Christianity'. If such a thing as an anti-Semite exists he might be one, for if the Jews are not Semites the Arabs undoubtedly are and he disliked them; his approved biography attributes 'racial predilections' to him and he said: 'I never saw any romance in the Arabs . . . They are a bitter, recalcitrant little people.' (A curious incident in his career occurred in 1920 when a sect of African Natives, who adopted the Jewish ritual and called themselves Israelites, encamped to celebrate the Passover at a place called Bullhoek and refused to leave it; these Israelites stood fast when troops sent by General Smuts's government advanced against them, nearly three hundred of them, and one white trooper, being killed.)

General Smuts appears to be more closely identified with Political Zionism than even any other Gentile politician of these four decades.

When he was made a Freeman of the City of London in 1917 (while the Balfour Declaration was in incubation) he publicly recommended the 'interesting military and political possibilities' of a Palestine campaign and spoke of 'silent, invisible forces'. He habitually used words of mystic fervour about Political Zionism and once said, 'Nothing in the whole bloody history of the human race compares with the history of the Jewish people'. Today the bloody expulsion of the Arabs from their native Palestine may be compared with another bloody expulsion in antique and barbaric times. However, he thought what has been done is just: 'It is not because I love the Jews better than other people that I support them; I love justice.' He became, as a Zionist writer said, 'the Jews' leading and accepted, perhaps their only active and consistent friend among the statesmen of the world' (in both these quotations 'Jews' should apparently be read as meaning 'Political Zionists').

Today these beliefs of General Smuts are clearly held by leading politicians in all English-speaking countries, and this will not quickly change because they have established successions loyal to this supreme, if mystic, theory. General Smuts's political heir was a Mr. J. H. Hofmeyr, who told Zionists, 'Hold fast to that Zionist ideal whatever happens, for it alone can save Jewry and the world'. Mr. Hofmeyr died but the succession passed to another Zionist champion. The same situation exists in America and Britain. President Truman upheld Political Zionism like Presidents Roosevelt and Wilson. Mr. Churchill, when he became Prime Minister, supported it like Mr. Lloyd George and Mr. Balfour, and Mr. Eden has avowed his respect for it. The thrall has spread to all other English-speaking lands. During the struggle at the United Nations Assembly to give a mock-legality to the partition of Palestine the Canadian, Australian and New Zealand delegations suddenly joined with General Smuts's South African one in ardent support for Political Zionism and in opposition to hard-pressed Britain; this was the first great dissension between Commonwealth nations, which in physical danger always immediately united.

The overriding allegiance spreads to all parties in all these countries, too, so that in this matter the English-speaking voter in America, Britain or throughout the Commonwealth countries has no choice. At the last American presidential election the Democratic candidate,

Mr. Truman, displayed the Zionist State as a trump card; but the Republican one, Mr. Dewey, appeared to think Zionist favour equally essential and at a Jewish ceremony 'donned a skull cap for the first time . . . since he sang in a synagogue choir as a young man'. Mrs. Eleanor Roosevelt, a leading Democratic personality, became vice-chairman of the 'National Christian Committee of the United Jewish Appeal' (which collects funds for Political Zionism); Senator Robert Taft, leader of the Republican Party, became another vice-chairman.

Both parties appear to believe the approval of Political Zionism so important that they will do anything to court it. If they win an election, they think they have won through a mass of votes 'delivered' by the Zionist interest; if they lose, they increase their efforts to gain that vote at the next election. Exactly the same situation exists in England. When the Second War ended (during which the Socialists spoke of 'encouraging the Arabs to move out and the Jews to move in') the masses of Jewry swung at once to Socialism. Suddenly Jews vanished from the Conservative benches; more Jews than ever before appeared on the Socialist ones and in the government (so that certain measures which cut deeply into the ancient British traditions of liberty and property were associated with the names of Ministers of Russian-Jewish origins).

Immediately the other party, the Conservative, redoubled its efforts, not to overthrow Socialism, but to gain Zionist support. It said it would support the Socialist Government's *foreign* policy, but when the Palestine dispute arose it moved a vote of censure on the Foreign Minister (Mr. Bevin) and Mr. Churchill's followers received the imperative three-line admonition to vote for it; in this matter *alone* was the government's foreign policy opposed (and a Conservative emissary appeared in Palestine). In 1950 a new election came and was fiercely fought in a neck-and-neck contest which brought the Socialist majority down from 140 to 6 seats.

Yet that homeric struggle, so eagerly watched by the world, was essentially bogus; I believe the Conservative Party management would risk losing an election rather than put up one candidate anywhere who does not accept Political Zionist supremacy and may have lost this election for that sake. The proof, I hold, is the case of Mr. Andrew Fountaine.

The deadliest word of our generation is 'Adviser'. 'Advisers' are now innumerable in British and American public affairs and where they appear power usually passes from the responsible figures to irresponsible ones whose motives cannot be scrutinized. The Conservative and Socialist Parties both have 'advisory committees' at headquarters which approve or reject candidates (again, the situation is similar in America). If voters ever learn of and become curious about these bodies they are briefly told that 'the best man' to represent them is thus selected; the mysterious advisers know better than the voter what he wants. (I first noticed during the war that the Conservative Party was sending avowed Political Zionist supporters as candidates to by-elections. Often the constituencies resented this foisting of strangers on them but were overborne; I knew a resident Conservative workingman of the highest record and quality who was thrust aside in this way.)

In 1950 one candidate, who was highly thought of by the voters of Chorley, fought without official Conservative approval, which was firmly denied him. This was Mr. Fountaine. In 1946, when the Conservative Party was in very low water, he was a delegate to the annual party conference at Brighton, and demanded that the party should 'root out' subversive influences in British public life. As at the touch of a button the reproach of 'anti-Semitism' came from the platform (I told the beginnings of this story in *From Smoke to Smother*, 1948) but the feeling of the meeting was strongly with Mr. Fountaine and the party-management agreed to 'an inquiry'. The promised report (at the next conference, in 1947) ignored the demand for action to 'root out' and blandly said the party-management 'should take certain steps to ensure that the conspiracy is closely studied'.

That was the familiar end of that, but not of the vendetta against Mr. Fountaine, on whom a taboo was laid. The 'advisory committee' implacably rejected him in 1950, though what he proposed was 'Conservative policy', so that he fought alone, receiving some 22,700 votes and losing the seat only by 361. With the backing of the party-machine he would obviously have won it, which would have reduced the Socialist majority to 4. If there were 10 other such cases (I should think there might have been more) the Conservatives threw away the election in this manner. If Mr. Fountaine stands again he will presumably have to fight the party-machine anew. However, immediately after his sensational feat at Chorley vigorous moves were begun from party-headquarters to have a Political Zionist put up as official Conservative candidate at the next election. The one good sign in all this was the extent of the voters' revolt.

In about seventy years Political Zionism, a movement of Russian Jews, has established its power over the masses of Jews everywhere and, through Gentile politicians, over the English-speaking nations, the major policies of which are clearly conditioned by it now. It was a thing born of an innate hostility to Gentiles which no act of Gentile mankind could alter. The success achieved can only be understood by considering the conspiratorial beginnings, among several million Russian Jews who lived self-secluded among Gentiles, who at school, university and in their careers pursued the Zionist ambition parallel with and through their education and professional activities. There is a science of mind-control and these men proved masters of it. They achieved dominance over Gentile politicians and split world Jewry as by atomic fission, reviving in it the doctrine of a peculiar people with a Messianic mission overriding other loyalties, overruling native interests, overlording public affairs.

The propagandist approach to the masses has worked wonders. The minds of men in the mass seem like screens, on which headlines produce an impression. In America, Mr. Albert Jay Nock thought that the increase in literacy (that is, the ability to read words) went parallel with a decrease in comprehension of what was read or what went on. In evidence he compared the American periodicals of today with the much superior ones of forty years ago (a comparison apt in England, too). For a decade at least the majority of Americans were as fearful of the words 'anti-Semitism' as an Alabama darkie might be of the evil eye; at that point, thought, reason and discrimination failed. Particularly, the words 'six million Jewish dead' seemed to atrophy the power to think. (A relevant reminiscence: at the Paris Peace Conference in 1919, after the First War, Dr. Weizmann maintained that 'as a group the Jews had been hit harder by the war than any other'. People still living may recall the huge casualties on all sides, the ruin in France, the massacres in Russia, the inflation-years in Germany and compare their sum with this statement.)

Mr. Nock may be right; a bench of Kentucky farmhands or Sussex gaffers, before they could read, probably would caustically have dismissed such rhetorical extravagances as this one of the six millions. During the Second War I noticed that the figures of Jewish losses, in places where war made verification impossible, were being irresponsibly inflated, and said so in a book. The process continued until the war's end when the figure of six millions was produced (and the Arabs were immediately chastised). A transparently worthless estimate was not only used for mass-delusion through newspapers, but even given official status! If by any turn of chance the American and British representatives who bandied it about at Nuremberg were ever called to answer for it, they might be hard pressed for a defence, for any impartial tribunal might tear it to pieces.

No proof can be given that six million Jews 'perished'; proof can be adduced that so many could *not* have perished. *Some* casualties in war can be precisely ascertained. Thus in six years the huge expenditure of human and mechanical effort by the Germans, Italians, Japanese and lesser foes killed 824,928 British, Commonwealth and American fighting-men, merchant sailors and civilians (Mr. Churchill's and General Eisenhower's figures). The reader may calculate how much more effort would have been needed to kill seven-and-a-half times as many people, separately. He might consider, too, the output of energy entailed, in the form of desk-work, detectives, constables, vehicles and the like, in the capture of one wanted man, say a felon or one who has lost his memory, and multiply that by six millions. Certain mathematical rules govern destruction on such a scale; you need pursuers, jailers, prisons, camps, transport, executioners in numbers inconceivable. The Germans would have needed, behind the fronts, armies perhaps ten times as great as all they disposed of, for such butchery.

In a matter where nothing is verifiable, one thing seems sure: that six million Jews were never even contained in German-occupied territories. Many Jews left Europe before the war began and the only large communities which remained were in Poland and Russia, countries from which trustworthy statistics are not to be expected. Many of those in Poland apparently welcomed the Communist invasion of 1939 and went into the Communist zone. A Jewish observer, Mr. Levine, returning to America from Russia in 1946, said: 'At the outset of the war, as we all know, Jews were among the first evacuated from the western regions threatened by the Hitlerite invaders and shipped to safety east of the Urals.' He said these privileged ones amounted to two millions.

Yet this massive assertion about the six millions was used by politicians in the highest places, by prosecutors at Nuremberg, and habitually by mass-newspapers which in lesser matters would print no statement unverified! In truth nobody outside Political Zionism knows how many Jews the world contains, partly because Jewry has always included a section which avoids prominence in statistics, partly because the numbers in the Soviet areas cannot be ascertained, partly because Political Zionism has been able to obscure population-movements. Rabbi Elmer Berger wrote in 1946, of the Jews in Poland and Russia, that he did not know how many had survived 'and no one knows'. Since President Roosevelt's time track has been lost of the increase of Jewish population in America; good observers believe it now to approach eight millions. In England the figure is similarly unknown; 'It is impossible in the absence of official statistics to do more than make an intelligent guess . . . The exact number of Jews in Britain remains a mystery' (the *Zionist Record*).

In my judgment the figure of six millions was a grotesque exaggeration which an unintimidated press would never have published, save to expose. In this matter the charges brought against the German leaders at Nuremberg cannot be substantiated, yet they were apparently presented as 'the crux of the case' (Captain Liddell Hart, alluding to the trial of Field Marshal von Manstein) and the men condemned were executed on the Jewish Day of Atonement.

If ever freedom of debate returns to the world, a board of impartial accountants might be set to study this matter of the six millions, stated by leading politicians of the West, and their representatives at Nuremberg, to have perished. Until then, all the student of the times can do is to try and trace their fate in such figures as are available to him. Figures, however, are curious things; though inanimate, they have a kind of life of their own, and if stretched too far may, like elastic, inflict painful stings and surprises.

Thus the seeker after truth today can only turn to those publications which, for many decades, have built up a reputation for supplying the most authentic and carefully scrutinized statistics in all important matters of the day. The chief of these, in the United States and Britain respectively, are the *World Almanac* and *Whitaker's Almanac*. In a question so shrouded in mystery as that of the number of Jews in the world they, with all others, are thrown on Jewish statistics, and they both state that the ones they present are supplied by Jewish sources, which thus are responsible for them.

Thus the *World Almanac* for 1947 (two years after the war's end) printed such Jewish-supplied 'estimates', which gave the world's population of Jews *in* 1939, when the war began, as 15,688,259. The population *after* 1945 was not then given. The *World Almanac* for 1950 and 1951, however, still quoting these Jewish estimates, gave the Jewish population of the world *in* 1939 as 16,643,120. The Jewish estimators gave no reason why they then found the Jewish population *before* the war to have *increased* by a million; it is a large difference in a relatively small figure. In the 1950 and 1951 editions figures for the Jewish population of the World *after* the war *were* given: according to these estimates they were 11,373,000 (1950 edition), or 11,303,350 (1951 edition).

If those estimates were correct, that would show the disappearance, if not of *six* million Jews, then of something over *five* million (assuming that the amended figure for 1939 is correct, and not the earlier one; in the second case, something over *four* million Jews disappeared, in these estimates).

Whitaker's Almanac for 1949 and 1950 gives total estimates, from similar Jewish sources, which approximately correspond with those printed in the *World Almanac* for 1950 and 1951. These state that the Jewish population of the world in 1939 was 16,838,000 and in 1948 11,385,200, a reduction of nearly *five and a half* millions.

But when the detailed estimates given in both almanacs are more closely compared a large discrepancy becomes apparent. The estimate of the Jewish populations of *separate countries*, given in *Whitaker's*, for 1949 and 1950, adds up to much more (13,120,000) than the total figure (11,385,200) given for the *world*! If this were correct, and if the larger figure for 1939 is also the right one, the decline in Jewish population would be something over *three and a half* millions, or *two and a half* if by any chance the lower estimate for 1939 were nearer the truth.

Where the real truth is, no man can ascertain, for the truth lies buried in those parts of the world where (as such careful publications wisely state in other sections) no trustworthy statistics can be obtained: Soviet Russia and the Eastern European countries forced into the Soviet area in 1945.

Thus the perspiring student will at length find, when he examines the figures for separate countries, the main reason for the large difference between the estimates published by the *World Almanac* and by *Whitaker's*. In the Jewish estimates for separate countries supplied to these publications, the Jewish population of the Soviet Union after the war is given at 2,000,000 (in the *World Almanac*, 1950 and 1951) and 5,300,000 (in *Whitaker's*, 1949 and 1950)! The first figure makes the sum, of vanished Jews, work out; in the second one, most of them reappear! That the second one is, in fact, the truer one is suggested by the fact that *Whitaker's* breaks down the Soviet population of Jews into *cities*, giving very large Jewish communities to such traditionally Jewish cities as Odessa and Kieff.

If these figures, as I believe, come much nearer to the truth, the figure of six millions, on the strength or weakness of which such grave things were done, was one which would not bear any scrutiny by independent investigators. It can never be so examined unless and until the Iron Curtain lifts or is smashed. However, if the estimates supplied to the *World Almanac* for its 1950 and 1951 editions were correct, they mean that only 2,600,000 Jews now exist in all Soviet Russia and the three traditional countries of large Jewish population in Eastern Europe (Poland, Hungary and Rumania) which at Yalta were forced into the Soviet area. Before the war this area contained between nine and ten million Jews, as far as can be estimated. According to the Jewish authority I quoted above Jews in it were removed from the regions threatened by Hitler in 1939 and 'shipped to safety east of the Urals'. He gave a figure of two millions, apparently for the Eastern European countries alone, without reference to Jews already in Soviet Russia.

Finally, as an illustrative footnote to this excursion into statistics, in 1948 the *New York Times* (a Jewish-owned newspaper) published what was offered as an authoritative, statistical article, which stated that the figure of the Jewish world population for the year 1948 was between 15,700,000 and 18,600,000.

In a time of such propagandist darkness the lot of the uneasy patriot is hard, in America as in England. Political Zionism openly shows its power, in ways wounding to native pride, in New York. Crowds of New Yorkers, flocking to hear a famous German pianist, were rudely thrust back by Zionist and Communist pickets who said he once played for Hitler; two hours before the concert was due to begin the Department of Justice (given untrammelled powers in such matters by the President) ordered him to leave the country. A Jewish magistrate refused to try young Zionists who threw refuse at a visiting Foreign Minister (Mr. Bevin). A rabbi, marrying a young woman twice found guilty by twelve jurors of Communist espionage (and at liberty pending appeal) wished her happiness with the words: 'Beyond mere conjecture there is neither proof nor certainty as to any act of disloyalty on your part.'

Literature and the drama come under the Zionist ban, which pauses at no name. *The Merchant of Venice* is in practice banned in New York (as by law in Moscow). The film of *Oliver Twist* was long taboo because the lesser of two rogues is a Jew and in this case the veto extended also to the American and British occupation zones of Germany; what Germans may see, hear or read is also coming under the spell of New York. The Gentile Americans number over 140 millions, but have no free choice from the mind's menu; the dishes are first tasted by the court official, as it were, and only those approved by him appear on it.

The press for years was almost closed to any reasoned criticism of Political Zionism, in editorial, news or letter columns. (In London, too, analogous conditions obtain. When a Zionist film about Palestine was shown there, and taken off at public protest, three leading London newspapers reported the matter at length without once mentioning the words Palestine, Zionists or Zionism.)

For nearly a decade there was in daily reality a very powerful censorship in this one matter. It produced widespread symptoms of mental claustrophobia among the American population and in 1949 began to relax a little under the stress of public exasperation, intuitive if not reasoned. It remains strong and produces a kind of mental twilight which is either that of dusk or dawn and must get better or get worse. Either the politicians of America (and Britain) will enact laws of lese-majesty in some form, to crush public discussion of the origins and aims of Soviet Communism and Political Zionism, or a more reasonable regime will return and the two great countries will take their destinies in their own hands again. I believe most Jews would welcome that, but at present they are all classed as Political Zionists by the leading Gentile politicians (rather as Mr. Churchill lumped all Germans together as '65 millions of these malignant Huns').

In this twilight period an important part is played by numerous semi-secret organizations which play on the fear of 'anti-Semitism'. They have public names and offices but are semi-secret in their methods of intimidation. A chief one is the Anti-Defamation League, originally a fraternal Jewish lodge but now a body of vast resources and endless activities. Its own description of its work is that it 'sends literature to various groups, works through the radio, the motion-picture industry and other media; subsidizes speakers' bureaus and publishes periodicals, pamphlets and books (from comic strips to literature), fostering goodwill and condemning discrimination, whether social, political or economic, encourages movements, meetings, programmes of all kinds, and uses every advertising media from newspaper advertisements to billboards'. This, it says, 'amounts to a high-powered educational programme geared to reach every man, woman and child every day of the year'. The Anti-Defamation League reported that in one recent year it transmitted 216 broadcasts a day, that it influenced 1900 daily newspapers with a circulation of 43,000,000, apart from rural, foreign language, negro and labour publications, that it placed 330,000 books in public libraries, as well as 9,000,000 pamphlets 'tailored to fit the audience', and distributed 40,000,000 comic-strip books to children and servicemen. Through approved lecture bureaus it presented approved lecturers to 30,000,000 people, and much more.

313

This is the public side of its work, and plainly represents the indoc-trination of public opinion on a scale greater than any commonly practised by regular political parties. The lesser-known aspect of its activities is the keeping of dossiers and black lists. Its spokesmen (some years ago it claimed 150 public relations committees in as many cities and 2000 key men in a thousand more) have been known to call on editors and publishers to persuade them against publishing material displeasing to it. The fear of losing advertising revenue is strong in America (as in England and the Commonwealth countries). This League for some years employed a man of many aliases who published a book 'smearing' thousands of people with the words 'Fascist', 'Anti-Semite' and the like. Three American courts convicted him of libel and one judge said, 'He would do anything for a dollar'. Under the complicated State laws the book continues widely to cir-culate.

Similar organizations, open in name but semi-clandestine in method, exist in other countries. Signs of their activity in England have been such things as the sudden deletion (until protest was made) of the term 'Christian name' from British registration forms in favour of 'fore-name' ('Christmas' and 'Xmas' might be analogous cases), and the servile and superfluous announcement of twenty-one East End candi-dates at the last British election that they 'pledged themselves to combat racial and religious prejudice' (the creation of the non-existent thing).

In France, again, a body called The Centre of Jewish Contemporary Documentation has been formed. The title suggests dossiers and black lists and inevitably awakens memories of Ochrana and Gestapo practices. A reception was held in London in 1950 to enlist the help of Anglo-Jewry in its work, so that its activities may now be spreading through England. It was first formed in France during the German occupation 'to gather documents and information'. This collection (the speakers said) 'now contained 75,000 documents of great impor-tance' and 'valuable use' was being made of these; the French delegation at Nuremberg 'depended entirely' on these documents and if the Centre had not existed 'the Nuremberg Trials would not have had the same result'. Thus the source of such charges as that about the six million dead is seen; the repute of American, British and French justice is involved.

All this gives the picture of a growing mechanism of power and indirect control. I said that for a decade at least the result has been almost to eliminate public discussion of Political Zionism, but that statement has one important exception. The ban runs for Gentiles only. Discussion is boundlessly free in the Zionist press. The perusal of this is somewhat humiliating to the Gentile reader who fears the hold which Political Zionism has gained over his leaders, for he finds in it all the arguments he would himself advance and would like to hear from his own representatives. The Zionist argument dominates, of course, but prudence, doubt, common humanity and reason all come to the word. The Zionist press contains all that is disallowed, in daily practice, in the Gentile mass-circulation sheets. It gives the true picture of world Jewry in renewed ferment, seeking the truth and its own soul.

The Zionist newspapers reminded me of a Jewish village in Ruthenia in 1938, where a man said to me, 'These Jews are the most disputatious people in the world among themselves, but at the approach of a stranger they close together like a sea urchin at the touch of a human finger'. In these publications I found the Jew who felt guilt because of the treatment of the Arabs; to whom the ruination of these poor peoples' homes and homeland by those who complained of homelessness was an awful thing. Next to him was the Jew who was tormented by the revived curse of dual loyalties; he did not want to become an Israeli or a Zionist-in-exile, but to remain a good American, Britisher, Frenchman or German. Next came the Jew who wanted it both ways, that is, to remain in the Dispersal and be a good Israeli; and the Jew who said, 'I supported Zionism as a Jewish Nationalist but now the Zionist State is here, for any who want to go to it, I am done with it; I propose to live as a Frenchman'. There was the Jew who wanted the new State to be one of a tribal religion, more exclusive than Hitler's, the Jew who wanted intermarriage with Gentiles, and the Jew who wanted it to be atheist and communist. There was a Berlin Jew who said five thousand of his fellow Jews there were saved by Germans and he would live nowhere else; Jews who longed to return to Europe and could not; Jews who hated Europe and adored the Communist destroyers of it. There were replies to all these opinions; the debate was open and endless.

Again, I found in the Zionist newspapers the open truth about the cry of 'anti-Semitism'. I knew it was a transferable label, moved about by the Political Zionists from one country to another in order to keep the Jewish masses on the rack; no Gentile newspaper would print that, but here it was candidly avowed. A leading Yiddish writer said the Political Zionists were keeping up the clamour of 'anti-Semitism' in order to undermine the morale, faith and hope of Jews in their American home. He said the Zionist intention was to keep Jews constantly on edge with the scare of anti-Semitism, not to let them forget the Hitler horrors, and to spread doubts, fear and despair about the future of Jews in America. Every manifestation of anti-Semitism, he wrote, was seized on and exaggerated to create an impression that American Jews stand on the brink of a catastrophe and that, sooner or later, they will have to run for safety.

He proved this by quoting a Hebrew writer in Jerusalem, who said, 'Upon us, Zionists, now lies the old responsibility of constantly raising the hair of the Jewish people, not to let them rest; to keep them for ever on the edge of a precipice and make them aware of dangers facing them' ('raising the hair' means 'making the flesh creep'). This method was explained again by a Zionist publication in Paris, which said that, while American Jews lived in a fool's paradise, they would never agree to regard that country as a place of transit for Israel, so that they must be 'propagandized'. By this means they would in time be brought to the Zionist State (where, as another Zionist writer recorded, a 'pronounced anti-Goyism' was emerging). As a companion piece to these candid Zionist statements, the Gentile mass-circulation sheets in 1948 and 1949 began to inform their readers that 'anti-Semitism' was rearing its head in the Soviet Empire (a quaint conceit). The Zionist newspapers quietly instructed their better-informed readers not to take these Gentile babblings too seriously; the Soviet remained the Jews' best friend in the world.

These quotations show that if the Jews of the world are not to be allowed peace, it is not the Gentile masses who will disturb them, though perhaps the top-line Gentile politicians in their submission to Political Zionism and its falsely Messianic aim of ruling the world from Jerusalem. As to that, the student of these things, as he goes along, may make astonishing discoveries about the age of the ambition and the strange Gentile places where it has earlier shown itself. In Salt Lake City, for instance, I found a Proclamation of the Twelve Apostles of the Mormon Church issued in 1845. This, in a chapter headed Armageddon, spoke of a battle in Palestine and of a victory of the Jews, attended with 'the personal advent of Messiah', which will 'change the whole order of things in Europe and Asia . . . The Jews as a nation become holy from that day forward, and their city and sanctuary become holy. There also the Messiah establishes his throne and seat of government. Jerusalem then becomes the seat of empire, and the great centre and capital of the world.'

I could not ascertain if this is still part of Mormon belief, or why; however, it is Political Zionism. Then I learned that President Lincoln, two years before his murder, received a mysterious visitor, said to have been a Canadian and a Gentile, who told him that, though the freeing of slaves was a good deed, 'There could be no peace in the world until the Jews were emancipated' (they were then as much emancipated as those among whom they lived). This visitor also canvassed the Political Zionist ambition. Mr. Lincoln, who had the Civil War on his hands, turned the matter aside (later generations of politicians found time to listen to such callers amid even greater preoccupations). Relevantly, one of the American Communist leaders tried in 1949 said Mr. Lincoln's election in 1860 was 'supported by American Marxists and international Marxists', thus placing the Civil War in the planned sequence of revolutionary and destructive ones of these 160 years, as I do; that strengthens the belief that Mr. Lincoln's conciliatory attitude towards the South at the war's end led to his murder by Marxist forces.

Then at the revivalist meetings in Denver, held under the sign of the cross, if in a rather unorthodox spirit, I was given a pamphlet which said, 'Just as God's earthly people, having finished their wilderness journeys, were about to enter the land of Canaan, a prophecy was uttered which has been fulfilled ever since and will have a fulfilment until Gentile dominion is overthrown and the Lord establishes His Millennial Kingdom, with the Jews at the head of the nations'.

The thing is aged, many-headed, many-coiled and has many lairs. What does it all amount to now? The dream of ruling the world from Jerusalem cannot seem too audacious today to men who have already achieved so much. The Zionist State has been formed. It has about as many inhabitants as Albania or Honduras and less than Haiti, yet Napoleon in all his glory was not treated much more deferentially. Clearly its size and might cannot make the world quail, yet no politician in any English-speaking country seems willing to take office or mount the hustings without salaaming towards it and, by symbolically washing his hands of 'racial discrimination', undertaking to obey its will. Some now even openly confess themselves 'Zionists'. The strength of this new State, so tiny in size, plainly lies in the English-speaking countries themselves, which are still the strongest in the world; in the power of the purse, which it wields in them; and in the ability to control masses through the control of politicians and parties. In peace this new State fills the people with unease and in war, begun no matter where, it will clearly form the core of conflict.

It was established by violence and can only expand by violence. As to that, the past is a signpost to the future. In 1919 Dr. Weizmann said, 'We do not aspire to found a Zionist State . . . We cannot hope to rule in a country in which only one-seventh of the population at present are Jews.' The Zionist State was set up in 1947 and a Zionist majority imposed by arms. In 1948 the first Zionist Premier said the new State contained barely ten per cent of the world's Jews and the ingathering of the exiles represented 'the real content of Zionism'. In 1950 the Zionist Foreign Minister said, 'A State has risen. It seems to be the crowning piece of our historic edifice . . . No, my friends, that crowning piece of the edifice must be turned into a new foundation for the still greater structure of the future' (and another speaker in reply said 'Let us bind ourselves this evening, not only to the people of Israel, but to the whole of world Jewry, whose aim is a greater State of Israel').

Politicians of the English-speaking countries have often demonstrated, implicitly or explicitly, that they will accept any expansion of the

Zionist State, if it is presented to them as an accomplished fact, or help such expansion with arms in future. The United Nations dictate of November 29th, 1947, which set up the Zionist State, assigned Jaffa, Acre, Ramleh, Lydda, Western Galilee, Beersheba and other areas to the native Arabs. The Zionists *took* these areas and when Count Bernadotte was sent to redress the matter he was almost casually murdered. The United Nations paid little heed to this killing of its emissary. While these violent annexations were in progress Dr. James MacDonald (later to become the first American Ambassador to the Zionist State) went to South Africa and there told a Zionist audience he did not think Israel was bound by the Partition limits (typically, the only protest against this, seen by me, came from a Jewish objector, who demurred that, deeply grateful as he was for Dr. MacDonald's friendship for Zionism, 'such statements at this juncture do not make it easier to reach a settlement in Palestine with the Arabs; and this must remain our considered policy, if disaster is not to overtake us').

Two years later, in September 1949, the American Foreign Minister, Mr. Dean Acheson, asked the United Nations to place at least Jerusalem, the Holy City, under international control, and this body agreed. The Zionist Premier forthwith announced that Jerusalem would be made the capital of the Zionist State and a mild request from the United Nations to revoke this decision was answered by the establishment of the Zionist Government in it and its proclamation as the Zionist capital. To Dr. James MacDonald, now American Ambassador, fell the paradoxical part of declining to attend, as the official representative of his country, the meeting of the Jewish Community Council in Jerusalem at which the United Nations request was derisively rejected, the Zionist Premier remarking that 'The fate of the Holy City was settled three thousand years ago, when it was made the Jewish capital'. In June 1950 the United Nations agreed that 'it was impracticable at this time to proceed with the statute for the internationalization of Jerusalem'.

In March 1950 the Zionist press reported that the Zionist army was larger than ever before and included a small army, navy, air force, paratroopers 'and other surprises' (this for a State of a million beings). They announced that 'impartial American aid, followed by a substantial

American development plan under President Truman's Fourth Point, would avert further trouble'. At that time British and American arms were not supplied to the new State and the junior Mr. Franklyn Roosevelt, at a Zionist gathering, demanded that none should be given to the neighbouring Arabs, while in New York also a Zionist rabbi accused the American Government of 'helping to keep the Jewish State weak in face of the mounting threat of the rearmament of the surrounding Arab countries'.

In April 1950 Mr. Dean Acheson stated that the arms embargo was lifted for the Zionist and Arab States alike though only for 'weapons of self-defence'. In June a spokesman of the British Foreign Office said Israel was 'the dominant military power in the Middle East and had greater air-fighter strength and tank-power than all the Arab States put together'. Also in June a high American Government official announced that Israel was being furnished 'with arms of American manufacture which the Arabs do not possess'. Simultaneously both great countries declared that no country in that area would receive arms if it displayed 'any aggressive intentions'. Aggressive intentions usually appear at the moment of aggression and the past history of this matter seems to make it improbable that the Zionist State would be declared an aggressor, or an Arab one the victim of aggression, in any imaginable circumstances.

All this, in my reading, plainly adds up the continued submission of American and British governments to the Political Zionist ambition, and to the preparation of Armageddon, leading to the Millennial Kingdom. However, in which sense the Millennial Kingdom will dawn events have yet to show, and I do not believe this strangling servitude of the English-speaking peoples, through their political leaders, can last much longer.

CHAPTER 3

COMMUNISM PENETRANT

SOVIET Communism penetrated into the edifice of the American Republic like the woodworm into furniture (which if unchecked will cause a massive sideboard to collapse). This happened also in England and the Commonwealth countries, that is, throughout the English-speaking area which is the world's last barrier against Asiatic rule. The extent of the rot is best shown by comparison with an event of thirty-seven years ago.

On March 2nd, 1913, the Austrian Military Intelligence opened two suspicious looking packets addressed to General Delivery (Poste Restante) at the Vienna Central Post Office from Eydtkuhnen on the Russo-German frontier. They contained banknotes worth $2700 (then about £540). They were re-sealed and detectives were set to watch who should call for them. Eighty-three days later, on May 24th, the postal clerk's alarm buzzer called the waiting detectives and they hurried to the post office, just in time to see a taxicab disappear. The trail was thus lost at the start but by chance they found the taxicab later and learned that its passenger had been taken to a café; in the cab they found the small leather sheath of a pocket knife. The trail faded again at the café, which was empty, but by a third chance they heard that a gentleman had recently been driven from it to an hotel. There the porter told them of four newly-arrived guests. They gave him the sheath and he asked each of these, as they came downstairs, if it were his. One claimed it.

He was Colonel Alfred Redl, Chief-of-Staff of the Eighth Austrian Corps at Prague. The detective rang the Political Police, who called Military Intelligence, of which Colonel Redl earlier (from 1900 to 1905) was Director. His successor, Captain Ronge, went to the post office and obtained the form which had to be filled in by persons collecting mail. He then returned to Military Intelligence and compared the writing with that of a notebook, containing the department's most

321

secret information, bequeathed to him by Redl on transfer to Prague eight years before. The handwriting was the same: Redl's.

Meanwhile Redl was being shadowed by detectives. Apparently suspicious, he tore up and threw away some papers. A detective collected and joined the pieces and took them to Captain Ronge, who found they were postal receipts for a money-packet sent to an officer of Uhlans and for letters to addresses in Brussels, Warsaw and Lausanne. These addresses appeared in a black list of foreign espionage agents prepared by Redl when he was in charge of Military Intelligence. The Chief of the Austro-Hungarian Secret Service, von Ostromiecz, was informed and at once went to the Commander-in-Chief, Marshal Conrad von Hoetzendorff.

Redl was visited at midnight in his room by von Ostromiecz and three officers. He bowed and said, 'I know why you have come. I have spoiled my life. I am writing letters of farewell.' He was given a revolver and left alone. He wrote, 'Levity and passion have destroyed me. Pray for me. I pay with my life for my sins. 1.15 a.m.; I will die now,' and shot himself.

When this happened the First War was but a few weeks distant. He may have changed its entire course or even have caused it. His rooms in Prague yielded proof that he was a spy for Russia for ten or eleven years. For a fortune, he sold the most secret Austro-Hungarian plans and also betrayed Austrian agents in Russia to the Russians; to strengthen his position the Russians arranged for him to 'capture' a Russian spy and expose a faked organization of espionage. Above all, he sold von Hoetzendorff's vital Plan Three to the Russians, who passed it to the Serbs. Time was too short to improvise entirely different plans and the Austro-Hungarian setbacks in the first campaigns were heavy, against an enemy apparently much inferior. Further, by substituting false papers for genuine ones procured by Austrian agents he misled both the Austro-Hungarian and the German general staffs about the number of new Russian army corps. Count Albert Apponyi, the Hungarian statesman, said long afterwards that, had the Austro-Hungarian and German general staffs known of those new Russian armies, they could have prevented their politicians from driving them into the First War.

Thus espionage and treason may have the direst results for nations. The vital comparison for today, however, is that *only a few hours* elapsed between Colonel Redl's call for his mail and his death. Once found out, no courts or judges were needed then; a man caught in such a deed did not wish to live. The same standard prevailed, pretty well, in all countries west of Asia. The case is different in 1950, and this difference seems to me the measure of what has happened to the English-speaking family since Communism emerged in Asia (inside the Communist Empire espionage and treason remain summarily punishable by death in peace or war).

This is what might happen if someone like Colonel Redl were detected in America, for instance, today. First, his responsible superiors might refuse to listen to evidence against him and he would remain at his post. If challenged he would not ask for a revolver but deny everything pointblank. He might rise in rank and gain greater access to national secrets. After five, or ten years uneasy patriots or penitent fellow-transgressors might force some public attention to the case. He would repeat all denials and his superiors would angrily rebuke his accusers as hysterical witch-hunters and Red-baiters. The investigators, thus finding themselves the accused, might produce *proof*! Would the culprit then collapse and the stable be cleansed? By no means; leaders of the party-in-power, judges, churchmen, newspapers and broadcasters would raise even louder clamour that he was a martyr. At last a trial might become unavoidable, and, proof brought, the verdict be of guilty. Would even that be the end? No; pending the final, supreme court utterance the chorus of 'witch-hunt' would become louder yet. The whole process might occupy more years than the hours that passed between Colonel Redl's detection and his death.

That points to an immense spiritual weakening of the West, more dangerous for the future than even the geographical changes which its leaders connived to bring about. If it continued the outcome of Armageddon would clearly be the victory of the old serpent.

Before the First War a traitor was, if not unknown in America or England, then rare enough to be the exception that proved a golden rule. Faith and loyalty were, both by inherent instinct and long teaching, matters of each man's private pride. Even reason preferred a candid allegiance to a secret disloyalty, which makes life an unhappy falsehood. In the 1920s, however, young people found themselves in a world where this suddenly changed. A method was found to corrupt them without their even being conscious of the gradual process, to the truth of which they only awoke in middle age, if at all, when they often could not retreat. They made no deliberate choice between loyalty and treachery; caught first in the outer strands of a web they felt then but a gentle constraint, and only later the lethal clutch. Their leaders were at fault; they were entrapped in 'the deception of nations'.

In America Communist penetration began at the end of the First War and continued after it. Misleadership at the top took the form of official encouragement, and the stealthy process continued step by step. In 1925 Congress, at some prompting, refused grants to the Department of Justice for investigative work. In 1931 a Congressional Report stated, 'The attitude of the War Department up to now has been that, Communism being a political question, it was not the function of the Army to maintain detailed knowledge of the activities of the Communists and it therefore relied on the Department of Justice to furnish the necessary information. The fact is that the Department of Justice has had no power or authority from Congress to obtain the facts regarding Communist propaganda and activities since 1925 and of necessity the War Department has been ever since hopelessly in the dark regarding these revolutionary activities directed against our domestic institutions.' Thus Military Intelligence and the Department of Justice were both hamstrung. That left only Naval Intelligence, which in 1935 issued 'a comprehensive survey of Communist activities in the United States'. Thereon President Roosevelt, prompted by a body called 'The National Conference of Jews and Christians', publicly forbade further Army or Navy reports.

The only remaining defences against Communist penetration were the efforts of individual officials, officers or civilians who continued vigilant and stored up information for a better day. Such men, publicly unknown, exist in all countries, and in England may have succeeded in keeping the Navy and Air Force at a level which, by a hairsbreadth, saved the island in 1940.

The support given by high places to Communism in America may remain for ever unexplained. Given this help, the picture of the time was favourable for its success among individuals. True, its aims were beyond doubt. Its leaders, from Stalin and Lenin back to Karl Marx and Adam Weishaupt and far beyond, all plainly stated that its object was to destroy Christianity and legitimate authority everywhere; that it existed long before Marx's Communist Manifesto of 1848 but until then as 'a secret society'; that, it must use 'the Trojan horse method of penetrating established governments and communities' and 'work illegally behind the screen of legality'; that its goal was 'the forcible overthrow of all existing social conditions' and so on.

Nevertheless, the white folk have a weakness (unless it is a strength) for wanting to see an evil thing proved before they will believe it and many remained in doubt. They were encouraged by their leaders to think that the Communist Revolution was the spontaneous uprising of oppressed Russians, which it was not, and the suppression of American and British official papers about that event helped delude them (I then fell for that deception and only realized the truth when I saw Soviet Russia and studied Communism there and elsewhere). Above all, from 1917 to 1939 Communism (having been thrown out of Poland, Bavaria and Hungary by the peoples there in 1918-19) was contained in Russia.

The circumstances of that time, then, left much room for confusion, especially in young minds. Strong national leadership, which could have shown them the right path, was denied them. In 1933 Mr. Roosevelt became President. Stricken by incurable bodily misfortune in 1921, he seemed to have dropped out of politics and appears to have invested substantially in a resort, Warm Springs in Georgia, where he went to seek better health. In 1928, however, he was induced to run as Democratic candidate for the Governorship of New York by friends who took over his financial preoccupations there, amounting to $250,000, and this led him to the presidency four years later.

His inauguration coincided with the bogus election in Germany by which, in the waning glow of the Reichstag fire, Hitler clinched his hold on the Germans. Mr. Roosevelt's first declamations also were Wagnerian, if not Hitlerian. One of the familiar 'Emergencies' of our time was in progress and Mr. Roosevelt (like many other politicians,

325

who are repudiated by statesmen of the classic mould) invoked it to claim 'Powers': 'In the event that the national emergency is still critical . . . I shall ask Congress for broad Executive power to wage a war against the emergency, as great as the power that would be given to me if we were in fact invaded by a foreign foe.' America (like England, though to a lesser degree of captivity) has never since escaped from those Powers. For twelve years Mr. Roosevelt ruled the Republic in that spirit, and in this time its foundation-timbers were much gnawed by termites, so that its major problem today (like England's) is the undoing of much that was done.

In finance, an era of prodigious deficit-spending was begun (to the cry of 'Down with the deficits'); Mr. Roosevelt spent three times as much public money as the entire line of presidents from Washington to his predecessor. A fundamental rule, laid down by the *Communist Manifesto*, for destroying society is 'A heavy progressive or graduated income-tax'. Mr. Roosevelt brought the Republic three-quarters of the way to the brink where Britain now stands, that at which the only remaining step leads to confiscation. Mr. Robert Sherwood, his admirer and ghost-writer, says this cornucopian expenditure 'offered more juicy plums in the way of political patronage than had ever before been known in peacetime'.

In foreign policy, his first act was to recognize the Soviet Empire, in 1933. The Soviet in return undertook to refrain from subversive activities in America and these immediately increased on a scale unknown before anywhere; Communist publications announced that the aim was to overthrow the Republic by force and 'recognition has not changed that'. The process was clearly prepared for years before and now, as at the opening of a sluice, a stream of picked men flowed into every department of the Republic's life. During the subsequent war a second and greater stream was released into places prepared by the first permeation.

The American masses remained as unconscious as if they were drugged of this planned infusion of Communism into the arteries of their State. It was an alien injection at the source, which swept many native Americans with it in its later reaches, and I have room here for only a glimpse of one aspect of it. During the Second War American broadcasting was put under the control of a body called the Federal Communications Commission. This set up a sub-department called the War Problems Division, and complaint about it grew loud enough for a Congressional Committee of Investigation to be appointed. This committee's Chief Counsel, Mr. Eugene L. Garey, said half-way through the war: 'This division was formed for the avowed purpose of unlawfully liquidating all the radio personnel in the foreign-language field that did not meet with its favour. A real Gestapo was created and a lawless enterprise was launched . . . In a time of war we are asked to place our trust in lately arrived aliens whose sole claim to trustworthiness is that because they have been unfaithful to old allegiances they will be faithful to new ones. The voices of these aliens go into our homes and the unwary are led to believe that they speak with authority and official approval. They even censor our Christmas and Easter religious programmes and tell us what music we may hear. Apparently we can still read the news in our press but we can only hear what these aliens permit to us. What next medium of communication will receive their attention? Obviously, the press . . . These destroyers of free speech are alien in birth, education, training and thought . . . If the radio can thus be controlled in August 1943, there is nothing to prevent that control from slanting our political news and nothing to prevent the colouring of our war aims and purposes when peace comes.'*

The last sentence accurately foretold the subsequent event. The subtle control did extend to other means of communication and then to high policy; the results of the war proved it. In 1913 President Wilson wrote, 'We know that something intervenes between the people of the United States and the control of their own affairs at Washington'. Whether he or Mr. Roosevelt, as war-time presidents, found what that something was and yielded to it, one cannot judge. Several Americans told me that a president's one concern is to remain president, and if that is so considerations of national interest are likely to suffer. Mr. Roosevelt had cause to know what Communism meant. He had to send troops to break a Communist strike at a Californian

* Apropos, an amusing experience befell me in England about the same time. I was approached to broadcast to Austria, a service for which I was equipped by experience and knowledge of German; later I received intimation that 'friendly aliens' already so employed would not feel comfortable if I appeared among them and the matter was dropped.

arms plant (before the Nazis and Communists fell out, of course). Also, he had at that period the experience, unique among American presidents, of being booed on his own White House lawn, when he told Youth Congress delegates gathered there that if any of them were Communists (apparently they all were) 'you have no American right, by act or deed of any kind, to subvert the Government and Constitution of this Nation'.

Nevertheless, his harshest rebukes, to the end, were kept for any who urged him to check Communist penetration. Mr. Martin Dies (chairman of the Congressional committee chiefly concerned, who was later 'smeared' into oblivion) was angrily told, 'There's no one interested in Communism, no one at all. There is no menace here in Communism'. Thus conditions were created, ideal for the subversion of a State by the agents of a foreign power.

The chief victims of this twilight period in America were young people, usually native-born Americans, who fell into the clutches of the trained organizers, mostly aliens. How were they to know if treason was evil, if their leaders made a treasonable party legal? They found themselves in a bewildering world, of which Canterbury today is perhaps the microcosm. There the Archbishop teaches the Christian lesson and the Dean upholds atheist Communism. Obviously the congregation must think that the house of God is but a debating-place where anything may be right, and this situation exists in all English-speaking countries now. If the great political, educational and religious shepherds differ so, the littlest lamb may know as well as or better than they. So it is today in many churches and more universities, especially American universities. The old notion was that university presidents, rectors and fellows knew more than the students and their teaching rested on certain principles, those of the Christian faith and of the American Constitution. The universities were themselves the products of Christian growth and their members imparted wisdom in that sense.

Now the thing has been turned into its opposite. The rule of 'free and untrammelled inquiry' prevails; at the educational bargain-counters religious, agnostic and atheist professors compete, the denials of science are opposed to the beliefs of faith, the economic bedlam of

Liberalism, Socialism and Communism dominates the classrooms, and from the pandemonium the pupil may choose what he prefers. The inference for the student is plainly that his instructors know nothing, as they all vary, and he must seek the truth when he leaves the university's argument. The teaching *corps d'élite*, carefully guiding young men towards a good life, has been disbanded; in its place is an anarchic chaos from which young folk emerge leaderless into the world. The spiritual distress which is so palpable in young Americans today begins at this source. The emergent graduate often falls into bad hands and only learns the truth, which wise instructors might have shown him, after ten or twenty years of bitter disillusionment.

Such a man was Mr. Whittaker Chambers, whose story epitomizes the decline of the West, under bad leaders, during these four decades. What happened to him could not have befallen any man before 1917; for thirty-three years now it has occurred to many men in many countries. The root evil is the legalization of the Communist Party in non-Communist countries, which is akin to legalizing murder in civil law; its prohibition is the only way of protecting young people from such ordeals as that of Mr. Chambers. As long as political leaders insist that an avowedly destructive party is legal young men and women will join it and find themselves forced into degradations which, for lack of instruction, they cannot foresee. For this their national leaders, who declaim against the assassin they set free, are in truth responsible.

In 1924 Mr. Chambers left a New York university contemplating suicide, which was natural enough. He was exceptionally gifted and, had his feet been set on the right path, might very soon have become a famous writer. Instead, the university years left him spiritually adrift and morbidly despairing and in 1925 he joined the Communist Party, then a semi-underground one almost completely alien in membership. He joined the New York *Daily Worker* and earned the praise of Moscow by his editorship of its Letters Page (today Letters Pages in the majority of newspapers claiming to be Conservative, Republican, Socialist, Democratic, Liberal or Independent are used by planted men to spread Communism through the selective presentation of correspondence; they should be read in that light). He gained further approval in Moscow through some revolutionary short stories, full of rifle volleys and bleeding proletarians, which were produced as plays by Communist groups in many countries. He was thought important enough for higher tasks and in 1932 was made editor of the Communist *New Masses*.

Then the screw was given the first turn. Communist emissaries from Moscow told him he was 'to go into the underground'; if he refused he would be expelled from the party. He accepted, was given the usual 'cover name' ('Bob' at that moment) and disappeared from the face of America as if he were dead. With wife and baby he moved about the land, constantly taking new identities and acting as transmission-man for stolen documents, money, and instructions from Moscow, and organizer of cells and underground groups. One method of changing identity was to search the obituary notices of newspapers for a man born in the same year, write to the Board of Health for a copy of his birth certificate, and with it to obtain a passport in the dead man's name from the State Department. Clearly centuries of experience lie behind such devices; they could not be quickly invented.

Two years later he was drawn a stage further into the net. In 1934 Mr. Roosevelt was president and the intensive penetration of the Republic's organism was in progress. Mr. Chambers was introduced by another Moscovite emissary to a junior government official about his own age, Mr. Alger Hiss. An acquaintance thus began which led to developments more astounding than the affair of Colonel Redl. Mr. Hiss, another bewildered university graduate of the 1920s, was brought into government service in 1933, when Mr. Roosevelt was setting up the 'Alphabetical Agencies', that is, bodies known as the AA., FWA., TERA., RFC., and so on, all of which had billions to spend on Projects supposed to spell death for the 'Emergency'. Great staffs were being recruited and within these new, unsupervisable organizations Communist infiltrants were helping each other towards the peaks of power in the manner of mountaineers roped together. The key-men, at strategic points, were nearly always of foreign birth or antecedents; the flies in the web were often young Americans. The directors sat in Moscow with charts of the Republic's government organization before them and moved their followers into control-posts. Miss

Edna Lonigan, an acute observer, wrote, 'First the network placed its economists and lawyers . . . Then it moved its men into public relations. As the leaders learned more about the workings of the bureaucracy, they put their people into jobs as personnel directors. Assistant directors proved even better for the purpose. These officials were never in the headlines. But they saw the incoming applications; they could weed out those with anti-Communist records, or 'expedite' those with key names and key experience to identify them . . . The duty of the ablest Soviet agents' (then) 'was not espionage. It was to win the confidence of those who directed policy . . . So, each year, the network moved its men into higher and higher positions.'

Such was the true picture, now revealed, of the Republic in the 1930s as it moved towards the Second War and, more important, the Second Peace; this is the reason for the shape that war and peace took. 'When war came the veterans of eight years of conspiracy reached the highest policy levels. Always an invisible force was pushing the favoured higher' (Miss Lonigan).

Mr. Chambers and Mr. Hiss became ever deeper involved. In Washington Mr. Chambers was ordered, by the Moscovite emissary, to form a 'special group' including several persons in rising government service; among them were Mr. Hiss and a Mr. Harry Dexter White, who was secretary to Mr. Henry Morgenthau junior (of the Plan for Germany). At this time the visible Communist Party in America was negligible, maintained in that small open form (as in other countries) to delude the public into believing this was all Communism amounted to. In fact, each new member of 'Carl's' group (Mr. Chambers was now just 'Carl', a trusted Communist agent, to the others) formed a fresh cell around him in the various government departments and agencies. These young Americans, of course, thought 'Fascism' was the opposite of 'Communism' and could only be destroyed with the help of Communism. Their Moscovite masters wished them to think that and their own political, religious and educational instructors had not enlightened them.

By 1936 all these young men (Messrs. Chambers, Hiss and White were but three of a great number) were involved beyond turning back. They were ordered to obtain secret documents from the State Department, where Mr. Hiss was by this time employed. Mr. Chambers acted as courier. The documents were either copied on Mr. Hiss's private typewriter or the originals were given to Mr. Chambers to take to Baltimore to be microfilmed; in either case the originals were back in their official files by next morning. This happened under the nose of an Assistant Secretary of State who fourteen years later remembered wondering why the 'trade agreements division' of his Department constantly asked for secret material that had nothing to do with trade agreements!

At that point the Moscovites used a final device of entrapment which appears in all these affairs. Communist Moscow does not bribe its agents with thousands, as Czarist Moscow did Colonel Redl. For its purpose the smallest thing is enough, a bottle of whisky, a few dollars, a fur coat. The victims are so encoiled that they do not desire, and would rather refuse such tokens, but the object is incrimination, not reward. Once they accept *something*, they are hopelessly committed and at that stage Moscow will not take nay. Mr. Hiss and Mr. Chambers each received the kiss of death in the form of a Bokhara rug. The paltriness of the gifts in these cases somehow adds to the captives' ignominy.

Once a week for a year Mr. Chambers took the military and diplomatic secrets of the Republic, and of Powers friendly with it, to the Moscovite agents. For fourteen years he had paid the penalty of the confusions implanted in his mind, at its most impressionable stage, by his university experience and his political leaders. Now awakening came. One day, 'with the terror of a Catholic contemplating mortal sin', he read Tchernavin's account of Siberian labour-slavery, *I Speak for the Silent*. When he finished it his Communism was finished. After losing fourteen years he realized that 'Communism is a form of totalitarianism, that its triumph means slavery to men wherever they fall under its sway and spiritual night to the human mind and soul'.

In 1938 he went underground in a different sense. First he bought a shack on a hilltop near Baltimore, whence he could watch all approaches. Then he took a vital precaution. He collected one more batch of documents from Mr. Hiss and had them microfilmed in Baltimore, but then, instead of conveying them to the Moscovite agent in New York, he disappeared with them, and his wife and family, into the shack. A few days later, in the hope of safeguarding his family if he were killed, he deposited this package with a relative in New York. Its contents, revealed ten years later, showed that Moscow must have known nearly as much of the most vital military and diplomatic secrets of the West as if they were its own.

After a year, in 1939, he felt secure enough to resume life as Whittaker Chambers and obtained a post with *Time* magazine. He was eaten with remorse but could not bring himself to inculpate men he liked, such as Mr. Hiss, until August 26th, 1939, when the news of the Hitler-Stalin pact exploded. Then this quiet man realized that he had purveyed the innermost secrets of the West, not only to Moscow but probably to Berlin as well! He could not remain silent but feared to go to the State Department, so much permeated with Communists. He tried instead to reach President Roosevelt and to that end dined with an Assistant Secretary of State, Mr. Adolf Berle, on September 2nd, 1939, when Stalin was about to join Hitler in destroying Poland. Mr. Chambers told his story and was later informed, he says, that Mr. Berle went to the President and was told 'to go jump in the lake, only in coarser language'. In following months repeated efforts were made to have the matter investigated, notably by a Jewish journalist, Mr. Don Levine, and Mr. William Bullitt, a former Ambassador to Russia, went personally with it to President Roosevelt but was equally rebuffed.

There the matter might have ended but for a series of astounding chances, occupying many years. While the Second War went on Mr. Chambers rose to Senior Editor of *Time*, and Mr. Hiss (though ignorant of foreign countries) advanced to assistant to the head of the Far Eastern Division; special assistant to the Adviser on Political Relations; Deputy Director of the Office of Special Political Affairs; and Presidential Adviser!

In this last capacity, in 1945, he accompanied the dying President to Yalta and helped draft the proposals for 'unity governments' in Eastern Europe which in effect abandoned that area to the Communist Empire (of course, no 'unity government' containing Communists would survive in those countries without the Red Army's presence, but that was also ensured at Yalta). Mr. Hiss himself said he helped formulate the Yalta Agreement and he was a signatory. Mr. Stettinius (an inexperienced man who was catapulted into the post of Foreign Minister at that time) wrote that he consulted Mr. Hiss about the Polish boundaries, a part of the world unknown to both. Mr. Roosevelt yielded to the Soviet demand for three votes at the United Nations against one American vote at a moment when he was closeted with Stalin, an interpreter and Mr. Hiss. To later objections Mr. Roosevelt replied, 'I know I shouldn't have done it, but I was so tired when they got hold of me. Besides, it won't make much difference.' Mr. Hiss next appeared as General Secretary, at the foundation meeting of the United Nations Organization at San Francisco and then, aged forty-one, was put in supreme charge of the Office of Special Political Affairs (which, according to a leading American newspaper, 'was a major voice in department affairs and a vital factor in formulating foreign policy'). At this moment Mr. Chambers's information against him had been in currency for nearly six years and the incriminating papers for that period had accumulated dust on top of a disused service-lift in New York.

In November 1945 the Canadian spy case broke and the Canadian Prime Minister flew to Washington to inform the new President, Mr. Truman, of grave matters in America, emerged from the Canadian investigations. Mr. Truman was told of something which the published Canadian Report did not disclose, namely, that Igor Gouzenko (the fugitive from the Soviet Embassy in Ottawa) stated 'the Soviet had an agent in the United States who was an assistant to the Secretary of State, Mr. Stettinius'. Mr. Mackenzie King's flights to Mr. Truman and Mr. Attlee led to no official statement, public investigation or effective action in either country, although the Canadian Prime Minister publicly spoke of the extreme gravity of his mission (he died in 1950 and 'left unfinished his last and cherished task: the writing of his memoirs').

In 1946 Mr. Hiss, still rising, went to London as principal Adviser to the American delegation to the United Nations General Assembly. However, the rumours about him were now becoming loud and embarrassing to the authorities and his star paled somewhat. He gained financially in leaving the American Foreign Service gracefully to become President, at $20,000 a year, of one of those bodies which Work For Peace (usually in the strangest ways): the Carnegie Endowment for Peace, in December 1946. The conservative-minded gentlemen who looked after this Endowment refused to examine charges that Mr. Hiss might be a Communist and indignantly defended his 'complete loyalty to our American institutions'.

At this moment the two young men who left universities in the 1920s with minds ravaged by the confusions there were both greatly successful. Mr. Hiss stood beside a dying president at a fateful moment in the world's story, in a place where he could give a decisive slant to world affairs. He was a complete Communist, instructed when he entered government service to deny his Communism, divest himself of all traces of his allegiance and avoid open association with it. Mr. Chambers was Senior Editor of *Time* at $30,000 a year. He had made good the lost years materially; spiritually he sought rehabilitation in religion, in the Christian and patriotic upbringing of his children, and in work on his farm. Mr. Hiss was publicly popular; Mr. Chambers felt enmity among his colleagues, who included many Communist infiltrants. The thought that the public structure of his country was riddled with Communist agents tormented him. He still hoped to expose that but still wished to keep the matter of actual espionage secret, for fear of harming men whose perfidy was but his own earlier one.

Apparently he never would have achieved what he desired but for the first of a long series of chances, which led to partial disclosures but not once to the lifting of the whole dark curtain. In 1945 a Miss Elizabeth Bentley experienced the same awakening as Mr. Chambers in 1938. She, too, was in the 'underground'. Hers was another story of adolescent confusions and, in her case, of love. She was a New Englander of good old stock but at the same New York university came under the same influences and was 'a card-carrying Communist' in 1935. Her enthusiasm being noticed, she was told in 1938 to 'destroy her card', dissociate herself from open Communist associations and begin more important work. Her chief was an East European and she fell in love with him. By 1941 she, too, was a courier for stolen documents and a recipient of information from people in high places, which she passed towards the centre of the web.

In 1943 her chief died suddenly. Until that time she was 'terrifically shielded from the realities behind this thing'; now she came in direct contact with the Moscovites and by 1944 wanted desperately to break loose. Like all such penitents, she thought official departments were full of Communists and dared not go to one. She went finally to a local branch of the Criminal Investigation Department (FBI.) in a small Connecticut city. She accused a Presidential Adviser, a high Treasury official, a State Department man and numerous lesser government servants. Her story was not taken seriously, but as she said she had an appointment with the First Secretary of the Soviet Embassy, a Mr. Gromoff, detectives were set, apparently without enthusiasm, to watch the meeting. Her masters were suspicious and at that very moment insisted that she take money, the substantial sum of $2000. The detectives saw it change hands. No haste was shown but apparently this incident helped move President Truman to approve the appointment of a Federal Grand Jury to investigate Communist espionage (in 1947!). By this time Mr. Chambers's information was eight years old; a full report of the Un-American Activities Committee of Congress had lain on two presidential desks for four years; the Canadian Prime Minister's warning was eighteen months old.

Now the matter seemed about to become public in the genuine sense. However, dilatoriness may be as effective as suppression. After a year, in April 1948, the Grand Jury still dragged on, while newspaper readers wearily wondered what to make of reports, often compiled by persons whose intention was to obscure the facts. Then the Grand Jury changed its course. The matter of espionage was dropped and the investigation turned away from hidden Communism in public offices to the question whether the *open* Communist Party 'conspired to overthrow the Government by force' (under that misleading head some open Communist leaders were later tried and sentenced). A presidential election approached and wiseheads said the matter was to be sidetracked.

Another chance brought it back to the rails. There are scrupulous journalists, and Miss Bentley, when she saw the stoolpigeons appear before the Grand Jury, communicated with one, whose newspaper at long last published her story, though without names. This enabled the ever-thwarted Un-American Activities Committee of Congress to sub-poena a number of persons involved. For the first time the American public gained some inkling of what was involved. Its curiosity was then foiled by another simple device. Nearly all the witnesses took advantage of a kink in American law which enabled them to reply to questions, 'I refuse to answer on the grounds that any answer I give may tend to be self-incriminatory'. Mr. Harry Dexter White denied everything, like Mr. Hiss, and with other witnesses turned the proceedings into an attack on the Committee's 'witch-hunt'. Once more inquiry seemed checkmated. Then, by yet another chance, another journalist recalled stories heard years before of state-ments made by a Mr. Whittaker Chambers. He urged the committee to sub-poena Mr. Chambers and this was done, Mr. Chambers saying wearily to a friend, 'I always feared I'd have to cross this bridge, but I hoped not to' (he had ever hoped to get the evil cured without involv-ing individuals in 'the ultimate perfidy of espionage').

Thus, after nine years, on August 3rd, 1948, Mr. Chambers was at last heard, and *publicly* heard. He told of his efforts of 1939 to move the authorities to action, saying 'At that moment in history I was one of the few men on this side of the battle who could perform this service'. He named the members of his former 'group', among them Mr. Hiss and Mr. White. He still did not mention espionage, saying the purpose at the time 'was not primarily espionage, but the Communist infiltra-tion of the American Government'.

The next day rabid vituperation broke loose in the newspapers, radio and Congress, against Mr. Chambers, not Mr. Hiss or the others. Two days later Mr. Hiss was heard. He denied ever knowing Mr. Chambers and any association with Communism at any time. He was presented in the press, not only of America but of the world, for journalism was thoroughly permeated too, as a national hero suffering martyrdom. The Committee was so greatly intimidated that it made to wash its hands of the whole business, but one more chance prevented this. A solitary committeeman doubted Mr. Hiss's denials and urged that a sub-committee be sent privately to Mr. Chambers to test by further questioning his claim to have known Mr. Hiss. On August 7th, 1948, this sub-committee saw Mr. Chambers and elicited such details of Mr. Hiss's household and affairs that the proof, who was lying, was plainly within reach. Nine days later, while a tremendous press campaign continued against Mr. Chambers (he was called 'mad' among other things, a familiar Communist trick) Mr. Hiss was called again. He repeated all denials, but his answers to questions, which confirmed Mr. Chambers's information in detail, showed that Mr. Chambers must have known him, his wife and child and stayed in his house. On August 17th, 1948, they were confronted privately. Mr. Hiss, after asking to hear Mr. Chambers's voice and look in his mouth, decided he was a man called Crosley who *had* once stayed in his house. He reiterated all denials about Communism and invited Mr. Chambers to repeat his statements outside the committee-room, so that he could be sued for libel.

That put the fat in the fire. Presumably Mr. Chambers, until this moment, felt certain Mr. Hiss would not drive him into the last corner by sueing for libel, while Mr. Hiss was sure Mr. Chambers would not dare to produce his proofs, or did not know he had them.

About this time Mr. Chambers resigned his senior editorship of *Time* (which in its columns treated him not much more kindly than the other publications); this threw up the question, what motive could a man have to sacrifice $30,000 a year and a brilliant career merely to defame another man unknown to him? The second confrontation, on August 25th, 1948, was public. When it came about Mr. Hiss was acclaimed by a host of friends throughout America; Mr. Chambers was a pariah. When one after another of Mr. Hiss's statements was broken down by evidence he denied having made them and attacked Mr. Chambers's character, as the press did outside. However, his friends cut off his last escape, for some sympathizers inveigled Mr. Chambers to a microphone, apparently to bait him, and dared him to repeat there that Mr. Hiss 'is or ever was a Communist', which Mr. Chambers promptly did. Thereon even the public wondered why Mr. Hiss did not sue and after a month he did, for $75,000.

Now Mr. Chambers could not turn back. He went to his relative in New York and retrieved the dust-covered envelope from the disused service-lift shaft. It contained forty-seven copies of official documents (proved to have been typewritten on Mr. Hiss's machine), five rolls of microfilm which recorded hundreds more documents in miniature, four memorandums in Mr. Hiss's writing and five in Mr. Dexter White's. He took the papers to his lawyer and put the microfilm rolls in a pumpkin on his farm, the top of which he removed and replaced. At the 'pre-trial hearing' Mr. Hiss's lawyer contemptuously asked if Mr. Chambers had 'any documentary proof of your assertions' and, after ten years, the papers were produced.

The affrighted lawyers agreed that the matter was now too big for them and sent the documents to the FBI. On December 8th, 1948, the Grand Jury, ageing fast, was once more convened. The investigators retained little faith in it and what they had vanished when an inspired newspaper announcement said 'The Justice Department is about ready to drop its investigation of the celebrated Alger Hiss-Whittaker Chambers controversy' (Americans often smile about the English gift for understatement, but the word 'controversy' has seldom been outdone, or underdone, even in England).

Even at that stage the matter looked likely to be shelved but for still another chance. A third journalist cabled to the persistent Congressman who previously rescued it from oblivion that he believed 'new evidence' was in currency; would the Committee reopen its investigation? The Congressman replied that he would have the Committee's hearings reopened 'if necessary to prevent Justice Department cover-up' and returned from a sea voyage to land by commandeered coast-guard aeroplane. The thing was a race for time now, for the Congressional Committee itself was about to die; an election was just over which increased the Democratic and reduced the Republican strength in Congress and soon the Committee's membership was to be re-arranged and its zeal curbed, like that of the Grand Jury. It was a matter of days.

The irrepressible Congressman, returned to Washington, had Mr. Chambers sub-poenaed to yield up any *other* material in his possession. Mr. Chambers led the committee's investigators to his pumpkin patch and his last proofs, the five rolls of microfilm. They too contained the most secret information of the American and other governments.

American Ambassadors in London and other capitals laid bare the minds of British and other Prime Ministers; private matters of military, naval and air forces abounded, and graver things still. The prints made a pile over four feet high. Not all these documents have been made public; even today their content is held too serious. They represented perhaps a fiftieth part of the whole mass of information which was conveyed to Moscow by this *one* group. Mr. White's memorandums were read to the House of Representatives and seriously incriminated himself and others. He died suddenly about this time, as did Mr. Laurence Duggan (a former State Department official also named in the business) and several other people. These deaths have never been publicly explained.

Of these documents an Under Secretary of State during the period concerned, Mr. Sumner Welles, said that their release to unauthorized hands in 1938 would have been 'in the highest degree prejudicial, and in the highest degree dangerous, to the national interest'. To have delivered them to a foreign power would have meant giving away also the means of breaking the most secret codes. An Assistant Secretary of State, Mr. Francis B. Sayre (whose testimony was not made public) said in comment on press suggestions that the documents were not of the highest importance, 'I violently disagree, not only because of the substance of these cables, but because some of them were in the highly confidential codes . . . And for these telegrams to get out at the time they did meant that other governments could crack our codes and that, I think, is indescribably horrible.' Another point, he added, was that 'some of these cables reveal sources from which information was obtained, sources planted in foreign countries. Now, you make a cable of this kind known, you cut off that source of information from another country, and you kill what you have been working on for years' (this is what Colonel Redl did, too).

The Un-American Activities Committee now tried once more to force the government's hand by publishing the news of the pumpkin-plot papers and vague indications of their import. The Grand Jury met, and on December 10th reported, sure enough, that it could find no grounds for an indictment! It also attacked the Congressional Committee for its irritating zeal. Then the last chance intervened. The

FBI., with professional energy, ran down letters written by Mr. and Mrs. Hiss on a typewriter since disappeared; they were found to have been written on the same machine which made the copies of secret documents, between their abstraction and return. At that Mr. Hiss was indicted for perjury, in denying that he furnished the copies to Mr. Chambers and that he ever saw or talked with Mr. Chambers at relevant dates (under the American statute of limitations Mr. Hiss was never charged with espionage or treason).

During this time the presidential office repeatedly referred to the matter as 'a red herring' or 'a hysterical outcry' intended only to discredit the party in power. Just before the Un-American Activities Committee passed from Republican control Mr. Chambers made a full disclosure to it of everything he knew and had done in espionage. This material was suppressed by the new committee; if published it might give the public mind a galvanic shock so great that purification would be forced.

Even at this stage the matter might have ended in public acclamation for Mr. Hiss but for that remarkable institution, the jury system. Mr. Hiss's first trial, in May-July 1949, was conducted by a judge who once referred to Mr. Chambers as 'the defendant'; who was new on the Federal bench and assigned himself to this trial; whose nomination was refused endorsement by the Association of the Bar of New York City and by the Federal Bar Associations of the States of New York, New Jersey and Connecticut; and was supported by only one group, the New York County Lawyers Association, of the judiciary committee of which Mr. Hiss's counsel was chairman. A justice of the Supreme Court (which would have to try any ultimate appeal) offered himself as character witness for Mr. Hiss. This was Mr. Felix Frankfurter, who was initially responsible for Mr. Hiss's entry into government service; his 'young men' of the Harvard Law School in the 1920s were numerously distributed in it. However, eight jurors voted for conviction against four for acquittal. The evidence was thought conclusive by most people and found so by the next jury, in 1950, which returned a unanimous verdict of guilty.

Mr. Hiss was sentenced to five years imprisonment and this was followed by one of the most remarkable incidents of the whole affair.

On hearing the news the Secretary of State of the day, Mr. Dean Acheson, called pressmen together to tell them, 'Whatever the outcome of any appeal by Mr. Hiss, I do not intend to turn my back on him'. To reinforce the solemn earnestness of his words, he spoke them with an open Bible at hand! The case of Colonel Redl filled from first to last about eleven hours; that of Mr. Hiss about eleven years, up to that point.

The Hiss case shows that by this mid-century a massive power has arisen in the world which is now able to corrupt and enslave young people in great numbers; secretly to sway politicians, political parties and major actions of State policy; and to prevent, delay or mitigate the exposure and punishment of treachery.

This state of affairs is not only an American one but exists, in varying degrees, in England and the Commonwealth countries; that is, throughout the English-speaking area. In England no action followed Mr. MacKenzie King's warning of the extent of treasonable infusion in 1946 (if Dr. Allan Nunn May was tried and convicted, this seems only to have been because his name emerged too clearly in the Canadian revelations to be ignored). The case of Dr. Klaus Fuchs apparently became public in 1950 solely because the FBI., in America, drew attention to it (it was less successful in obtaining action about similar cases in America). Yet the British Government was warned in 1933, according to Mr. Attlee, that Dr. Fuchs was a Communist, and Dr. Fuchs's own counsel at his trial said he was always 'a known Communist and never pretended that he was anything else'. His name was one of five sent to the British Government by the Canadian one in 1946, when 'the responsibility for further investigation rested on the British Government' (the Canadian Minister of External Affairs). Yet he was allowed to continue his vital work and was enabled, by the grant of British citizenship, to take part in, and betray, atomic research work in America. In both the May and Fuchs cases the judicial comments at the trials were ignored (the Lord Chief Justice said, 'Dare we now give shelter to political refugees who may be followers of this pernicious creed and who well may disguise themselves to bite the hand that feeds them?' and he was rebuked by the *Daily Telegraph, Manchester Guardian* and *Spectator.*) The Prime Minister said that, save by totalitarian methods, 'There were no means by which one could have found out about this man', despite the Canadian warning of four years before. Here is a span of seventeen years of treason unchecked, and in the persons of Drs. May and Fuchs only the fringe of the destructive organism was touched. In America (which received a list of 165 names from Canada) the President spoke of 'hysteria'.

Newspapers of the most respectable pretensions join in obscuring the matter and preventing exposure; possibly their owners and editors often do not even understand what goes on in their own columns. Any man who tries to expose the evil is 'smeared' as a 'character assassin', 'Red-baiter', 'witch-hunter' or 'anti-Semite' by newspapers from London to Manchester, Durban to Cape Town and Johannesburg, Sydney to Auckland, New York to Los Angeles. The 'smear' once attached to the accuser, the *facts* of the charge or inquiry are suppressed or obscured. This is the result of the systematic permeation of the press during the last twenty-five years by trained Leftist writers whose allegiance is not publicly known. A leading American journalist, Mr. Arthur Krock, wrote of 'The increase in the number of syndicated writers from Washington of Leftist persuasions. Their opinions and their versions of the facts and factors in public affairs reach millions of readers. And like-minded radio commentators are skilled in the use of inflections and tones to produce desired effects on listeners while adhering to a neutral text.' In England, a case of this kind became public when Reuter's Chief Correspondent in Berlin resigned and transferred to the Communist sector, then giving a propagandist interview to the Communist press there. He, too, was a known Communist. The fact only became public, however, because of his public action, which was apparently ordered for propagandist effect; and here, again, but one tiny corner of a great dark curtain was lifted; the general condition remains.

I was travelling in America during the first Hiss trial and saw that the American public had no means of judging the facts. Not only the judge referred to the accuser as 'the defendant'. Leading political personages, writers and broadcasters put it that way (Mrs. Eleanor Roosevelt said 'Mr. Chambers is on trial and not Mr. Hiss'), and I believe many people thought that the actual case. American newspapers in the great majority are assembly-line jobs. They are made up of 'agency reports', prepared by the 'syndicated writers of Leftist persuasions' to whom Mr. Krock referred, which are widely distributed and universally used. The planting of a few trained men at these sources of news-supply enables the whole stream of information to be infected, far outside America; I satisfied myself that British and Common-wealth readers, too, could gain no authentic view of the matter. Mr. Hiss's case was not an isolated one. During 1949 and 1950 at least half a dozen major scandals of the kind deeply alarmed masses of Americans, but with each new one the clamour of 'Drop the witch-hunt' grew louder from leading public personages, newspapers and the radio.

The Hiss case is symbolic. Mr. Chambers and Mr. Hiss in their opposed figures represent the inner conflict which threatens to disrupt the English-speaking family as it awaits the final assault of Asiatic barbarism, the last stage of Armageddon. In the 1920s they were the earliest guinea-pigs of Communism in the Christian West. Now they stand, one an unregenerate Communist, ready to conspire and lie to the last for the sake, or fear, of his alien allegiance; the other a regener-ate who would rather die than see that cause triumph, who has returned to religion as well as patriotism. The dark background is the political heaven in which there was no joy over the sinner who repented, but only praise and friendship for the one who did not. Somewhere in that clouded Olympus behind the two men lies the shape of the coming decision.

As to that, the whole future of America is at stake. Dr. Charles A. Beard (in *President Roosevelt and the Coming of the War, 1941*; published 1948) said, 'At this point in its history, the American Republic has arrived under the theory that the President of the United States pos-sesses limitless authority publicly to misrepresent and secretly to control foreign policy, foreign affairs, and the war power. More than a hundred years ago, James Madison, Father of the Constitution, pro-phesied that the supreme test of American statesmanship would come about 1930. Although not exactly in the form that Madison foresaw, the test is here now — with no divinity hedging our Republic against Caesar.'

If President Madison and Dr. Beard are right, the result of the test, under Mr. Roosevelt's presidency (he was elected in 1932) was that power in the Republic passed by penetration largely into foreign hands, and did not leave them when the next president succeeded. The power of American presidents has become so much infected before they use it that even a war against the Communist Empire could be turned to serve the ends of these occult controllers; to judge by the course of the Second War it would be diverted at decisive moments to serve the destructive plan in some way. President Roosevelt's actions, particularly at Yalta, show that. His own words, and abundant other evidence, prove that he was not, alone and by himself, the wielder of power, but that this was exercised by ascendant groups around him.

Whether he knew, all the time, some of the time, or none of the time, whither they were pushing him may never become clear. Towards his end (when Mr. Churchill in the House of Commons said 'The United States is now at the highest pinnacle of her power and fame' and Mr. Sherwood, the ghost-writer, urged the President to quote this in a speech), Mr. Roosevelt said, 'What Winston says may be true at the moment, but I'd hate to say it, because we may be heading before very long for the pinnacle of our weakness'. The 'strange statement' perplexed Mr. Sherwood but was a truer picture than Mr. Churchill's, whether Mr. Roosevelt realized this or was simply fey. Once Mr. Churchill, with similar rhetorical inexactitude, spoke of 'the hospitable and exhilarating atmosphere of the White House and of the American nation, erect and infuriate against tyrants and aggressors'. The American nation desired to be in that heroic posture, and perhaps thought it was, but under President Roosevelt the reality was other than the appearance.

What real purpose did Mr. Roosevelt promote through the way he used his imperial powers? He furthered the main principles of a plan for the redistribution of the earth published in 1942 (but clearly prepared much earlier) by a mysterious 'Group for a New World Order', headed by a Mr. Moritz Gomberg. What this group proposed was startling at the time but proved farsighted. The main recommendations were that the Communist Empire should be extended from the Pacific to the Rhine, with China, Korea, Indo-China, Siam and Malaya in its orbit; and that a Hebrew State should be set up on the soil of 'Palestine,

Transjordan and the adjoining territories'. These two projects were largely realized. Canada and numerous 'strategic islands' were to pass to the United States (the reader should keep these 'strategic islands' in mind). The remaining countries of Western Europe were to disappear in a 'United States of Europe' (this scheme is being vigorously pursued at present). The African continent was to become a 'Union of Republics'. The British Commonwealth was to be left much reduced, the Dutch West Indies joining Australia and New Zealand in it. The scheme looks like a blueprint of the second stage in a grand operation of three stages, and substantial parts of it were achieved; what was not then accomplished is being energetically attempted now.

Certainly President Roosevelt would not publicly have owned such a plan, but his actions all furthered it. The fighting leaders in America (and in England) both thought they saw plainly what they fought for; to sustain each other. On the eve of America's entry into the war the Chief of Naval Operations, Admiral Stark, prepared a memorandum which stated, as the major national objectives, 'defence of the Western Hemisphere and prevention of the disruption of the British Empire, with all that such a consummation implies'. The same dominant aims were declared in another memorandum, jointly prepared by the two Chiefs of Staff, General Marshall and Admiral Stark. The fighting leaders in England, and the political ones, in reverse circumstances would clearly put 'the prevention of the disruption of the United States' at the head of the list. President Roosevelt, the potentate, in truth thought differently. In 1950 his speeches and papers were published; being edited by a Mr. Samuel Rosenman, one of the three ghost-writers who prepared his speeches, they are of especial authenticity. Mr. Rosenman records that, in answer to a journalist who asked if Mr. Churchill expected the British Empire to remain intact after the war, Mr. Roosevelt said, 'Yes, he is mid-Victorian on all things like that . . . Dear old Winston will never learn on that point.'

Then what were Mr. Roosevelt's private ideas about the British Commonwealth, his ally, and how far did Mr. Churchill understand them? Mr. Roosevelt's views seem to have been constant and different from what was publicly supposed; he wanted to redistribute the Commonwealth, in collaboration with the Soviet and to enlarge the Communist Empire. Mr. Churchill seems to have moved about between incomprehension of this and sudden, irritable perceptions of it. Mr. Roosevelt may or may not have understood the ultimate purpose of destroying *all* nations; his experience was not great. Mr. Churchill, more widely travelled and deeply versed, knew it well. That appears from his own words: 'No sooner did Lenin arrive in Russia than he began beckoning a finger here and there to obscure persons in sheltered retreats in New York, Glasgow, Berne and other countries, and he gathered together the leading spirits of a formidable sect, the most formidable sect in the world'; and, 'The citadel will be stormed under the banners of Liberty and Democracy; and once the apparatus of power is in the hands of the Brotherhood all opposition, all contrary opinions, must be extinguished by death. Democracy is but a tool to be used and afterwards broken; liberty but a sentimental folly unworthy of the logician. The absolute rule of a self-chosen priesthood according to dogmas it has learned by rote is to be imposed upon mankind without mitigation progressively for ever.' No shred of doubt, then, remains in Mr. Churchill's case that he knows what it is all about.

These two men in the 1940s wielded, or outwardly appeared to wield, imperial power, untrammelled. Mr. Churchill says this was the office he liked best: 'Power in a national crisis, when a man believes he knows what orders should be given, is a blessing.' To me it seems a curse, in the light of the two wars. However, it set them both free to pursue purposes which the masses inferred to be those of preserving their own countries, first, and sustaining their allies, second.

One of Mr. Churchill's first actions seemed oddly aberrant; the offer, as France fell, to merge the British and French nations. It would have meant the surrender of national identity in one direction while it was being defended to the last in another; to this day I am grateful to the Frenchmen who rejected it. The idea was not Mr. Churchill's. He says he was 'by no means convinced', and 'the implications and consequences' of this 'immense design' were not in any way thought out; yet he made the proposal. (A prime mover, he says, was M. Jean Monnet of France, who in 1950 was a prime mover in an analagous project, that to unite British, French and German heavy industry under 'a supreme authority'. In this form the plan of the Group for a

New World Order goes on and it seems to me all in tune with the aims of the Brotherhood.)

Mr. Churchill was a heroic figure then, yet the British Islanders, had they been told more, might have been disturbed at some of the things he contemplated. As France collapsed he told these islanders, 'Our Empire beyond the seas, armed and guarded by the British Fleet, would carry on the struggle'. Yet later Mr. Harry Hopkins reported to President Roosevelt, 'Churchill believed that if the United Kingdom fell, the Empire would be ended, at least temporarily, and the leadership of the remaining units of the British Commonwealth would pass to Washington'.

Had that happened, Canada would presumably have passed to the United States (as the Group for a New World Order foresaw), but why should it have happened? At that time the British Government urged the French Government with all its might to withdraw with its fleet to the French overseas empire and continue the battle from there. Marshal Petain was even accused of treachery for not doing so (and as I write the nonagenarian is still in a fortress on that account). No reason offers why the King, government and fleet should not have gone to Canada to fight on from there. The British Islander today may be more than ever grateful to Lord Dowding and all those who resisted the pressure to have the last British fighters sent to France. At that time several messages from Mr. Churchill to President Roosevelt spoke of the British fleet 'crossing the Atlantic' (not 'going to Canada') in the event of a successful invasion of Britain, and at one point the Canadian Prime Minister and British Ambassador in Washington seem both to have taken alarm.

Then the curious matter of the 'strategic islands' arose (which the Group for a New World Order also foresaw to pass to America: the ruling idea may be that the World-Government-to-come can best hold the world in thrall from this chain of ocean strongholds). Mr. Churchill suggested to Mr. Roosevelt that the Republic should acquire on 99-year leases naval bases on certain British West Indian islands, in return for the use of fifty old destroyers. He says, 'There was, of course, no comparison between the intrinsic value of these antiquated and inefficient craft and the immense *permanent*' (my italics) 'strategic

348

security afforded to the United States by the enjoyment of island bases'.

Much later (November 1942) Mr. Churchill seems to have been seized by sudden suspicions, for he said, 'Let me make this clear, in case there should be any mistake about it in any quarter. We mean to hold to our own. I have not become the King's First Minister in order to preside over the liquidation of the British Empire . . . Here we are and here we stand, a veritable rock of salvation in this drifting world.' However, if that needed saying Mr. Churchill's earlier actions may have caused the need. Apart from the islands, there was his strange pronouncement of August 1940, 'The British Empire and the United States will have to be somewhat mixed up together in some of their affairs for mutual and general advantage . . . I do not view the process with any misgivings. I could not stop it if I wished. Like the Mississippi, it just keeps rolling along. Let it roll.' I never found, in America or my own island, any who wanted the two countries 'mixed up', unless they were hangers-on of 'the most formidable sect in the world' which desires the destruction of all nations.

Mr. Churchill in 1940 may have overestimated his knowledge of what was in President Roosevelt's mind; this would explain his somewhat aggrieved later protest, for by that time he was enlightened. In June 1942 a Mr. Molotoff visited Washington and President Roosevelt told him there were, all over the world, 'many islands and colonial possessions which ought, for our own safety, to be taken away from weak nations' ('our' apparently meant the Communist Empire and the United States. These islands were nearly all in possession of the Republic's fighting allies, particularly the British Commonwealth). The President was specific: the Japanese should be removed from the formerly German islands they administered 'but we do not want these islands and neither the British nor the French ought to have them either. Perhaps the same procedure should be applied to the islands now held by the British. These islands obviously ought not to belong to any one nation'. Mr. Roosevelt, then, did not want the 'strategic islands' for the American Republic, but for the New World Order.

Mr. Roosevelt then turned from islands to mainland 'colonial possessions' (which, the reader will recall, the Group for a New

World Order allotted to the Communist Empire). The President 'took as examples' Indo-China (French), Siam (*not* a 'colonial posses-sion' but an independent kingdom), and the Malay States (British), and proposed changes of authority there. Mr. Molotoff was favourably impressed. Mr. Churchill seems to have become restless when he learned about these proposed dispositions (extended later also to India and Hong Kong). Thereon Mr. Eden, visiting Washington, was moved to mention that President Roosevelt did not suggest any com-parable American gestures and to inquire about the President's con-stitutional powers for reshaping the world while it was still at war. Mr. Hopkins then consulted an Assistant Secretary of State (Mr. Berle), who reported that the President could do anything he liked 'without any Congressional action in the first instance' and 'the hand-ling of the military forces of the United States could be so managed as to foster any purpose he pursued'.

Such evidence is conclusive but if it were not the last nail of proof is driven home in a book published in 1950 by Admiral William D. Leahy, personal Chief of Staff to Presidents Roosevelt and Truman (*I Was There*). This shows plainly that Mr. Roosevelt's grand design was for a large apportionment of the globe between the Communist Empire and the United States, at the expense of the British Common-wealth and French Empire. Support of Communism in China, too, was primarily intended to prevent a British revival there and in the planning of the Pacific campaign everything was done to exclude the British and make China and Japan into a Soviet-American sphere of influence. Admiral Leahy shows that President Truman, when he succeeded, accepted and applied this policy without question. The results of it confront America today. Charity in search of motive might conclude that President Roosevelt's inexperience and super-ficial knowledge of world affairs and ill-health blinded him to what he did and that his facial expression at the end reflected an awakening inner consternation about the purposes for which he was used.

In fact he furthered the aims of the 'formidable sect' and perilously weakened his country at home. He is the great example of the appar-ently powerful man, used by others for ulterior aims. In reality he was not even president at fateful moments. Mr. Hopkins was that and he was like a blind man playing with high tension wires. History shows no stranger partnership than this, which built up the Communist Empire to its present peak of menace.

I told how Mr. Roosevelt emerged from political oblivion to become, first Governor of New York, then President, wielding exceptional Powers against a permanent Emergency. Constitutional restraints irked him from the start; if he did not, like Hitler, proclaim himself 'the supreme magistrate', yet in a similar spirit, when his actions were challenged, he attacked his Supreme Court and threatened to pack it with compliant justices. His and Mr. Hopkins's assaults on the obstructive judges because they were 'elderly' read oddly thirteen years later; years in those cases denoted physical health, but neither Mr. Roosevelt nor Mr. Hopkins were to live long enough to be accused of old age. Immediately he became Governor, in 1928, Mr. Roosevelt began a huge programme of welfare expenditure which he inflated from a State to a national one when he became President. In 1928 he first chose Mr. Hopkins, then a little-known charity-appeal organizer, to conduct this spending which later, again, swelled into a worldwide distribution under the name of 'Lend-Lease'. Mr. Hopkins never enriched himself but sovereignly dispensed more money than any man, or probably any thousand men, in the world before, free from all supervision. What manner of man, then, was this Mr. Hopkins?

He, too, was a typical product of the years of confusion. Born in humble circumstances, he emerged just before the First War from a small college where his favourite professor was a man who, during years in England, fell in with the London Economic Club and the Fabian Society and who believed 'the democratic nations would learn to co-operate through a United States of the World'; the familiar influences appear at the start. Another professor, from whom he first learned about 'the strange, remote, gigantic mass that was Russia', was a converted Jew from Bohemia who conducted a course on Applied Christianity. Mr. Hopkins was 'permanently influenced' by what he thus learned of 'the Christian ethic and the teachings of Tolstoy'.

Arrived in the outer, bewildering world Mr. Hopkins (through the second professor) obtained a small post with a mission in the East Side slums of New York, which were then (1912) full of Eastern European gunmen of the Peter the Painter or Stern Gang type. Four men ('Gyp the Blood, Dago Frank, Lefty Louie and Whitey Lewis') were executed for the murder of a gaming-house owner, Herman Rosenthal, and one day, when Mr. Hopkins lectured on civic betterment to a boys' club, a lad rose and said 'I move that the whole club stand up for two minutes in honour of the four gunmen who died today'. Mr. Hopkins was 'profoundly puzzled' but, typically, concluded that 'society' must be to blame. He had a hard life, enlisted in the organized claques for Caruso and Geraldine Farrar at the Opera House, joined the Red Cross in 1917, returned to charity-appeal work in 1921. Employers or colleagues of that period depict 'an ulcerous type, intense, seeming to be in a perpetual nervous ferment, a chain-smoker and black coffee drinker. Most of the time he would show up at the office looking as though he had spent the previous night sleeping in a hayloft. He would wear the same shirt three or four days at a time'; 'Harry never had the faintest conception of the value of money. But then, that is true of most social workers. Although in no sense personally dishonest, they can become unscrupulous in the handling of funds. They can convince themselves that the worthy end justifies the means.'

Thus the later global replanner and dispenser of untold billions. From 1933 on he was 'in all respects the inevitable Roosevelt favourite'. In 1937 he spent six months in hospital, a large portion of his stomach being removed, and in 1938 was told by Mr. Roosevelt he would be the next president, or at least Democratic candidate. Further illness possibly prevented that; in August 1939 he had 'about four weeks to live', but recovered and 'was taken into the White House to live in May 1940'. From then until the war's end he was in decisive matters 'the de facto President' or in others 'the second most important individual in the United States Government during the most critical period of the world's greatest war, yet he had no legitimate official position nor even any desk of his own except a card table in his bedroom' (Mr. Robert Sherwood, his biographer, who was also brought into the White House by Mr. Hopkins).

Mr. Sherwood, though an admirer, calls him 'a profoundly

352

shrewd and faintly ominous man' and says when he entered the White House 'he was to all intents and purposes physically a finished man who might drag out his life for a few years of relative inactivity or might collapse or die at any time'. However, not inactive, he lived in President Lincoln's study, which was the best guest room, assigned to King George VI during his visit in 1939; 'it was conveniently located for Churchill, being right across the hall' from the room occupied by Mr. Churchill during his visits.

A dying president delegated to another dying man such authority that he became in fact, all unsupervised, the president. Unhindered power to dispose of the money, arms, manufactures and military operations of America was his, or anyone's who could control his mind. Today's map shows the results. Mr. Hopkins lacked training and knowledge for a task involving the fate of hundreds of millions of beings. He cultivated crudeness in thought, manners and speech, and talked of 'cracking down on the bastards' if he were opposed. This appealed to Mr. Roosevelt, who liked to put on the Common Man air (the widespread American weakness to which Mr. Somerset Maugham alluded). The two men especially liked to deride professional members of the American Foreign Service as 'pansies', 'striped-pants' and 'cookie-pushers'.

Mr. Hopkins entered on his empire with the birth of Lend-Lease and reigned for four years. Mr. Churchill says that by November 1940 Britain had paid to America, in cash or British-owned shares requisitioned from their owners, nearly 5,000,000,000 dollars, so that its resources were almost exhausted and further American supplies could not be paid for. Hard bargains were driven. At American request the British Government sold the Courtauld business in America to the United States Government for a low figure and it was then sold through the markets at a much higher price. An American warship was sent to Cape Town, despite Mr. Churchill's appeals, to carry away British gold gathered there. After that the barrel was empty, and 'Lend-Lease' appeared. Under a statute of 1892 the American Secretary of War might 'lease army property when in his discretion it will be for the public good'. This was invoked (December 1940) to help Britain, President Roosevelt saying in a 'Fireside Chat', 'If Britain should go down, all of us in the Americas would be living at the point of a gun'.

Appearances belie realities; not Britain was to be chiefly succoured. The Lend-Lease Bill was passed against the protests of many Americans who wanted to help Britain but feared their money might in the end arm the Red Army. *Three months later* that became the case. In June the Fascists red and brown turned against each other and Lend-Lease became an inexhaustible supply-line to the Communist Empire. The sums which passed through it (say, over £20,000,000,000,000) are beyond human comprehension, and where it all went is hard to determine. Mr. Sherwood appears to say that about a fifth went to the Soviet Empire, but the share might be much larger if the countries it was helped to annex were included.

Some idea of the possibilities is given by the Report of a Congressional Committee on Military Expenditure for the year 1949, which asked, 'What became of the vast quantities of war material on hand at the end of hostilities?' The American Army, it stated, then had material sufficient to equip only eighteen fully-equipped divisions 'although at the end of the war it had some eighty-nine fully equipped divisions and great additional quantities of material in the pipe line'. The Report also asked what happened to the 86,000 tanks produced during the war; in 1949 the Army could only produce 16,000, most of them obsolete.

After the Second War's end this vast quantity of arms disappeared, somehow, somewhere. Private soldiers may not lose a button without reprimand. The direction in which most of it went seems obvious. The American Army was precipitately disbanded, Western Europe left almost undefended, the Soviet Empire up to Berlin gorged with soldiers and weapons.

Mr. Hopkins, though without formal title, was put in sole charge of this stupendous distribution. That meant world power, for it meant the control of foreign policy. He decided who should have weapons, and also merchant shipping, vehicles, food, fuel, industrial equipment (among other things, plans of the Tennessee Valley Authority's great power plants were supplied, and machines built from these are now being used in atom-bomb and other production in the Soviet fastnesses). The State Department in Washington and American Ambassadors abroad were excluded from the daily business of foreign relations; the foreign missions besieged the bestower of gifts, Mr. Hopkins. He appointed his own 'Expediter of Lend-Lease' in London, so that the functions of the American Ambassador there (as Mr. Walter Winant sadly complained) virtually ceased. Mr. Churchill, with messages for President Roosevelt, would cable to Mr. Hopkins and receive replies from him. The experienced Foreign Minister (Mr. Cordell Hull) sometimes received polite notes enclosing copies of Mr. Hopkins's cables 'for information'. A Cabinet Committee (representing the State Department, Treasury, Army and Navy) at first expected to supervise this gigantic diffusion of money, arms and goods, but it was thrust aside and Mr. Hopkins became supreme arbiter.

The results now show how he used the power. Right at the start (July 1941) he went to Moscow to discuss deliveries. He told Stalin that the American Government would be unwilling to send really big stuff, like tanks, aircraft and artillery, until 'the relative and strategic interests of each front, as well as the interests of our several countries' were fully and jointly explored in conference.

This seems the first and last time any suggestion was made that the causes and outcome of the war should be discussed before the Soviet Empire was put in a position to ignore any conditions. Thereafter supplies were continuous, increasing and unconditional, though pious hopes about this or that were sometimes expressed.

In tackling Stalin, Mr. Hopkins was the opposite of the picture painted of him by Mr. Roosevelt: 'When he's talking to some foreign dignitary, he knows how to slump back in his chair and put up his feet upon the conference table and say, Oh yeah?' Mr. Hopkins said 'Oh yes!' not 'Oh yeah?' He emerged from the presence in a state of awe that remained with him, so that a friend had to remind him he was a down-to-earth American, as good as any man if not better.

Thus supplies began without any irritating condition save one: that repayment should begin five years after the war's end (I doubt if this matter was strictly pressed, in 1950). Only one obstacle remained. Mr. Hopkins, now 'Chairman of the President's Soviet Protocol Committee', was in 1942 irritated by a committee-member who urged that 'before we extend further aid to the Russians we should demand that they provide us with full information concerning their military situation as the British have consistently done'. Italics should be sparingly used but Mr. Hopkins's reply deserves them because it explains what truly went on and what confronts the world today:

The United States is doing things which it would not do for other United Nations without full information from them. This decision to act without full information was made with some misgivings but after due deliberation (whose deliberation, Mr. Hopkins did not mention; presumably Mr. Hopkins's). *There is no reservation about the policy at the present time but the policy is constantly being brought up by various groups for rediscussion. I propose that no further consideration be given to these requests for rediscussion.*

That was final, and fateful for America and the world. Mr. Sherwood says, 'The repeated warnings of possible Russian perfidy that Roosevelt received in 1941 and throughout the years that followed only served to make him increase his efforts to convince the Russians of America's incontestable good faith', and presumably Mr. Hopkins was the master-mind in this. At this point Mr. Hopkins, to judge by such words, seemed only to desire the triumph of the Soviet Empire and I wondered if he ever stated what he thought the war *was* about. I found he repeatedly described the grand purpose. It was, in splendid simplicity, 'to defeat Hitler'. Mr. Churchill elaborates: 'There he sat, slim, frail, ill, but absolutely glowing with refined comprehension of the Cause. It was to be the defeat, ruin and slaughter of Hitler, to the exclusion of all other purposes, loyalties or aims.'

These are hard words, used in praise, but apparently true, especially the ones about 'exclusion of all other loyalties' (which might almost form an indictment). If Mr. Hopkins's refined comprehension reduced the Cause to the slaughter of one man he was sorely disappointed. One of his last experiences on earth was to hear from Stalin's august lips scornful disbelief of Hitler's death, and Stalin should have known, because by that time his soldiers were in exclusive possession of the place where Hitler committed suicide, omitting to leave his body behind. On his return to Berlin Mr. Hopkins was apparently the first American citizen to be allowed into this place. He had told the sceptical Stalin he hoped to find Hitler's body there. He found only some books in Hitler's office, which he took for souvenirs.

'The exclusion of all other loyalties'; those are remarkable words indeed. Did the master of rhetoric who used them realize, on this occasion, how precisely they described the sober but sinister truth? A man in Mr. Hopkins's position ('de facto President') should have but two loyalties, the primary one to his country and the secondary one to his country's allies. These cannot be 'excluded' (and Mr. Churchill is not one to use words carelessly) without other loyalties taking their place. Mr. Hopkins did in fact put loyalty to the Communist ally (so recently Hitler's own ally) above loyalty to all his country's other allies; his own words testify to that. Therewith he also put it above loyalty to his own country; whether his mental and physical health enabled him to see that or not, the event proved it for his country was left facing another and worse war. In effect his actions advanced the aims of that 'Brotherhood' or 'most formidable sect in the world' which Mr. Churchill so well understood, and it is hard to see why Mr. Churchill thought so highly of his comprehension.

'Other loyalties' indeed suffered grievously after Mr. Hopkins entered the war. In its later years the picture behind the scenes was rather like that of a supper party at the Borgias, culminating in the toxic banquet at Yalta. The Communist Empire had a primary and a secondary aim. The first was to add as much territory as it could to its domains through the war. The second was to prevent the rise of men, or groups of men, in the remaining European countries who would become national heroes of liberation there, forming strong cores around which those nations would rally in the third stage of Armageddon. The weaker and more leaderless those remaining nations were left, the easier would the final triumph be. The actions of Messrs. Roosevelt and Hopkins, and unhappily those of the British leaders, also lent themselves to this process, which was to make a third war harder to prevent and more difficult to fight if it came.

The reader may remember how thankless the lot became, as the war went on, of any who at the start threw in their lot with the enemies of the man whose 'defeat, ruin and slaughter' was the Cause. King Leopold of the Belgians was called traitor because he stayed with his army to the last and did not join his government in exile. King Peter of Yugoslavia was dethroned because he formed a government in exile and did not stay with his army to the last ('He asked me,' says Brigadier Fitzroy Maclean, Mr. Churchill's emissary to the Communist usurper, Tito, 'what prospect I thought he had of recovering his throne after the war. I replied, None, unless he could somehow go back and take part in the war of liberation, side by side with his people, as his father had done in the last war'). King George of Greece sinned mortally by staying with his army to the last *and* then forming a government in exile; after that his allies insisted that he should not remount his throne without a public referendum.

General de Gaulle, having fought with us from the start, was pictured as a nuisance and probably 'a Fascist'. Otto Strasser, the one German who fought Hitler in Germany and in exile from 1933 on, was held a virtual prisoner in Canada and as I write is still forbidden even to return to his country, where men who crushed attempts to kill Hitler are allowed to organize political parties. As to Poland (Mr. Churchill wrongly calls a section of *Their Finest Hour*, 'Alone!'; the Poles then fought with us on land, at sea and in the air) it was 'the first to fight' and its liberation intact was pledged by Mr. Eden on July 30th, 1941. Yet it was handed to the Communist Empire; the Poles, logically, did not appear at all in the ultimate Victory Parade. Mr. Churchill even thought, by 1949, that the Poles 'doomed themselves by their follies' to 'awful slaughter and miseries' (from a sea-girt island it may appear folly to live in a country squeezed between the Rooshans and the Prooshans).

In China Chiang Kai-shek incurred the odium generally attaching to allies. His troubles began during Mr. Hopkins's reign. The accumulated evidence of the various inquiries and exposures which have occurred since the Second War ended now overwhelmingly suggests that Communist infiltration in American government departments and more particularly in the war-time agencies which were set up, was strong enough for the Communists to delay Lend-Lease deliveries to Chiang Kai-shek, or rather, to ensure that he received no deliveries. When the great flow of supplies to the Communist Empire began the Chinese emissary in Washington protested to Mr. Hopkins, 'I have now been in the United States over fourteen months pleading for help of planes ... In these fourteen months not a single plane sufficiently equipped with armaments and ammunition so that it could actually be used to fire has reached China.' By November 1942 Madame Chiang Kai-Shek told Mr. Hopkins, 'Everyone in China is afraid that the United States is going to sell them down the river', a prescient fear. Mr. Roosevelt's arrangements at Yalta, and subsequent American support for the Communist demand to be taken into Chiang Kai-Shek's government, did what else was needed.

Mr. Churchill's part in such affairs shows curious alternations, as if different lights played on him. His offer to 'release' Greece from its own intention to fight the Nazis if attacked, in 1941, horrified the British Ambassador and military commander, who knew the Greeks meant to fight in any circumstances, against any comers, for their own honour, without any other's leave or objection. Had Greece accepted the proffered 'release' it would presumably be now part of the Soviet Empire, and the general situation that much worse. Mr. Churchill averted that through his heroic interventions in 1945, when the Communists tried to clinch the matter by invasion and massacre.

The Yugoslav affair seems beyond reasonable explanation. Knowing the Balkans, I think only future tribulation can come from the political course Mr. Churchill pursued there, apparently with the support of Messrs. Roosevelt and Hopkins. After the war he complained of the 'Iron Curtain', but Communist Yugoslavia is its southern pin, and he put it there. His emissary's account of the abandonment of King Peter ('to whom the British Government was morally under a definite obligation, who had thrown in his lot with Great Britain in her hour of need, and to whose government they were politically committed') will remain painful reading for all time. While Britain had few arms to give, King Peter's general was supported; when they were in lavish supply, the Communist leader was supported; at the end the King's general was shot by Communists in khaki uniform using British or American weapons — it is gruesome. Some words of Mr. Churchill (used about the abandonment of Czechoslovakia in 1938, by Mr. Chamberlain's government) might apply in this case: 'There is one helpful guide, namely, for a nation to keep its word and to act in

359

accordance with its treaty obligations to allies. This guide is called honour.'

In all that the American and British masses had no say or authentic information. Mr. Churchill's dictum, 'At no time was the right of criticism impaired', is substantially misleading. The *right* may have continued, but the public expression of criticism, at the time when it might have done good, was in practice much restricted. The press and broadcasting, in England as in America, were controlled by official agencies which effectively operated to reduce criticism to a minimum, and quite apart from that, the newspapers and radio were thoroughly permeated by Communists. Writers of my own experience and knowledge were virtually excluded, or they would have said, much earlier and in suitable terms, what Brigadier Maclean's American top-sergeant said when he saw that Red Army trucks rolling into Belgrade in 1944 were American ones: 'It makes you sick to think of these unprintable unmentionables having all this good American equipment.' At that time the world did not know of atom bombs and when it did learn of them was for some years told that America had a monopoly, but in fact, under 'Lend Lease', atomic compounds also went to the Communist Empire and no doubt remains now that secrets of manufacture also travelled that way, from sources American and British. Further, the industrial capacity of the Soviet Empire, behind the Urals, was being greatly expanded in the same manner, and that was something not so important for the outcome of the Second War as for preparing a third.

Nevertheless, up to the very last one means remained of making good these deeds and forcing the Communist Empire to conclude the war in the spirit in which it was begun, namely, by liberating the nations overrun. This was to send the American and British armies right across Germany and beyond and let them do the liberating. However, that possibility was foreseen too, and arrangements made to prevent it. In 1943 Mr. Hopkins thought 'there was no understanding between Great Britain, Russia and ourselves as to which army should be where' after the defeat of Germany. Either this lack of understanding was carefully nurtured until the Red Army stood on the Berlin line, which meant the bisection of Europe and a third war unless the grace of God should avert one (man would not be able to), or an understanding to that effect was reached.

In that last stage Mr. Hopkins, possibly all unknowing, was acting as the chief instrument of a mechanism of power controlled and permeated by Communism. Soon after the invasion of Normandy he telegraphed a warning to President Roosevelt against meeting Mr. Churchill 'without Uncle Joe'. The vital matter of who should occupy what 'zone' dragged on in some committee and eventually settled itself in the shape visible today: the extension of the Communist Empire to Berlin. The British and American military commanders, given free hand, could have occupied all Germany and much beyond.

At last, as if Stalin himself were planning every detail, Mr. Hopkins's four years approached their climax. In October 1944, when the last coup alone remained in doubt, Mr. Cordell Hull resigned the American Secretaryship of State (Foreign Office). He was the one experienced professional still near the hub of affairs and for years had been by-passed, Messrs. Roosevelt and Hopkins sending their dispatches through military channels so that they should not reach his eyes or those of American ambassadors abroad. All checks and restraints were now slipped. A man of standing, Mr. James Byrnes, might have been appointed, but some years before had told Mr. Hopkins to 'keep the hell out of my business'. A completely unqualified one, Mr. Edward Stettinius, was therefore selected; his part was to do what Mr. Hopkins said.

This determined the shape of the American delegation to the vital Yalta Conference, where all that had been hatched was to pop out of the egg. Its four leading members were President Roosevelt, Mr. Hopkins, Mr. Stettinius and Mr. Alger Hiss; three had but a short time to live and the fourth was a Communist. Mr. Hopkins was in reality the chief delegate. He only left his bed to attend full meetings; the American delegation otherwise gathered in his bedroom. The place of meeting (in Soviet territory) was chosen by Mr. Hopkins, who over-rode all objections of Mr. Roosevelt's other advisers. Mr. Hopkins says that President Roosevelt was already unclear of understanding; nevertheless he remembered to tell Stalin 'privately' that the British ought to give Hong Kong back to the Chinese, who were already abandoned in Mr. Hopkins's and presumably in Mr. Hiss's minds to the Communists. Then Mr. Stettinius, prompted by Mr. Hopkins, revived the proposal for relieving Britain of colonial possessions and 'strategic islands'. This angered Mr. Churchill, who also fought hard for 'the rights of small nations', at that stage unhappily a cause already largely lost, in Yugoslavia among other places.

Mr. Sherwood thinks President Roosevelt 'would not have agreed to that final firm commitment' (he appears to mean the betrayal of China) 'had it not been that the Yalta Conference was almost at an end and he was tired and anxious to avoid further argument'. These reasons might explain concessions in a matter of a few dimes but seem inadequate in one of such dimensions. The documents suggest that Mr. Roosevelt at that moment was beyond knowing what he did or resisting any pressure from those around him. The American Republic, materially, was at its greatest strength; through its President it was spiritually at its weakest.

The Yalta Conference must surely be unique in history. Acted as a play in a theatre, it would challenge credulity to such extent that the playgoers might laugh it off the stage. It had a strange sequel, a little human footnote still not legible. It was the end of the Roosevelt-Hopkins partnership! The last meeting over, President Roosevelt wanted Harry the Hop to help him write his speech to America, on the homeward voyage. Suddenly Harry the Hop would not comply! He 'sent word' that he must leave the ship at Algiers, rest, and then fly to Washington. Mr. Roosevelt was 'disappointed and even displeased'. His farewell (when Mr. Hopkins emerged from his cabin to go ashore) 'was not very amiable'. The two men never met again; the great partnership ends in a row of dots, a query mark and the present ordeal of mankind.

Mr. Sherwood writes for nine hundred pages as an ardent admirer of both men. At the end he seems suddenly to shrink, Dorian Gray-like, from the picture of America under their sway which he has drawn. He finishes the amazing tale by expressing the hope that 'a phenomenon like Franklin D. Roosevelt will not recur . . . in the interests of the nation and indeed of the entire world, which must never again be in the position in time of peril of placing so much reliance on the imagination, courage and durability of one mortal man' (nevertheless America, and Britain, are more than ever in that position now). Mr. Sherwood was left in an 'alarmed awareness of the risks that we run of disastrous fallibility at the very top of our Constitutional structure'. He says there is 'far too great a gap between the President and the Congress' and adds that 'the extraordinary and solitary Constitutional powers of the President remain and, in times of crisis, they are going to be asserted for better or for worse'. He particularly mentions (and in my observation this is a most vital point) the added power, to lead or mislead, which was given to Mr. Roosevelt for the first time among presidents but remains with his successors: that of commanding a direct audience of many millions through broadcasts.

Mr. Roosevelt, and the man who in fact supplanted him at decisive moments, both were made the instruments of Soviet Communism, which had penetrated the roost on which they stood to a degree they probably never knew. They refused ear to all arguments against subversion at home or the probity of the Communist Empire. Their minds had been moulded to think that such honest misgivings were but the emanations of 'racial discrimination', 'Red-baiting' or 'anti-Semitism'; so perverse are the top-line politicians of our time that they would make it treason to denounce treason, and this is both an American and an English situation.

The power which deluded these men grew up, like Political Zionism, among Russian Jewry. To that Dr. Weizmann's book, among much other evidence, appears to be conclusive testimony. Communism is the product of the revolutionary son (as Zionism was that of the nationalist son) in those households. The directing forces of both movements remain Russian-Jewish; each new disclosure reaffirms that and many more Jews than Gentiles have spoken to it. Dr. Oscar Levy wrote in 1920, 'Jewish elements provide the driving force for both Communism and Capitalism for the material as well as the spiritual ruin of the world'. Mr. Maurice Samuel wrote, 'We are trying to rebuild the world to our needs and unbuild it for the Gentiles . . . We, the destroyers, will remain destroyers forever . . . Nothing you will do will meet our needs and demands. We will forever destroy because we need a world of our own.'

Such statements, made by non-Jews, would today be denounced as racial defamation but are true of the group of Russian Jewry which produced Soviet Communism. It did *not* include *all* Russian Jews; once again, Russian Jews have attacked it more strongly than Gentiles, and have been ignored by leading Gentile politicians just as the established Jews in England and America were ignored. For instance, a Russian Jew, Mr. J. Anthony Marcus, in 1949 gave evidence for a United States Senate Committee which was appointed to consider matters of Immigration and Naturalization, with particular reference to 'Communist Activities among Aliens and National Groups'. He said, among much else:

I am here because I owe an eternal debt to this country, as do many millions more immigrants. I came here from Czarist Russia as a lonely immigrant boy in 1910, seeking the freedom, economic and educational opportunities which were denied to me in the country of my birth . . . Here in America such opportunities were mine for the mere asking and on equal terms with the native-born citizens. Within four years after landing here with the munificent fortune of $14.28, with an English vocabulary of three words ('street' and 'hurry up') I not only made my way from modest beginnings in industrial plants to a post in the United States Immigration Service but had managed to save up enough money to bring over from Russia my widowed mother and six brothers and sisters . . . The life of a person is entirely too short to enable him to repay so great a debt to the generous, warm-hearted and fair-minded people of America . . . In a modest way I have tried through the years to make some repayment . . . Ever since landing on American soil I have felt that since my ancestors had contributed nothing to make this country free, prosperous, generous, progressive and cultured; since my ancestors did not struggle and die in the process of clearing the wilderness, fighting the Indian wars, freezing in the covered wagons as they blazed a trail from coast to coast for future settlers, suffering hunger and thirst while building this great continent, the least I could and should do is to help preserve its liberties for all time to come. The same duty devolves upon every immigrant here.

Prior to the First World War, countless thousands of immigrants came here without any intention of becoming full-fledged members of this democracy. They were bent on exploiting our political and economic opportunities and returning to their homelands as soon as America had served their purpose . . . Since the conclusion of the First World War, a new type has made his way here. Some have discovered that one did not have to labour in factories, mines, mills or fields to earn a living. One could earn a much better living, and satisfy their exaggerated ego besides, by stirring up political and labour trouble among their compatriots, promising paradise on earth à la Stalin to the uninformed, unthinking and ungrateful. This is very important, because there are hundreds and hundreds of organizations in the United States that have very large memberships and . . . they are being pressed by their relatives abroad, who are being pressed by their respective totalitarian governments, to do their bidding on our soil . . . Reluctantly, I must confess that too many of my fellow immigrants, both naturalized and those still aliens, are largely responsible for the subversive movements plaguing this country today . . . They remained aliens to our language and at heart.

. . . The presence here of large bodies of ethnic groups, alien at heart and spirit to our way of life, is the outgrowth of lax immigration laws . . . On the basis of nearly thirty years of close contact with the operations of the Soviet Government here and abroad, I most earnestly urge you to heed this warning . . . Bad as it was prior to the Second War, since its conclusion matters have taken a turn for the worse. The satellite nations — Czechoslovakia, Poland, Hungary, Rumania, Lithuania, Latvia, Bulgaria and so forth — have millions of their former nationals in this country, some naturalized and many not. They, in turn, have millions of relatives and friends in their former homelands . . . By bringing pressure to bear on those relatives overseas, by reprisals or threats thereof, they [the Communists] can and do exert pressure on their American relations to do the biddings of their Communist governments . . . As a former immigrant, I deem it my duty to speak frankly to fellow immigrants who in these troubled times, by omission or commission, fail to show their appreciation of what this country has done for them. . . .

Such statements apply, not to World Jewry, but to the cohesive body of Russian Jewry, non-Semitic in origins, which has thrown up

the two destructive movements of today, and has in effect landed armies
of political paratroopers in America and England. Until now, and for
thirty years past, words like those of Mr. Marcus have had no effect
on the Gentile political leaders who facilitated the process and the
bulk of Jews and Gentiles alike are caught in this destructive mechanism.
Indeed, the most rabid hatred is kept for Jewish objectors to it. An
American rabbi, Mr. Morris Lazaron, once said, 'There is no room in
this country for any race, Italian, Russian, Polish or Jewish, to set itself
up as a private community and build a wall around itself'. The sober
opinion received an inflammatory reply from a particularly fanatical
Political Zionist leader, the late Rabbi Stephen S. Wise, who said,
'This Jewish apostle of Christian-Jewish goodwill stands exposed in
the nakedness of his bitter and unyielding anti-Jewishness. If there were
such a thing as decent public opinion in America, Rabbi Morris Lazaron
would nevermore be permitted to stand before a Jewish meeting.'

That violent group of Russian Jewry, from all I have seen as I have
come through the decades, is the one which has perfected two methods
of gaining political control over leading politicians of the West and
over the masses of Jewry. I believe the majority of Jews, and very
few Gentiles, understand this, and I think most Jews would join with
Gentiles in opposing something equally harmful to them both, if they
could. Both are thwarted in that by the present permeation of political
machines in great countries, especially America, by these political paratroopers from afar. The actions of President Roosevelt and Mr. Hopkins appear to represent their greatest success in mind-control to date.
They have shown stupendous skill in their work; had this been applied
to improving relations between men a dazzling prospect of betterment
might face the world today. But their driving force is essentially
hatred, and for that reason I believe they must fail in the end. Their
dupes are inwardly the unhappiest folk I know, for their lives are
living lies. Serving no positive purpose, but only a destructive one,
they are the victims of 'the deception of nations' and in time must
destroy themselves.

However, as matters stand today in the political parties, they can
only be checkmated by some counter-movement sprung from the
loins of the masses. I think this birth, or renascence, is occurring now.

CHAPTER 4

LOOKING BACK

FROM the deck I watched the lights of New Orleans, of the Mississippi's banks and of the last land slip past until the night was black; the ship was out at sea and America was astern. So that was that; I knew the whole area, from Moscow to San Francisco, where the destiny of the world is being forged. Now I had seen everything.

All the world is waiting for the sunrise; there was more truth in that trite ballad of the Second War than its writer or hearers knew. Since 1914 the world has been waiting, and it must wait awhile yet. This feeling of a world waiting to know its own fate, like a prisoner while the jury is absent, has accompanied me everywhere I went. I felt it first in Berlin in 1929 (and today it must lie heavier than ever on that city); it hung over Vienna when I went there in 1935, and over Prague and Budapest and Belgrade and Warsaw in 1938 and 1939. It was more tangible than ever in Paris in early 1940, and heaviest of all over my own London a month or two later.

Still the unanswered question presses on all the peoples, and ever more onerously, and in America it was tangible and vibrant, too. Men know in their hearts, though few of them admit, that the ordeal which began in 1914 is not over but continues; it must continue until the ambition which has been pursued during these four decades succeeds or fails, until the Western nations are free again or have been wholly enslaved, not through defeats in battle but by the alien conspirators at home to whom they have opened their gates.

The feeling of constant suspense which troubled Europe between the wars has spread to the American Republic. Its people intuitively know, if they do not consciously realize, that in the next stage of the process they will be in the thick of the clash. But what the process is very few of them perceive. I think personal experience, of the actual event, is necessary to that. They are in a clutch which they feel but do not understand. They are like the Berliners in 1932, the Viennese in 1937. Only their anticipation is palpable.

To my mind, they are in a similar boat to the British Islander, though not yet quite so far downstream. They are being steered, under pretence of going to fight 'emergencies' and wars of arms, towards the serfdom of the World State with its terrible great sword and its oceanic watchtowers. But only at a high level of enlightenment, like that of Mrs. Alice Duer Miller in *The White Cliffs* and of Professor J. Frank Dobie in *A Texan in England*, does a perception of that inexorably-linked destiny, or doom, survive. Professor Dobie wrote, 'It is not only their common language, their common inheritance of the noblest literature on earth and many common material and national interests that dictate a decent partnership between America and the British nations; it is a common civilization'.

That is in fact the stake, but I do not believe that the forces which have become so strong behind the American and British governments desire the continuance of that civilization. They wish to destroy it and the time seems to me to be ripe for the culminating attempt.

I found in America, if my eye was true, at this time a great bewilderment, a sense of premonition and a spiritual leaderlessness, all things which I knew from Europe and my country, between the wars and after the second one. The structure of government and all the means of public information have become so infested that the masses of men simply cannot tell where truth or native interest lie. The machine has taken charge, and only when men see with their own eyes whither it takes them will they now know whether this was good or bad for them, and turn to resistance if they still can. America, my own country and what remains of Europe are, I thought, in one ship now, and it is being steered towards the harbour lights, or the wreckers' light, of the World State. I think those lights false ones, set up on rocks. To judge what this great scheme portends for mankind, you need to know the men who are truly behind it. I think I know them, after these twenty-five years of political exploration. However, all should be able to form an opinion about that before very long.

Meanwhile, it was a fine experience and I was the better and happier for it. I looked back with regret as the last of America faded astern, and turned my face towards new travels.

POSTSCRIPT

I FINISHED this book in June 1950 and a few days later American troops were sent to South Korea to fight Communists from North Korea. The book was meant to be a picture of America on the eve of events which, I thought, clearly impended. Now they have begun; I think they are intended to start the third stage of Armageddon.

In the year that followed I travelled far and wide again, in Africa, then in Canada, and once more into the United States. Thus I often saw The Boys as they set out on one more journey: splendid Rhodesian fighting-men and South African airmen (Boer and British) sailing from Durban; Canadians entraining at Montreal; my own fellow-islanders training for the fray in Canada; Americans reporting for duty. Fine men all, the very best; the breed does not deteriorate, but improves.

But for what *purpose* were they being sent? Watching them, I recalled those ominous words of President Roosevelt's legal adviser: 'the handling of the military forces of the United States can be so managed as to foster any purpose you pursue'. That applies, also, to British, Canadian, Australian, New Zealand and all other military forces, in these times.

Though I feel myself still in the first flush of youth, I come to feel myself also like the Old Man of the Sea when I watch these departures of The Boys. 1914 . . . ! 1917 . . . ! 1939 . . . ! 1941 . . . ! 1950 . . . ! In these first contingents are always many who go for sheer love of a campaign; behind them, later, come the masses.

As I foresee them, the events which began with the landing in Korea will comprise the third and probably the final stage in Armageddon and will continue from now on without genuine interruption, whether the Korean affair for tactical reasons is allowed to subside, or is inflated into a third world upheaval. The purpose pursued, by those who truly wield power in the world now, will in my opinion be to reduce America and Britain, both, to slave-status in a World Federation dominated by 'that most formidable sect in the world' to which Mr. Churchill once alluded. This brotherhood has in the last thirty years become so powerful in America and Britain that its chances of success are good. 'When the fox hath once got in his nose, he'll soon find means to make the body follow', said Shakespeare, and this particular fox has in Washington and London got in much more than its nose.

That at least is my opinion, but before adding such argument as I can to support it I beg the patient reader's ear for some explanation of myself. The man who has closely followed these things from their open beginning in 1914, as I have, and has broken away from daily journalism because hidden restraints prevent both the accurate reporting of facts and the unimpeded building of opinion on them, treads a curious path. He becomes a free and thus a happy man. But the very reason that moved him to this self-liberation is that the times are bad and infested with falsehood. The tale he freely tells, therefore, is one of a bad time getting worse, before it can get better; the only difference is that he can at least say what he sees.

This exposes him to the danger that 'the nature of bad news infects the teller'. He has to beware of that contagion, to which such as the late Mr. H. G. Wells succumbed (who was so oppressed by the sense of coming evil that he at last thought the end of the world was at hand, whereas only his own impended).

A trained journalist is better equipped to write of such matters than a novelist who turns to moralizing. I am not tempted to moralize, only to report. My training shows me the deep truth of Shakespeare's warning about the contaminatory danger of bad news, so that I try to shun the personal infection while telling bad news from book to book (at the moment there is no other news), and I hope one day to report the happier sequel.

Merely to shout warnings is also useless, for 'by a divine instinct men's minds mistrust *ensuing* danger'. (Who but that Founding Father of wisdom would have seen the *divine* root of what seems, in the passing instant, a devilish inertia?) Nevertheless, a v riter should write, though he should always remember those two great truths, and I write to try and show the true shape of current events behind the smoke-screens thrown out for the masses.

Dogmatism is another danger. My native way of saying things sometimes gives an abrupt shock to the reader's newspaper-born notions of what goes on in the world, stinging him to sharp cries of grief or rage. A man who has seen as much as I have of the sequence of events that began in 1914 is easily moved to impatience at the false public presentation of them and the surrender of the mass-mind to transparent falsehoods. However, no mortal is qualified to cry, 'Lord, what fools these mortals be!', so I want to curb my natural spleen, and in offering my opinions about far Korea to the reader to say, 'Come, let us reason together'. Then he can make up his own mind.

My *opinion*, then, is that the Korean affair, whether it remains localized now or is puffed up into a third universal war, is either the beginning of the end, or the end of the beginning, of Armageddon. I think the 'military forces' engaged, and their operations, will be 'handled' to pursue certain 'purposes', and I think the overriding purpose is to enslave all The Boys, on all sides, to a tyrannous world authority, for which the present United Nations Organization is a rehearsal. In two earlier books (of 1948 and 1950) I said that, in view of the outcome of the Second War, no faith could be put in any third war begun as one of 'The West against Communist aggression', or the like, unless the political leaders of America and Britain were set free from the secret thrall which they have in recent generations accepted. With that as the basis of my argument, I hope the persevering reader will scrutinize with me the beginnings and present stage of the Korean episode.

In the sequel to Mr. Roosevelt's imperial gift of 'special rights in China' to the Communist Empire (which, under further American pressure, by 1950 had extended to include *all* China save an island yet unconquered, Formosa), the Korean peninsula was partitioned like Europe and Palestine. North Korea was occupied by Soviet and South Korea by American troops.

Events then followed the pattern now familiar. An American expert, General Wedemeyer, was in 1947 sent to Korea and in that year reported to President Truman that the Communist North Koreans would be sent by the Russian Communists against the South Koreans once the Soviet had 'induced' the United States to withdraw its own troops from South Korea. On that, United States forces *were* withdrawn (1948); the North Korean Communists *did* invade (1950); and President Truman (without consulting the American commander, General MacArthur), ordered the American forces to return, broadcasting that this event 'makes it clear beyond all doubt that the international Communist movement is willing to use armed invasion to conquer independent nations . . . The free nations face a worldwide threat. It must be met with a worldwide defence'. The United Nations Organization was hurriedly called together to proclaim the President's action a United Nations one. In England, the Prime Minister spoke of 'a worldwide conspiracy against the way of life of the free democracies' and his Attorney General said South Korea was 'one of the lighthouses of liberty, which we cannot serenely allow to go out' (Sir Hartley Shawcross, one of the prosecutors of Nuremberg, also referred to 'the world conscience').

Up to that early stage in the affair, then, it could be interpreted in two ways. Either this sudden war against 'Communist aggression' was genuine or it was false. Either the leading politicians of the West had suddenly awakened to the true nature of Communism; or military operations were being begun and would be 'handled' to allow certain other, overriding 'purposes' to be pursued.

What are the signs either way, of genuineness or falsity? The genuine motive can only be tested when the world is able to survey what comes of it all, and that might be some time yet. Many things, however, meanwhile pointed to a continuation of the false one.

First, only five years earlier eight separate European nations, and half of Germany, were surrendered to 'Communist aggression' through secret arrangements made by President Roosevelt which limited the Anglo-American advance in Europe in 1944-45. These countries were forced, by the arrival of the Red Army, to submit to Communist governments, appointed by Moscow. The United Nations Organization, today eager to check 'Communist aggression', in fact sanctioned those aggressions and annexations by admitting the puppet-governments to full membership, so that each Soviet vote was echoed by several dummies. All these governments, with the parent one, remained members of the United Nations Organization when it set out to punish 'Communist aggression'; indeed, for some time the American Commander's operational reports, and requests for reinforcements, were rendered to the Soviet delegate there, who was for the time president of the Security Council!

Second, soon after the Korean campaign against Communist aggression began, the American President sanctioned large loans to Yugoslavia, a Communist State. True, its head was *supposed* to dislike and be disliked by Stalin, but it was beyond any question a *Communist* state. Was the war, then, to be one against Communism in one place and for Communism in another?

Third, and most important, Korea was a geographical pendant of the Chinese mainland, and at American insistence a Communist Government had been foisted on China, too (the Secretary for War under whom General MacArthur operated, General Marshall, but a year or two before had played the chief part in that). Now all that remained non-Communist was this South Korea and the island of Formosa, where the Chinese anti-Communist leader, Chiang Kai-shek (who had been fighting Fascism *and* Communism longer than anybody else in the world) stood with his last forces. He at once offered an army of trained troops to fight 'Communist aggression', and this aid was promptly refused by the American President, who also forbade him to attack his enemies on the mainland.

No reasonable man, I think, can in all this find any genuine sign of a resolve to stamp out Communist aggression or to liberate the world, at last. The picture is that, of saying one thing and doing another, of declaring A Cause to the masses but 'handling' military operations to pursue other 'purposes', which caused the political loss of the Second War, after it was militarily won.

That was particularly clear in the case of Chiang Kai-shek. His unpopularity, in the parliaments and newspapers of the West, could not have been greater had he been a Communist aggressor; indeed, I think it would then have been much less. Having fought all comers for twenty years, and being now embattled in his last island stronghold, he had no friends anywhere. The same process began, of 'smearing' a national leader, which was used (if the patient reader will cast his memory back) with *every* anti-Fascist ally during the Second War. To be on the side of the West, to fight valiantly against Hitler, was a political death-warrant, and sometimes a mortal one. Generals Bor and Anders of Poland, Mihailovitch of Yugoslavia and his King, King George of Greece, General de Gaulle of France and Otto Strasser of

Germany, and many more, all received 'the treatment' in this way; now Chiang Kai-shek's turn came. The campaign against him proved the complete infestation of the newspapers of the West, whatever political label they display; and behind it was the massive fact, that he could have thrown large armies into the battle to take the brunt off The Boys from America, from Britain and the British countries overseas. *That was not allowed!*

Next came the turn of the American commander, General MacArthur. He believed it his duty to destroy the enemy and win battles; outside America, and even in large parts of that country, the mass-newspapers, now so largely controlled by the conspirators of these times, made him as unpopular as Chiang Kai-shek. He did not stop at the 38th Parallel (I hope one day to see a fighting, advancing army perform the delightful military exercise of stopping at an imaginary line, particularly if a good position for the enemy lies on the other side of it); he wanted to bomb the enemy, even to use Chiang's soldiers! In a war against 'Communist aggression' these were clearly disgraceful, almost mutinous ideas; he was dismissed.

I heard his tumultuous public welcome and his speech to Congress from a ship at sea, and landed in North America while the furore continued. General MacArthur is a soldier of a well-known American school. When you have been trained at West Point around 1900 by instructors whose own instructors were still fighting the War of Independence, you see everything in terms of redcoats and continue to fight all your battles against King George III; it is an amiable weakness that only disappears in the course of several centuries. Thus General MacArthur in 1945 did not want the British 'to assume control of any territory that we recaptured from the enemy' and 'refused to use any British divisions until after an assault on the Japanese mainland was under way'. In his speech to Congress General MacArthur, while putting all cogent facts of the Korean affair plainly before America, also contrived to suggest that it was all, in some odd way, mixed up with British 'colonialism' (he did not explain what this had to do with an American President's decision, first to leave Korea and then to reoccupy it). However, that is unimportant. The important thing was his gigantic public welcome, which to my mind sprang spontaneously from the hearts and throats of the great mass of Americans who feel, though they cannot understand, the falsehoods that have beclouded the matter from its start. *If* they are to fight Communism, they wanted to fight it, destroy it, and get the thing done; if not, then they wanted to get out. General MacArthur's orders from Washington (they must count among the most curious of all military history) were merely to 'ensure the security of his command'.

General MacArthur may have been mistaken about the date, thinking it to be 1775, not 1951, but in the main matter at issue he was a symbol of truth among falsehood, and a genuine one. For that reason his tremendous welcome came from the great mass of Americans who felt and feared the falsehoods and longed for truth.

If he was sent, without being asked, against a 'Communist aggressor', he wanted to fight successful battles, destroy and drive back the enemy, win the campaign. When he felt a hand reach out from behind and arrest him each time he tried to do those things, he thought it was a treacherous hand, and protested loudly. He did his country and the world a great service, for by his stand and dismissal large numbers of people for the first time had the brutal contrast, between what the politicians said and what they did, put luridly before them.

Also, The Boys might at some stage in these proceedings wonder to what end they are being used, if any commander who seeks to destroy the enemy is to be dismissed. It is a piquant reflection, that the final success of the Plan for Mankind can probably only be averted now by the recurrence of similar incidents, by the loud protest of a politician here and a general there against the deception of nations. General MacArthur's dismissal was presented to the public masses as the necessary assertion of 'the civil authority over the military', a phrase once valid. Today, when 'the civil authority' in all great countries has clearly passed into other hands than those of the visible politicians, it is an artful deception.

General MacArthur went the way of every politician and soldier, for many years past, who has rebelled against this occult rule. To the close student of the records, General Wavell's relegation from the battlefield, during the Second War, looks very much as if it was the penalty for his reluctance to have any truck with the major disaster which was being prepared in Palestine. The dismissal of General Sir Frederick Morgan (the chief planner of D-Day, and 'an exceptionally fine officer' according to General Eisenhower) *was* openly the consequence of his public warning that, in the confusion following the fighting's end in Europe, mass-movements of Eastern Europeans were being made to bring about that new centre of world-unrest in Palestine. General Marshall resigned after opposing the recognition of Israel; and only reappeared in the American scene after lending himself to the enforced Communization of China. Mr. Bevin, the only statesman of the last thirty years, was pursued to his deathbed for his opposition to the Palestinian adventure, being described in Zionist newspapers just before his end as 'a symbol of anti-Jewishness almost as definite as Hitler'!

General MacArthur's dismissal was, I thought, certain from the very start of the Korean affair unless he understood and accepted the meaning of a certain event at its outset. He was made, *not* the commander of the American, or of Allied forces, but 'the United Nations commander', and as a pledge of that status he was sent a United Nations flag. This was indeed a retreat from Old Glory and, knowing something of his character, I was at the time surprised that he submitted. The United Nations flag is in the same colours as that of the new Zionist State, and is almost indistinguishable, in colouring and device, from one used by the Soviet State for its 'International Peace Movement'.

But that was not all. This particular banner, bestowed on General MacArthur, was an especial one: that carried by Count Bernadotte, the emissary of the United Nations murdered on a mission of peace to Palestine! His death went unpunished; it was tacitly overlooked by the United Nations; his proposals were ignored and their opposite accepted.

Thus no more arrogant and open emblem, not of 'The United Nations Organization' as visible to the masses, but of an inner authority ruling it, could have been chosen to present to General MacArthur. There is a sardonic and obviously deliberate symbolism in such episodes as this.

To my mind, the choice of that banner clearly meant that any commander, in the Korean affair or any later one that might grow out of it, must without question carry out his orders received or expect dismissal. It is a great gain to the world that the first commander thus involved did prefer dismissal and did obtain the world's eye for a moment with his public exposure of the inherent falsity of the situation. This is not a matter of the supremacy of 'the civil' over 'the military' authority, but of that of 'The United Nations Organization' and of whatever forces in truth control that body, of which Mr. Alger Hiss was a founding father. The answer to that question supplies itself: on the very first line of this organization's first ledger-page stand two fatal entries written in red: the expulsion of the defenceless Arabs from their native Palestine, with the proclamation of a Zionist State; and the mock-legalization of the Soviet Union's annexation of half Europe.

Thus any commander who intends to keep a 'United Nations' command, while this state of affairs continues, must carry out *any* orders, no matter what his military knowledge or national pride tell him he ought to do. Up to the present the picture of a commander who conforms to that idea is given by General Eisenhower, of himself, in his book, *Crusade in Europe*. At the time, when the thing was in its beginnings, he may well have failed to see its true shape. I do not think that can be hidden from any future commander, who will have before his eyes the way military victory in Europe was converted into political defeat, and the obvious reappearance of symptoms of that same result in Korea.

It fell to General Eisenhower to obey orders to make the Anglo-American advance in Europe, in 1944-45, conform with the Soviet advance from the east, so that in the end Communism swallowed half of Europe. The Anglo-American military commanders, left to pursue purely military ends, could have averted that calamity by pressing right through Germany, and beyond. General Eisenhower repeatedly mentions recommendations by Mr. Churchill in some such sense, but says he had to oppose them because they were 'political', where he was tied to 'military' considerations. However, the supreme order to let the Red Armies get to the Berlin line first was the greatest *political* one of these 1951 years, in my judgment.

Instructively, General Eisenhower refers to General Montgomery's reputation for excessive caution. He mentions this only to refute it, but by alluding to it at all gives the rumour further currency. Then he mentions two occasions on which General Montgomery, after the Normandy landing, urged a quicker and more vigorous advance; on both occasions General Eisenhower declined! The second occasion was in September 1944, when General Montgomery urged that, if given full support, he could rush right on into Berlin and end the war. 'I would not consider it,' General Eisenhower says; and the picture of Europe today may be the result.

In 1951 General Eisenhower is Supreme Commander in Western Europe, and events might have shown him that situations arise when a commander would do better to demur than yield. Of General MacArthur's dismissal, he said 'When you put on a uniform, there are certain inhibitions which you accept'. In his book, however, he said, 'The American soldier . . . is an intelligent human being who demands and deserves basic understanding of the reasons why his country took up arms and of the conflicting consequences of victory or defeat . . . Belief in an underlying cause is fully as important to success in war as any local esprit or discipline induced or produced by whatever kind of command or leadership action.'

The question arises from that, whether the American soldier, surveying Europe as the Allied victory in 1945 left it, and Korea after the first year's fighting, has any clear 'basic understanding of the reasons why his country took up arms', or of 'the underlying cause'. I do not see how a belief in those essentials can be reconciled with unquestioning submission to orders which might blatantly conflict with 'the reasons' or 'the cause', and think it might be grave if General Eisenhower took with him into his second Supreme Command an inflexible respect for 'certain inhibitions'.

For what *was* the result of General MacArthur's dismissal? How far did it clarify 'the cause' or improve the prospects? The answers may be learned from the remarks that were made about it by leading men who approved of it. First, President Truman himself announced that his country 'would not strip itself of allies in order to follow General MacArthur into direct war on Communist China' (the Chinese Communists, as I have neglected to mention, by this time were making war on General MacArthur, and his successor). But if anyone 'stripped' the American forces of allies, it was apparently President Truman, who from the first forbade Chiang's anti-Communist Chinese to fight the Chinese Communists, and refused the aid of their armies! Words lose all meaning in these debates.

Then the British Defence Minister, a Mr. Shinwell, announced that General MacArthur's dismissal had opened the way for the United Nations and Red China 'to get together'. Red China, with its puppet North Korea, was 'the Communist aggressor' against whom this enterprise was originally launched. Now the aim was 'to get together'.

Then, while American cheers for General MacArthur still resounded, the Canadian Minister for External Affairs, Mr. Lester Pearson, declared that it was 'a mistake to say the United Nations forces were fighting in Korea to defeat Communism. The purpose there is to defeat aggression by Communist states'. He added that 'until the war is ended there can be no question of even discussing whether Formosa should be handed over to the Peking regime' (the Communist Government foisted on China) 'and the same view holds in regard to the recognition of the Peking Government'.

That is clear. It means that when the war *is* ended there *can* be 'a question of discussing whether Formosa should be handed over' to the Communists, and there *can* be 'a question of recognizing the Chinese Communist Government'.

That would mean rewarding 'Communist aggression' by handing over to the Chinese Communists the last unsubdued anti-Communist stronghold, and a further reward in the form of recognition. That would be a repetition of the events of 1945 in Europe: the expansion of the Communist area, the increase of Communist voting-strength in the United Nations Organization, the abandonment of the anti-Communist (or anti-Fascist) leader. It would be the exact opposite of 'the reasons' and 'the underlying cause' proclaimed to the masses when the war was begun!

That should explain the mass of American enthusiasm for General MacArthur. He was seen as the symbol of truth against untruth. At the time the statements were made, which I have quoted above, ten thousand Americans had fallen in Korea, and mounting numbers of British, Canadian, Australian, New Zealand, South African, Greek, Turkish and other soldiers. Surely at some point The Boys must learn for what they are sent to fight? To masses of Americans, in any case, it must have seemed that the exposure of a Mr. Alger Hiss (and to numbers of British Islanders, that of a Dr. Nunn May, a Dr. Klaus Fuchs or a Dr. Bruno Pontecorvo) was wasted energy, if events were to follow such a course as this.

I do not see how to escape the conclusion that, at any rate up to this point, military undertakings were once again being 'handled' to pursue the 'purposes' of groups which have become supremely powerful in America and England, and that these purposes were the opposite of any 'cause' publicly proclaimed. I think the aim is so to direct events that the last obstacles to the setting up of the despotic World State shall be broken down; and these are, the remaining rights of property and liberty in the American Republic and the British Island.

For the great secret which has been discovered in the Twentieth Century is this: that once you can get The Boys marching you can behind their backs destroy all these remaining obstacles. You can do anything at all! The solution to all problems lies in the magic words, Emergency Powers.

In England this process has been carried half-way to completion, or perhaps a little more; only the last coup is needed. Income-tax is already nearly half of income, and taxation only begins there. Men may no longer freely buy food, choose their occupations or build homes. They have as yet the right to fair trial. All these inroads on property and liberty were begun under Emergency Powers in the First War and enlarged under those taken by Mr. Churchill in the Second War. The restoration of those rights was promised but in the event the Socialist Government of 1945 prolonged the Emergency Powers *temporarily*, from year to year. The Korean enterprise once begun, they were made *permanent* at once! Now they can only be thrown off by some great change or upheaval in England; the people are half-way back to where they were centuries ago.

America almost escaped from President Roosevelt's Emergency Powers after 1945. Save for the great increase in taxation, they mostly fell away. The Korean enterprise once begun, President Truman reintroduced his predecessor's 'State of National Emergency', and

America followed England on to the downhill path, though some distance behind.

In both countries the chief device recommended by Karl Marx's Communist Manifesto for reducing a free country to slave status ('a progressive income-tax') was at once applied. President Truman announced that his country 'must be taxed until it hurts'; in England a Mr. Strauss, Minister of Supply, foretold 'severe new taxation', and this quickly followed.

The Plan goes on, by the methods now tried and tested. I do not now see much likelihood that effective public opposition to it will arise before it is completed, because there is no effective public realization of it. The chief reason for this is the astonishing submission of the world's newspapers to it. They are now so very largely served by news-agencies and political writers working from a central source that their infestation by news and views, all coloured to serve the hidden purpose, is almost absolute. Since I first set foot in a newspaper office thirty years ago the deterioration in this matter has been fantastic; since I shook that dust from my feet twelve years ago I have watched it constantly increase in speed.

I do not believe that far Korea has much more than the importance of a starting-button in these events. A few years from now men will have forgotten where it is, and have to jog their memories to recall that, like Poland, it was once proclaimed to be 'a lighthouse of liberty'. I think the events which will grow out of this event will prove to be mainly concerned with a different territory, the one known to biblical prophecy as Armageddon.

Already tomorrow's events are taking shape there. 'If the war should spread' (wrote a Zionist newspaper, while all the world and his wife looked at Korea) 'the Middle East is seen as a potential danger zone, and new talks have taken place in Washington between Israel representatives and the United States State Department on the subject of arms shipments to the Near East and protective measures if Israel is threatened'.

Why is that particular piece of the globe held so vital by those who, quite transparently today, control the acts of great governments? I think the answer is contained in some words spoken in 1950 to a Zionist audience by the World Zionist leader, Dr. Nahum Goldman (once again I am obliged to a Zionist newspaper for knowledge of them). He said of Israel. 'The state has been established in one of the most difficult geographical positions in the world. It is very hard to find an explanation, but it is a unique geographical position. In the days when we were trying to get the Jewish state with the consent of the British Government and at one of the private talks I had with Mr. Bevin, he said: "Do you know what you are asking me to do? You are asking me to deliver the key to one of the most vital and strategic areas in the world." And I said, "It is not written in either the New or Old Testament that Great Britain must have this key".'

That applies to any other country in the world today, not alone Great Britain.

Of the many methods by which these great ambitions are pursued, far behind the scenes visible to the public masses, I can offer one other small but vividly illuminating glimpse (also from a Zionist newspaper). At the time of the numerous exposures of Communist agents in British and American atomic research in 1950 (the case of one 'Professor Pontecorvo' was in discussion at the moment), a Zionist publication printed these statements:

'The matter has brought into question, though still in a friendly and rather delicate manner, the position of other foreign-born scientists, the overwhelming number of whom are Jews from different parts of Europe. In fact, investigation has now revealed to the public that atomic research is to a large extent a Jewish science . . . It is of some interest to disclose that before the war a proposal was put forward to Dr. Weizmann to bring together some of the most noted Jewish scientists in order to establish a team which would bargain with the allies in the interest of the Jews . . . Only recently I saw the project as originally outlined . . . by a scientist who had himself achieved some renown in the sphere of military invention.'

In the picture of such larger ambitions the Korean affair dwindles to the size of a speck, or perhaps of a starting-button. As to that enterprise, whether it is to grow into a third world war or not, no confidence can in my opinion be placed in any military or verbal campaign against 'Communist aggression' while the victims of such aggression are represented by Communist commissars in the debates of the United Nations Organization; while the Communist Party is left legal in the great countries supposed to be united against Communist aggression; while Communist permeation remains unchecked and unexposed in their countries and while their peoples are by the screw of Emergency Powers ground ever deeper towards Communism.

The Korean undertaking could not at its start be accepted, until proof appeared, as a genuine bid to punish 'Communist aggression' or check Communism; the political leaders of the two great countries chiefly concerned, America and Britain, had for many years done their utmost to prevent the exposure of Communist infiltration into their own governmental machines and today still continue to cloak it, while publicly accusing and abusing 'the worldwide Communist conspiracy'. The conversion was therefore too sudden to be accepted without proof by deed. The first year of the Korean affair, however, at every stage gave greater cause to doubt the genuine conversion and genuine motive, and to suspect the continuance of the secret, false one.

If the real motive is to increase the authority of the United Nations Organization over peoples, and to tighten the submission of peoples to it, the forward-looking reader should bear in mind that among its delegations Communist voting-power is very strong and will be made stronger, as the direct result of the Korean episode, if that is to lead to the abandonment of Chiang Kai-shek and the mock-legalization of the Chinese Communist Government by its admission to the United Nations.

Quite apart from that aspect, anyone who knows the permanent staff of the United Nations Organization would smile at the notion that it would wholly and genuinely support any attempt to check, repress or punish Communist aggression. The permanent staff was assembled in those days of greatest confusion which surrounded the fighting's end in Europe; the days when Mr. Alger Hiss was Presidential Adviser and first Secretary-General of the new world directorate. It is permeated through and through with Eastern European Communists and Zionists, the spiritual kith and kin of the persons who have appeared, as at the turning of stones, in those fragmentary exposures of espionage and subversion which have occurred in the last five years in the United States, America and Britain. This particularly applies to those organs of it, called 'Unesco' and the like, which are clearly intended to be shadow-ministries of the future World Government.

In these circumstances, any World Government arising out of the United Nations Organization in its present form would be a tyrannous, despotic thing comparable only, in my judgment, with the carpet-bagger-and-scallawag regime which the North inflicted on the prostrate South after the American Civil War, or the Soviet on prostrate Eastern Europe after the Second War of this century. If the U.N. stables ever were truly cleansed, that might alter, but they have not yet been and no sign appears of any true intention to purify them.

Beyond that, to my mind, lies the point where hopeful portents appear in the darkening, downhill process. Until the Western world sees the actual reality of what threatens, it will not believe, for authentic information is now denied the masses and in any case men's minds disbelieve dangers yet to come. But when the plan succeeds and the thing happens, men will at last see its face, and know its clutch. Not all the carpet-baggers and scallawags could prevent the American South from putting itself together again; the South survived and revived. That is the later stage to which I look now in the greater picture.

The picture is that of 'the deception of nations'. Revelation says that the final attempt will fail and the old serpent be put in chains. That final attempt seems to be beginning now and in its last stage, as I judge, aims at the disintegration of the American Republic and the British Commonwealth, not at that of the Communist Empire. However, the happier outcome is yet to follow, and I expect by way of later travels, farther and wider, one day to come to and witness that liberation from the thrall which began in 1914.

BETWEEN the writing of the Postscript and the publication of this book came the event which calls for the Post-Postscript: the truce-parley in Korea.

This event was foreshadowed in an allusion on page 369: 'whether the Korean affair for tactical reasons is allowed to subside, or is inflated into a third world upheaval'. For tactical reasons which I think obvious, the intention as I write seems to be to allow the Korean affair to subside. The reason appears to me to be that the Korean war was coming too near to achieving its declared aim: a heavy defeat for 'Communist aggression'. I do not believe that result was ever genuinely desired by the forces which began it, and think the major facts of the year's fighting, 1950-51, plainly demonstrate this.

Before the truce-talks were even announced an American commentator, Senator Joe McCarthy, in a speech which was suppressed by nearly all newspapers everywhere, said, 'This Administration, which has given us this caricature of a war, is now bent on an even worse horror: a phony and fraudulent peace.' I think this opinion accurate and borne out by the facts now available. If that is so, it equally vindicates one I expressed in two books published after the Second War (*From Smoke to Smother*, 1948, and *Somewhere South of Suez*, 1950): that the great governments of the West are at present plainly servient to or infested by the agents of two super-national forces, Soviet Communism and Zionist Nationalism, which pursue overriding ambitions; and that while this condition continues no confidence can be put in any war proclaimed at its outset to be one of 'The West against Communism'. I thought that any such war would in the event be 'handled' to destroy the last defences of personal liberty and property in the English-speaking countries and to enslave them all to a bogus World State which would in truth be a Communist-Zionist directorate.

That would be the continuation of the process begun at Yalta, where the military victory of the West was transformed into the political victory of these overriding forces, so that the major results of the war were the expansion of the Communist Empire and the erection of the Zionist State, both through the political leaders and military strength of the English-speaking countires. The course of the Korean campaign, in my view, showed that these overriding forces remain powerful enough to bend all military operations to their overriding ends (whether the truce now in negotiation is completed or the fighting is renewed).

The theory may be tested against the facts now known. The Korean war is unlike any other in history. Its course, like that of the Second War after the Communist Empire changed from alliance with Hitler to alliance with the West, seems to me to have followed 'a secret pattern to which we do not as yet have the key'. The words, again are those of Senator McCarthy in his speech of June 14th, 1951, before the United States Senate, which I hold to be the most important document made public (though suppressed by newspapers) since the Canadian Spy Report of 1946 and any who wish to understand the real war that has been in progress since 1939, or 1914, should obtain it. I think, however, that my theory, given above, provides 'the key'.

I support the statement that the Korean war was, or is, unlike any other in history with the following arguments.

It was begun, on his own authority, by an American president without any consultation of the American people. That in itself is not new in history; despotic rulers have often sent their people into war so. What is new in history is that the American representative at the Nuremberg Trials, instructed by the same president, made this very thing a capital charge against the Nazi leaders. He pressed for and obtained from the chief defendant, Goring, an admission that the German people were not consulted when Hitler decided to make war on Soviet Russia. This point was laboured in order to lay emphasis on the criminal irresponsibility of the Nazi leaders, and the consequent guilt of individual German generals in following it.

Similarly, the British and other peoples were not consulted when they, too, were sent into the Korean war, following the Americans. All these English-speaking peoples have now surrendered their birth-rights to the dogma of 'emergency powers', set up during two world wars, under which governments in the English-speaking world may at any instant throw their peoples into foreign war, or domestic servitude, without further explanation than that of 'an emergency'.

The supreme importance of that, to my mind, is *not* so much that these peoples can now be drawn blindfold into war, for, unlike most others, I do not see war in itself as the supreme evil. The greater importance of it is that they have also surrendered the power to scrutinize their governors' motives for beginning a war, the conduct of military operations, or the political outcome. The campaign may be so 'handled' as to produce their own political defeat at the moment of military victory, which means that the men of the English-speaking countries can be marched, through 'emergencies', to their own enslavement.

When I first visited America, in 1949, one of my earliest acquaintances, an American who seemed at first sight a simple man, surprised me by a deeply perceptive remark. He spoke of the machine of mass-suggestion which has been built in the last twenty years and said, 'I guess this country could be brought to fight any other country in the world after one month's propaganda treatment by the politicians, press and radio.'

He erred, however, by thirty days. Not even thirty seconds of propagandist preparation now are necessary to set English-speaking soldiers on the march, from the American Republic, the British island, the English-speaking countries oversea. Again, the supreme importance of that is not so much that they are sent to fight, willy-nilly, but that they have no insight into or control over true motives or real results. When they have fought and won, under this system, the political triumph can be handed to their enemies.

General Eisenhower, who carried out the order which left half Europe in the Communist clutch, wrote in his book that soldiers demand and deserve the truth about the reasons for a war they fight, and need 'belief in an underlying cause'. In Korea the valid reasons and the credible cause were not to be perceived. The war 'against Communist aggression' there was begun by governments, in the United States and Britain, which for five years (since the Canadian Prime Minister's urgent flight to and warning of the American President and the British Prime Minister in 1945) refused to expose the

Communist infestation of their own departments, agencies and services; they always indignantly denied that the condition existed when some public expostulant called attention to it.

The exposures of it which occurred in the United States and Britain before and during the Korean war (such as that of Mr. Alger Hiss and many others in America; of 'Professor Pontecorvo', Dr. Klaus Fuchs, Dr. Alan Nunn May and others in England) were *in every case* brought about by outside action, such as the persistent denunciations of a repentant Communist agent, or imperious summonses from Moscow to desert), and *never* by the act of the London or Washington Governments.

From the moment of the Canadian Prime Minister's warning (and in the case of America much earlier, for President Roosevelt was given proofs in 1939) the concealment of this situation by those governments has been a clear sign that no 'war against Communist aggression' undertaken by them could be held genuine, unless its course and outcome proved this. If the infestation were not admitted, exposed and removed, the hidden forces clearly, from the outset of any new war, would work for the political victory of the alien power to which they owed allegiance. Yalta was the first major proof of their strength; Korea has yet to prove or disprove whether it is to be the second. Obviously, until Communism is outlawed in the English-speaking countries, and the general condition altered, of which the sporadic revelations have given only the most partial glimpses, political defeat must be feared as the outcome of any war into which the men of the English-speaking countries are sent, no matter how complete their military victory.

What were the signs of a genuine determination to arrest 'Communist aggression' in Korea? I do not know of a clear one, but the causes for continued misgiving, until unmistakable reassurance is given, were innumerable. The Korean campaign was waged under a Defence Secretary, in the United States, who was earlier responsible for enforcing Communism on China, through pressure brought on the anti-Communist leader, Chiang Kai-shek, and the cessation of supplies to him. Politically, it was begun under a Foreign Secretary there who publicly proclaimed that he would 'not turn his back' on the convicted Communist agent (President Roosevelt's chief adviser at Yalta) who had been exposed in his own Department.

The war was conducted as one of 'The United Nations Organization'. This was clearly the first *political* defeat of the forces from the English-speaking countries which chiefly fought it, for the Communist parentland and all the countries thrust into its grasp by this very United Nations Organization in 1945 were full members of it. When the American commander in the field claimed his immemorial military right of 'hot pursuit' of enemy aircraft, the American Secretary of State claimed that this could not be demanded from the United Nations Organization because the Communist Empire, from its seat, would veto this military action! Thus the commander in the field was in vital operations subject to the enemy's orders!

That is new in history, and even newer was the case of Formosa. This island was the last stronghold of the Chinese anti-Communists. In past history none would have presumed to deny their leader, Chiang Kai-shek, and his armies their natural right to fight the Chinese Communists, even before these joined the Korean Communists in the attack on South Korea, ordered by the common masters in Moscow.

Chiang Kai-shek's offer to fight the Chinese Communist aggressor, however, was refused by the President who rebuked General Mac-Arthur for actions liable 'to strip the United States of allies'. That was not all. The American Seventh Fleet was ordered to protect the Chinese Communist mainland from any attack by the Chinese anti-Communists on Formosa! The order simply stated that the Seventh Fleet should immobilize the anti-Communist leader on his island and prevent any landings by him on the China coast.

Thus of two American brothers, sent out in the name of 'an emergency', one might have been sent to Korea to fight Chinese Communists and the other, if he were a sailor with the Seventh Fleet, have had the duty of protecting them! That might equally apply to two British brothers; for all I know British naval units may have shared in the blockade of the anti-Communists on Formosa.

It is in respect of this transaction, particularly, that I used the words, 'The Korean war is unlike any other in history', and venture to think of it as transparently suspect in its motives and conduct.

The Korean war ended (in saying this I am assuming that the truce will be completed and the fighting not be renewed) with the dismissal of the American commander who wanted to win it. As soon as he was gone the word 'truce' began to echo through the corridors of the United Nations Organization, the Communist Empire's representative then pronounced it as publicly as he would have uttered the veto on 'hot pursuit' of Communists, there was a mysterious journey of the American Defence Secretary to Japan, and, as suddenly as the war began, the truce-parleys started. The picture is that of semi-secret agreement among master-minds on both sides of the supposedly opposed lines; it looks to be like a discussion at the board of directors of a chainstore undertaking about rivalry between local branches.

The case of General MacArthur becomes more instructive as it recedes in time. He asked in his speech to Congress, 'Where is the merit in fighting an enemy merely in order to give him military advantages?' A commander of that mind might have found himself unable to carry out the order of 1945 in Europe, to 'let the Russians take Berlin'; had there been such a general, and had he been dismissed, the state of the world today would fully have vindicated him.

The British reader may not realize that General MacArthur is but one of a number of American generals who have been relegated, have resigned, or have not received the promotion that seemed due to them, apparently because they felt and rebelled against 'the impossible dilemma between duty and conscience' which is recurrently thrust on generals in these days of overriding, occult powers. To my mind, this dilemma arises from the fact that, in those mysterious, higher circles, the notion prevails of 'handling military operations' to produce other results than those which the military commanders and the masses believe they fight for. They feel the inhibitions from above, the restraining hand, the falsity of the situation into which they are thrust, the danger to their men and their victory.

Another reason why, I feel, the Korean war may be called unlike any other in history is that General MacArthur was dismissed for questioning his orders just when the last German generals were being hanged for unquestioningly obeying orders! The words I quoted above, 'an impossible dilemma between duty and conscience', are those of a great authority, Lord Hankey, when he commented in the House of Lords on the Nuremberg Trials. The American representative there, Mr. Justice Jackson, with the approval of President Truman set up the principle, new in International Law, that 'the fact that the defendant acted pursuant to order of his government or of a superior shall not free him from responsibility'. The German leaders and generals were hanged, among other ostensible things, for obeying 'the obsolete doctrine that orders from an official superior protect one who obeys them'.

The highest appointments in the American fighting services, as a result of the Korean war, apparently went to generals who accepted this 'obsolete doctrine' of unquestioning obedience. General Marshall, the present Defence Secretary, once told Congress that in enforcing Chiang Kai-shek's submission to the Communists he merely carried out the instructions of an authority higher than himself, and this answer seems to have been taken as conclusive. (It was General Marshall who in 1942 proposed that the United States should withdraw from the war in Europe unless the British agreed to a cross-Channel invasion that year. Hardly any American troops or craft then were ready to take part in such an operation, to which Mr. Churchill's dictum of the time applies, that a hasty, reckless invasion might have proved 'the only way in which we could possibly lose this war').

Similarly General Eisenhower, commenting on General MacArthur's dismissal, spoke of 'certain inhibitions' which a commander (presumably, other than a German commander) must accept. The phrase must be taken to cover the last stage of operations in Europe in 1945, which were subordinated to the order of President Truman (given on the advice of General Marshall and the other Chiefs of Staff) 'to let the Russians take Berlin'.

Another point in which the Korean war, I think, may fairly be said to be unlike any other in history is that on three separate occasions before it began the American Foreign Secretary, Mr. Dean Acheson, stated that neither Formosa nor South Korea fell within the American defence perimeter. As the Communist invasion of South Korea then was immediately met by an American counter-landing, the observer can only surmise that American opinion was at that time becoming restless, so that a token of apparently genuine anti-Communist senti-ment was thought in high political circles to be necessary. The greater fact remains, however, that the American commander was not allowed to make the countermove effective.

It seems to me clear that all these political and military moves were directed, by agreement on the higher levels of all countries concerned, to some ambition not yet revealed. I think it to be the progressive sub-jugation of the English-speaking countries to the World State. I might be wrong. Is there any sure test by which the genuineness or fraudu-lence of the Korean war may be judged?

I think one offers: the question of Formosa and that (linked with it) of Communist China's admission to the United Nations Organization over the body of Chiang Kai-shek and his anti-Communists.

Here is another matter in which the Korean war may, without fear of challenge, be called unlike any other in history.

At its start and for some time thereafter the official spokesmen of the American, British and Canadian Governments (the three chiefly engaged) repeatedly recommended that Formosa should be handed over to Communist China (as China itself had been handed over to Communism); that Chiang Kai-shek's government should be aban-doned as the Polish and many other governments were abandoned during the Second War; and that Communist China should be given membership of the United Nations Organization in place of the anti-Communists, then, and as I write still, the representatives of China there.

It seems to me astounding, even in these times, that this proposal to fight a war 'against Communist aggression' for the purpose of reward-ing Communist aggression with territory and power should have been so openly made in such high places, and have been so supinely received by the peoples of the three countries.

The observer of these times may see an intentional and sardonic cynicism in the terms which are currently used to describe soldiers from the English-speaking countries. If they can openly be put to such purposes as this, it may not be accident that they are coming to be spoken of as 'bodies' (a word against which Mr. Churchill was moved vehemently to protest during the Second War), 'General Issue Joes', or beings 'expendable'. It was in tune with this growing practice (also new in history, I think) that an official American spokesman, in June 1951, said that after the glorious inauguration of the World Force in Korea, American contingents would in future be 'earmarked' for United Nations service. 'Earmarking', I believe, is a term hitherto used about cattle.

As the Korean war went on, however, a new factor arose in the situation, with which the planners at high levels may not sufficiently have reckoned. This was the casualty-lists. The death of thousands of American soldiers made an impression in America, painful enough to disquieten party-managers, who live with thoughts of the next congressional or presidential election. The martyrdom of the Black Watch and the Gloucesters, also, was vibrantly felt throughout the British Island and Ulster.

From this moment a change occurred in the allusions made by leading politicians to Formosa, the desertion of Chiang Kai-shek and the elevation of Red China. In Britain and Canada no retraction was made, but the politicians became quieter about the matter. In America, however, where the bereaved were much more numerous, a complete alteration was made. The government's official spokesman said, frequently, publicly and plainly, that the United States would not allow Formosa to be thrown to the Communist wolves on the China coast, or Communist China to be received in triumph at the building of the Board of Directors in New York.

That is the point at which all may test the matter for themselves. If in the sequel, sooner or later, Chiang Kai-shek is abandoned like so many before him, if Formosa is handed over to his enemies and these are admitted to join the other Soviet puppets in New York, then the Korean war was fraudulent in its motives from the start, and the only genuine thing about it was the casualty-list of English-speaking soldiers, and those from Turkey, Greece and elsewhere.

I believe that this was in truth the issue at the root of the whole affair. As long as Formosa remained an anti-Communist stronghold, China was not wholly Communist; the Communist area could not be further expanded; and the number of Soviet satellites in the United Nations Organization would not increase. Islands are notoriously difficult to conquer, as the British Islander should know. The plan existed (the official statements of members of the governments leagued to check 'Communist aggression' exist to prove it) to save Communist China the pains of conquering Formosa by using the United Nations Organization to make another mock-legal transfer, in the name of a war against Communist aggression!

I do not believe that plan has been dropped; I think the truce parleys in Korea are a sign that it will be pursued by other methods. It may not be quite so easy now, given the suspicious and resentful state of American opinion, to complete the transaction, but the attempt will in my judgment be made, and by its success or failure the shape of the future may be known. If a truce is called in Korea, memories in the English-speaking world will cool; in America the Communists will repeat the 1945-46 campaign to 'bring the boys home'; soon the stage may be clear for another Yalta.

All that is in flux at the moment, with the approach of an American presidential election probably the decisive factor. The Communist Empire slightly prefers, on balance, to have the Democrats in office there, rather than the Republicans, and for that reason might delay its hand until after November 1952. The party-managers in America might calculate that Formosa could be handed over and Communist China honoured before that, and an election yet be won.

Whatever the moment and the method, the powerful forces which at present clearly can bend leading politicians of the English-speaking countries to their will, and use the United Nations Organization as their instrument, plainly hold Formosa and the strengthening of Communist China to be of major importance in their plans. I think they will not desist from the attempt to enthrone the Chinese Communists on Formosa and in New York, and they will have strong support in London, Washington and Formosa.

Korea, then, was the first full and open test of the uses which will be made of the fighting-men from the English-speaking world, if their governors continue to subordinate them to the United Nations Organization. As they were sent to fight they were in fact plainly told that the aim was to help the enemy to military and political successes; General MacArthur was right about that, even if he merely felt and did not fully perceive it. This is the result of surrendering national sovereignty and national interests to a coterie or committee, housed on New York's East River, which claims to represent The World. A 'secret pattern' is being woven there and in its design the armies of the English-speaking world would be but puppets. Another, greater war, waged under these auspices, would in my opinion merely repeat the history of Korea on a greater scale, if Korea is to repeat that of Yalta. Ominously, as the Korean truce-parleys began, a report came from Washington that General Eisenhower desired 'an Allied army with a single flag, uniform and command to defend Western Europe'. The flag, presumably, would be that under which Count Bernadotte was murdered and General MacArthur was dismissed; to what effective extent Western Europe would be defended may unhappily be judged by the example of Korea, which has been largely destroyed and seems likely to be left in the Limbo-like state of Europe, at the best.

That might be inferred, too, from the words of the American President when the Korean truce-parleys began. I heard him make a speech to a listless audience, which was more interested in the fire-crackers, on July the Fourth, 1951. He did not proclaim the victory of the cause he had proclaimed when he ordered American troops into Korea a year before, but that of another, quite different cause, and as I judge the true one: 'Men of the armed forces in Korea, you will go down in history as the first army to fight under a flag of a world organization in the defence of human freedom.'

That was 'the victory' then: that for the first time in history men were brought to fight under the flag of an organization calling itself a world one. How far they were allowed to defend human freedom, they may judge by what yet comes of the Korean episode. If it leads to a further increase in their enemies' strength within the 'world organization', the lesson would be plain, quite apart from what happens to the Koreans.

This surrender of English-speaking troops to the purposes of 'a world organization', the motives and ambitions of which are unknown to them, was only part of the successes which were won, through the Korean affair, by the World-Planners. Another part was the further diminution of personal liberty in the American Republic and the

British island. All the American President's speeches, after the truce-talks began, followed the line begun by President Roosevelt nineteen years before: the 'emergency' continued, there must be more and more taxation, more and more 'controls', less and less 'human freedom'. The American Republic is being dragged down the road descended, before it, by the British people.

The 'emergency' goes on and clearly will continue until the forces which now dominate national governments succeed in their aim of reducing the English-speaking world to slave status within their World State, or are exposed and defeated. In that grand design of the twentieth century Korea is but a stepping-stone towards the final stage of Armageddon.

By 'partitioning', through this bogus United Nations Organization, three flashpoints for the culminating struggle have been made: in Europe, on the bisection line; in the Far East, in Korea; and in the Near East, in Arab Palestine.

The great centre of the conclusive conflict, in my judgment, is to be the Near East. This part of the world's surface, in my opinion, is 'earmarked' to be the true seat of world government, and the people who live there realize this much more clearly than the English-speaking peoples who have been and will be used to conquer it.

The Prime Minister of the Zionist State has recently declared (in New York) that 'the Jewish State is not the fulfilment of Zionism'; that the present small state 'has jurisdiction only over the Jews living in it' whereas 'Zionism embraces all Jews everywhere' and 'we are still very far from the Zionist ideal'; that within the next ten years four million Jews must be brought to the Zionist State.

The perceptive reader may survey for himself the future prospects which are opened by these ambitions. Two world wars and thirty-four years of local Arabian warfare have been needed to set up the Zionist State and to transport a million Jews to it. There are not four million Jews in the world who wish to go to the Zionist State. To enable this new transfer of populations the cry of anti-Semitism would have to be raised anew, probably in the later stages of some new war. To gain the true perspective the reader should bear in mind the vast sums of American money which are being poured into this part of the world, in order 'to increase the ability of the recipient countries to defend themselves' (the words are those of an official American Government spokesman), and the lengths to which American party-managers, on both sides, apparently feel themselves forced to go, in the competition for the Zionist vote.

The signs of the outcome are clear to see, from the anti-British outbursts in Persia to the assassination of King Abdullah of Jordan (the only Arab ruler who ever showed an inclination to make a deal with Zionist Nationalism). The Near East is the great powder-keg, and the World Planners are dancing round it with spark-scattering torches. At present few signs offer that the leading politicians of the English-speaking countries will shake off the thralls which have led them, for thirty-four years or more, to support by their deeds (whatever their words) the two exterior forces which have brought about the present situation: Soviet Communism and Zionist Nationalism. Until they outlaw the one and break loose from the other, the twentieth century and the English-speaking peoples must move relentlessly towards their final test in the place called in the Hebrew tongue Megiddo.

I can imagine that some future historian, writing perhaps a hundred years from now, might say something like this: 'In considering today the events which enabled conspiratorial sects from Asia and Eurasia to gain power over the then mighty nations of the West and bring about the short-lived but bloody fiasco of the World State, from the cruel effects of which they are even now but slowly reviving, the historian is struck by the apparent absence of protest or resistance among the leaders of those Western nations, which thus were deprived of what they had gained during two thousand years. Very rarely, from what one can now tell, did a leading man see what impended or succeed, if he saw, in making his voice heard. The Canadian Prime Minister, in 1945, was ignored by the American and British leaders. A British Foreign Minister, Mr. Ernest Bevin, in 1945-51 seems to have perceived the immense omens of the Zionist State and vainly to have tried to keep his country from lending countenance to it. A British general, Sir Frederick Morgan, at one phase tried, equally vainly, to call public attention to the grave danger of that enterprise. An American general, one Douglas MacArthur, at a later stage (the astonishing campaign of

1950-51 in Korea) was dismissed for his resistance to the hindrances that were placed on his leadership. In all countries a rare politician, soldier or writer tried to stem the Gadarene stampede, but on the whole the process seems to have been one of infatuated self-surrender to the forces of destruction. So much has been lost of the truth of those days that today's historian is himself at a loss to account for much that was done or was not done, and for public acquiescence in it all, but even when that is said two things remain to puzzle him: the fewness of the public men who resisted the occult forces which were truly in control, and the apparent lack of public response even to their warnings.'

To any such comment I offer a reply across the century to come: 'At the mid-twentieth century the forces conspiring to enslave all the countries of the Christian West, especially the English-speaking ones, were so greatly in control of public information, of every kind, that the masses knew next to nothing of what went on and what impended. Public men, by the mid-century, had come to fear these inhibitors too much to tempt their wrath, and any who did risk that ire were defamed by so powerful a machine of the spoken and written word that even the masses, after lending an eager ear of hope renewed for an instant, in the nature of masses then dully turned their backs on the speakers and shunned them, thinking they must be evil after all. In that way they were brought again and again to pit themselves against each other, always in the name of "freedom", for their own mutual destruction and enslavement; thus the shortlived but bloody fiasco of the World State came about. Only when they experienced it did they know the truth and rise; and God must have willed it so, good scribe of the year 2051, for "by a *divine* instinct men's minds mistrust *ensuing* danger".'